HOW PARTI
ORGANIZE

Change and Adaptation in Party Organizations
in Western Democracies

Edited by

Richard S. Katz and Peter Mair

SAGE Publications
London • Thousand Oaks • New Delhi

In memory of
Rudolf Wildenmann

Editorial arrangement © Richard S. Katz and
Peter Mair 1994
Chapter 1 © Peter Mair
Chapter 2 © Richard S. Katz and Robin Kolodny 1994
Chapter 3 © Wolfgang C. Müller
Chapter 4 © Kris Deschouwer
Chapter 5 © Paul D. Webb
Chapter 6 © Lars Bille
Chapter 7 © Jan Sundberg
Chapter 8 © Thomas Poguntke
Chapter 9 © David M. Farrell
Chapter 10 © Luciano Bardi and Leonardo Morlino
Chapter 11 © Ruud A. Koole
Chapter 12 © Lars Svåsand
Chapter 13 © Jon Pierre and Anders Widfeldt
Chapter 14 © Luciano Bardi

First published 1994

SAGE Publications Ltd
6 Bonhill Street
London EC2A 4PU

SAGE Publications Inc
2455 Teller Road
Thousand Oaks, California 91320

SAGE Publications India Pvt Ltd
32, M-Block Market
Greater Kailash – I
New Delhi 110 048

British Library Cataloguing in Publication data

A catalogue record for this book is
available from the British Library.

ISBN 0 8039 7960 6
ISBN 0 8039 7961 4 (pbk)

Library of Congress catalog card number 94–068658

Typeset by Photoprint, Torquay, S. Devon
Printed in Great Britain by The Cromwell Press Ltd,
Broughton Gifford, Melksham, Wiltshire

Contents

Contributors

Luciano Bardi Dipartimento di Politica, Istituzioni e Storia, Università di Bologna

Lars Bille Institute of Political Science, University of Copenhagen

Kris Deschouwer Centrum voor Politicologie, Vrije Universiteit Brussel

David M. Farrell Department of Government, University of Manchester

Richard S. Katz Department of Political Science, The Johns Hopkins University

Robin Kolodny Department of Political Science, Temple University

Ruud A. Koole Department of Political Science, University of Leiden

Peter Mair Department of Political Science, University of Leiden

Leonardo Morlino Facoltà di Scienze Politiche, Università di Firenze

Wolfgang C. Müller Institut für Staats- und Politikwissenschaft, Universität Wien

Jon Pierre Department of Political Science, Göteborgs Universitet

Thomas Poguntke Fakultät für Sozialwissenschaft, Universität Mannheim

Jan Sundberg Department of Political Science, University of Helsinki

Lars Svåsand Department of Comparative Politics, University of Bergen

Paul D. Webb Department of Government, Brunel, University of West London

Anders Widfeldt Department of Political Science, Göteborgs Universitet

Preface and Acknowledgements

This volume emerges from a long-standing international research project on party organizational change and adaptation. The project was devised with two principal goals. The first was simply to document the nuts and bolts of organizational developments since 1960 in twelve Western democracies, and thereby to fill what had been a major gap in the data base from which analysts of party politics have been able to develop their ideas. This goal was largely accomplished in the first volume of the project series, *Party Organizations: A Data Handbook on Party Organizations in Western Democracies, 1960–90* (Sage, 1992), which focused almost exclusively on what we called 'the official story', drawing primarily on party and party-related documents and reports in order to outline party rules and structures as well as to record data concerning membership and finance.

The second goal of the project, once having established the official story, was to move beyond it by adding politics to the raw data, and hence to understand the contexts in which parties develop their organizational structures and the reasons why they change or why they remain the same. There are two complementary ways in which this problem can be addressed. One is on the basis of a country-by-country analysis, which is the approach adopted in this, the second volume of the series; the other is on the basis of a cross-national analysis, which is the focus of a projected third volume in the series.

There are a number of reasons why it is useful to begin with a country-by-country approach. The authors of these chapters were themselves responsible for the original data collection, and so they are particularly sensitive to what these data mean within the different national contexts and to how they should be interpreted. In this sense they are very well placed to offer what might be called the 'real [national] story'. Moreover, while the unit of analysis throughout this project has always been the individual political party, we are also very much aware that each party is part of a party system, and that these party systems are structured on a national basis. Thus while some adaptations in party organizations might be expected to derive from factors which affect most, if not all, Western democracies, such as the mass media revolution or the peculiarities of post-industrial society, and while other adaptations may be specific to individual parties, there nevertheless remain many stimuli to which parties must respond which differ across countries but which are shared by all parties within the same country. In this sense, the national context clearly matters, with different parties within each country being subject to the same national regulations, operating within the same constitutional and social structures, and sharing the same electoral market.

Given that the studies in this volume are the first to use the wealth of systematic empirical data which has been gathered by this project, they offer a unique insight into party development over the past thirty years. It is for this reason that we felt it inappropriate to tie the contributions down by means of strict preconceptions or models. Rather, each of the authors was given a free hand to organize their contribution as they saw fit, and each was encouraged to emphasize whatever was deemed most central to an understanding of the individual cases. For reasons of space, the authors were also asked to avoid reporting details of the data which are already available in the data handbook. At the same time, however, regardless of the individual emphases, a common purpose was asserted by requiring each author to address a number of key questions or themes. Thus the authors were asked to assess the prevailing conceptions of party, both from the points of view of the parties themselves as well as from the point of view of the state, and were also asked to assess the development of parties as membership organizations, which involved looking at the extent of party membership, at the role of ordinary members in party decision-making, and at the relative importance of members to the organization as a whole. Other common themes concerned the development of party as a professional organization, including the size and organization of party staff and the role of professional advisers and consultants; the development of party finance, with particular reference to the relative importance of the members and of the state as sources of party revenue; and the relationships between the various components of party, with particular reference to the standing of the parliamentary party. More generally, authors were also asked to address the problem of changes, if any, in the relationship between the parties, civil society and the state.

The project from which this volume derives was first developed within a Research Group of the European Consortium for Political Research (ECPR), and subsequent meetings of the project members in both the University of Limerick and the University of Leiden were held on the fringes of the ECPR Joint Sessions of Workshops. For both of these reasons, we would like to thank the ECPR for its long-term support. The project was funded primarily by the American National Science Foundation under grant number SES-8818439, with additional financial support being provided by the *Forschungsstelle für Gesellschaftliche Entwicklungen* (FGE) of the University of Mannheim, as well as by various national foundations. We are grateful to all of these organizations for their generous help. Thanks are also due to our departments in Johns Hopkins and Leiden, which wittingly or unwittingly provided much of the material infrastructure and support which was required to link researchers from so many different countries.

Finally, we would also like to record a special thanks for the help which we received from Rudolf Wildenmann, who, in his various capacities as chairman of the ECPR executive, as director of the FGE and as a long-term friend and adviser to us both, offered this project his constant support, both practically and intellectually. Rudolf saw and seemed pleased with our first volume, the data handbook, but sadly died before this particular volume was completed. Like many other political scientists throughout Europe, we owe much to Rudolf, and we now dedicate this book to his memory.

Richard S. Katz
Peter Mair

1

Party Organizations: From Civil Society to the State

Peter Mair

Party organizations and the problem of party decline

The study of parties and party systems still constitutes one of the largest and most active subfields within comparative politics (for example, Janda, 1993). It is also a study which continues to present an immensely varied landscape, ranging from work which explores the relationship of parties to the wider society, through work which is concerned with the role of parties in government, to work which, often at a more theoretical level, deals with the interactions between parties and with the dynamics of party systems. We now know a great deal, for example, about cross-national developments in the ties which bind, or fail to bind, parties to their voters, whether this be expressed in terms of the stability and change of electoral preferences (see, for example, Bartolini and Mair, 1990; Crewe and Denver, 1985; Dalton et al., 1984), or in terms of the sociology of party support (see, for example, Franklin et al., 1992; Rose, 1974). We also know increasingly more about parties in office, both in terms of processes of coalition formation (for example, Laver and Schofield, 1990; Pridham, 1986), and in terms of the role of parties in policy-making and in government more generally (for example, Budge and Keman, 1990; Castles and Wildenmann, 1986; Katz, 1987; Laver and Budge, 1992). Most recently, comparative analysis has also been addressed to the question of parties as strategic actors and as campaigners (for example, Bowler and Farrell, 1992; Butler and Ranney, 1992). And to all of this work can be added the more wide-ranging and ever-expanding volume of studies on party families and party systems (see, for example, the now dated bibliography in Mair, 1990: 353–60).

At the same time, however, there are also imbalances, with the ever-growing cumulation of knowledge in some areas contrasting sharply with surprisingly evident lacunae in others. The empirically grounded study of parties as organizations, which provides the focus for this volume, has long constituted one of the most obvious of these lacunae (see also Katz and Mair, 1992b). This is notwithstanding the fact that much of the pioneering work in the field of party research, by Michels and Ostrogorski in particular, was focused precisely on this area, and also notwithstanding some more recent theoretical discussions which have speculated on differing models of party and party change (for example, Panebianco, 1988). Thus while we now know a great deal about parties and their voters, about parties and their governments, and about parties and their competitors, there continue to be severe limits to the comparative understanding of precisely how party organizations work, about how they change, and about how they adapt.

One of the most obvious symptoms of this long-term neglect of comparative research on the development of party organizations is that much of the thinking on the subject still remains caught within a set of terms of reference which was established almost a generation ago. More specifically, and despite the occasional emphasis on more modern variants, much of this thinking remains predicated on the assumption of 'the mass party' as model (see Katz and Mair, 1994). In this view, party organizations are defined primarily with reference to their relationships with civil society; party organizational strength is measured primarily with reference to the size of the membership and the capacity of the party to close off (often pre-defined) sectors of the electorate; and party structures are understood and assessed primarily in terms of modes of internal representation and accountability. It follows therefore that the attenuation of any of these elements – such as occurs through the privileging of leadership groups inside the party, through the downgrading of the role of members, or through the development of programmes aimed at the voters at large rather than at the party-attached or even party-incorporated clientele – involves also the attenuation, and decline, of party per se.

The problem with this line of reasoning begins when the decline of the mass party is treated as signifying the decline of party more generally. In this sense, the mass party is not only the model for what has gone before, but also remains the model almost in perpetuity, such that parties which may be indifferent to membership, which may emphasize the power of their leadership, and which may develop less self-consciously democratic processes of internal decision-making, are somehow also parties in decline. Kirchheimer (1966), for example, who was one of the first authors to signal the demise of the mass party, and who pointed to the emergence of the newer 'catch-all' party, did so with regret, in that he envisaged the new type of party possibly becoming 'too blunt to serve as a link with the functional powerholders of society' (p. 200). Pizzorno (1981), who also emphasized the passing of the mass party, and who depicted it as the now redundant creature of a specific time, was led to advance a series of hypotheses seeking to explain how parties as such could survive thereafter. Even Panebianco (1988), who argues that the mass party had been superseded by what he refers to as the 'electoral-professional party', suggests that this may also involve the weakening of the position of party 'in every arena' (p. 269). The period of the mass party can therefore be seen to coincide with 'the golden age' of parties, and since then everything has been downhill. Indeed, it was probably this sense of decline which discouraged empirical research in the field of party organizations during the past twenty years, in that it seemed more useful to devote one's research efforts to those 'emerging alternative organizations', such as new social movements, which were increasingly regarded as threatening to displace parties as the active intermediaries between the citizenry and the state (see, for example, Lawson and Merkl, 1988).

There are also other problems associated with this mass-party centred argument. In the first place, much of the speculation about the passing of the mass party and about the imputed decline of party more generally has ensued without much reference to empirical evidence, not least because of the sheer difficulty involved in gathering the sort of data which might bolster or even challenge this thesis (see, for example, Bartolini, 1983; von Beyme, 1985; Katz, 1990). Second, and notwithstanding the insights which have been provided by much of the more theoretical reasoning, the precise way in which different models of party organization may be distinguished still remains relatively unclear. For while these models are certainly useful when seeking to make quite long-term generalizations about party organizational development, they nevertheless prove very difficult to treat in a more specific way, or as genuinely empirical constructs (for example, Dittrich, 1983; Krouwel, 1993; Sjöblom, 1981). Third, and not least as a result of the legacy of the mass-party model, there still remains a tendency to evaluate party organizations in terms of their relations with civil society. Alternative aspects of party organization, on the other hand, particularly those which relate to the party in parliament (cf. von Beyme, 1983; Heckscher, 1953: 149–59), or to the party in central office, still often tend to be ignored.

New perspectives on the development of party organization

In the context of the wider research project on change and adaptation in party organizations, of which this particular volume forms part, there are two principal strategies which have been adopted in order to deal with these problems. The first, and probably the more important of these strategies, aims at going beyond the classic work of Janda (1980) and at remedying the dearth of empirical evidence about party organizational developments by means of a systematic collection of cross-national data over time on all relevant party organizations in a variety of Western democracies. Over and above information concerning the electoral and governmental history of the almost eighty parties in the twelve countries included in this project, data were also gathered on the development and structure of party membership; on the numbers and allocation of party staff; on the internal distribution of power and the organization and functions of internal party organs; and on party finance, including information on the provision of state subsidies for parties. These data have since been published in a separate handbook (Katz and Mair, 1992a).

The second strategy involves an attempt to move away from the conception of party as a unitary actor, and especially to move away from the almost exclusive concern with the relationship between parties and civil society, by disaggregating party organizations into at least three different elements, or faces, each of which interacts with the others. The first of these faces is the *party in public office*, that is, the party organization in government and in parliament. The second is the *party on the ground*, that is, the membership organization, and also potentially the loyal party voters. The third face is the *party in central office*, which is organizationally distinct from the party in public office, and which, at least in the traditional mass-party model, organizes and is usually representative of the party on the ground (see Katz and Mair, 1994).

Both strategies facilitate the adoption of a more differentiated and at the same time more grounded approach to the study of party organizational change and adaptation. Both also allow a more sensitive understanding of the broader question of party decline. The availability of cross-national data, for example, not only allows us to test whether any such decline is real or imagined but, by distinguishing between the different faces, also allows us to pinpoint more precisely where change is taking place, and to find out whether, say, decline in one of these elements is perhaps countered by growth at other levels of the party. Indeed, a central hypothesis which emerges from this project has been that it is really only the party on the ground which is becoming less important or which is in decline, whereas the resources of the party in central office, and especially those of the party in public office, have in fact been strengthened. In this sense, we argue that the emphasis on party decline *tout court* may be misplaced.

Even this narrower version of the party decline thesis, which hypothesizes that decline may be largely limited to the party on the ground, cannot wholly be sustained by the data, however. There are two reasons for this. First, when looking at the actual numbers involved, it appears that the most important decline in levels of party membership has been that which has occurred in *relative* terms, in the sense that membership levels have often simply failed to keep up with the dramatic expansion in the size of national electorates (see also Mair, 1993). As can be seen from Table 1.1, for example, almost all of the countries for which long-term data are available register a decline in the proportion of electors who are party members, ranging from the remarkable erosion from more than 21 per cent of electors to just less than 7 per cent of electors in the case of Denmark, to the more muted fall of less than 1 per cent in Sweden across the same period. Only two of these countries, Belgium and Germany, register an increase in the party membership share of the electorate (from 7.8 per cent to 9.2 per cent, and from 2.7 per cent to 4.2 per cent, respectively). That said, it is also necessary to recognize that some six countries register an overall increase in the *absolute numbers* of party members (Belgium,

Table 1.1 *Development of party membership*

	Beginning of 1960s		End of 1980s	
	N ('000)	% of electorate	N ('000)	% of electorate
Austria	1380.7	26.2	1311.8	21.8
Belgium	468.8	7.8	654.4	9.2
Denmark	599.1	21.1	260.5	6.5
Finland	513.1	18.9	520.1	12.9
Germany	1001.9[a]	2.7	1907.5	4.2
Ireland	na	na	129.3	5.3
Italy	4332.8	12.7	4405.2	9.7
N'lands[b]	648.4	9.4	326.4	2.9
Norway	363.7	15.5	432.0	13.5
Sweden	1092.1	22.0	1343.3	21.2
UK	3258.8	9.4	1426.3	3.3

[a] Includes estimate of 50,000 for FDP membership.
[b] Includes estimate of 10,000 for CPN in 1963, and includes Green Left in 1989.

Source: Katz and Mair, 1992a

Finland, Germany, Italy, Norway, Sweden), in contrast to only four which register an overall decline in absolute numbers (Austria, Denmark, the Netherlands, the United Kingdom).

Second, the impression of decline in the importance of the party on the ground must also be tempered by the relatively widespread evidence cited in the chapters of this volume which suggest that, far from marginalizing their members, a variety of different parties are actually ceding them more decision-making power (see also p. 15). In 1970, for example, the Belgian PSC introduced direct membership elections for the party president, and followed this in 1980 by stipulating that membership ballots take place for all internal party mandates. In 1981, for the first time, the British Labour Party allowed representatives of the membership a direct vote in leadership elections, and is currently moving towards a wholesale 'one member, one vote' procedure. In Ireland, the recent commission on the organizational renewal of Fine Gael also recommended a direct vote for party members in leadership elections. The role of the membership in the selection of candidates for public office has also often been enhanced. Party members in Denmark, for instance, now have a greater role in candidate selection as well as a voice in the approval of party programmes. In Germany, the SPD is now emphasizing the need for greater *Basisdemokratie*, including the introduction of binding membership ballots. Candidate selection was also decentralized in the Netherlands in the late 1960s and early 1970s, although this trend has recently been reversed. Finally, in both Finland and Norway, a variety of attempts by the party leadership to gain more control over the candidate selection process were successfully resisted by the local parties, who still retain a powerful voice.

As our central hypothesis indicates, however, the most powerful evidence which can be marshalled against the party decline thesis comes when we move away from the party on the ground, and begin to look at the resources available to the party central offices and to the parties in public office. In the first place, and most obviously, more and more parties are gaining access to public office, and in this sense they are also gaining access to more resources, on the one hand, and to alternative means of legitimation, on the other. There are now very few parties which are marginalized in this regard. The Finnish Communists and the German Social Democrats joined their first post-war coalitions in the 1960s, and it was also in the 1960s that the first post-war bourgeois coalition was formed in Norway. By the end of the 1970s, parties such as the Belgian Rassemblement Walloon, Volksunie and Front Démocratique des Bruxellois Francophones had been admitted to government for the first time, as had the Dutch D66. The 1970s also witnessed the first bourgeois coalition in Sweden, and the advent to office, after sixteen years of opposition, of the Fine Gael and Labour parties in Ireland. By the end of the 1980s, the governing ranks of European parties had expanded further to include then the Austrian Freedom Party, the Danish Centre Democrats and Christian People's Party, as well as the Finnish Rural Party (see Katz and Mair, 1992a; Woldendorp et al., 1993). Other than many of the recently mobilized 'new politics' parties of the left, and virtually all of the 'new politics' parties of the far right, therefore, the only substantial parties which have long remained outside government at a national level are the British Liberal Party, which nevertheless formed a pact with the minority Labour government in the late 1970s; and the Italian Communist Party, the majority of which has now reconstituted itself as the reformed and increasingly coalitionable Democratic Party of the Left (PDS).[1] Governing, even if only sporadically, is therefore by now a standard experience for most parties, and the resources which this brings now constitute an important means of sustenance.

Second, as can be seen from the summary figures reported in Table 1.2, the overall resources of the various parties for which comparable data are available have grown in almost all the countries included in this project. The numbers of party staff have increased universally, ranging from the massive 330 per cent increase in Ireland (and almost the same in Germany), to the more modest increases in Britain and the Netherlands. In these terms at least, parties now have much greater resources at their disposal than was the case some two decades ago, and even these figures leave aside the countless additional personnel resources which are available through government appointments, on the one hand, and through the contractual employment of specialist consultants, on the other. The incomes of party central offices have also grown almost everywhere in the last fifteen years or so, increasing by more than 300 per cent in the German case, by more than 200 per cent in the Austrian case and by more than 100 per cent in the Irish case. Only in Sweden, which registered a marginal decline, and in Italy, where the 'official', but now admittedly highly misleading, figures reveal a decline of almost 25 per cent, has central office income actually fallen in real terms.

Table 1.2 *Development of party resources*

	Growth in number of staff employed by parties[a] (%)	Growth in income of party central offices[b] (%)
Austria	+ 61	+ 286
Denmark	+ 112	+ 50
Finland	+ 55	+ 6
Germany	+ 268	+ 350
Ireland	+ 330	+ 123
Italy	+ 140	− 25
N'lands	+ 17	+ 41
Norway	+ 50	+ 14
Sweden	+ 55	− 4
UK	+ 24	+ 46
USA	na	+ 145

[a] The change refers to the difference between the position in the late 1960s or early 1970s and that in the late 1980s; only those parties are included where it proved possible to make a direct comparison over time.
[b] The change refers to the difference between the income (in constant prices) in *c.* 1975 and that in 1989/90; only those parties are included where it proved possible to make a direct comparison over time.

Source: Katz and Mair, 1992a

Parties and the state

Both aspects are of course related, in that it is often real or potential access to public office which has enhanced the ability of parties to accumulate organizational resources such as staff and money. In this sense, the state, which is often the source of these resources, becomes a means by which parties can help ensure their own persistence and survival. Indeed, if there is one single theme which is to be drawn from the diversity apparent in the chapters included in this present volume, it is that the understanding of party organizational change and adaptation requires us to pay at least as much attention, if not more, to the linkage between party and state as to the linkage between parties and civil society. At the same time, however, it is also clear that it is precisely this particular linkage which has tended to be either ignored or undervalued in previous assessments of party change and stability which, as noted above, have tended to focus almost exclusively on party relations with civil society (see, for example, Lawson, 1988, and Sainsbury, 1990; for one notable exception, see Müller, 1993).

What is also clear from the chapters included in this volume is that it is in the last decade or two that the relevance of the linkage with the state has tended to become particularly important. In a sense, then, the increasingly top-down style of party organizational life which was emphasized in Kirchheimer's depiction of the catch-all party, and especially in Panebianco's depiction of the electoral-professional party, and which implied an erosion of the party–civil society linkage, may also be said to have coincided with correspondingly greater emphasis on the linkage between party and state, with the latter offering the potential to compensate for the former. This is also in fact the dynamic which was hypothesized in an earlier paper which was developed in the context of this project (Katz and Mair, 1992c), in which it was argued that parties had moved from an earlier, post-suffrage stage (the classic 'mass party' phase) in which they had represented the interests of civil society vis-à-vis the state, to a stage in which they acted almost as independent brokers between state and civil society (the classic 'catch-all party' phase), and in which, in Downsian or Schumpeterian terms, they behaved more as competing teams of leaders, to a new and more recent stage, in which they actually move closer to becoming part of the state, and remain at quite a remove from civil society. The balance of linkage has therefore changed, as have the parties themselves.

Taken to extremes, any such movement might well require us to modify the conventional conception in which parties are seen as intermediaries between civil society and the state, a conception which may perhaps have been better suited to those phases in which the parties either represented the interests of civil society or simply acted as a broker for these interests. Instead, by linking themselves more closely to the state, and especially by relying on the state for their resources, they call to mind a more useful heuristic conception in which the state itself might be seen as the intermediary between the parties and the citizenry. This is, to be sure, an extreme and somewhat abstract conception; nonetheless, it does help us to get away from the increasingly frustrating and often misleading emphasis on the parties' own links with civil society, and does help us to recognize the importance of their ties with the state. In the Italian case in particular, for instance, as can be seen from Bardi and Morlino's discussion of *partitocrazia*, a conception of the state as intermediary can also help to illuminate the processes by which parties seek to survive.

Almost all of the chapters in this volume emphasize how the state, as opposed to simply civil society, has become unquestionably important for the survival of political parties, both in terms of the legitimacy which public office confers, as well as in terms of the resources and capacities which are either offered, or regulated, by the state itself. There are a number of ways in which this may be illustrated. In the first place, and most simply, there are now few if any parties which still maintain their own partisan channel of communication, be this a party press, a party broadcasting system, or whatever. Rather, they now rely almost exclusively on a combination of independent, usually printed, media, on the one hand, where the access afforded to an individual party depends on whether it can either buy space or convince editors; and, on the other hand, publicly owned and/or controlled broadcasting networks (television and radio), where access, which is becoming increasingly important, is usually guaranteed by law and strictly regulated. As far as this latter outlet is concerned, the manner in which parties present their message, and the relative frequency with which it can be presented, therefore clearly depends in large part on rules and procedures devised by the state.

The second, and significantly more direct, way in which the state helps to ensure the position of political parties can be seen in personnel resources. As noted above, for example (see Table 1.2), the numbers of staff working for parties have expanded substantially in the past two decades, and much of this increase can be accounted for by the growth of parliamentary party staff who are paid largely, if not exclusively, from state funds. Indeed, with the exception of Italy (and perhaps also of the UK, where comparisons over time are difficult to measure), the growth of parliamentary party staff has consistently outstripped that of central office staff. In a number of cases (for example, Austria, Finland, Germany, Norway, Sweden), parliamentary staff numbers have actually grown by three to four times as much as those in party central offices; in Denmark, the increase in parliamentary staff has been ten times that in central office staff, while in Ireland the ratio is more than twelve to one.

This is not to suggest, however, that there has been a wholesale shift in personnel from the more 'private' party world of the central offices to the more 'public' party world of the parliaments. On the contrary, while the ratio of parliamentary party staff to central office has increased with time, and while the parliamentary bias is therefore certainly being accentuated, it is nevertheless still only in a minority of countries (Denmark, Germany, Ireland, the Netherlands and the US) that the overall numbers employed in the parties' parliamentary offices now exceed those employed in the central offices. That said, it must also be emphasized that even central office growth may itself be partially explained by the greater availability of state resources, in that a majority of countries now offer direct (and sometimes indirect) public subventions for party central offices, a system which was introduced either at the same time (Finland, Sweden) or slightly later (Austria, Belgium, Denmark, Germany, Norway) than that for parliamentary party offices. Moreover, the parties can also benefit in staff terms from the generous provisions which are often made available to parties in government, allowing them to appoint partisan advisers and consultants to (temporary) senior positions in the public bureaucracy (see, for instance, the discussion of Belgium, Finland and Ireland in this volume). In general, therefore, much of the organizational capacity available to the parties in staffing terms can be traced to resources which are increasingly provided, either directly or indirectly, by the state.

Third, and following from this, the state is also increasingly important to the parties in sheer financial terms. In Austria and Denmark, for example, *total* state funding for the parties at the national level more or less matches the amounts which they generate from all other sources of income taken together, while in Finland, Norway and Sweden, the total state subsidies received by the parties significantly exceed their total recorded incomes from other sources. In Ireland, where state subsidies officially do not exist (except for the so-called Oireachtas Grant), the total sums received by the parties from the state in 1989 actually amounted to almost half as much again as that received as a result of their own fund-raising efforts. In the

German case, once the subsidies for the various party foundations are included, state subsidies account for a sum which is more than ten times greater than that accounted for by other sources. Indeed, it is only in the Netherlands, the UK and the US that 'private' sources of party funds (membership fees, members' donations and so on) still constitute a larger source of revenue than that which comes from the public purse.

Fourth, as is also evident from a number of chapters in this volume, much of the character of contemporary party organization and party activity is increasingly shaped by state regulations, many of which were adopted in the wake of the granting of state subventions. As Poguntke emphasizes, the German case is perhaps the paradigmatic case of state regulation of party life, especially since the promulgation of the Party Law in 1967, and the regulation of a variety of principles of intra-party democracy. In Sweden, as Pierre and Widfeldt argue, the process of organizational convergence which has occurred since the 1970s owes much to the new rules regarding state subventions, while the advent of what Koole refers to as 'a parliamentary party complex' in the Netherlands also followed from the introduction of state subsidies, which in this case were directed to the parties in parliament. In Norway, long-standing laws which offer state financial support for nomination meetings which are conducted in a particular way have encouraged the parties to adopt a uniform procedure of candidate selection. In Austria, the constitutional principle of the 'free mandate' effectively prevents any formal attempt to bring the party in public office under the control of the extra-parliamentary party. More broadly, the very structure of party organizations is determined at least in part by the structure of the state itself, even to the extent that changes in the number of party basic units (or branches) is sometimes simply a response to a process of municipal reform (as, for example, in Belgium and the Netherlands).

Finally, it also seems to be the case that parties in public office have been increasingly willing to take advantage of public resources in order to reward their supporters. While the evidence here is necessarily sketchy and is sometimes nebulous, there is nevertheless a degree of consistency which suggests that party patronage, exercised through the state, is becoming an increasingly prevalent (or at least noticeable) phenomenon. The most obvious illustration is provided by the Italian case, and the widespread party corruption which was uncovered by the *mani pulite* investigations. Other, less compelling evidence of patronage is referred to in this volume in the cases of Austria, Germany, Finland and Belgium; in Ireland, questions have been raised in connection with government favours to the beef industry, while in Britain concern has been expressed about the associations between the Conservatives and some potentially corrupt financiers, on the one hand, and about the appointments policy of the Conservative government itself, on the other. In all of these cases, it would seem, support for, and/or membership of, a party may possibly be translated into the receipt of public honour or publicly funded benefits. At the same time, however, from the perspective of the parties themselves, this is also clearly a risky and potentially costly strategy, which can well provoke an anti-party backlash. The Italian evidence is unequivocal in this regard, as is the evidence of increasing popular disenchantment with the style of the traditional parties, and their *Parteibücher*, in Austria.

The potential exploitation of state resources for patronage purposes also highlights a more general problem with the wider conception of state aid for parties. To be sure, as the above points indicate, the state plays an important role in party survival, and increasingly so. Nonetheless, the fact that parties now place greater reliance on state-regulated channels of communications; that they increasingly staff their organizations on the basis of facilities offered through public office; that state subventions constitute an ever-growing proportion of party income; that party life is increasingly regulated by state laws; and that state patronage may offer an expanding source of selective benefits for party supporters, should not simply be taken to imply that parties have suddenly discovered some sort of external drip-feed from which their otherwise ailing organizations can draw more and more nourishment. In other words, these various developments should not be interpreted simply in terms in which 'the state' itself would be seen as an exogenous factor influencing party life. On the contrary, regardless of whether we are dealing with state regulations, or party laws, or levels of state subventions, we are always dealing with decisions which have been taken by the parliament, and by the political class, and therefore by the parties themselves. Thus, as the German discussion makes clear, while any one party may regard this regulatory context as an exogenous factor to which it must adapt, it is the parties as a whole, or at least as a majority, which have usually devised and determined the character of these regulations. In this sense, rather than thinking in terms of 'the state' helping the parties, it is perhaps more useful to think of it being the parties which are helping themselves, in that they are regulating themselves, paying themselves and offering resources to themselves, albeit in the name of the state.

If the parties can then be seen as helping to lay the basis for their own survival, they can also be seen to be laying the basis for their own mutual assimilation and convergence (see Katz and Mair, 1993). All parties in any given country are obliged to conform to the national rules regarding state subventions and to the increasingly pervasive party laws; all face the increasing communality of circumstances associated with communicating through the broadcast media rather than their own individual partisan channels; all tend to rely increasingly on the common font of state funding rather than on their own idiosyncratic modes of revenue raising; and, within the wider arena, all rely increasingly on the professional skills and expertise of the same group of marketing managers and consultants. In this sense, as exemplified perhaps most strongly in the case of Sweden, and to a lesser extent in Finland and Norway, the parties are beginning to look more and more like one another in terms of organizational character and style; and to the extent that the rules and procedures which govern party life also become more and more similar across national boundaries (not least through the internationalization of Saatchi and Saatchi's campaigning techniques – see Farrell, 1993), then we can also perhaps anticipate a more pronounced pattern of transnational convergence, even if, as Bardi notes, we have yet to see the emergence of genuine transnational parties.

Changing parties

Whatever is happening to the party on the ground, therefore, there is little to suggest any sense of decline of the party in public office, and hence there is also little to suggest any sense of party decline *tout court*. What we see instead are *changing* parties, in which the balance between the different faces is shifting, and in which, perhaps, they are also becoming more autonomous from one another. In the Netherlands, for example, it is possible to speak of the 'parliamentarization' of the parties; in Austria, it would seem more appropriate to speak of their 'governmentalization'. This shift towards an emphasis on the party in public office and its autonomy is also encouraged by systemic features, such as the need to negotiate delicate coalition arrangements in countries such as Belgium and, increasingly so, Sweden. At the same time, however, this shift in the balance of internal party resources also begs two important questions: first, how does this affect the position of the third face of party organization, the party in central office? Second, where does this leave the membership?

The party in central office

The party in central office was crucial to the conception of the mass party in that it was seen as the voice, or guardian, of the party on the ground, and as the means by which the party in public office could be held accountable to the mass membership (see Katz and Mair, 1994). More recently, however, although the evidence is difficult to interpret unequivocally, it would appear that both of these features may be eroding. In the first place, there are quite a number of parties which now reveal an increasing tendency for membership of the central office organs, and particularly the various national executive bodies, to be made up by representatives and/or *ex-officio* members of the party in public office rather than by representatives of the party on the ground. These include many liberal parties (for example, in Austria, Belgium, Denmark and Germany), as well as social democratic parties (for example, the Irish Labour Party) and conservative parties (for example, the Norwegian Hoyre). The evidence here is far from consistent, however, in that the statutes of other parties continue to include strict limits on the number of public office holders who can become members of party executive bodies, limits which, in certain cases (for example, the Dutch PvdA, the Danish Socialist People's Party and the Finnish National Coalition), have actually become stricter over time. In other cases, of course, such limits have been eased, and for many parties there are no such formal restrictions at all. Even then, however, it is often difficult to assess changes in the actual extent and influence of public office representation in internal executive organs. Indeed in Belgium, for example, as Deschouwer suggests, the inclusion of representatives of the party in public office on the parties' national executives need not be interpreted as a sign of the increasing influence of MPs, but rather as a means by which the party in central office maintains control over its public representatives.

Secondly, there is evidence to suggest that much of the more important work of the party in central office is increasingly being carried out by professionals and consultants, rather than by traditional party bureaucrats or even party activists. The 'accountability' of such staff would seem to matter less than their expertise, and therefore any attempt to assess the workings of such a professional central office in terms of how well it represents the views of the party on the ground (or even the party in public office) may well be misplaced. In this case also, it is the question of increasing central office autonomy which appears to be the most relevant. That said, this new professionalism certainly appears to indicate a shift from a situation in which many of the activities of central office were directed towards the organization and maintenance of the party on the ground (a key concern in the mass party), towards one in which they are now increasingly directed towards the mobilization of support in the electorate at large (as in Panebianco's electoral-professional party). More-over, once this shift takes place, it is clear that central office will necessarily orient more towards the views and demands of the party leadership and the party in public office than to those of the party on the ground.

In one scenario, therefore, the party in central office becomes simply more autonomous; in a second scenario, it becomes more subject to the control of the party in public office; in yet another scenario, as its resources become transferred across to the offices of the party in parliament, it is simply marginalized. Only rarely, it seems, is there evidence of a reaffirmation or a strengthening of its traditional position as representative or guardian of the party on the ground.

The paradoxical role of party membership

The second question, as to where all of this leaves the membership party, or the party on the ground, is more complex. On the face of it, a strengthening of the position and of the resources of the party in public office, and the marginalization of, or greater autonomy afforded to, the party in central office, would appear to offer little scope for an enhance-ment of the position of the party on the ground. In this sense, we might anticipate that party members would themselves be marginalized, being deemed unnecessary, or even ignored (see Katz, 1990; for an alternative view, see Scarrow, 1994). In practice, however, despite the relative decline in membership levels in most countries (see Table 1.1), the evidence does suggest that many parties still consider membership to be of value (see, for example, Müller's discussion of the Austrian case).

In the first place, despite the widespread introduction of state subventions, membership fees and donations still constitute an important source of revenue for many parties and, as Koole emphasizes in the case of the Netherlands, this is particularly true for what might be defined as the 'modern cadre party'. Even beyond the Netherlands, however, where state subventions remain relatively limited, members also contribute quite substantially to party incomes. In Austria, for example, the most recent figures suggest that membership fees account for an average of some 27 per cent of the head office income of the SPÖ and ÖVP; in Denmark, income from members and branches accounts for an average of almost 45 per cent of the head office income of the SD, RV, SF and KRF; in Germany, the average for the SPD and CDU is almost 20 per cent, while in Ireland, in the case of Fine Gael, income from members, branches and constituencies accounts for a very high 80 per cent of income. Thus, even though membership fees may often no longer constitute the main source of party revenue, they nevertheless remain important, and the loss of this income would almost certainly weaken the parties. For this reason alone, membership appears to remain an asset. Indeed, when discussing the balance between income generated from the membership and that generated via public subsidies, it is particularly interesting to note the case of Germany, where some of the reforms of public financing which are currently being discussed include provisions which would base the level of subsidy partly on the size of the party's membership, thus offering parties an additional incentive to boost their position on the ground. That said, in cases such as Norway and Sweden, where state subventions are among the highest in Europe, and where parties such as the DNA (in Norway) and the Social Democrats and Moderates (in Sweden) derive only some 10 per cent of their head office income from their members, the costs of maintaining the membership organization may well exceed the revenue which it generates.

Second, as Sundberg emphasizes at length in his discussion of the Finnish case, and as Müller points out in the Austrian case, members are also of value to the parties simply as warm bodies which can occupy official positions, both inside the party itself, as well as in public positions. In the Finnish case, for example, it is estimated that more than 55,000 persons are required by the parties to serve on internal party boards; that more than 60,000 persons are required to stand as party candidates in municipal elections; that more than 31,000 candidates are required to stand for parish council elections; and that upwards of 300,000 persons occupy 'positions of trust' in the local administration, including positions on the various boards and councils. To be sure, Finnish democracy, which is an increasingly organized democracy, may be an extreme case in this regard. Nonetheless, even at a more muted level, this syndrome may be regarded as having a wider validity, and as requiring parties to maintain a membership simply in order to influence public decision-making. Sundberg's conclusion is certainly generalizable beyond Finland: the more a party wishes to influence what goes on in society, and on the ground, the more it will need a mass membership. Warm bodies are important, and are not really substitutable.

Third, as emphasized in a number of these chapters, members can still prove important for organizational and political purposes. As Pierre and Widfeldt underline in the Swedish case, for example, the parties continue to rely on their membership levels to maintain at least the *image* of a mass party, and as proof that they are seen as viable channels for political representation. Members in this sense are also legitimizers, and it is such a perspective which clearly helps to explain the thinking behind the proposed reforms in the public financing of the German parties. In a related way, members are also useful in that they may help to mobilize voters. This function is, to be sure, less important than was once the case, in that parties now have at their disposal alternative techniques and networks of communication which can prove at least as effective as anything which is done by the membership. As Müller notes in the case of the Austrian SPÖ, for example, the leadership has appeared to grow increasingly sceptical about the value of the party organization as a means of communicating to the electorate as a whole. On the other hand, however, there is also the case of the Norwegian Conservatives, who have only recently begun to stress the benefits of membership as a means of electoral mobilization, an argument which is also sustained by Seyd and Whiteley's (1992) comprehensive analysis of British Labour Party membership. Either way, whether as legitimizers or as active campaigners, membership can continue to constitute an important resource in the process of inter-party competition, and hence it comes as no surprise to see that a number of parties, as in Britain and Ireland, still emphasize the need for membership drives. For all of these reasons, then, it does not seem likely that parties will willingly shed their members or discourage them from involvement in intra-party decision-making. Members might sometimes prove a nuisance, but they can also bring tangible, as well as intangible, benefits.

Moreover, as noted above, it also seems that many parties are attempting to give their members more say rather than less say, and that they are empowering rather than marginalizing them. Many parties now afford their ordinary members a greater voice in candidate selection than was once the case; in addition, more and more parties now seem willing to allow the ordinary members a voice in the selection of party leaders. The somewhat curious pattern that is developing, therefore, seems to be one in which the party in public office is afforded more power or more autonomy; in which the party in central office is becoming more professionalized; and in which, at the same time, through enhanced democratization, the ordinary members themselves, albeit sometimes fewer in number, are being afforded a greater role. This pattern would certainly seem to characterize the changes in a variety of parties in countries such as Austria, Denmark, Germany, Ireland, and the Netherlands.

At the same time, however, this pattern is also ostensibly paradoxical, in that it suggests that *both* the party on the ground and the party in public office are growing in importance. Conventional wisdom, on the other hand, would suggest more of a see-saw effect, in which the growth in importance of one necessarily involves a decline in the importance of the other. So how are we to understand this apparent paradox? How can parties democratize while at the same time affording more autonomy and power to the party in public office? How can they pursue these two apparently contradictory paths at one and the same time?

One possible answer is that the parties are actually making a careful and conscious distinction between different elements within the party on the ground, in the sense that the process of intra-party democratization is being extended to the members as individuals rather than to what might be called the *organized* party on the ground. In other words, it is not the party congress or the middle-level elite, or the activists, who are being empowered, but rather the 'ordinary' members, who are at once more docile and more likely to endorse the policies (and candidates) proposed by the party leadership and by the party in public office. This is, in fact, one of the most commonly observable trends across the range of countries and parties included in this volume: ordinary members, often at home, and via postal ballots, are increasingly being consulted by the party leadership, and are increasingly involved in legitimizing the choices of the party in public office, a process which is facilitated by the increasing use of centralized registers of party members. The more organized membership party, on the other hand, be it represented in congress or even in central office, as in the case of the Austrian parties and the Dutch denominational parties, for example, tends to become less relevant. Thus it is not a question of a simple see-saw, in which the gains of the party in public office must be compensated for by the losses of the party on the ground, or vice versa; rather, both can ostensibly become more important, while the activist layer inside the party, the traditionally more troublesome layer, becomes marginalized. Nor is this necessarily a problem for the party leadership, for, in contrast to the activists, these ordinary and often disaggregated members are not very likely to mount a serious challenge against the positions adopted by the leadership (see, for example, Zielonka-Goei, 1992). It is of course difficult to pin down precise figures on this. Moreover, as can be seen in the evidence of membership pressures on the leadership in the Finnish and Swedish cases, it is certainly not a universal phenomenon, and even the more passive members may well prove willing to challenge their leaders on issues such as membership rights. Nonetheless, as the British Labour Party would certainly appear to believe, it may well be the case that a fully democratized party is more susceptible to control by the party in public office than is a party in which the ordinary member (but not the activist) is effectively marginalized.

In a related vein, it might also be argued that the process of intra-party democratization is often meaningless and/or illusory. Thus, for example, while ordinary members may be given the right to vote in the leadership selection process, they are nevertheless often offered only a limited or constrained choice. The Dutch D66 now includes with its postal ballot on candidate selection an advisory list with an ordering proposed by the national committee of the party. Ordinary members in the British and Irish Labour parties now have a direct vote in choosing between the competing candidates for party leader, but the initial nomination of candidates remains the preserve of the party in public office, and the candidates themselves can be drawn only from within the ranks of the parliamentary parties. In Belgium, despite the introduction of direct elections by the PSC, the PRL and the new VLD, and despite an increase in the number of 'real' leadership elections, the party executive bodies still continue to have the strongest effective decision-making voice. In Denmark too, the election of party chairman is usually more managed than open. Moreover, at other levels within the parties, the opening up of the candidate selection process to a greater membership role, or even to a wider electoral involvement, as in the case of the occasional new 'primaries', for example, can nevertheless still be accompanied, as is the case in Austria, by the effective imposition of strong controls and strong discipline on those candidates who manage to become members of the parliamentary party. Democratization on paper may therefore actually coexist with powerful elite influence in practice.

Finally, as indicated above, the whole question of which face of the party is becoming more powerful and which less powerful may itself be misleading, in that we may actually be witnessing a process of mutual and growing autonomy. In the classic mass-party model, the relationship between the different faces was essentially hierarchical, with the party on the ground delegating power to the party congress and thence to the party executive, and with both congress and executive scrutinizing and controlling the activities of the party in public office. Even in the catch-all model, the relationship was hierarchical, albeit in reverse flow, with the party in public office emerging to dominate the party in central office and the party congress and, in so doing, effectively marginalizing the party on the ground. But while no clear single 'model' of party is apparent from the discussions in this volume, there is nevertheless a quite widespread consensus that the relevant relationships are now more *stratarchical* than hierarchical, and that each face of the party is now increasingly autonomous of the others. Thus, for example, while local input into the national party in a more hierarchical model was focused on the party congress and, through that, on the party central office, it seems now increasingly focused on the selection of local candidates, who, in turn, will eventually constitute the party in public office and will devise their own autonomous codes of discipline and behaviour. Of course, it may also be the case that mutual autonomy will develop to a degree in which the local party will become essentially unconcerned about any real input into the national party (and vice versa), and will devote itself primarily to politics at the local level.

All of this might suggest that the European parties are drifting towards what might be termed an 'American' model of party which, as depicted by Katz and Kolodny, is almost wholly decentralized and candidate-centred. This would be clearly misleading, however. For despite the apparent decline in the 'partyness' of European society, which is noted throughout this volume, there has certainly been no decline in the 'partyness' of the European state. On the contrary: given the extent, indeed, the increasing extent, to which parties organize the affairs of state and public decision-making in the European polities, they can in no sense be regarded, like their American counterparts, as 'empty vessels'. American parties matter as governing organizations, but only within very severe limits, and once we separate out the specific role of candidates, then these limits do not appear to go much beyond the initial organization of committees in Congress. In Europe, by contrast, where modern government continues to be party government, and where modern democracy continues to be party democracy, the party vessels are far from empty.

Party self-sufficiency and anti-party politics

From an organizational perspective, at least, a conception of party *change* or *adaptation* therefore seems much more appropriate than the rather misleading conception of party decline. Parties are in fact changing in two important respects. In the first place, party structures are tending to become increasingly stratarchical in character, with the party on the ground, the party in public office, and possibly even the party in central office, each stressing its own freedom of manoeuvre. In this sense, and significantly so, we can also witness the erosion of a sense of linkage even inside party itself. Second, parties, and especially the face of the party in public office, are becoming increasingly state-oriented, and are correspondingly less firmly tied to civil society, a process which is particularly evident in terms of the resources which are used by the parties in order to ensure their own survival and legitimacy. Indeed, this increased dependence of parties on the state can also be interpreted as the increased dependence of parties on themselves, since it is the parties themselves which, to all intents and purposes, are the state, or, at least, are those who devise the rules and regulations promulgated by the state, and who inevitably privilege their own position.

The outcome of both of these processes, at least in the short term, is therefore a greater sense of party *self-sufficiency*, especially at leadership level. To be sure, parties still need their voters. In many cases, as we have seen, they also still need their members. Increasingly, however, as the different faces of party become more autonomous of one another, and as the party leaderships increasingly turn towards the state for their resources, the relevance of linkages which are based on trust, accountability and, above all, representation, tends to become eroded, both inside and outside the parties. Thus while the parties may become more privileged, they also become more remote. It is this particular combination of developments that may well have provided the basis for the increasingly widespread anti-party sentiment which now characterizes mass politics in Western democracies.

One of the most striking electoral changes in many Western democracies within the last decade has been the emergence of what might be called 'anti-party' politics. At one level, and perhaps most commonly, this has been reflected in the growing popular scepticism about the integrity and honesty of the political class, and in the increasingly widespread belief that the established politicians are potentially venal, self-serving and even corrupt. At another level, as was seen in the recent campaign of American presidential candidate Ross Perot, and in that of the Canadian Reform Party, this has been reflected in the attempted mobilization of a reformist populism, which assumes that all of the established alternatives have failed irredeemably, and that the party system itself needs to be replaced. At yet another level, however, and more dangerously, this attitude has also been reflected in the rallying cries of new extreme-right forces, ranging from the National Front in France, to the Vlaams Blok in Belgium, to the Republicans in Germany and to the longer established but now increasingly strident Freedom Party in Austria.

This new wave of right-wing anti-party protest, from which virtually no Western democracy is currently immune, clearly derives its momentum from a variety of different factors. Among these are the slowdown in economic growth and the perceived inability of policy-makers to make more than small adjustments within an internationally determined economic order, on the one hand, as well as those particular tensions which are rooted in a re-awakened racism and xenophobia, on the other. At the same time, however, it is also possible to suggest that one of the key elements underlying this protest has resulted from the actions of the parties themselves, which, by becoming more self-sufficient and inward-looking, and often by turning their backs on civil society, have begun to widen the gap between the citizenry and the established political class.

In this sense, and perhaps ironically, the problem is not one of party decline per se, as is often imputed to be the case; rather, it appears to be one in which the parties are at once stronger, but also more remote; at once more in control, but also less powerful; and at once more privileged, but also less legitimate. Albeit less specifically, this picture also resembles the image of the dying years of the traditional Italian parties which is drawn by Bardi and Morlino in this volume, an image which rightly emphasizes those long-term preconditions of transformation that preceded the catalytic *mani pulite* investigations. The Italian case, to be sure, is exceptional, as is the sheer extent of party-system transformation which subsequently ensued. At the same time, however, the crisis which was evoked in parties which had become far too entangled with the state, which had neglected to adjust to changes in civil society, and which had become almost entirely

caught up with their own internal manoeuvrings, is one to which the
established parties in all Western democracies could well pay heed.

Note

1 Indeed, shortly after its formation, in April 1993 the party had actually joined Carlo
Ciampi's new reformist government, but withdrew 24 hours later following the refusal of the
Chamber of Deputies to allow the prosecution of the discredited Socialist leader, Bettino
Craxi.

References

Bartolini, Stefano (1983) 'The membership of mass parties: the social-democratic experi-
ence', in Hans Daalder and Peter Mair (eds), *Western European Party Systems*. London:
Sage. pp. 177–220.
Bartolini, Stefano and Mair, Peter (1990) *Identity, Competition and Electoral Availability:
The Stabilisation of European Electorates, 1885–1985*. Cambridge: Cambridge University
Press.
Beyme, Klaus von (1983) 'Governments, parliaments and the structure of power in political
parties', in Hans Daalder and Peter Mair (eds), *Western European Party Systems*. London:
Sage. pp. 341–68.
Beyme, Klaus von (1985) *Political Parties in Western Democracies*. New York: St Martin's
Press.
Bowler, Sean and Farrell, David (eds) (1992) *Electoral Strategies and Political Marketing*.
Basingstoke: Macmillan.
Budge, Ian and Keman, Hans (1990) *Parties and Democracy*. Oxford: Oxford University
Press.
Butler, David and Ranney, Austin (eds) (1992) *Electioneering: A Comparative Study of
Continuity and Change*. Oxford: Clarendon Press.
Castles, Francis and Wildenmann, Rudolf (eds) (1986) *Visions and Realities of Party
Government*. Berlin: de Gruyter.
Crewe, Ivor and Denver, David (eds) (1985) *Electoral Change in Western Democracies:
Patterns and Sources of Electoral Volatility*. London: Croom Helm.
Dalton, Russell J., Flanagan, Scott C. and Beck, Paul Allen (eds) (1984) *Electoral Change in
Advanced Industrial Democracies: Realignment or Dealignment?* Princeton: Princeton
University Press.
Dittrich, Karl (1983) 'Testing the catch-all thesis: some difficulties and possibilities', in Hans
Daalder and Peter Mair (eds), *Western European Party Systems*. London: Sage. pp.257–66.
Farrell, David (1993) *The Contemporary Irish Party: Campaign and Organizational Develop-
ments in a Changing Environment*. PhD thesis. European University Institute, Florence.
Franklin, Mark, Mackie, Tom and Valen, Henry (eds) (1992) *Electoral Change: Responses to
Social and Attitudinal Structures in Western Countries*. Cambridge: Cambridge University
Press.
Hecksher, Gunnar (1953) *The Study of Comparative Government and Politics*. Westport:
Greenwood Press.
Janda, Kenneth (1980) *Political Parties: A Cross-National Survey*. New York: Free Press.
Janda, Kenneth (1993) 'Comparative political parties: research and theory', in Ada W.
Finifter (ed.), *The State of the Discipline II*. Washington, DC: American Political Science
Association. pp. 163–92.
Katz, Richard S. (ed.) (1987) *Party Governments: European and American Experiences*.
Berlin: de Gruyter.
Katz, Richard S. (1990) 'Party as linkage: a vestigial function?', in Diane Sainsbury (ed.),

Party Strategies and Party–Voter Linkages, special issue of the *European Journal of Political Research*, 18 (1): 143–61.

Katz, Richard S. and Mair, Peter (eds) (1992a) *Party Organizations: A Data Handbook on Party Organizations in Western Democracies, 1960–90*. London: Sage.

Katz, Richard S. and Mair, Peter (1992b) 'Introduction: the cross-national study of party organizations', in Richard S. Katz and Peter Mair (eds), *Party Organizations: A Data Handbook on Party Organizations in Western Democracies, 1960–90*. London: Sage. pp. 1–20.

Katz, Richard S. and Mair, Peter (1992c) 'Changing models of party organization: the emergence of the cartel party', paper presented to the Workshop on Democracies and the Organization of Political Parties, ECPR Joint Sessions, University of Limerick.

Katz, Richard S. and Mair, Peter (1993) 'Varieties of convergence and patterns of incorporation in West European Party Systems', paper presented to the Workshop on Inter-Party Relationships in National and European Parliamentary Arenas, ECPR Joint Sessions, University of Leiden.

Katz, Richard S. and Mair, Peter (1994) 'The evolution of party organizations in Europe: three faces of party organization', in William Crotty (ed.), *Political Parties in a Changing Age*, special issue of the *American Review of Politics*, 14: 593–617.

Kirchheimer, Otto (1966) 'The transformation of West European party systems', in Joseph LaPalombara and Myron Weiner (eds), *Political Parties and Political Development*. Princeton: Princeton University Press. pp. 177–200.

Krouwel, André (1993) 'The organizational dimension of the catch-all party', paper presented to the Workshop on Inter-Party Relationships in National and European Parliamentary Arenas, ECPR Joint Sessions, University of Leiden.

Laver, Michael and Budge, Ian (eds) (1992) *Party Policy and Government Coalitions*. Basingstoke: Macmillan.

Laver, Michael and Schofield, Norman (1990) *Multiparty Government*. Oxford: Oxford University Press.

Lawson, Kay (1988) 'When linkage fails', in Kay Lawson and Peter Merkl (eds), *When Parties Fail: Emerging Alternative Organizations*. Princeton: Princeton University Press. pp. 13–38.

Lawson, Kay and Merkl, Peter (eds) (1988) *When Parties Fail: Emerging Alternative Organizations*. Princeton: Princeton University Press.

Mair, Peter (ed.) (1990) *The West European Party System*. Oxford: Oxford University Press.

Mair, Peter (1993) 'Myths of electoral change and the survival of traditional parties', *European Journal of Political Research*, 24 (2): 121–33.

Müller, Wolfgang C. (1993) 'The relevance of the state for party system change', *Journal of Theoretical Politics*, 5 (4): 419–54.

Panebianco, Angelo (1988) *Political Parties: Organization and Power*. Cambridge: Cambridge University Press.

Pizzorno, Alesandro (1981) 'Interests and parties in pluralism', in Suzanne Berger (ed.), *Organizing Interests in Western Europe: Pluralism, Corporatism, and the Transformation of Politics*. Cambridge: Cambridge University Press. pp. 249–84.

Pridham, Geoffrey (ed.) (1986) *Coalitional Behaviour in Theory and Practice: An Inductive Model for Western Europe*. Cambridge: Cambridge University Press.

Rose, Richard (ed.) (1974) *Electoral Behavior*. New York: Free Press.

Sainsbury, Diane (ed.) (1990) *Party Strategies and Party–Voter Linkages*, special issue of the *European Journal of Political Research*, 18 (1).

Scarrow, Susan E. (1994) 'The "paradox of enrollment": assessing the costs and benefits of party memberships', *European Journal of Political Research*, 25 (1): 41–60.

Seyd, Patrick and Whiteley, Paul (1992) *Labour's Grass Roots*. Oxford: Oxford University Press.

Sjöblom, Gunnar (1981) 'Notes on the notion of party adaptation', paper presented to workshop on Party Adaptation, ECPR Joint Sessions, University of Lancaster.

Woldendorp, Jaap, Keman, Hans and Budge Ian, (1993) *Political Data 1945–1990: Party Governments in 20 Democracies*, special issue of the *European Journal of Political Research*, 24 (1).
Zielonka-Goei, Mei Lan (1992) 'Members marginalising themselves? Intra-party participation in the Netherlands', *West European Politics*, 15 (2): 93–106.

2

Party Organization as an Empty Vessel: Parties in American Politics

Richard S. Katz and Robin Kolodny

Conventionally, the United States is described as having two parties – the Democrats and the Republicans. At one level, this is accurate. In 1991, all one hundred senators, 434 out of 435 members of the House of Representatives, and the president and vice-president had been elected either as Democrats or as Republicans, as had 49 of the 50 state governors. Indeed, what was remarkable about the 1990 and 1992 congressional elections was the high number (that is, one) of candidates elected who were not Democrats or Republicans – the highest number since 1952. With a few minor exceptions, the Democratic and Republican labels dominate state and local politics as well. While many American ballots appear notable for the large number of candidates and parties, it is very rare that more than two candidates – the Democrat and the Republican – are of any real significance.

Not only do the Democratic and Republican labels dominate American politics today, they have done so for an extremely long time. The last president who was not either a Democrat or a Republican was elected was 1848, and in only five presidential elections since 1864 have the Democratic and Republican candidates failed between them to receive at least 90 per cent of the vote (1892, 89 per cent; 1912, 65 per cent; 1924, 83 per cent; 1968, 86 per cent; and 1992, 81 per cent). The last time (and the only time since 1860) that the Democrats and Republicans did not between them hold at least 95 per cent of the seats in the House of Representatives was 1896.

Yet the persistence of this two-party system is curious for two reasons. First, the parties themselves have undergone dramatic shifts, both in their ideological orientations and constituent support bases. Second, one of the most notable features of American politics is the degree to which competition is framed in terms of individual candidates rather than partisan affiliations. Neither of these phenomena is new, but arguably they have become more significant since 1960. Together they offer grounds for arguing, with only moderate exaggeration, that rather than having two parties, or six parties (the organizations associated with the Democratic and Republican national committees, plus those associated with the Democratic and Republican conferences/caucuses in each house of Con-

gress – that is, going one step beyond James MacGregor Burns' (1965) idea
that congressional and presidential parties ought to be considered separately, and considering as separate the parties in the House and Senate as
well) – or one hundred parties (the two parties independently organized in
each state with the so-called national parties being no more than umbrella
organizations), the United States actually has no political parties at all.[1]

The view advanced here is that, from a structural perspective, American
national parties are best understood as being two loose alliances, each
consisting of three fundamentally independent organizations. From a more
substantive perspective, each of the six organizations exhibits such a low
degree of 'partyness' (Katz, 1986: 22–42) that they do not, in fact,
constitute national parties.

A complete analysis of this view must contend with three sets of related
questions. The first concerns the meaning of 'party' in American politics.
What is the official conception of party, and how do the parties conceive
themselves? How do parties relate to American understandings about and
expectations for democratic government? Most particularly, how are these
conceptions of party manifested, both in the internal organization of the
parties and in the role they play in the organization of government?
Second, given the picture of party weakness and incoherence that will
emerge in response to the first set of questions, why does the form of a two-
party system persist even in the absence of much substance? And why not
just any two parties, but precisely the Democrats and the Republicans?

Obviously, as we move from the first set of questions to the second, the
answers must become more speculative and interpretative. This is even
more the case with the third set of questions: what are the consequences of
the way American parties, and the American party system, are structured?
What is the impact of this way of organizing electoral competition on the
performance of the parties in government? And, most speculatively of all,
to what extent are the trends of the 1980s likely to be reversed with the
return, in 1992, of Democratic control of both the White House and the
Congress?

As these questions are too interrelated to permit individual consideration of each, the discussion which follows will proceed somewhat fluidly.
To begin, three fundamental aspects of American politics which have
significantly influenced the place and meaning of American parties will be
explored. These are the presidential system and the concomitant doctrine
of separation of powers, a basic ambivalence about parties, and federalism.

Fundamental features of American politics

Separation of powers

One of the basic tenets of American political thinking is that 'ambition
must be made to counteract ambition' (*The Federalist Papers*, no. 51). To

further this, the executive and legislative branches were made quite distinct from one another, and yet with each one involved in the exercise of those powers that logically belong to the other. The election of the president, although held concurrently with congressional elections, does not depend on their outcome, and in any case only one-third of the Senate is chosen at the same time as the president, and the House of Representatives is renewed halfway through the president's fixed four-year term. Although appointments to the president's cabinet require confirmation by the Senate, this has evolved into a judgement on the nominee's competence and moral/ethical suitability, not the policies of either the president or the nominee, and once confirmed there can be no vote of 'no confidence' leading to resignation or replacement. Analogously, while it is possible to talk about 'presidential coat-tails' affecting the outcome of congressional elections, there has been decreasing evidence of such an impact. It continues to be the case that the president's party tends to lose seats in the House at mid-term elections, but the very regularity of this loss makes it doubtful that these elections can be treated as referenda on presidential performance. The president cannot dissolve Congress and call for new elections; members of the legislative branch are as independent of the executive as he is of them.

Furthermore, the two houses conduct most of their business independently. Each party has two completely separate organizations and two completely independent sets of leaders, one in the House and the other in the Senate. To the (quite limited) extent that the congressional parties as organizations are capable of taking positions or reaching accommodations, the positions of a party in one chamber may well be repudiated by its nominal co-partisans in the other.

The veto power makes the president a major player in the legislative process, while his power of appointment gives him important leverage in local, as well as national, politics. At the same time, Congress retains tremendous power not only over the general content of legislation, but especially through detailed control of appropriations, over the particular geographic pattern of federal spending, and over the conduct of the bureaucracy. Thus it is both politically practical for Congress to act independently of the executive and reasonable for voters to apply different criteria to the choice of president and the choice of representatives. And once the voters do apply different criteria for different offices, it is also reasonable for politicians, both as candidates and in office, to respond accordingly.

One consequence of the separation of powers and independent election of the president, House of Representatives and Senate is the possibility of divided government (each party in 'control' of at least one of those organs). Divided government is not a new phenomenon: different parties controlled at least one of the three organs of government for twenty-eight of the hundred years between 1868 and 1968, but this was always a relatively short-lived situation (in no case was there divided control for more than six consecutive years) and, moreover, one that could cut either way. Since 1968, however, divided government in the specific form of a Republican president and a Democratic majority in the House of Representatives (and usually in the Senate as well) became the norm, with the four years of the Democratic Carter presidency the only exception and with general consensus not only among political analysts, but among party politicians themselves, that there was little prospect either for the Democrats to win the White House or to lose control of the House of Representatives in the foreseeable future. While the election of Bill Clinton as president in 1992 proved this consensus to have been wrong, the belief that the Republicans were the natural party of the presidency and the Democrats the natural party of Congress has strongly shaped the organization and behaviour of both parties. Even before this, however, the separation of powers was reflected in the organization of the parties, as will be discussed below.

Ambivalence toward parties

American political culture is profoundly ambivalent about political parties. The Founding Fathers wasted no time in organizing political parties to oppose one another, but 'if there was one point of political philosophy upon which these men, who differed on so many things, agreed quite readily, it was their common conviction about the baneful effects of the spirit of party' (Hofstadter, 1970: 3). On one hand, something to transcend the divisions wrought by the separation of powers is necessary if there is to be any effective government at all, while on the other hand, party can represent the seed of precisely the kind of national majority faction against which a large and diverse republic was supposed to protect.

Ambivalence about party is reflected in American attitudes toward representation. Members of Congress see themselves, and are seen by their constituents, primarily as agents of their districts or states, rather than as members of national organizations taking collective responsibility for government. Even presidential candidates, whose constituency is national, and who are expected to attend to the national interest, are seen more as individuals than as partisans. In most democracies to say 'I vote for the candidate, not the party' would be regarded as evidence of political immaturity; in the United States it is exactly the reverse. Indeed one explanation for the persistence of divided government in the 1980s stems from the different expectations of the people for the two branches of government coupled with their failure to see the collective records of the parties as more important than the individual records of the candidates. Given a choice between representing local interests and remaining loyal to the position of a national party, there is little doubt in the minds of either voters or members of Congress that party should give way. In contrast to the British understanding of elections as contests between cohesive teams, the American understanding is that there are many circumstances in which a member who placed party loyalty above constituency interests would be betraying the trust of the voters.

Especially with the rise of urban (and occasionally rural) political machines in the late nineteenth century, a second ambivalence about political parties came to the fore, that is a perception that party organizations illegitimately interposed themselves between the people and their representatives, and, moreover, were fundamentally corrupt and self-serving. This feeling had two particular roots beyond the obvious experience with organizations like Tammany Hall in New York. One was the belief that the relationship between representative and constituent should be direct and should also exist between the representative and all citizens in the constituency, not just those who had voted for the winner; hence it should not be mediated by divisive organizations like parties. The other was the identification of party with those who voted for it, rather than with formal members or even less with committee members or other party officials, many of whom held no publicly elected office at all. More generally, antipathy toward party organizations in the Populist and Progressive eras of the late nineteenth and early twentieth centuries was part of a wider antipathy toward all concentrations of power. At the same time, the Populists and Progressives recognized that parties were necessary to structure elections, especially in a context in which many offices were to be filled. Thus they adopted the same approach toward political parties that they applied to railroads and other 'public utilities'; while nominally left in the private sector, they were subjected to a battery of regulations that in some respects appended them to the state apparatus. Like the separation of powers, this ambivalence about party and particularly the imposition of state authority on parties, is reflected in their organizations.

Federalism

The most fundamental point about federalism as a factor conditioning the character of American parties is simply that the states are extremely important, both as loci for political careers and as independent decision-makers. Although there are more than 500,000 directly elected officials in the United States, fewer than 600 of these hold office at the federal level (Department of Commerce, 1991), and only two, the president and vice-president, contest elections which are truly national in orientation. The vast majority of appointive offices also are located in state and local governments. Moreover, while the presidency clearly is the top political job, career histories suggest that a state governorship is generally considered preferable to a seat in the House of Representatives and in some cases the Senate. One reason is that the states are, in fact, quite powerful. The national government has few supervisory powers with regard to the states beyond those embodied in the 'strings attached' to various federal programmes of grants-in-aid. The states remain important loci of power and independent decision-making in a wide range of policy fields, including many of the most emotionally charged.

The second point about American federalism is that it has engendered conflicts of interest between the federal government and the governments of the states. While this is true to some extent in all federal systems, its significance is heightened in the United States by the fact that those in office in the states generally do not expect to move to the national level, and thus are singularly unlikely to be sympathetic to the federal position. In particular and most recently, as the Reagan and Bush administrations tried to balance the federal budget by shifting responsibilities, but not the revenue to discharge them, to the states, the interests even of Republican state governors diverged significantly from those of the president of their own party.

Separation of powers, federalism and party organization

Although it is common in talking about American national parties to look particularly at the national committees of the parties and their staffs, the separation of powers and federalism that characterize American government are also reflected in the organization of the parties. With regard to separation of powers, it is more accurate to say that the United States has six parties at the national level rather than two, three parties calling themselves Democratic and three calling themselves Republican, but all in fact independent. Often, the national committee (corresponding to the central committee or national executive of the typical European party) of each party is taken to be 'the' party organization, and at least implicitly credited with the functions and achievements of other independent party organs (for example, Cotter and Bibby, 1980). In fact, there is a proliferation of party bodies, most of which are *not* responsible to others, and the party national committees are only the 'national executives' of the presidential parties. Each of the national party labels is also applied to an organization in each house of Congress (here referred to as 'caucuses', although officially all but the House Democratic Caucus are 'conferences'). These are not just the 'parliamentary' wings of a single national party, however, but autonomous organizations with their own professional bureaucracies that independently perform most of the functions normally associated with parties writ large – policy formulation, fund-raising, organizing and managing campaigns, recruiting candidates, etc.[2] There is no claim that the party platform adopted by the national *presidential* nominating convention is binding on either of the corresponding congressional parties, let alone on their individual members, nor is the presidential party represented in the caucuses when (and if) they adopt policy positions. While the three 'branches' (House, Senate and presidential/ national committee) of each party would prefer to have more rather than fewer candidates with the same party label elected in the other arenas, and share some expectation of mutual sympathy, aid and understanding and, at least in general terms, some extremely vague ideological orientations, the similarities end there. Both their constituencies and their objectives are quite distinct. One consequence is that the two party national committees, or the two party organizations in one of the houses of Congress, resemble one another far more in both structure and in operation than do any pair of 'branches' in the same party.

The federal nature of American government is also reflected in the organization of the parties. Genetically, the parties of the national committees are loose federations of state parties that came together in the last century to nominate and support presidential candidates, while the congressional parties are equally loose alliances of congressmen and senators formed even earlier to organize their respective chambers and allocate such things as committee assignments and staff. In all of this, the state remains the basic unit. In both presidential parties the national nominating convention and the national committee are made up of delegates and officers of the state parties. The primacy of the state parties is illustrated by the fact that although their representatives in the conventions or national committees can amend the rules, and thus alter the structure, of the national party, the national party cannot impose any uniformity of either policy or structure on the state parties (except with regard to their delegations to the national conventions and committees – and even this right has only been asserted effectively since the 1970s).

The importance of the state as a political unit is also manifested in the congressional parties (particularly in the House of Representatives, given that there are only two senators from each state). The state delegation, for example, is the basic unit of representation for both the Democratic Congressional Campaign Committee (DCCC) and the National Republican Congressional Committee (NRCC – see p. 43), and while not every state is directly represented on the caucus committees on committees (which assign members of their parties to the standing committees of the corresponding chamber), state delegations (for example, Democratic Representatives from Michigan) are still the basic units grouped to form the constituencies of members of the committees on committees.

While parties are defined at both the national and state levels, the state role is by far the more important. It is the fifty states, rather than the national government, that primarily regulate the conduct of elections at the federal, state and local levels. States started regulating parties far earlier, and the range of party structures and activities governed by state regulations is far broader. Federal involvement in the definition of party really only dates marginally from 1946 or more substantially from 1971, and is primarily the indirect consequence of the regulation of campaign finance.

State conceptions of parties

In broad terms, the states' 'official conceptions' of parties are concerned with two subjects – the nature of the party system, and the organization and operation of individual parties within that system. With regard to the first of these, the states have attempted to institutionalize not just a two-party system, but a system dominated precisely by the Democratic and Republican parties. Although only Delaware and Oklahoma explicitly put the Democrats and Republicans first and second on the ballot, all but four (Alabama, Idaho, Mississippi, Virginia) of the other states using party-oriented ballots implicitly achieve the same result by requiring parties to be listed in order of their voting strength at the last election, by requiring that the 'major' parties be listed first, or by allowing an elected state official (that is, a Democrat or a Republican) to determine the order of parties on the ballot. In all states, parties with a set number of registrants and/or votes in the previous election (usually only the Democrats and Republicans) are guaranteed a place on the ballot. New or minor parties generally need to submit petitions signed by substantial numbers of voters before every election. The magnitude of this bias is particularly acute when these state requirements are cumulated to the presidential level. For example, for a new party presidential candidate to have appeared on the ballot in all fifty states plus the District of Columbia in 1992 required at a minimum a total of over 640,000 petition signatures, plus an additional 79,300 registrants (in states for which the number of registrants required is smaller than the number of nominating petition signatures).

Along with advantageous ballot access, the 'major' parties are also subject in most states to detailed party laws, establishing their structures and controlling their choice of candidates. In both respects, these laws generally reflect the Progressive era's hostility to closed party organizations, and tend to treat parties more as semi-public agencies for the organization of elections than as private bodies (agencies of civil society) advocating particular programmes. Moreover, in regulating even the selection and behaviour of state delegations to the national party conventions, they implicitly assert both the confederal nature of the parties and the superiority of state over national authority in the control of parties.[3]

In general terms, each of the 'major' state parties (regulation of 'minor' parties often is different or non-existent – indicating that they are not considered 'real' parties) has a state central committee (ranging in size from under two dozen to nearly 1000, often with an executive committee, and chosen by county committees, state conventions or primary elections), a state chairman (formally elected by the central committee or a state convention, although frequently in effect named by the governor for his/her own party) and one or more lower tiers of county, city, ward, district or precinct committees (most often filled by primary elections) (Beck and Sorauf, 1992). Since participation in the primary elections or local caucuses that form the base of all the many state variants on this theme is open to any voter who meets quite minimal requirements (themselves set by state law rather than by the parties and in some cases allowing participation by people who need *never* make any pretence of party affinity or affiliation), the possibility of a strong, stable and professional party organization might appear to be limited. In addition, the independence of American elected officials from their party organizations, and the use of the direct primary to determine partisan nominations, means that the party organizations have very restricted direct relevance to government or policy. On the other hand, elections of party officials and participation in party caucuses is generally of such low salience that a relatively stable group of party activists usually remains in control.

Although this structure might suggest strong affinity between American party organization and the mass membership party model, there is a fundamental difference with regard to the notion of party membership. The states generally adopted the Progressive era equation of party registration, or even more of party voting, with party membership. However, party affiliation on the electoral register differs from membership in several important respects. The parties exercise no control over registration; they cannot impose requirements or expel disloyal 'members'. Although affiliation with a party entails a public declaration of intent to affiliate, no other form of commitment is required; party registrants pay no dues, generally make no declaration of loyalty and need attend no meetings (indeed, there rarely are any meetings). Registrants often acquire no special position within the party's decision-making structures; although nominations generally are made by primary election, in only twenty-six of the fifty states is participation in the primary restricted to those who have previously (in some cases as little as ten days before) affiliated with the party. In many states there is no partisan registration at all, leaving the notion of party membership even more vacuous. Indeed, in a recent court case that indirectly speaks volumes about the parties' conceptions of themselves, the Supreme Court ruled that the state of Connecticut could not prohibit the Republican Party from allowing voters registered as independents from voting in its primary elections (*Tashjian v. Republican Party of Connecticut*, 479 US 1024 [1986]).

This 'empty vessel' conception of parties is also clear with regard to candidate selection. For all major offices except the presidency, this is virtually always by primary election (again with the right to participate, either as candidate or as voter, beyond the control of the party organizations). Indeed, far from being able to name, or even veto, nominees, in a few cases state law has prohibited the party organizations even from endorsing particular candidates in the primaries. The result, and the *intended* result, is that basic electoral competition is with few exceptions between two candidates, one called the 'Democrat' and the other called the 'Republican', but neither chosen by a party with any organizational control over their selection, campaigns, or actions in office. As Ripley observes (1983: 76, emphasis in original), Congressional elections are less national contests than they '*are local events with national consequences and (sometimes) [. . .] influenced by national events*. Local candidates by and large are responsible for their own electoral fates. . . .'

The federal conception of parties

Federal involvement in the definition of party revolves around four, not entirely consistent, themes. The first is a clearly non-party conception of politics. For example, the only regulation of political broadcasting is the 'equal access' rule of the Federal Communications Act, which refers only to legally qualified candidates. Similarly, the primary reporting unit for the Federal Election Campaign Act (FECA) is the candidate committee, and indeed compliance with the law requires that candidates form their own committees rather than relying on pre-existing party organizations; spending by a party on behalf of one of its candidates is not regarded as a 'normal' party activity, but rather as a contribution to the candidate's own campaign.

The second, and somewhat contradictory, theme appears in the composition of the independent regulatory commissions, like the Federal Communications Commission or the Federal Election Commission. Here a bipartisan conception of politics is enshrined in the requirement that no more than half the members of a commission come from the same political party. One result is that the president may have to appoint members to fill positions allocated to the other party. The third theme is the institutionalization of the division of the national parties into separate national committee, House and Senate organizations. Since the Legislative Reorganization Act of 1946, the Democratic and Republican parties have received public financial support for their congressional policy committees. This support is not channelled through the party national committees, however, but goes directly to the party organizations in the two chambers of Congress. The fourth, and most important, part of the federal 'official conception' of parties is embodied in FECA. In the course of regulating the activities of *candidates* for federal office, FECA has a number of provisions which collectively suggest federal, but nonetheless broadly coherent, parties, each headed by its national committee. In addition, FECA reinforces the bias already noted in state laws in favour of the Democratic and Republican parties.

FECA provides public funding for party activities in conjunction with presidential campaigns under three headings. First, each major party is entitled to $2 million plus cost of living adjustments since 1974 for its presidential nominating convention; in 1992, this amounted to about $11 million for each party. Second, presidential candidates who voluntarily accept FECA's general election spending limits ($20 million adjusted for inflation; in 1992, $55 million), receive that amount as a grant from the government. Third, candidates for a party's presidential nomination can receive federal funds to match money raised in private donations. This is available to any candidate, of any party, who meets in each of twenty states the requirement of having raised at least $5000 in donations of less than $250 each. For the first two types of support, however, FECA distinguishes among 'major parties' (those whose presidential candidate received at least 25 per cent of the popular vote in the previous election, that is, the Democrats and Republicans), 'minor parties' (those whose candidate received more than 5 per cent but less than 25 per cent of the popular vote, that is, generally none), and 'new parties' (all others, for example, Libertarians, or in 1992 Ross Perot). Major parties and their candidates receive full and equal funding in advance; minor parties and their candidates receive proportionately reduced funding, also in advance; new party candidates can receive general election funding based on their share of the vote in the current election, if they receive at least 5 per cent of the vote in that election (and thus qualify as minor parties for the next election as well), but this money is paid only after the fact.

The general election subvention is paid to the candidates' own campaign committees, not to their parties, and so while reinforcing the hegemony of the Democratic and Republican labels it does not strengthen the parties as organizations, and indeed is suggestive of a no-party conception of presidential elections even as it entrenches the existing two major parties. Other FECA provisions, however, were explicitly intended to strengthen the parties as organizations, and reflected discontent (at least among professional party politicians) with the success that the Progressive reforms and earlier federal finance legislation had in eviscerating the parties. In addition to providing public funding for presidential campaigns, the law regulates both contributions to political committees and candidates for any federal office as well as expenditures on behalf of such candidates. In doing so, however, the law distinguishes between party committees and other political committees or individuals. With regard to contributions, national and state party committees are allowed to make unlimited contributions to one another, while all other donors are limited in what they can give. Moreover, FECA allows an individual to contribute up to $20,000 per year to a political party, but only $5000 per year to a Political Action Committee (PAC) and $1000 per year to a candidate. Nonetheless, by subjecting each individual's total political contributions to a $25,000 annual limit, the law makes it unlikely that individuals will give anything like the full legal amount to a party, since that would only leave $5000 for all candidates and PACs where individuals might expect their contributions to make a greater difference to the causes they wish to support.

Looking at expenditures, the law distinguishes two categories of expenditure: independent and coordinated, the difference lying in the 'knowledge and consent' of candidates and their organizations. On the premise that a candidate bearing a party label and that party's organization(s) are necessarily in communication with each other, the law assumes that expenditures made by political parties on behalf of candidates cannot be without the candidates' knowledge and consent. Therefore, party expenditures are considered to be 'coordinated' with the individual campaigns, and carry absolute (although reasonably generous) limits in the law. On the other hand, non-party organizations (read: PACs), which do not nominate candidates, are assumed to be able to make 'independent' campaign expenditures for or against a candidate without his/her knowledge and consent. Since 1976, when the Supreme Court ruled limitations on independent expenditures to violate the First Amendment, these expenditures have been unlimited (*Buckley v. Valeo*).

As originally understood, the language of FECA allows only 'the national committee of a political party and a State committee of a political party, including any subordinate committee of a State committee' (*2 USC § 441a*) to make coordinated expenditures. In 1982, however, the National Republican Senatorial Committee (NRSC, the congressional campaign committee of the Republicans in the Senate, but, like the other three committees, technically an extra-congressional organization, not simply a committee of the Republican Conference) won the right to spend the amount of money legally allowed for 'coordinated expenditures' by the national and state parties, provided the national committee and state parties agreed to the arrangement. It was a relatively simple matter to get both the national and most of the state committees to enter into these agency agreements; they simply did not have the time, desire or money to pursue congressional coordinated expenditures themselves.

The original law clearly implied the dominance of the national committees. The development of agency agreements, however, reinforced the separation of congressional campaigns both from the national committees and from the state party organizations. Although formally they made the Congressional Campaign Committees (CCCs) agents of the national committees and state parties, in practice they took both the principals out of the congressional campaign business altogether. Rather than begging for funds from the national committees and state parties and offering advice on how party funds should be allocated, the CCCs became agents for the raising of money as well as its disbursement, and once they had developed their own fund-raising operations the CCCs directed the disbursement of the funds raised without further reference to their nominal principals.

Finally, FECA is most pro-party in what it fails to limit. Expenditures by state and local parties for voter registration, get-out-the-vote drives and other party-building purposes are exempted from the limits applied to other activities, effectively allowing individuals, PACs and, in some cases, corporations and unions to make unlimited contributions. Moreover, since 1979 the national parties have been able to use this exemption (known as 'soft money') to accept unlimited contributions provided that they are passed through to the states. As a result, in 1988 at least 375 people were able to contribute $100,000 or more to one or the other of the major parties (Magleby and Nelson, 1990: 19).

Despite the complexity of this picture, there is an important element of commonality that runs throughout both the state and the federal conceptions of party. That is, American parties are officially conceived as organizations that provide services, both to candidates and to democracy, but not as organizations that themselves run campaigns. They are seen as providing a framework for the choice of candidates (which in some cases they are legally barred from trying to influence); as structuring electoral choice both through the physical organization of the ballot and through campaigns asking for undifferentiated support of the primary winners, whoever they may be; as getting out the vote; as helping candidates raise money; and as acting as a wholesale provider of services for candidates. The actual direction of campaigns, however, is presumed to be the province of the candidates acting as individuals.

The organization of American national parties

Presidential parties

On the surface, the two presidential party organizations are quite similar, and closely follow the 'normal' model of a membership-based party. Formally, the highest governing body of each of the two presidential parties is its quadrennial national convention. The convention chooses the presidential and vice-presidential nominees (and thus the closest approximation in the American system to *the* party leader), approves the party platform drafted by one of its own committees, and installs the party's national committee to conduct the party's business between conventions. Until 1972, the conventions also had sole power to amend the national party rules; since then, the Democrats have allowed the Democratic National Committee (DNC) to amend the party charter by a two-thirds vote (as opposed to simple majority in the convention). Each of the party national committees in turn elects the party's national chairman, and each also has an executive committee composed of a small number of national committee members, plus representatives of other party-affiliated organizations.

At a deeper level, however, the similarity between American presidential parties and the European membership party model rapidly begins to fade. Most fundamentally, as observed above, there are no party members in any real sense. Although there are a variety of ancillary organizations, many of these are associations of elected officials rather than ordinary citizens (for example, the Democratic Governors Conference) or exist only on paper for the purpose of giving the appearance of ethnic or other representation. Others are 'clubs' of contributors, whose members have no special rights within the party except the right to be solicited for even larger contributions.

In their self-conceptions, the national parties are associations of state parties. Convention delegates are apportioned among the state parties with regard to state population, but also (perhaps reflecting the equation of electoral supporters and members) to previous support for the party's candidates. The allocation rules have changed frequently, ostensibly to improve the fairness of the process and to improve the competitive quality of the eventual nominee, but more generally to try to cement the position of whatever group is currently on top. One constant, however, is that in neither party does partisan registration, as the closest American equivalent to party membership, have any bearing on state delegation size. Over the period from 1960 through 1990, the Democrats have gradually increased the weight given to states with strong records of support for the presidential ticket while the Republicans have increased the weight given to population (in the guise of number of congressional districts); moreover, while the Democrats have averaged success over the three previous presidential elections, the Republicans have considered only the immediately preceding election cycle and have given (since 1976) bonus delegates to states electing Republican senators, governors and House delegation majorities as well as to states whose electoral votes went to the Republican presidential nominee. Thus, as divided government became more firmly established, each of the parties rewarded those states in which it had done well, but with particular weight given to the arena (presidential or congressional) in which it was doing poorly overall.

At the beginning of the 1960s, the national conventions were in a real sense assemblies of the delegates of state party organizations. Through 1968, thirty-eight states chose all or a substantial part of their national convention delegates in state conventions or state party committees; only fifteen states (plus the District of Columbia) had primary elections in which the names of the presidential candidates themselves appeared on the ballot, and in only six of these was the result binding on the state delegation.[4] Even when primaries chose the delegates, a whole slate generally was chosen together, and so was likely to vote as a bloc; indeed, until 1968, the Democrats permitted a state party to instruct its delegation to vote as a bloc, regardless of the wishes of the minority. Party officials and office-holders loomed large in the delegations.

Beginning after the Democrats' 1968 loss, a series of reforms altered this process and the composition of the Democratic convention. The most substantial Democratic reform was to require state parties to 'assure that such delegates have been selected through a process in which all Democratic voters have had full and timely opportunity to participate' (Commission on Party Structure and Delegate Selection, 1970: 14–15). This not only reduced the power of the state organizations, and emphasized the absence of any sense of formal party membership, but far more than was true in the past made the selection of delegates hinge almost entirely on popular preference among presidential candidates. Beginning in 1976, the Democrats in fact have required proportional representation for supporters of all presidential candidates (counting 'uncommitted' as a separate candidate) receiving at least 15 per cent support in the state's selection process, be that primary election or local caucuses. The Democrats have also required (since 1972) each state to have an affirmative action plan leading to delegations that reflect the demographic characteristics of the state's Democratic voters, and (since 1980) equal representation for men and women; as a result, the female proportion of convention delegates rose from 13 per cent in 1968, to 40 per cent in 1972, and 49 per cent in 1980. The need to comply with these rules then led to greatly expanded use of primaries as the principal selection method (in 1988, thirty-one states either selected their Democratic delegates by primary, or so as to reflect the result of a presidential preference primary). It also threatened to leave the party's public office-holders out altogether. To avert this possibility, and to increase the weight given to professional politicians (who presumably would value electoral attractiveness over ideological purity), the Democrats have, since 1980, reserved an increasing number of delegate positions for pledged (and since 1984 also for unpledged) 'super-delegates'. Continuing the emphasis on states as the basic units of the national party, these additional delegates are regarded as part of their states' delegations, even if they are chosen elsewhere (for example, by the Congressional caucuses).

The formal structure of the Republican convention has changed far less than the Democratic, in part because the Republicans have maintained the rule that only the National Convention can change the rules for subsequent conventions, but also because their string of presidential victories until 1992 gave them less incentive to reform their rules. In place of the Democratic requirement of gender equality, the Republicans in 1976 adopted equality as a target, supplemented in 1980 by an explicit statement that this target was not to be taken as a quota. Reflecting this difference, the female proportion of Republican delegates has never exceeded 44 per cent, and in 1988 had fallen to 35 per cent. On the other hand, because many of the changes in Democratic Party rules could only be implemented by changing state election laws, they have come to affect the Republican Party as well. Thus, primary elections have become the principal determiner of Republican convention delegates, although in many states the Republicans have retained some form of winner-take-all system, rather than the proportionality required by Democratic Party rules. As a result, in neither party is it any longer possible (as it clearly was in the 1950s and early 1960s) for a candidate to 'skip the primaries' and still be nominated; nor, given the winnowing of the candidate field through the protracted primary and caucus process, does it appear credible that there will be in the foreseeable future a convention that does other than ratify on the first ballot the pre-ordained choice.

Although the form of the state delegation remains, one effect of these reforms has been to change fundamentally the role of the delegates, from representatives of state parties to representatives of individual candidates and those candidates' own campaign organizations. Often, for example, state election laws now require a prospective convention delegate to have the prior nomination or approval of the candidate (s)he pledges to support. Especially in the Democratic Party, this changed orientation is directly reflected in the committees of the national convention as well. Each of the national conventions has (with slight variations in nomenclature) three major standing committees: credentials, rules and platform.[5] Until 1972, each state had equal representation (one man and one woman) on each of the Democrats' standing committees. In 1972, ninety-five additional members were allocated in proportion to the size of the states' convention delegations (again equally divided by gender). The crucial change came in 1976, when allocation of committee seats was made proportional to support for presidential candidates, with each candidate permitted to nominate candidates (who need not be delegates to the convention) for the slots allotted to his supporters. Finally, in 1984 a second tier of committee members was added, elected by the Executive Committee of the Democratic National Committee from among 'Party Leaders and Elected Officials'. The Republicans have retained the principle of equal state representation (from 1964, one man and one woman) on standing committees, but the spread of primaries has also made these far more than in the past the direct agents of presidential candidates.

Although the national conventions nominally install their parties' national committees to act for them between conventions, the national committees' structures reflect the formal nature of the parties as federations of state organizations, and their operation reflects the real nature of the parties as essentially empty frameworks within which individual presidential candidates and their supporters contend for position. Each state nominates members in accordance with party rules for ratification by the national convention. For the Republicans, these rules simply specified that state law or custom be observed, and this has meant tremendous stability in the size and composition of their national committee membership. Since 1960, each state or territory has been represented by one man and one woman. In 1960 and 1964, state party chairmen were also granted membership, provided that state demonstrated its Republican voting strength based on one of several measures. Since 1968, state party chairmen have been members automatically. Thus the size of the Republican National Committee membership fluctuated between 148 in 1960 and 165 in 1988. Until 1968, the Democratic National Committee was similarly structured, and party rules similarly deferred to local practice in the selection of national committee members. Since then, however, the DNC has been in a state of flux. From 1960 through 1968, the DNC consisted of one man and one woman from each state and territory. From 1972 on, the committee has been constituted along the same lines as delegates to the national convention. The state party chair and highest ranking opposite sex member of the state party are automatically members, with 150 additional members being apportioned among the states based on the same formula as specified in the call to the convention for delegates. Also beginning in 1972, an increasing number of representatives of party elected officials, and beginning in 1976 an increasing number of representatives of affiliated organizations (Young Democrats, National Federation of Democratic

Women) were given seats on the DNC. Finally, allowance was also made for a number of at-large members to provide 'balanced' representation. Altogether, the DNC had grown to 403 members in 1988.

The real administrative head of the presidential party organization is the National Chairman, who, in particular, hires the staff of the national (committee) party headquarters. Although nominally selected by the national committee, in the president's party the national chairman is effectively a presidential appointee. The basis of this appointive power is not the party rules, but the dominance of the president's supporters within the party as evidenced by his victory at the last national convention and as cemented by the conversion of supporters of his erstwhile opponents within the party. Since the primary purpose of the party as embodied in the national convention and national committee is to choose and support a presidential candidate, it stands to reason that a successful candidate – additionally armed with the president's power of appointment in the governmental sphere – would dominate the national committee organization. The dominance of the defeated presidential candidate, however, disappears with his defeat; hence the chairmanship of the out-party's national committee is more seriously contested, but primarily as a trial of strength among prospective presidential candidates and would-be kingmakers.

In practical political terms, the national committees and their chairmen are of some real importance. In the first place, the DNC has the power to change the party's rules, in particular the rules regarding delegate allocation and selection for the next national convention; in doing so, they obviously can advantage some candidates at the expense of others. Secondly, in both parties, the chairman and national committee staff are in regular contact with, and able to provide a variety of resources (especially money and access to money) and services to state parties. In doing this, they can, at least to a limited degree, favour those who are likely to support the 'right' candidate/position at the national level, and more generally can build a base of local information, contacts, and reciprocal favour-doing that can be invaluable in the next campaign for the party's presidential nomination. Thirdly, the national chairman is well positioned to gain access to the media. Particularly when a story calls for presentation of the 'Democratic' and 'Republican' positions, the national chairmen make ideally equivalent spokesmen. Especially here, however, it is also important to underline the limits of the national chairman's power. In neither party can the chairman make binding – or even seriously considered advisory – policy decisions. In the president's party, the national chairman (if he wants to keep his job) can do nothing except serve as a mouthpiece for the White House, although in some cases this may mean docilely repeating the White House line, in others serving as the ostensible source of 'trial balloons', and in still others serving as one of the many faces a president may want to present to the various elements of a fragile supporting coalition. In the out-party, the chairman has somewhat more freedom in what he says, but it is a freedom born of marginality and he still can speak for the party only as a well placed insider, not as an authoritative decision-maker.

Congressional parties

In most democratic political systems, the parliamentary party is simply one aspect of the governing face of a national party organization. In the United States, however, the congressional parties are, as already observed, free-standing and independent organizations, in particular performing for their members in their own spheres both of electoral competition and of government the functions performed by the presidential parties for presidential candidates and the president himself. While the congressional parties are represented on the national committees/executive committees of the corresponding presidential parties, this representation, like the committees themselves, is more symbolic than substantive.

Congressional parties also differ from most parliamentary parties in that party discipline is virtually unknown. Relatively few votes divide a majority of one party from a majority of the other, and the average party unity scores (the percentage of the time the member votes with the majority of his/her party) on those votes that do divide the parties generally is barely half way between the theoretical minimum of 0.5 and a perfect 1.0. One reason is that there are virtually no sanctions for breaking party ranks, even when there is an official party (that is, caucus) position – deviants retain their committee and subcommittee chairmanships, office space and staff, as well as their claim on party resources in seeking re-election. As for party leaders denying a rebellious member renomination, that is not within the realm of legal possibility. Indeed, there is not even a particularly strong aspiration toward party unity. Among the four congressional caucuses, the only rules obliging members to support caucus decisions are the House Democrats' rule requiring party unity on the election of Speaker and other officers of the House, and the House Republican rules obliging the ranking Republican member of a committee to 'ensure that each measure on which the Republican Conference has taken a position is managed in accordance with such position' and all members of the Republican leadership 'to support positions adopted by the Conference'.

This is not to say that there are no broad differences between the parties. In Congress, as in the presidential arena, Democrats generally are more ready to use public rather than private means to solve economic problems, while Republicans are more ready to use the power of the state to enforce conformity with social norms; economically, Democrats tend to prefer 'trickle-up' policies (for example, policies like increasing the personal income tax exemption to stimulate demand), while Republicans tend to prefer 'trickle-down' policies (for example, policies like capital gains tax cuts to stimulate investment). There are, however, many apparent exceptions in both parties, and in campaigning, as in Congressional policy-making, while the positions taken by party leaders may become identified as the 'party' positions, members are free to depart from them whenever their own perceptions of electoral expedience or desirable policy so dictate. Moreover, the position enunciated by the leaders is likely to be the result of negotiation and brokerage (trying to find a position that most members will accept) rather than centralized decision, and on many important issues there is no party position at all, even in this limited sense.

While the leaders of the presidential party (that is, the presidential candidates) are chosen by the parties' primary voters or state and local caucus participants, the leaders of the congressional parties are chosen by the caucuses themselves. That is to say that although they have consti-tuents in their own districts or states and must win re-election there like any other member of Congress, their only 'constituents' as leaders are the other sitting Senators or Representatives. In this the congressional parties are like many other parliamentary parties. Where they differ is that the leaders chosen by the congressional parties do not in any substantial sense become the leaders of the party outside Congress. Even if party label and image are significant electorally, no congressional candidate is likely to believe that the identity of the party's leader in Congress will make a difference to his/her own fate at the polls. Congressional party leadership and congressional elections are generally independent of one another – except that the 'pork barrel' opportunities, and the required moderation and compromise, of leadership positions can respectively be electoral assets or liabilities for the leaders themselves in their own districts. The closest to an exception is the slight tendency to consider overall party success in deciding whether to retain the chairman of one of the Congres-sional Campaign Committees. This choice, however, is made after the new Congress has been elected, and hence only those members who were themselves (re)elected, regardless of how disastrous the overall result may have been, can vote.

Each of the caucuses chooses candidates for Speaker (House) and President *pro tempore* (Senate) and elects the party floor leaders, whips, chairmen of the caucuses (*not* the same person as the Speaker/majority/minority leader except for the Senate Democrats) and of the various caucus committees. In the Democratic caucuses, these caucus committee chairmanships are all held by the Speaker (except the chairmanship of the House Democratic caucus) or floor leader, while in the Republican caucuses, they are spread among different individuals, perhaps because as the majority party the Democrats have all the standing committee and subcommittee chairmanships to divide among themselves (making party offices appear relatively unimportant) while for the Republicans chairman-ships of the various caucus committees are the best offices available. Additionally, the caucuses may meet during the Congress to adopt party policy positions, which, however, are not binding on anyone.

The most important policy-relevant decision of the caucuses is the assignment of their members to the standing committees of the full chamber, at the beginning of each Congress. For the Democrats, committee assignments are controlled by the two Steering Committees, which are chaired by the Speaker in the House and the Majority Leader in the Senate. The Republicans have a separate Committee on Committees, but basically follow the same procedure, the most significant element of which is that it only applies to new members and senior members seeking new committee assignments. Returning members have a presumptive right to reappointment to the committees on which they served in the previous Congress unless 'bumped' by a reduction in the party's share of the committee seats. Because the committee assignments are based on party, those who are neither Democrats nor Republicans get what is left over at the end – a powerful incentive even for those few candidates elected as independents or on minor party tickets to join either the Democratic or Republican caucus. While this makes party affiliation crucial to the organization and operation of Congress, however, it does not make the party organizations themselves powerful. First, the party caucuses exercise the greatest discretion with freshman members, who have no record of party loyalty for which they can be rewarded or punished. Second, the caucuses are constrained by a variety of norms, for example requiring geographic balance among committee members, that limit their discretion even in the assignment of freshmen. More important, however, is the simple fact that within the congressional parties unity is less important to leaders and followers alike than is the maintenance or achievement of a nominal partisan majority; thus members generally are assigned to the committees that will allow them to be seen attending to their own constituents' needs and interests, even if this is detrimental to overall party cohesion.

Since the mid-1970s, the Democratic (majority) caucus has also designated the chairmen of the standing committees. (The minority Republican House caucus began this practice for the ranking minority member in 1971.)[6] Previously, committee assignments and chairmanships were awarded strictly on the basis of seniority. In fact, seniority still is rarely violated, and then only in extreme cases. Analogously, since 1973 Democratic subcommittee chairmen have been designated by the relevant Democratic committee caucuses, rather than by the committee chairmen, although again generally following a seniority rule. While this marginally increased the power of the caucus, its real effect was to decrease the individual power of committee chairmen, making the process more egalitarian rather than more partisan. Virtually all members of the majority party in the Senate and about half the members in the House chair one or more subcommittees. Especially given this diffusion of chairmanships, caucus members do not want to be bound by party discipline, and thus do not try to impose it on others.

What most underlines the status of the congressional parties as more than simply two additional faces of a single national party in government, is that each has its own, independent, agency for conducting and coordinating campaigns (that is, for performing the extra-parliamentary functions of a political party) separately from, and sometimes in opposition to, the national committee of nominally the same party. These are the four Congressional Campaign Committees (CCCs): the Democratic Congressional Campaign Committee (DCCC: House Democrats); the NRCC (National Republican Congressional Committee: House Republicans); the DSCC (Democratic Senatorial Campaign Committee: Senate Democrats); and the NRSC (National Republican Senatorial Committee: Senate Republicans). The CCCs originated in the 1860s to help congressmen campaign independently from the president, and they continue to reflect the electoral separation of the legislative and executive branches today. Originally, they organized speaking tours in support of congressional candidates and sponsored the preparation of issue books laying out and defending policy positions. Later they also 'laundered' contributions from potentially sensitive donors, often accepting contributions in cash, and then passing it on as a cheque drawn on a party bank account. The finance reforms of the 1970s led to significant changes in the CCCs, however. Many of their traditional functions (speaker's bureau and issue books) had already been marginalized. Now their main residual function, the 'laundering' of contributions, became illegal. Moreover, the CCCs became responsible for their own overheads, and they no longer could have subsidized office space in the Capitol, or employees who were paid by the Sergeant-at-Arms or from left-over slots on congressmen's clerk-hire allowances.[7]

As it became clear that the national committees were not prepared to devote 'adequate' resources to congressional candidates, or to allow the advice of the CCCs to direct the allocation of those resources, one result was the agency agreements discussed earlier. Another was for the CCCs dramatically to strengthen their own fund-raising capacity. With autonomous fund-raising came renewed independence from the national committees. The initial breakthrough came in 1978 with a direct mail campaign instigated by NRCC chairman Guy Vander Jagt. This was so successful (in terms both of money raised and Republican electoral success) that the NRCC was able to aid the debt-ridden NRSC, whose new chairman, Robert Packwood, got on the direct mail bandwagon. The initial Democratic response, based on their continued control of Congress, was, on the one hand, to continue fund-raising as usual (that is, through an annual dinner) and, on the other hand, to attempt to legislate away the CCCs' right to raise money at all. When the legislative attempt failed, and a subsequent attempt to prevent agency agreements by lawsuit also failed, the Democrats emulated the Republicans in soliciting direct mail and PAC contributions.

Structurally, each of the CCCs in the House has at least one member from each state in which the party has representation, although the party leaders may appoint additional members. The chairman and vice-chairmen are selected from among the committee members by a formal vote of the entire party caucus; for the House Democrats, this election is simply the pro forma ratification of the Speaker's choice; the other three caucuses may have serious contests for these positions.

In Herrnson's (1988: 48) view, the CCCs are important because they 'provide their candidates with both direct and brokered services and thereby function as the most important aggregators, distributors, and directors of campaign services and resources in congressional elections'. Two important points must be emphasized, however. First, although the dollar totals provided by the parties to their candidates appear impressive on their own, they are only about 10 per cent of the total spent by candidates. The other services provided by the CCCs may also be less significant than they appear. Indicatively, even former NRSC chairman John Heinz 'preferred to use costly outside consultants rather than free "in-house" advisers in his re-election campaigns. "He never used the services of the NRSC when he ran" ' (Luntz, 1988: 140, quoting Republican media consultant John Deardourff). Second, the primary criteria influencing the distribution of CCC resources are incumbency and 'winnability'; notable by its absence is any consideration of party loyalty, either in congressional behaviour or in campaign platform. Moreover, the 1990 NRCC experiment with channelling resources to targeted open seats (and thus away from incumbents) has been interpreted as one of the stimuli to a challenge to Guy Vander Jagt's re-election as chairman. Although the challenge was unsuccessful, the experience is likely to result in even greater concentration on incumbents in the future. Again, those who are re-elected without CCC help are unlikely to be grateful (an incentive to give to incumbents, who are likely to win), while those who are defeated (most challengers) cannot vote for caucus leadership positions. All of the CCCs offer advice about the selection of issues and issue positions. What is most striking about this advice, however, is that it is tailored to the candidate's own position. While pre-packaged issue papers are made available to candidates who request them, a candidate who opposes the party's position will be given help in advancing his own, contrary, position – although, more often, a candidate who does not accept the position identified with the party will simply seek advice elsewhere.

By most standards, it is hard to call congressional parties 'parties' rather than 'cliques'. In one arena, party discipline is absolute: the organization of the chambers, and therefore the selection of committee and subcommittee chairs. But, unlike policy, these are basically individual, rather than collective, rewards, and so cooperation among co-partisans in competition with the other party is easy. The organizing function itself is performed at the beginning of each Congress, and is in effect over by the next day; only its consequences for the subsequent operation of Congress and for its ultimate policy decisions, profound though they may be, but also indirect and in some respects even unintended, linger on.

Party staff

The two key features of American party bureaucracies are transience and personal ties. There is virtually no permanent staff. Although vast numbers of people are employed in American 'party' politics (for example, the budgets for administrative and legislative assistance of the eight senators representing the four smallest states total to more than the staff budget of the entire British Labour party), most are not employees of any of the party organizations per se, but rather are employed by individual representatives or working as independent contractors, and even those individuals who are nominally employed by the parties more often in reality work for individual leaders. American parties, at least as represented by the staffs of their national committees and congressional caucuses and CCCs, are less permanent organizations than they are blank organization charts or, even better, empty suites of offices waiting to be filled from a pool of political professionals who float between various party structures, the personal staff of individual politicians and independent consultancy, but who have no fixed attachment to the party as a permanent organization. And reflecting the division of American parties among presidential, senatorial and House organizations, these suites of offices are physically separated – on separate floors in the case of the DNC, DCCC and DSCC, and in the case of the RNC and NRCC, but with a completely separate building in the case of the NRSC.

Looking first at the staff of the national committees, what the winner of an American presidential election gets from the party is not the use of a pre-existing staff, but the use of the party headquarters building to house his own staff, as well as access to the party's bank accounts to pay them. The people working at RNC headquarters in 1991 and 1992, for example, did not describe themselves as the staff of the Republican National Committee, but rather as the staff of *George Bush's* National Committee. On the Democratic side, on the other hand, the DNC was staffed by people who had little previous connection with Bill Clinton, and Clinton's campaign was conducted essentially without reference to the national party organization. Even for such non-sensitive questions as the candidate's schedule, one had to contact his own headquarters in Arkansas, and the DNC chairman, Ron Brown, was reduced to doing 'colour commentary' after one of the candidate debates on public television.[8] By 1996, however, one can predict that the DNC will have become Bill Clinton's organization, and will be populated by many of the people who in 1992 were working in Little Rock.

The staff of the congressional parties is more fragmented than that of the national committees. The vast majority are staff aides to individual members of congress. Reflecting the absence of a strong hierarchy of congressional leadership, some staffers work for the party (majority or minority) leaders, some for the parties (caucuses) per se (which is to say for their chairmen, who, except in the case of the Senate Democrats, are *not* the majority or minority leaders), and still others for the CCCs (again effectively for their chairmen). Just as the election of a new president results in virtually complete turnover of the national committee staff (as does the election of a new national chairman after a presidential defeat), these congressional aides all expect to be replaced whenever the relevant leadership position changes hands.

Complementing the relatively limited job possibilities and the insecurity that this implies, the United States has a large and expanding market for ex-party bureaucrats as independent consultants, lobbyists and news media commentators. Indeed, far from being a career, working within one of the three organizations of each of the parties is more generally an apprenticeship, during which the experience and contacts required for a subsequent independent career are acquired. Generally speaking, therefore, the functions normally performed by long-term officials employed by a party organization in other systems are performed in the United States by independent contractors in the short-term employ of individual candidates. This is probably the one area in which the partisan nature of American politics is often understated, however. While these independent consultants have no formal ties to party organizations, they are not for the most part people with no independent convictions available for hire by the highest bidder. Rather, there are Democratic pollsters and Republican pollsters, Democratic media consultants and Republican media consultants, and they advertise themselves as such, for example, in the campaign-professional trade press. But, like the congressional parties, these party ties are often more nominal than substantive, and refer more to vague tendencies than to concrete ideologies or fixed policy positions.

Why does the two-party system persist?

Given the weakness of the two American parties just described, one might well wonder why they persist at all. In part the answer has already been given. The two parties enjoy a panoply of important advantages, and benefit from a variety of institutional barriers to the entry of any new parties. Officials elected on the slates of the two parties are, of course, the ones who gave themselves these advantages. In doing so, however, they could justify what were essentially self-serving actions with reference to a strong cultural understanding of democracy as being best served by a choice between exactly two alternatives.

The nature of media coverage of campaigns also contributes to the two-party monopoly of public office. Since no free time is provided to candidates, candidates must rely on the editorial decisions of journalists to gain exposure beyond that which they can afford to buy. Although broadcasters do not restrict coverage to the candidates of the major parties on those grounds, they do tend to limit coverage to candidates that they regard as 'viable', which is usually the same thing. In 1992, for example, four candidates for president – Bill Clinton (Democrat), George Bush (Republican), Ross Perot (Independent) and Andre Marrou (Libertarian) – appeared on the ballot in all fifty states. Only the first three received serious news coverage, however, the first two as the major party candidates, and Perot largely because his wealth allowed him direct access to both the media and the public.

The impact of these factors is reinforced by the absence of any significant countervailing pressures. It is almost always easier for an insurgent to secure a place on the primary ballot of one of the major parties than to get on the general election ballot as an independent or new party candidate, and to win both the primary and then the general election as a major party candidate than to win the general election as a minor party candidate. Yet to pursue the major party route to office requires no sacrifice of independence. Thus, American general elections remain primarily a series of simultaneous contests between pairs of party-labelled, but not party-bound, candidates.

Ironically, however, while the two parties have built themselves virtually impenetrable barriers against challenge by new parties, they are both terribly vulnerable to being taken over from within. At the presidential level, this can be illustrated by considering the success of 'outsider' Jimmy Carter in winning the Democratic nomination in 1976, the reaction of conservative Republicans to Ronald Reagan's failure to obtain the party's nomination in the same year, or the strategy of Jackson Democrats in the 1980s. For other offices, the legally imposed openness of the parties can leave their leaders unable to prevent the party's label from being appropriated by candidates they view as loathsome, as is demonstrated by the 1990 senatorial and 1991 gubernatorial campaigns of former Nazi and Ku Klux Klan Grand Wizard, David Duke, under the Republican banner in Louisiana (and his subsequent entry into several 1992 Republican presidential primaries).

Questions for the future

Whether or not the old saw that American parties are like two bottles on a shelf, one labelled 'whiskey' and the other labelled 'milk', but both empty, accurately describes the policies of the Democrats and the Republicans, it surely fits their organizations. Moreover, the two bottles, although each quite complicated and variegated, are remarkably similar to one another. In one important respect, however, the two party bottles have become more different, at least in the period from 1968 to 1992. Although political scientists kept looking for a realignment of party identification that never came, there nonetheless developed an expectation born of experience that the Republicans would control the White House and the Democrats would control Congress. This expectation arguably had important consequences for the parties and their leaders.

For the Democrats, permanent Republican control of the White House meant that the congressional leaders became accustomed to an adversarial rather than a collaborative relationship with the president and, moreover, to a relationship in which their majority forced the president to treat them with considerable respect and deference. The idea that the national chairman might be a first rank party leader never being seriously entertained, they also became used to being the highest authorities in the party, with no expectation that they ought to support 'the leader of their party'. Therefore the first question to be asked now is whether the Democrats in Congress will be prepared to accept the less prominent role of supporters of a Democratic president or whether, alternatively, they have become so accustomed to the independence and power of their majority-in-opposition status that they treat a Democratic president in much the same way they treated Republicans. The latter case, which was foreshadowed by relations between Jimmy Carter and the Democratic Congresses he faced, would clearly further the six-party model. (At the same time, one lesson that might be drawn from the Carter years is that the price of failure to hang together is twelve years of Republican presidencies, and this might deter repetition of the experience.)

The behaviour of 'ordinary' members of the Democratic caucuses was also affected. Although other factors also contributed to the trend, the absence of a Democratic presidential programme to support contributed to the fragmentation of congressional authority (for example, the proliferation of subcommittees and the devolution of power to their chairmen). Divided control contributed to the opportunities for individual deals as the Republican White House tried to build support that of mathematical necessity had to cut across party lines and thus for the tendency of members of Congress to emphasize constituency service and the delivery of particular economic benefits (that is, the kind of 'quid' the White House could offer in exchange for the 'quo' of roll-call support) both in Congress and in their campaigns. To the extent that this continues under a Democratic administration, it would favour the no-party, or empty framework, model.

Under a Democratic administration, the Republicans have been freed from any expectation of supporting a president who was forced to compromise with the Democrats and are more able to unify as a principled opposition. Moreover, since there continues to be no appreciable chance of Republican majorities in Congress, national power for Republicans, as individuals as well as collectively, requires that they recapture the White House. This, in turn, should encourage even members of Congress to address the national, presidential, constituency (at least more than the Democrats, who are more prone to address their individual, local, constituencies). If they do this, it would further the two-party model. Alternatively, however, denied the possibility of influence through the White House (in exchange for loyalty) or the patronage resources of the executive branch, Republicans in Congress could see that their permanent minority status means they will be completely marginalized unless they come to individual arrangements on individual issues. In this case, the result would further the no-party model. This alternative is the more consistent with previous experience. But as with the Carter experience, there is an evident downside. One clear consequence of the accommodating attitude of Republicans who had come to terms with their permanent minority status was the 'Reagan revolution' at the primary ballot boxes that displaced many of them.

Underlying, and reflected in, these observations is perhaps the most important consequence of persistent divided government. It meant that partisan conflict between Democrats and Republicans came to coincide with rather than cross-cut institutional conflict between the legislative and executive branches. This is significant in the context of party organization because emphasis on, or dominance of, the presidential wing of a party is more consistent with the two-party model while emphasis on, or dominance of, the legislative wings of a party is more consistent with the six-party and, indeed, the no-party models. The implication of this, that the Republicans should have become more party-like and the Democrats less so over the twenty-four years from 1968 to 1992, is true in general terms. The question is whether this tendency will continue, especially if 1992 marks the return of extended Democratic dominance rather than simply another four-year hiatus.

Notes

1 This chapter is concerned with state parties only to the extent that they are constitutive parts of the national parties. Thus, the hundred-party model is only of indirect concern. The central focus is on the distinction among the two-party, six-party, and no-party conceptions as relevant in national (presidential and congressional) politics.

2 The degree to which the congressional parties in general, and the congressional campaign committees in particular, perform these functions actually is quite limited (Katz and Kolodny, 1992). The point is that the national committees are no more effective in performing these functions, either at the congressional or presidential levels, because American political campaigns are overwhelmingly candidate- rather than party-oriented.

3 Although state law continues to control the selection of national convention delegates, the courts have ruled that the national parties may impose rules to which state selection processes must conform, and that the national conventions may refuse to seat delegations selected otherwise.

4 In addition, presidential preference primaries were optional in Alabama and Arkansas. In the latter case, the outcome would be binding on the delegation.

5 The Republicans have, and the Democrats until 1972 had, a standing committee on permanent organization as well.

6 The ranking minority member is the senior member of the committee from the minority party. In general, this person has control over the part of the committee staff assigned to the minority (as the committee chairman has control over the rest of the staff).

7 It is for this reason that the CCCs technically are not committees of the caucuses.

8 In the context of American television coverage of the debates, for Ron Brown to have appeared on public television indicates that none of the 'real' networks, including CNN, thought he was important enough to interview.

50   *How Parties Organize*

References

Beck, Paul Allen and Sorauf, Frank J. (1992) *Party Politics in America*. New York: Harper Collins.

Burns, James MacGregor (1965) *The Deadlock of Democracy: Four-Party Politics in America*. Englewood Cliffs, NJ: Prentice-Hall.

Commission on Party Structure and Delegate Selection (1970) *Mandate for Reform: A Report*. Washington, DC: The Commission.

Cotter, Cornelius P. and Bibby, John F. (1980) 'Institutional development and the thesis of party decline', *Political Science Quarterly* 95 (Spring): 1–27.

Department of Commerce (1991) *Census of Governments 1987*. Washington, DC: Bureau of the Census.

Herrnson, Paul (1988) *Party Campaigning in the 1980s*. Cambridge, MA: Harvard University Press.

Hofstadter, Richard (1970) *The Idea of a Party System: The Rise of Legitimate Opposition in the United States, 1780–1840*. Berkeley: University of California Press.

Katz, Richard S. (1986) 'Party government: a rationalistic conception', in Francis G. Castles and Rudolf Wildenmann (eds), *Visions and Realities of Party Government*. Berlin: de Gruyter, pp.31–71.

Katz, Richard S. and Kolodny, Robin (1992) 'The USA: the 1990 congressional campaign', in Shaun Bowler and David M. Farrell (eds), *Electoral Strategies and Political Marketing*. New York: St Martin's Press, pp.183–203.

Luntz, Frank (1988) *Candidates, Consultants, and Campaigns: The Style and Substance of American Electioneering*. New York: Basil Blackwell.

Magleby, David B. and Nelson, Candice J. (1990) *The Money Chase: Congressional Campaign Finance Reform*. Washington, DC: Brookings Institution.

Ripley, Randall (1983) *Congress: Process and Policy*. New York: Norton.

3

The Development of Austrian Party Organizations in the Post-war Period

Wolfgang C. Müller

This chapter is concerned with the post-war organizational development of the four parties which have been represented in the Austrian parliament since the mid-1980s: the Social Democrats (SPÖ – before 1991, the Socialists), the People's Party (ÖVP), the Freedom Party (FPÖ) and the Green Alternative (GA – also known as the Greens).[1] Three other parties which have also been (or still are) represented in parliament during the post-war period – the Communist Party (KPÖ), the League of Independents (VdU), which was the predecessor of the FPÖ, and the Liberal Forum (LF), which was established as a breakaway from the FPÖ in 1993 – have been largely excluded from the analysis on grounds of relevance and/ or access to reliable information. Throughout the chapter, I am concerned with the questions of whether these organizational developments can be said to involve processes of *étatization* (Katz and Mair, 1992b) and professionalization; whether there has been a process of organizational convergence; and whether there have been significant differences in the extent and pace of organizational change. I first outline the challenges to party organizations which emerged during the past half century and discuss the party responses to these challenges; I then go on to discuss those changes in the parties' environment which were introduced by the parties themselves. The remaining sections are concerned with the changes in the parties' organizational 'philosophy', in their formal organizational structures, in their membership, finance and staffing, and in their internal power structures.

Before going on to address these themes, however, I would first like to point to three general and quite striking features of Austrian party organizations. In the first place, the parties as membership organizations are the largest in Western Europe in relative terms; and, despite the small size of the country, they are also among the largest in absolute terms. This applies both to the party system as a whole when compared to other party systems, as well as to each of the individual parties when compared to other members of its respective political family. Second, post-war politics in Austria has been *party* politics par excellence, in which the two major parties (SPÖ and ÖVP) in particular have established a substantial grip on political institutions and civil society. Scarcely any relevant appointment or decision has been made without the major parties, or in a truly 'non-party' spirit, while society itself has been colonized by party to an extent in which almost all societal organizations (from the automobile associations to the major conservationist organizations) bear a party label or have close links to one of the two major parties. To be sure, the principal interest groups refer to themselves as being 'above party'; in practice, however, they are 'all party' (that is, the parties organize within them), and each is dominated by a faction of one of the major parties. Third, the four parties with which we are concerned evidence a wide-ranging structural variation. Indeed, examples drawn from almost the entire universe of the organizational patterns developed by political parties in Western Europe can be found in the four parties dealt with in this chapter.

Party organizations and the challenge of environmental change

Looking at the post-war period as a whole, it is possible to identify four major environmental changes which have constituted challenges to party organizations, the severity of which has depended on both the nature of the links between the individual parties and their environment and their individual internal structures.

The first of these is the *change in the citizenry*, in which industrialization and the growth of the tertiary sector has effected a thorough transformation in the social structure and culture. The potential voters and members of parties have experienced a period of unprecedented affluence, with increasing access to higher education, more leisure time (and more ways in which to spend it) and better welfare services than ever before. The resources of the citizens have therefore changed considerably, as have their preferences, with, for example, traditional bread-and-butter issues becoming augmented by environmental concerns and a desire for increasing political participation. In addition, and despite the social and economic successes of the post-war period, it has also been possible since the 1970s to witness a growing disenchantment with the main political parties and politicians. In 1982, for example, a survey reported that 69 per cent of the population drew negative associations from the term *Parteibuch* (party membership card)[2] (Plasser, 1987: 127) and, although we lack relevant survey data on this particular question more recently, there is nothing to suggest the term now enjoys any greater popularity. Thus the 1992 presidential election resulted in the triumphant victory of a candidate who not only pushed his own party affiliation completely into the background, but who also made the critique of party a major issue in his campaign. In a similar vein, a survey in 1989 found that some 69 per cent of respondents agreed that 'politicians were corrupt and bribable', as against little more than half that figure barely a decade previously (Plasser et al., 1992: 27; Plasser and Ulram, 1991: 136). Surveys among younger people reveal an even greater degree of alienation.

Second, there is the *change in the political community*, in which the representational monopoly of the major parties and their linked interest groups has been increasingly undermined since the late 1960s by alternative organizations and movements (Gottweis, 1991), which have less defined organizational structures, represent previously 'silent' groups (such as the disabled, clients of public services and consumers), and are often concerned with 'new demands'. Third, there is the process of *technological change*, which includes the establishment of television as the most important means of mass communication and, more recently, the introduction of satellite and cable channels which have undermined the monopoly of the public broadcasting corporation. Fourth, there has been *institutional change*, which has involved the use of more direct democracy, a greater role for those governmental institutions where partisan control is relatively weak, and a greater autonomy from the party organization of politicians in representative institutions (Müller, 1992b; see also pp. 70, 73).

The legal regulation of parties and party finance

The party law which was enacted in 1975, the first such, is a very liberal law, which introduced a rather generous scheme of state party finance while not restricting the activities of parties and demanding only minimal formal requirements for party registration. Indeed, the only real attempt to regulate the parties involved some SPÖ-backed amendments requiring the publication of information regarding large financial donations. In effect, the new law therefore confirmed the status quo for those parties which had founded the Second Republic in 1945 (the SPÖ, ÖVP and KPÖ), while making life somewhat easier for other parties and for new parties (Müller, 1992a: 26f).

State subsidies had begun to be given to the parliamentary Fraktions in the early 1960s, when these were the only party institutions positively recognized by law. The amounts involved were small, however, and were not even enough to provide what could be seen as the minimum requirements for a parliamentary Fraktion, although they were later increased by unanimous decisions of the parliament. State financing of the party organizations had been demanded by senior ÖVP politicians as early as 1959, and in 1967 the ÖVP single-party government had already prepared a party finance bill which, due to SPÖ resistance, was not actually enacted. Being able to rely on a solid income from membership fees, and being critical of the ÖVP government's budgetary policy, the SPÖ was unwilling to share responsibility for what was seen to be a somewhat unpopular initiative. In 1972, however, two years after it had returned to government, the SPÖ finally accepted the principle of state party finance. The new system began by transferring the training of party activists and functionaries from the party organizations to newly created and state-funded political education institutes. This decision was agreed unani-

mously and, in order that it would win popular acceptance, it was also
agreed that these institutes would provide services for the general public.
Since public funding of the training of party functionaries was accepted by
the media and the public, in 1975 the parties were ready for the next step,
which involved the introduction of state financing for the party organizations themselves. The parties' need for additional money generally
resulted from the new and expensive campaign techniques which had
begun in the late 1960s and from the need to modernize and professionalize
their organizations. More immediately, the parties had experienced a
series of cost-intensive national election campaigns during the first half of
the 1970s, consisting of three parliamentary elections (1970, 1971, 1975)
and two presidential elections (1971, 1974). And while they first had to
regulate their legal status in order to introduce state funding (see Müller,
1992a: 26f), this was simply a by-product of the desire for public money,
with the result that only one paragraph of the party law is devoted to the
legal status of parties, while thirteen others are concerned with financial
aspects. Political controversy was again avoided and the decision was
adopted unanimously, with favourable press coverage being helped by its
being coupled with a rather generous scheme for subsidies to the press.
Amendments to the party law in subsequent years, which increased the
amounts of money and/or redistributed it among the parties, were usually
made in parliament in the early hours of the morning when a minimum of
media coverage could be expected (Müller and Hartmann, 1983).

Since 1975 all parties which poll more than 1 per cent of the vote have
been entitled to receive state subsidies in election years while the parties
represented in the *Nationalrat* are entitled to receive these funds permanently. Parties with at least five MPs receive a fixed amount of money, the
remaining funds being distributed according to the parties' share of the
vote. The main means of redistribution of state party finance among the
parties has been the fixed amount which has varied from AS 4 million in
1975 to AS 14 million in 1982, dropping back to AS 3 million since 1987.
The higher the fixed amount, the better off are the small parties, and as
long as the FPÖ was required as an actual or potential coalition partner by
the SPÖ, the dominant party during this period, the fixed amount
increased. After the grand coalition of SPÖ and ÖVP was formed in 1987
and the Greens had established themselves in parliament, the fixed amount
was reduced to an all-time low. On the one hand, the FPÖ, under its new
aggressive leadership, was not required for coalitions any longer, and was
not to be privileged; on the other hand, the maintenance of the old rules
would have led to a substantial reduction of the funding for the SPÖ and
the ÖVP, since a fourth party was now represented in parliament
(Sickinger and Nick, 1990: 76–8). The latter problem could have been
solved, of course, by an increase of the total available funding, but this was
not deemed appropriate in a time of budgetary restraint.[3]

Subsidies to the parties are also provided at the *Land* level, where funds
are allocated to the *Land* party organizations, the *Land* diet Fraktions, the

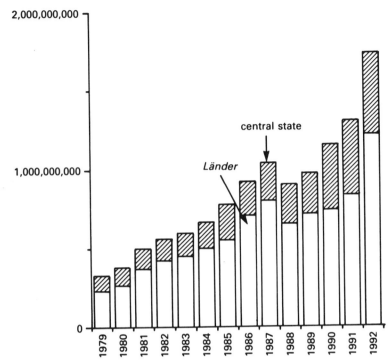

Figure 3.1   *Public subsidies for parties, 1979–92, in Austrian Schillings at constant 1987 prices* (Compiled from Dachs, 1985, 1992b; Müller, 1992a)

regional party press, etc. In contrast to public party finance at the national level, which is entirely based on specific laws, several of the *Land* subsidies have been granted on the basis of ad hoc decisions by the respective *Land* diet or *Land* government, and have thus received less publicity (Dachs, 1985, 1992b). As can be seen in Figure 3.1, however, subsidies at the *Land* level are of greater importance than at the national level, and between 1979 and 1990 were almost three times as big (despite the fact that the *Länder* had less than half the total budget; see Dachs, 1985, 1992b; Müller, 1992a). Public funds for parties are also provided at the local level, and while no systematic information is available at this level, it can nevertheless be assumed to be considerably less important than the public subsidies at the national and *Land* levels.

The parties as organizations

The *SPÖ*, which was established in 1945 as the successor of the Social Democratic Workers' Party (SDAP), has tended to regard itself for most of the post-war period as a party in a predominantly alien environment, made up of bourgeois forces consisting of the traditionally powerful social groups with their own means of mass communication, informal networks and political organization. Up until the 1970s, the Communist Party was also considered as a relevant threat, in relative rather than in absolute terms, in the sense that it could potentially endanger the SPÖ's capacity to monopolize the left. This view of itself as being besieged produced the attitude that 'those who do not belong to us are against us', with only formal party membership being seen as a proof of 'belonging'. In consequence, the party has aimed to organize its sympathizers comprehensively, to provide a strong feeling of solidarity among its members, activists and leaders, and to inculcate a strong sense of duty among these groups vis-à-vis the party as a whole. These features have characterized the SPÖ for most of the post-war period, but have tended to erode since the 1970s. Moreover, it must be emphasized that the party has spent only four years in opposition during the entire post-war period, a record which also has considerable consequences for its identity. During its participation in the old grand coalition (1945–66) it increasingly became a party of government (Müller, 1988b), and this process was completed during its period of single-party government (1970–83), when party policy changed from one oriented towards serving its own clientele to one which appealed to the population at large. Finally, in 1993, the territorial principle of organization which was central to its traditional mass-party style was augmented by a so-called 'issue principle', designed to make the party more attractive for young people. Although this new principle has not yet had a major impact on the party's organization, party headquarters believes that it will become dominant in the longer term.

Although the *ÖVP* succeeded the Christian Social Party (CSP), which up to 1934 had been the party-political expression of the Catholic-conservative *Lager*, it was nevertheless founded as a *new* party in 1945, differing from the CSP in at least two organizational respects. First, the ÖVP is a mass membership party, while the CSP was more a party of notables. Second, the ÖVP did not regard the CSP's centralized character as an appropriate model (Graf, 1947). The CSP had not organized masses of members because it could rely on interest groups such as the Bauern-bund, the Gewerbebund and the Christian trade unions, and the organizational framework of the Catholic church in general. In the post-war period, however, despite the development of special organizations by the party, the integration of these groups into the party was limited, in that the previously independent groups were keen to maintain a high degree of autonomy. The result was the very decentralized structure adopted by the ÖVP, which is reflected by the fact that the associated Leagues are not only parts of the ÖVP but also independent associations (*Vereine*). This means that they may withhold their resources from the party if appropriate and, in a worst-case scenario, have an easy exit option (Müller and Steininger, 1994a).

Being able to build up the party in 1945 on the backs of three 'corporatist' organizations, the Farmers' League, the Business League and the Workers' and Employees' League, was a major advantage. First, their functionaries had been able to maintain contact through the Nazi era and on this basis were able to rebuild their respective organizations within a very short time. Second, in contrast to the core of the CSP, the Leagues as such had not been associated with the setting up of the dictatorship in 1934 and the bulk of their functionaries had not been discredited (cf. Graf, 1947). However, not all of the ÖVP personnel in 1945 were recruited from the Leagues, some functionaries and many staff members being also recruited from the Austrian resistance movement. The alternative of building up the ÖVP as a party rather than a political peak organization of interest groups was promoted by most of the young resistance fighters and some of the incumbents of central party functions. However, in 1945, when the definitive arrangements for the party organizations were made, it became clear that the power within the party rested with the Leagues. Pushing the point to an extreme, the party as distinguished from the Leagues can be reduced to the party chairman, the general secretary, the leader of the parliamentary Fraktion and the staff of the party head-quarters.

The official political position of the ÖVP is that of a non-socialist catch-all party (*bürgerliche Sammlungspartei*), which means that the party aims to represent all individuals and groups who are not socialist as well as the most relevant democratic non-socialist ideologies, that is, Catholic social doctrine, conservatism and liberalism (Müller, 1988a, 1991; Müller and Steininger, 1994b). This also means that it cannot be monolithic in organizational terms, and hence it sees itself more as an umbrella organization for the three Leagues (and, more recently, for the three other constituent organizations, those of women, young people and the elderly). A second feature of the ÖVP view of itself as an organization is that it is a party of government par excellence. Its predecessor had ruled throughout the inter-war period and the ÖVP itself had dominated national government in the first twenty-five post-war years, and after having lost its governmental status at the national level in 1970 it took a long time to accommodate to the role of opposition. Even then, however, as a major parliamentary party, as a governing party in most of the *Länder*, and as the dominating force in two of the three major chambers, the ÖVP – or parts of the ÖVP – continued to participate in the making of authoritative decisions. Indeed, one consequence of the ÖVP being a party of government was that the party as such was not really concerned with many aspects of mass organization during this period.

The *FPÖ* is the manifestation of two quite different organizational traditions. While the 'third *Lager*' traditionally expressed itself through 'party of notables'-type parties, the Nazi period was a crucial experience for the *Lager* and in particular for the so-called 'front generation', which soon occupied the leadership positions in the FPÖ. There was a striking contrast between the mass organization, the discipline and the *Führer* principle which, at least on the surface, characterized the Nazi party, and the limited membership, open internal fights and dispersed power structure of the German-national parties Austria had experienced up until then. The FPÖ managed to combine both traditions. While aiming at a comprehensive organization, the party was able to organize only the hard core of the 'third *Lager*', and while the party statute granted considerable powers to the national leadership bodies and to the party leader in particular, the FPÖ in practice has turned out to have a dispersed power structure, with the *Land* party organizations enjoying a high degree of autonomy. This statement must be qualified, however, by making reference to the most recent phase of party history. Party chairman Jörg Haider, who is undoubtedly *the* electoral asset of the FPÖ, has managed for the first time to make full use of the competencies granted to the party chairman by the party statutes (Luther, 1991), and while the FPÖ previously saw itself as a party of individualists who may or may not agree with each other, the new activists and functionaries have nevertheless introduced a strong element of leader-orientation. What remains constant is the party's view of itself as one in which that which holds it together is not the promise of material rewards, as is often the case in the SPÖ and the ÖVP. On the contrary, to be an FPÖ-member in 'red-black' Austria has traditionally been seen as an indication of the readiness to accept personal disadvantage as the price for political belief. That said, however, the recent electoral successes of the FPÖ have introduced a bandwagon effect, and have created the possibility that personal rewards associated with inclusion in the leader's in-group will become a source of incentives inside the party.

In many respect the *Greens* see themselves as the antithesis of 'traditional' political parties. In organizational terms this means, first, the careful avoidance of the word 'party' in the statutes, in publications, and in statements by officials, and a favouring of 'movement' or just 'the Greens' or 'the Green Alternative'. Second, the Greens stress that they are an 'open' party, and that participation does not require a formal membership (a *Parteibuch*) or the payment of a fixed membership fee; rather, what is decisive is a belief in the goals of the Greens and a willingness to participate. Third, internal democracy is claimed to be more substantive than in other parties, with a more powerful and frequent party congress, strict rules of incompatibility between different party functions and between party functions and elected offices, restrictions in the number of terms, and other statutory provisions, being intended to bypass 'the iron law of oligarchy'. Fourth, the constitutional principle of the 'free mandate' is upheld against the principle of party democracy. Fifth, the Greens claim to be the most transparent party (in terms of party finance, internal decision-making and so on). Sixth, gender relations within the Greens are characterized by total equality, with the aim of total gender parity in party and elected offices.

From the beginning, however, several of these principles have proved disadvantageous in the context of party competition, as, for instance, in the general election of 1990, when the Greens nominated no less than four 'top candidates' in order to satisfy their understanding of internal democracy (Müller and Plasser, 1992). Electoral defeats, in particular at the *Land* level, have therefore led to pressure to accept some of the common wisdom of party competition and to adapt organizational principles accordingly. As a consequence, since 1991, the Greens have reduced their reluctance to be represented by single persons and to allow them to speak on behalf of the party without extensive prior internal discussions. Likewise, the Greens have professionalized other aspects of their public relations and, in 1992, they eliminated the rules of incompatibility between party functions and elected offices.

The structures of the parties

All Austrian parties have a relatively complex organizational structure which is largely territorial in character (the ÖVP also has a functional organization) and which follows the state structure in its hierarchical levels, thus having local, district, *Land* and national organizations. All 'traditional' parties also maintain networks of affiliated and partly ancillary organizations.[4]

Representation within the *SPÖ* is based first and foremost on the number of members, the importance of which is however reduced by the granting of minimum quotas to organizational and political units at all levels. As far as the national party is concerned it is the district level and the *Land* level which are the most important. While the bulk of national party congress delegates is nominated at the district party congresses, the *Land* party organizations have become particularly important since 1967 for the recruitment of the national executive bodies. In contrast to the other parties, the SPÖ maintains ancillary organizations and its affiliated organizations are also closer to the party. Since the 1970s, however, several affiliated organizations have become formally neutral, even though they continue to have a socialist group, representatives of which occupy leadership positions. This development, which was accepted rather reluctantly by the SPÖ, was initiated by the affiliated organizations themselves, which felt that a party label might impede their ability to attract apolitical members, and thus might constitute a competitive disadvantage vis-à-vis the corresponding organizations which are close to the ÖVP.

The *ÖVP* itself is an indirect party with a pyramidal organizational form (each level delegates to the level immediately above). Representation within the party is based on both the number of members and the number of votes. While the Leagues (the functional organizations) are entitled to nominate party congress delegates (at all levels) according to their numbers of members, the number of delegates of the territorial organizations are based on the number of votes won by the party in the last election at the relevant level. Moreover, while the three Leagues and the three other constituent organizations exist at all levels, the territorial organizations function as peak organizations. In recent years the local level has been an exception to this rule, since in this case it is only the Farmers' League which has managed to maintain its organization, while the other constituent organizations mainly lack the critical mass of activists required for a separate organization. For most aspects of intra-party life, however, functional organization is more important than territorial organization. Thus, for example, the nomination of delegates by the territorial organizations is de facto carried out by the Leagues at the respective level. Compared to the SPÖ, the ÖVP has relatively few officially affiliated organizations, although it is also clear that the Leagues and constituent organizations fulfil the functions which affiliated organizations play in other parties. Moreover, there are also many organizations which are linked to the party in more informal ways and which mainly belong to the network of Catholic organizations. Thus while the network of organizations linked to the party is not really smaller than that of the SPÖ, it is less party-centred, a feature which has advantages as well as disadvantages for the ÖVP (Houska, 1985). On the one hand, these organizations have a lower barrier of entry than their Socialist equivalents and are therefore better fitted to recruit 'apolitical' citizens. On the other hand, however, both the functionaries and the members have a double loyalty, to the Catholic church as well as to the ÖVP. And while this was not a problem as long as the positions of party and church were largely identical, problems have arisen more recently, and the party's relationship with Catholic organizations has become less harmonious (Müller and Steininger, 1994b).

The parties as membership organizations

As might be expected for parties which are characterized by such large membership bases, both the ÖVP and the SPÖ have genuinely nationwide organizations, with branches in all relevant communities. The ÖVP is, however, the more extensive of the two, with a support structure which is dominated by inhabitants of villages (in particular farmers) and small towns. That said, the gap between the two parties has narrowed with time. Thus the number of ÖVP units appears to have declined between the mid-1950s and the early 1970s, partly as a result of local government reforms and the merging of hundreds of small villages into larger communities, and partly in consequence of the different counting rules applied by the party in this period. Since then, however, this decline has been reversed, partly as a result of the greater organizational efforts made by the party during its period in opposition.

In the immediate post-war period, the SPÖ managed to set up local party organizations in its traditional strongholds of Vienna, the large towns, the industrialized areas and the important railway bases in the countryside. The number of organizational units grew continuously, paralleling the long-term increase of members and voters, until the mid-1960s. A period of organizational decline was then followed once again by an all-time high in the early 1970s, a cycle which can be interpreted as an outflow of the party's electoral fortunes, coinciding with its opposition period (1966–70) and then its return to governmental power in 1970. During its 'golden age' period in the 1970s and most of the 1980s, the SPÖ was able to maintain a very high degree of organizational presence; since the late 1980s, however, the decline of the party's fortunes and the general uneasiness with political parties in Austria seem to have introduced a period of organizational decline.

While the ÖVP is represented virtually throughout Austria by basic party units, and while the SPÖ is represented everywhere except in some rural villages, there remain many blank spaces on the map of the FPÖ's organizational representation. This is not only due to the fact that the FPÖ and its predecessors were always small parties, but also because of the more specific circumstances involved in the period of Allied occupation (1945–55), when the Soviet sector, and the countryside in particular, proved an unsuitable territory for organizational activities on the part of the FPÖ's predecessor, the VdU. The party has never caught up from this delayed start. That said, the FPÖ lags behind the two big parties much more in terms of members than it does in terms of organizational units. This is partly because about half of the FPÖ's basic units are only support bases (*Stützpunkte*) which nowadays require less than ten party members.[5]

Membership development

As noted above, the Austrian parties have proved to be extremely effective in recruiting party members. Even in terms of absolute numbers, for example, and despite the small size of the country, membership of the SPÖ and the ÖVP exceeds that of many of their respective sister parties in Western Europe (Katz and Mair, 1992a).[6] That said, the ÖVP figures in particular are difficult to estimate with any real accuracy. Until the 1980s, for example, only the *Land* organizations of the Leagues and the other constituent organizations (*Teilorganisationen*) collected data on membership, and while figures were reported to the *Land* party organizations and to the national headquarters of the Leagues and constituent organizations and thence to the central party organization on a regular basis, nevertheless little effort was made to store this information. Moreover the definition of membership varies substantially across these units and thus makes comparison with the other parties difficult, particularly insofar as the so-called 'family members' are concerned. Thus while about half of the Farmers' and the Business Leagues' members are 'family members' only between 10 and 20 per cent of the members of the Workers' and Employees' League belong to this category, and while a change towards individual membership for 'family members' was made in 1980, this was not implemented in all *Land* organizations of the respective Leagues until

1990. Multiple membership in two or more of the constituent organizations is also very common, and thus the simple addition of the figures reported to the party congress inflates the overall figures. The reporting of too many, or even too few, members is also part of a wider intra-party game. Since financial obligations and the number of party congress delegates depend in part on membership figures, the Leagues tend to downplay their membership levels when it comes to the payment of membership contributions, and tend to over-report when it comes to the allocation of delegates to the party congresses. Similarly, if the party congress is expected to be a 'normal' one, and without contested elections, the central party is more likely to accept the number of members as reported by the Leagues and the other constituent organizations than is the case when a controversy at the party congress is expected, and when the number of delegates allocated to the respective intra-party groups may prove to be relevant. In short, the total membership figures of the ÖVP have to be estimated, and while the estimates used here are based on substantially more information than in any previous attempt, the problem nevertheless remains that the quality of these data is much lower than in the case of the SPÖ and the FPÖ.

According to both the maximum and the minimum versions of membership size (the former includes 'family members'), social structural changes have clearly influenced the composition of the ÖVP's membership. However, while the number of persons engaged in the agricultural sector was reduced from about a third of the population in the immediate post-war period to less than a tenth in the 1980s, the share of the Farmers' League in the ÖVP has not declined at a similar rate, and absolute numbers have remained quite stable. And although the ÖAAB managed to become the League with most members (if 'family members' are excluded), the ÖVP nevertheless still remains dominated by traditional groups long after their numerical importance in the electorate has been substantially reduced (Müller and Steininger, 1994a). More generally, as can be seen in Figure 3.2, the ÖVP managed to increase its membership until the 1970s (according to the minimum version) or even until the early 1980s (according to the maximum version). Since then membership figures have declined considerably. Taking the minimum version, for example, which is the rough equivalent of the membership figures of other parties, membership declined by about 100,000 from the mid-1970s until 1992, when it totalled approximately 460,000.

The SPÖ in the immediate post-war period had recaptured almost all of the organizational strength it had enjoyed prior to 1934, and then experienced a long growth period, paralleling the party's gains in votes (but not vote shares), which continued until 1960. Thereafter, membership figures fluctuated slightly around an average of 700,000 during the 1960s and 1970s, before falling back again after 1979, since when the party has lost some 160,000 members. Membership figures are expected to continue to decline further, and experts in and around the party headquarters suggest that membership will settle at around 300,000 members.

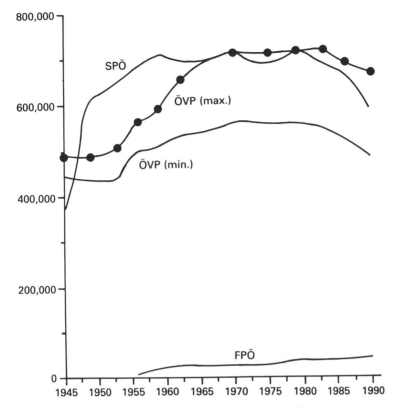

Figure 3.2   *The development of party membership, 1945–90*
(Müller, 1992a)

The FPÖ, by contrast, has never been a 'membership party', that is, a party which organizes a substantial (by Austrian standards) part of its voters. That said, however, and with the exception of the time when the party participated in government, membership figures have been constantly rising, reflecting in part the party's attempts to catch up with what the 'third camp' had missed in the immediate post-war period. More recently, it also reflects an increasing organizational capacity of the party (especially through the increase in party staff which, in turn, was made possible by the introduction of public subsidies). Since the party under its new leadership returned to a protest strategy in 1986, however, membership recruitment, which is not given first priority, has not been able to keep pace with the winning of new votes (party membership increased by 15 per cent between 1986 and 1992, while the number of FPÖ voters increased by 66 per cent between 1986 and 1990).

The overall ratio of party members to the electorate for the three main parties is reported in Table 3.1, which also includes summary figures showing the overall membership–electorate ratio. The figures for the immediate post-war period must be read with the qualification that they

Table 3.1   *Degree of party organization: party members as percentage*
of electorate, selected years

Year	SPÖ	ÖVP/max	ÖVP/min	FPÖ	Total/max	Total/min
1945	10.37	14.21	12.78		24.58	23.16
1953	14.32	11.01	9.61		25.33	23.94
1962	14.54	13.63	11.07	0.56	28.73	26.17
1979	13.91	13.88	10.80	0.72	28.51	25.42
1986	12.27	12.73	9.67	0.68	25.67	22.60
1990	10.44	11.90	8.67	0.75	23.09	19.86

Source: Calculated from Müller, 1992a

exclude the Communist Party, which in the early years organized up to 150,000 members (Ehmer, 1991), and the League of Independents, the predecessor of the FPÖ (1949–56), which did not organize masses of members but certainly had as many as the FPÖ when it started. Other parties, including the Greens, the members of which have also not been included, have not had a significant impact on the dimension of the overall degree of party organization. Having said this, and using the restrictive definition of party membership in the case of the ÖVP, it can be seen that about a quarter of the adult population has been organized in political parties for most of this period, although the figure fell to about a fifth of the adult population at the beginning of the 1990s. That said, and as far as the bulk of the members in the two major parties in particular are concerned, the concept of membership is not associated with specific political activities. According to surveys conducted between 1976 and 1985, for example, only roughly a third of the ÖVP members and a quarter of the SPÖ members work occasionally for their party (Plasser, 1987: 125), while a major party-commissioned survey among SPÖ members in 1986, an election year, suggested that only 13 per cent of the members occasionally engaged in party work, with only 7 per cent doing so on a regular basis (SPÖ, 1987).

Finally, reference should be made to the development of the party press. Due to the influence of the political parties in the allocation of paper in the immediate post-war period, the SPÖ and ÖVP newspapers enjoyed a major early advantage, and even by the early 1950s still accounted for roughly a third of the total daily newspaper circulation. Since then, however, the readership of the party press has continuously declined, such that there was no longer any relevant party newspaper by the late 1980s. This development is particularly striking given the extraordinarily high party membership levels, and indeed the party press would still flourish even if only a quarter of the party members subscribed. The effective disappearance of the party press is thus not only a further sign of the decline in the *size* of party organizations, but also indicates a *qualitative* change, in which the parties are no longer able to convince their members to avail thenselves of party-filtered information, and hence are also no longer able to encapsulate their respective clienteles.

The rationale of party membership

The extraordinarily high level of party membership cannot be explained by reference to the existence of greater political interest on the part of citizens in Austria as against those in other Western democracies – indeed, Austria is certainly not exceptional in this regard (cf. Plasser, 1987: 283f; Plasser and Ulram, 1991; cf. Verba et al., 1978: 348). Rather, and from the perspective of the party members themselves, it is family tradition, ideology, social factors and, in particular, patronage, which appear to count most heavily. Indeed, it is interesting that when asked about their own motives for becoming members, respondents tend to place most emphasis on ideology and family tradition, whereas when asked about the motives of members other than themselves they tend, perhaps more accurately, to place most emphasis on the importance of patronage (Deiser and Winkler, 1982, 94–8; Müller, 1989).

Parties have indeed provided patronage services on a large scale throughout the post-war period, although they have also become more sceptical in recent years both about the effectiveness of patronage in creating party loyalty and about the overall effects of an extensive patronage system. Unless it is also sustained by other sources of loyalty and, in particular, by the sort of sense of subcultural belonging which was still quite strong during the first post-war decades, patronage may only create long-term loyalty if it is *not* of a one-off character. Thus only those clients who require *permanent* patronage (for example, promotion during a career in the public service) are likely to maintain their party membership, while those requiring one-off benefits may turn away once they have received what they wanted (for example, public housing). The overall effects of an extensive patronage system also have to include the reactions of those citizens who do not receive patronage benefits or who even suffer from it (in the sense of not being promoted, or not receiving public housing). And given that the parties in recent years have found that more and more citizens are in fact alienated by patronage, it would then seem that it produces little, if any, net benefit for them (Müller, 1989), especially at a time when patronage resources have become more scarce due to privatization and budgetary restraint. As a result, and since the 1980s, the parties are becoming more reluctant to offer themselves as a source of patronage, with the Vienna *Land* executive of the SPÖ, for example, recently deciding that party membership will no longer be relevant for the allocation of public housing.

At the same time, it is clear that the political parties would not have been able to arrive at and maintain their extraordinarily high levels of member-ship without an enormous recruitment effort. In the case of the SPÖ, for example, membership recruitment campaigns have been conducted regu-larly over the whole post-war period, with the central party setting a goal in terms of new members to be recruited for the *Land* or district parties. In the ÖVP it is the constituent organizations at the *Land* level which engage

Table 3.2   *Party income (percentages per electoral cycle)*

	Members	State	Party taxes[a]	Other
SPÖ				
1975–78	42.8	44.8	3.0	9.4
1979–82	43.2	37.8	1.6	17.3
1983–85	41.6	33.6	0.2	24.6
1986–89	36.4	33.2	0.1	30.4
ÖVP				
1975–78	21.1	62.7	–	16.2
1979–82	22.9	42.0	–	35.1
1983–85	25.3	57.5	–	17.2
1986–89	23.3	54.5	–	22.2
FPÖ				
1975–78	5.0	56.6	4.7	33.7
1979–82	4.9	61.2	4.8	29.1
1983–85	4.2	73.3	6.3	16.2
1986–89	2.4	76.0	10.7	10.9

[a] Contributions of office-holders and political appointees.

Source: Calculated from Müller, 1992a

in similar efforts to increase or maintain their membership. But why do the parties make these efforts (cf. Kofler, 1985)? There are four factors which seem relevant here and which merit brief attention.

The first of these concerns the value of party members as secure voters, which has been of particular importance for the SPÖ, which, at least until the late 1960s, believed that its organizational efforts would reap electoral dividends. Only members were seen as secure voters and, according to the party's rough formula, each member would bring two additional voters, and thus with an effective organizational build-up the party could automatically be ensured of winning a parliamentary majority. Since the late 1960s, however, the party, or, more precisely, its leadership, has tended to rethink its attitude. Bruno Kreisky, for example, who led the SPÖ from 1967 until 1983, was sceptical about the value of the party organization as a means of communicating to the population at large (Müller, 1994a), and also sought to develop a particular appeal to non-socialists, who would stay with the SPÖ only for a while (*'ein Stück Weges mitgehen'*) and would not become party members.[7]

Second, party members may also be valued for financial reasons. Indeed, traditionally the SPÖ has stressed that it derives its income from the contributions of its members and therefore does not need to respond to individual or collective donors who remain unknown to the public, and, underlining this claim, the SPÖ has had a long tradition of reporting its budget to the party congress.[8] According to Table 3.2, which is based on the income of the party head offices plus the state subsidies to the parliamentary fraktions and to the parties' political education institutions, the parties, or more precisely the national party organizations, clearly differ in respect of the financial relevance of party members. While income from party members is the most relevant income category for the SPÖ, it ranks only second in the case of the ÖVP and has only marginal importance in the case of the FPÖ. Conversely, the state has become the most important source of finance for the national organizations of both the ÖVP and the FPÖ. However, since public subsidies also figure prominently in the accounts of the SPÖ, it seems fair to conclude that Austrian parties, at least financially, have moved closer to becoming 'parties of the state'. The FPÖ has clearly moved furthest down this road: in 1986–89, for example, more than 85 per cent of the national party's income came from the state, either directly or indirectly (via party taxes from the salaries of elected office-holders). The third major income category, 'other income', may effectively be translated as 'donations', and ranks as the second most important source of income in the case of the FPÖ and the third in the cases of the ÖVP and the SPÖ. Bearing in mind the general character of the parties, this rank-order is not unexpected; what is surprising, however, is the actual share of the party income covered by donations, and, in particular, the increase in the SPÖ from less than 10 per cent in 1975 to more than 30 per cent in 1989, a figure which now exceeds that of either of the 'bourgeois' parties.[9]

Third, party members may serve as a reservoir for potential candidates. As interviews with party functionaries suggest, the behaviour of members inside the party can be observed over a long period and their suitability as potential candidates assessed; then, once elected, they may be more likely to act according to the party's expectations (they should be sufficiently talented, should not discredit the party, should maintain party discipline and so on). Austrian parties certainly need a lot of candidates, in that there are three levels of representative and governmental institutions, the lowest of which is almost amateur, and in that there are also the (interest group) chamber elections, in which candidates are fielded by the party factions (the ÖVP Leagues) or ancillary organizations (in the case of the SPÖ). Fourth, party members are also a resource in intra-party politics, a rationale which is most important in the case of the ÖVP, and which is also relevant in the SPÖ, where district organizations play a role similar to that of the Leagues and engage in a kind of contest to recruit party members. In order to adapt to the new 1992 electoral law, however, the ÖVP decided to introduce open primaries as a basis for the drawing up of the candidate lists, a decision which *potentially* allows the electorate to replace the party organization in this process.

Causes of party membership decline

Party membership decline can be explained first and foremost by changes in the citizenry and the political community and by the failure of the major parties to adapt to these changes. Social-structural and cultural changes have substantially reduced the ease with which groups of citizens can be organized and, while extensive welfare services have also created new dependencies, their overwhelming effect, and that of affluence, has been to reduce the relevance of politics for individual 'life chances'. Moreover, new demands regarding environmental protection and political participation, the satisfaction of which has not figured prominently among the achievements of the 'established' political parties, have also become more prominent in recent years. Developments in civil society are only one side of the equation, however. In their role as bureaucratic institutions, as well as through their involvement in scandals, the political parties themselves have also contributed to their organizational decline. Moreover, although they are by and large still interested in maintaining high membership levels, the parties have also become more reluctant to apply previously effective methods of membership recruitment, especially patronage. Either way, it appears from the Austrian case, as more generally (Katz, 1990: 158), that the costs and benefits of party membership have shifted and that this shift has made membership less attractive for both party elites and ordinary citizens.

The party leadership and the parliamentary party

In contrast to the situation which often prevails in other countries, all of the parties in Austria have clearly defined, and quite easily identifiable, leadership bodies (Müller and Meth-Cohn, 1991). While most of the members of these bodies are elected at the national party congresses, some may also be recruited by appointment. The major exception to election by the party congress has been the ÖVP before 1980 and since 1991, when the party chairmanship and a few other positions were filled by the national party congress, while the bulk of party executive members were ex-officio representatives of the constituent organizations of the party and holders of important state functions. What is most striking in the Austrian case, however, is the sheer variety of executive bodies, ranging from meetings of more than a hundred people to smaller groups of just eight to ten people.

The party statutes ascribe major functions to the executive bodies of the parties which, over time, have increased at the expense of the party congress. Shifts of functions between the different executive bodies have occurred quite frequently (see Müller, 1992a), as have changes in the size and titles of the leadership bodies. Moreover, all parties have tended to increase the number of party executive members over time in order to satisfy demands for representation from the *Land* party organizations, as well as from ancillary and affiliated organizations. Gaining representation in the party executive by an expansion of its size, however, constitutes an example of the declining marginal values of 'goods' which become available to more people, and hence being a member of the 67-strong *Parteivorstand* of the SPÖ in 1992 is not nearly the same as having belonged to the 20-member *Parteivorstand* in 1945. The parties have applied two methods to counter the 'law of growing party executives'. First, they have created new, additional executive bodies with a substantially smaller number of members than the old executive body. The smaller body formally takes over some of the functions previously assigned to the larger body and de facto tends to pre-empt the latter's decisions even in respect of its remaining competencies. The second method used to combat the growth of party executive membership has been the occasional reduction in the number of members with the intention of making the party bodies more effective. Indeed, the larger executive bodies meet only a few times a year and have little impact on real decision-making. Moreover, in practice, much decision-making occurs outside formal party bodies. As one cabinet minister from the SPÖ has put it:

> I have been a member of all party executive bodies, of the *Parteivorstand* and the *Parteipräsidium*, both at the *Land* and at the national levels. But I would like once to be a member of a body which really decides. In all these party executive bodies I have been faced with proposals which had been agreed by smaller circles before.

Such inner circles have probably always existed and will be found in any formal organization. But while the existence of inner circles which have a factional character and which are based on personal or ideological ties have remained largely secret, those which are based on formal party positions have often been granted a semi-official status. Examples of this include the 'big five' in the ÖVP, consisting of the party chairman, general secretary and the chairmen of the three Leagues; the 'round of fourteen', consisting of the 'big five' plus the chairmen of the *Land* party organizations; and the 'round of seven' in the SPÖ in the mid-1980s, consisting of the party chairman, his deputies residing in Vienna, the two central secretaries of the party and the leader of the parliamentary Fraktion.

The power of the party leaders vis-à-vis the party members has also increased during the post-war period (Müller et al., 1992). First, the intervals between the party congresses have become longer, and in the SPÖ and the FPÖ the term of party leadership has been increased from one to two years, while in the ÖVP it was first increased from two to three years, and later, in 1991, from three to four years. Second, the length of the meetings of the party congresses have been reduced. Third, their character has been changed from a forum for open intra-party debate to a carefully prepared media event which may not be distorted by criticism from the rank and file. Indeed, analyses of the leadership elections over the whole post-war period have demonstrated that most elections are not contested and the candidates receive majorities which come close to 100 per cent approval (Müller and Meth-Cohn, 1991; Müller et al., 1992). Moreover, the party leaderships have also proved remarkably successful in winning rank-and-file acceptance of the imperative of vote-maximization at the expense of 'pure' party goals.

Austrian party leaders have enjoyed a great deal of autonomy from their rank and file. This is a result of both the encapsulation and mutual hostility of the political subcultures (cf. Luther, 1992: 65–71) on the one hand, and the motivation structure of party members and activists on the other. Mutual hostility increased the support for leaders who represented the party in the daily parliamentary, governmental and interest group struggles, and being under fire from other parties tended to silence intra-party criticism. Indeed, there are several cases in which it was precisely the fire from other parties which kept politicians in office, sometimes deliberately so. Encapsulation also left the rank and file without much information about the 'outside' world, and allowed the leaders to combine polemics directed against the elites of other parties in the intra-party arena with a strategy of constructive negotiations with these same elites outside the party. The prominence of patronage and social contacts as motives among the party membership has also allowed the parties more of a free hand to engage in ideological or policy manoeuvring. At the same time, the party activists tend to be preoccupied with maintaining the party organization (this has become a goal in itself for many activists in the SPÖ in particular), and with the extraction and allocation of patronage resources from office-holders in their respective parties (Müller, 1989). Party leaders have, moreover, proved very effective in controlling intra-party democracy. That said, the recent decline in both encapsulation and patronage may now imply a change in the relationship between leaders and members, and may lead to the emergence of more strained and hence more 'normal' relations in the future. It is certainly the case that signs already exist which suggest that party activists are less willing to accept the decisions of their leaders.

The relationship between party organization and parliamentary party

The statutes of the parties either make no mention at all of the parliamentary party, or mention it only briefly and without any substantive reference, which, in itself, stands in stark contrast to the otherwise comprehensive and detailed regulations of intra-party life. This 'silence of the statutes' is due to legal reasons. Since the constitution includes the principle of the 'free mandate', that is, that MPs are 'bound in the exercise of their function by no mandate' (Art. 56), any formal subordination of the parliamentary Fraktion to extra-parliamentary party bodies would violate this rule. Nor do the two major parties have separate statutes for the parliamentary party, which reflects their intent to maintain as much flexibility as possible. Finally, although parliamentary parties had a clear legal status and were funded earlier than the party organizations, in practice they have always been the instrument of their respective party organizations or, more precisely, of the leadership of the party organizations.

Control over the parliamentary party is exercised in three ways, the first of which involves the selection and list-ranking of parliamentary candidates, which is subject to the veto power of the higher executive bodies in the party (Müller, 1992a: 100–4); even primaries, which were not wide-spread until the 1990s, are not generally binding (Nick, 1992). Most of the candidates have proven their loyalty to the party through many years of party work (Fischer, 1974; Stirnemann, 1989) and, once elected to parliament, they remain dependent on the party for their political career, with renomination or promotion requiring that MPs be both loyal and disciplined. Open conflict with the party would not only ruin the political career of an MP (there is no example of a successful independent candidate) but in many cases would also damage his or her career more generally. This is, of course, most obvious in the case of party employees but, given the importance of party in Austrian daily life, it is also partly true for almost all occupational groups.

The second way in which control is exercised is through the issuing of recommendations to the parliamentary Fraktion by the party congress and the party executive. While most congress recommendations are concerned with the initiation of legislation, there are also rare but important cases in which the party executive may recommend certain voting positions to its MPs. In most cases, however, communications from the top bodies of the party organization to the parliamentary Fraktion are not formalized, but are rather ensured by means of interlocking leaderships. Moreover, senior representatives of the party organization are also entitled to ex-officio participation in the decision-making of the parliamentary Fraktion, and while it is sometimes difficult to get MPs to support the policy of the party leadership, opposition can be overcome by means of appeals to authority and to party solidarity. That said, party discipline has declined quite substantially since 1986, and individual MPs or groups of MPs, such as, for example, those ÖVP deputies who belong to the Business League, quite regularly vote against the party or demonstratively abstain (Müller, 1992b, 1993).

Control is finally exercised through the recruitment of the leader of the parliamentary Fraktions. In the case of the SPÖ, and until 1967, it was usual for the party chairman to be automatically elected as Fraktion leader; and, since the leader used to be the party's senior representative in government, acting leaders of the parliamentary party were also nominated by the party executive and approved by the Fraktion. In 1967, however, when Kreisky was elected party chairman in a contested election, he allowed his predecessor as party chairman, Bruno Pittermann, to retain the position of parliamentary party leader for the remaining legislative period. In 1970, the SPÖ returned to the practice of combining the two leadership positions while having an acting leader of the parliamentary party who was nominated by the party organization and formally confirmed by the Fraktion. Then, in 1983, the new party chairman, Fred Sinowatz, abandoned the claim to formal parliamentary leadership, and the leader of the Fraktion has since been elected by the MPs, although this still continued to be done on the basis of an official candidate proposed by the party executive, who was always elected without difficulty. In 1990, however, when a number of MPs expressed interest in becoming leader, the party executive did not intervene by making a formal proposal, but the party chairman did convince some of the MPs to withdraw their candidacies in order to get his own candidate elected by as large a majority as possible. In formal terms, therefore, the influence of the party organization on leadership recruitment has been reduced; in practice, however, the chairman continues to exercise an important role.

The ÖVP traditionally separated the positions of party leadership and parliamentary party leadership, with the position of the latter being used to balance power between the Leagues. This was effected within the party executive which issued a formal recommendation to the Fraktion which, in turn, elected the respective politician as leader. The practice of a formal recommendation by the party executive for the leadership of the Fraktion changed only in 1971 when a contested election was held, and in the early 1970s there arose a number of conflicts between the parliamentary party and the party organization or, more precisely, their respective leaders, in which the party organization turned out to be the more powerful of the two (Kriechbaumer, 1981: 299–302). In order to avoid conflicts with a separate parliamentary leader, and also to strengthen his own power base, the party chairman in 1978 combined the two positions, a practice which continued with his successor. In 1986, however, when the ÖVP returned to government, it proved politically (though not legally) impossible for the party chairman to combine parliamentary leadership with government office. On this occasion the party executive did not formally recommend a candidate as Fraktion leader, but the preferred choice of the chairman did succeed to the position on the basis of a contested election. In 1990, and again in a contested election, he was then defeated by a candidate who had been recommended by the new party chairman. Thus, while it is clear that the autonomy of the ÖVP Fraktion has increased, the informal means of influencing recruitment are nevertheless also relevant, and the fact that elections have been contested, and closely so, indicates an even deeper level of change than in the SPÖ.

The FPÖ Fraktion leader was always elected by the MPs, and since the party chairmen were initially not MPs, they were therefore ineligible to become Fraktion leaders. Since 1966, however, chairmanship has mostly been combined with membership of parliament, and since 1970 the two leadership positions have sometimes been combined. In 1991, however, a controversy about the possible return of party chairman Jörg Haider – at that time not even an MP – to the leadership of the parliamentary party demonstrated that the Fraktion was keen to defend its autonomy in electing its own leader. Haider eventually returned to parliament and became leader of the parliamentary Fraktion in 1992, but this was eased by the resignation of the incumbent leader, who wished to avoid a confrontation in which the party chairman might have threatened to resign.

In all three parties, therefore, there have been periods in which the leader of the party organization has also been the leader of the parliamentary party, and whenever a party leader wished to take over the parliamentary leadership, this was always possible. The only qualification which has to be made is that party leaders have normally done so only when a vacancy arose, and have not sought the displacement of an incumbent leader.[10] More generally, however, and also when looking at the other means of control, it is clear that the parliamentary parties have increased their autonomy, a development which is likely to be enhanced by the new 1992 electoral law, which places a greater emphasis on the importance of individual candidates. This is, nevertheless, a far cry from 'parliamentarization' (that is, a shift of power by which the parliamentary party becomes the power centre of the party), and it may well be more correct to speak of 'governmentalization', with a shift of power from the party organization to the party's team in government, both in policy and career terms (Müller, 1994b; Müller and Philipp, 1987).

The party staff

The size of party staff has increased substantially during the post-war period. In the inter-war period, for example, the Social Democrats employed just nine persons in party headquarters, a figure which rose to about sixty in the late 1940s and to eighty-five in 1990. At the same time, however, this is only the tip of the iceberg (Müller, 1992a): thus while there were seventy employees in ÖVP headquarters in 1990, for example, the constituent organizations and *Land* organizations employed a further 750 persons, and even more were 'lent' to the party by interest groups and firms. Taking everything into account, ÖVP insiders have estimated a total of some 1500 party staff in 1990.

This growth of staffing in the main parties has been caused by the greater demands involved in such functions as propaganda and public relations, and also by increased specialization. What used to be one of several jobs carried out by a single employee three decades ago is now the exclusive occupation of one or more staff members. It has also been necessary to assign duties to party employees which used to be exercised by party activists or functionaries. On the one hand, the availability of activists has declined; on the other hand, they are less and less qualified to provide the party with the required services. Life for party functionaries, in particular at the higher levels, has also become more difficult, and the need to be available to the media in particular seems to occupy a substantial proportion of their time and thus prevents them from engaging in other activities which, in turn, now have to be carried out by staff members (Müller, 1983). Activities have also been 'contracted out', especially propaganda activities, which have been largely transferred to professional agencies (Müller and Plasser, 1992). The same is true of public opinion research, which has been carried out for the parties by professional pollsters since the 1960s.

The accession to power by those who were originally meant to be party instruments only is a familiar theme in the Austrian debate (for example, Hartl, 1986: 96ff). Indeed, in the SPÖ, most politicians began their career as secretaries, and of the five party chairmen since 1945, two were secretaries of the parliamentary *Fraktion*, one was a *Land* party secretary and the remaining two served as secretaries to members of the executive. The incumbent party chairmen of the ÖVP and the FPÖ also served as party secretaries during their career. But while the current senior party secretaries are first and foremost the servants of their party leaders, this has not always been the case. In the SPÖ, for example, in the 1940s, 1950s and 1960s, when there existed a more collective party leadership, several of the central secretaries had an independent power base of their own (such as a powerful district party organization) and their point of reference was the party executive as much as the party chairman. They thus held onto their positions even when the party leadership changed. Since Kreisky, however, they tend to be subordinated much more to the party leader. In the ÖVP, the position of the general secretary has been weakened institutionally by several successive party reforms. Traditionally it was a position to be filled by a party congress vote which was formally independent of the election of the party chairman (in effect the party chairman and the general secretary formed a joint ticket which was based on intra-party coalitions). In 1980, however, in an attempt to strengthen the party chairman, it was decided that the general secretary has to be elected on the basis of a proposal of the party chairman, and then in 1991 the election was transferred from the party congress to the party executive. In the case of the FPÖ, the position of general secretary was introduced only in 1978, and has tended to be occupied by important intra-party allies of the respective leaders or by those who lack a personal power base but nevertheless enjoy the trust of the leader.[11]

Conclusion

The main feature of Austrian party organizational development in the post-war period is continuity. The formal organizational structure of the three 'traditional' parties is still roughly the same as at the time of their foundation, and the numerous amendments to the party statutes and the 'organizational reforms' which have occurred on a regular basis have not led to fundamental changes. Moreover, the major parties have managed to maintain their enormous size and their networks of ancillary and affiliated organizations. Continuity also characterizes the internal power structure of the parties, with the party leadership enjoying a great degree of autonomy from the rank and file and with the party organization proving to dominate over the parliamentary party.

That said, it is necessary to point towards several important changes which have occurred. The organizations of the major parties reached a peak in the 1980s and are now in a period of decline, with both the ÖVP and the SPÖ losing a considerable number of members. This trend continues. The number of party activists has also fallen, and the age structure of party members and activists suggests that this decline will be progressive.[12] Furthermore, the party press has effectively disappeared. At the same time, all of the parties have increased their staffing levels considerably, and have assigned to party employees many activities which were previously carried out by party functionaries and activists. Despite this, however, the parties have also been forced to place increasing reliance on outside expertise, particularly in the fields of research and propaganda. Even before the decline in numbers, however, the relevance of the membership had begun to erode. Members were no longer a principal means of communication with the wider electorate, and were no longer so relevant in the provision of financial resources, which were now increasingly drawn from public subsidies.

The internal power structure of parties has also changed. The increase in the numbers of undecided voters,has forced the parties to reduce further the impact of their rank and files. In this process the mass media, which now constitute the principal linkage between the party and the electorate, have played a crucial role (cf. Müller, 1983). Moreover, in order to be successful, the parties have also been obliged to recruit personalities who are able to come across well on television, to professionalize their propaganda and communication techniques, and to grant their leaders more and more power. Institutional changes, including the introduction of new forms of direct democracy, have certainly facilitated this process. That said, the increased emphasis on the role of leaders applies not only to the national level, but also to the *Land* levels. The result is that the national leaders have become more powerful only in respect to national party politics, while *Land* party politics have become increasingly autonomous. This trend has also been reinforced by the extremely generous public subsidies at the *Land* level. At the same time, however, and perhaps paradoxically, there has been an unprecedented degree of party competition at the national level since the mid-1980s. For although they are largely autonomous in matters of intra-party politics, the fortunes of the *Land* parties now depend to a considerable extent on those of the national parties. Finally, while *étatization*, professionalization and the increasing role of electoral leaders have contributed to a trend towards convergence, it is at the level of organization that one still sees some of the main differences between Austrian parties.

There are a number of different models which can be drawn on in attempting to typify the prevailing mode of party organization in Austria, including those of the mass (integration) party (Duverger, 1954; Neumann, 1956), the catch-all party (Kirchheimer, 1966), the cartel party (Katz and Mair, 1992b), and the modern cadre party (Koole, 1992, and also in this volume), the last three of which have been elaborated in order to categorize precisely the developments in the period under consideration in this chapter. At the same time, however, in all of these models, there are a number of different dimensions which are relevant, but not all of which necessarily point in the same direction.

In terms of the electoral arena, for example, it is clear that Austrian parties can no longer rely on the mobilization strategy of a mass party, and yet do not contain competition in the way which is suggested for the cartel party. Rather, as is the case with the catch-all party and the modern cadre party, the dominant pattern is one of electoral competition. Austrian party work and party campaigning is also no longer as labour-intensive as in the case of the mass party, nor as capital-intensive as is the case for the cartel party. Here again, then, the catch-all party and the modern cadre-party models, which lie in between these two extremes, would appear to be the most appropriate. Thus the SPÖ and partly also the ÖVP still rely heavily on their activists in order to maintain their mass membership organizations, even if they adopt a more capital-intensive approach in other respects. For their part, the FPÖ and the Greens do not require much activist labour, and have tended to remain more amateur in style. In terms of resources, the Austrian parties bear little similarity to the mass party, which relies exclusively on membership fees, but do correspond more closely to the catch-all party, which draws on a wide variety of sources. The SPÖ, to be sure, which still relies on membership fees as its single largest source of income, has preserved a little of its mass party heritage, but it is the two most 'anti-cartel' parties, the Greens and the FPÖ, which actually follow the cartel-party model in relying most heavily on the state.

No Austrian party grants its members the influential decision-making role which is suggested by the mass-party model. At the same time, however, none would correspond to the cartel-party suggestion that party members are irrelevant. As far as the major parties are concerned, it is probably true to say that members are marginalized, as in the catch-all party, while the Greens, where party leaders are accountable to the party congress, and not only in a formal sense, best approach the modern cadre-party model, in which members maintain a sort of 'negative' influence. Moreover, the other element of the catch-all model, which suggests that membership is neither cultivated nor homogeneous, also tends to fit the SPÖ and ÖVP, while both the FPÖ and the Greens, with their relatively small or almost non-existent membership, tend to approach the position of the modern cadre party. Finally, Austrian parties can no longer be seen as mass parties in the sense that they now fail to provide their own channels of communication, and in this respect the major parties approach the cartel-party model through their privileged access to state-regulated channels of communication. Even then, however, they still have to compete with each other and with the other parties, and there also now exist channels of communication which are not regulated by the state and which are becoming more important. In this sense, the catch-all and modern cadre-party models might again be most appropriate.

In sum, it would seem that it is the catch-all-party model which best fits the major parties (see also Müller, 1992c), whereas the smaller parties, the FPÖ and the Greens, approximate more closely to the modern cadre party. Despite some evidence of convergence, the Austrian parties have, therefore, retained much of their distinctiveness.

Notes

The author is grateful to G. Heindl, A.K. Konecny and in particular to P. Mair, D. Meth-Cohn and A. Stirnemann, for comments on an earlier draft.

1 The organizational development of these four parties is discussed mainly on the basis of data which are reported in full detail elsewhere (Müller, 1992a).

2 It is worth noting that the typical connotation of the *Parteibuch* is patronage (colloquially it would be said that one needs to have a particular *Parteibuch* to get a particular job etc.).

3 Individual parliamentary candidates or MPs did not receive any public subsidy before 1992, when a new law provided individual MPs with financial resources for the employment of personal staff.

4 The smaller parties need to be commented on only very briefly. The organizational form of the *FPÖ* is pyramidal, with representation being based on the number of members. The number of affiliated organizations is small and their relations with the party are loose. The most important feature of the formal structure of the *Green Alternative* is the relevance of the *Land* organizations. Representation at the party congress is based on the size of the population of the *Länder*. Within the larger leadership body of the party, the *Bundesausschuß*, all *Land* party organizations enjoy equal representation.

5 Because of its loose and decentralized party structure, no data on the number of Green party units are available. In many local communities the Greens are represented by citizen initiatives and local groups which may run in local elections under a variety of names.

6 Full details of the membership levels are reported in Müller (1992a: Tables II.b.1.a–d).

7 There is also not much objective evidence about the electoral effectiveness of the party organizations and, indeed, there are electoral districts where one of the major parties has more members than voters (Dachs, 1992a: 245). Surveys have also demonstrated a substantial decline in the electoral loyalty of party members in the period from 1978 to 1985 (Plasser, 1987: 124).

8 It was not until the introduction of substantial public funding in 1975 that the accounts of the other parties became available.

9 It should be emphasized that this inter-party comparison refers only to the *national* party organizations. Since the parties differ in their internal structure and the relative importance of the central party organization vis-à-vis the subordinated territorial levels (and functional organizations in the case of the ÖVP), these differences may not be representative of the parties as a whole. The ÖVP's complex structure, for instance, requires more resources for other levels than the central party. Likewise the traditional autonomy of the FPÖ's *Land* party organizations has prevented them from providing much of their income from members to the national party organization.

10 When the Greens first established themselves in parliament there was initially no corresponding party organization, and thus no alternative to the election of the parliamentary leader by the MPs. Since 1990, however, the party organization is represented ex officio in the parliamentary fraktion by one of its leaders. Until 1992, the party statute declared that the holding of party and elected offices was incompatible.

11 To the best of my knowledge there has been only one successful coup attempt by a party secretary against his chairman during the entire post-war period (when *Land* party secretary Jörg Haider replaced the chairman of the Carinthian FPÖ).

12 The Vienna SPÖ, which in 1992 still organized 30.8 per cent of the SPÖ members,

78 *How Parties Organize*

constitutes the most drastic example: it has more members above the age of 90 than below the age of 20.

References

Dachs, H. (1985) 'Öffentliche Parteienfinanzierung in den österreichischen Bundesländern', *Österreichisches Jahrbuch für Politik 1985*: 439–54.
Dachs, H. (ed.) (1992a) *Parteien und Wahlen in Österreichs Bundesländern 1945–1991.* Vienna: Verlag für Geschichte und Politik.
Dachs, H. (1992b) 'Vom öffentlichen Parteiengeld in Österreichs Bundesländern', *Österreichisches Jahrbuch für Politik 1992*: 695–723.
Deiser, R. and Winkler, N. (1982) *Das politische Handeln der Österreicher.* Vienna: Verlag für Gesellschaftskritik.
Duverger, M. (1954) *Political Parties.* London: Methuen.
Ehmer, J. (1991) 'Die Kommunistische Partei Österreichs', in H. Dachs, P. Gerlich, H. Gottweis, F. Horner, H. Kramer, V. Lauber, W.C. Müller and E. Tálos (eds), *Handbuch des politischen Systems Österreichs.* Vienna: Manz, pp. 275–85.
Fischer, H. (1974) 'Die parlamentarischen Fraktionen', in H. Fischer (ed.), *Das politische System Österreichs.* Vienna: Europaverlag, pp. 111–50.
Gottweis, H. (1991) 'Neue Soziale Bewegungen in Österreich', in H. Dachs et al. (eds), *Handbuch des politischen Systems Österreichs.* Vienna: Manz, pp. 309–24.
Graf, F. (1947) *Die organisatorischen Aufgaben der Österreichischen Volkspartei.* Vienna: Österreichischer Verlag.
Hartl, R. (1986) *Österreich oder der schwierige Weg zum Sozialismus.* Vienna: Orac.
Houska, J.J. (1985) *Influencing Mass Political Behavior.* Berkeley: Institute of International Studies.
Katz, R.S. (1990) 'Party as linkage: a vestigial function?' *European Journal of Political Research*, 18: 143–61.
Katz, R.S. and Mair, P. (eds) (1992a) *Party Organizations: A Data Handbook on Party Organizations in Western Democracies, 1960–90.* London: Sage.
Katz, R.S. and Mair, P. (1992b) 'Changing models of party organization: the emergence of the cartel party', paper presented to the Workshop on Democracies and the Organization of Political Parties, ECPR Joint Sessions, University of Limerick.
Kirchheimer, O. (1966) 'The transformation of the Western European party systems', in J. LaPalombara and M. Weiner (eds), *Political Parties and Political Development.* Princeton: Princeton University Press, pp. 177–200.
Kofler, A. (1985) *Parteiengesellschaft im Umbruch.* Vienna: Böhlau.
Koole, R.A. (1992) *De opkomst van de moderne kaderpartij.* Utrecht: Het Spectrum.
Kriechbaumer, R. (1981) *Österreichs Innenpolitik 1970–1975.* Vienna: Verlag für Geschichte und Politik.
Luther, K.R. (1991) 'Die Freiheitliche Partei Österreichs', in H. Dachs et al. (eds), *Handbuch des politischen Systems Österreichs.* Vienna: Manz, pp. 247–62.
Luther, K.R. (1992) 'Consociationalism, parties and the party system in Austria', *West European Politics*, 15 (1): 45–98.
Müller, W.C. (1983) 'Parteien zwischen Öffentlichkeitsarbeit und Medienzwängen', in P. Gerlich and W.C. Müller (eds), *Zwischen Koalition und Konkurrenz. Österreichs Parteien seit 1945.* Vienna: Braumüller, pp. 281–315.
Müller, W.C. (1988a) 'Conservatism and the transformation of the Austrian People's Party', in B. Girvin (ed.), *The Transformation of Contemporary Conservatism.* London: Sage, pp. 98–119.
Müller, W.C. (1988b) 'SPÖ und große Koalition', in P. Pelinka and G. Steger (eds), *Auf dem Weg zur Staatspartei.* Vienna: Verlag für Gesellschaftskritik, pp. 23–46.
Müller, W.C. (1989) 'Party patronage in Austria', in A. Pelinka and F. Plasser (eds), *The Austrian Party System.* Boulder: Westview Press, pp. 327–56.

Müller, W.C. (1991) 'Die Österreichische Volkspartei', in H. Dachs et al. (eds), *Handbuch des politischen Systems Österreichs*. Vienna: Manz, pp. 227–46.

Müller, W.C. (1992a) 'Austria (1945–1990)', in R.S. Katz and P. Mair (eds), *Party Organizations: A Data Handbook on Party Organization in Western Democracies, 1960–90*. London: Sage, pp. 21–120.

Müller, W.C. (1992b) 'Austrian governmental institutions: do they matter?' *West European Politics*, 15 (1): 99–131.

Müller, W.C. (1992c) 'The catch-all party thesis and the Austrian Social Democrats', *German Politics*, 1 (2): 181–99.

Müller, W.C. (1993) 'Executive-legislative relations in Austria 1945–92', *Legislative Studies Quarterly*, 18: 467–94.

Müller, W.C. (1994a) 'Die Organisation der SPÖ, 1945–1993', in W. Maderthaner and W.C. Müller (eds), *Die Organisation der österreichischen Sozialdemokratie*. Vienna: Löcker (forthcoming).

Müller, W.C. (1994b) 'Models of government and the Austrian cabinet', in M. Laver and K.A. Shepsle (eds), *Cabinet Ministers and Parliamentary Government*. Cambridge: Cambridge University Press (forthcoming).

Müller, W.C. and Hartmann, M. (1983) 'Finanzen im Dunklen: Aspekte der Parteienfinanzierung', in P. Gerlich and W.C. Müller (eds), *Zwischen Koalition und Konkurrenz. Österreichs Parteien seit 1945*. Vienna: Braumüller, pp. 249–79.

Müller, W.C. and Meth-Cohn, D. (1991) 'The selection of party chairmen in Austria: a study in intra-party decision-making', *European Journal of Political Research*, 20: 39–65.

Müller, W.C. and Philipp, W. (1987) 'Parteienregierung und Regierungsparteien in Österreich', *Österreichische Zeitschrift für Politikwissenschaft*, 16: 277–302.

Müller, W.C., Philipp, W. and Steininger, B. (1992) 'Wie oligarchisch sind Österreichs Parteien?' *Österreichische Zeitschrift für Politikwissenschaft*, 21: 117–46.

Müller, W.C. and Plasser, F. (1992) 'Austria: the 1990 campaign', in D.M. Farrell and S. Bowler (eds), *Electoral Strategies and Political Marketing*. London: Macmillan, pp. 24–42.

Müller, W.C. and Steininger, B. (1994a) 'Party organisation and party competitivenenss: the case of the Austrian People's Party, 1945–92', *European Journal of Political Research*, 26: forthcoming.

Müller, W.C. and Steininger, B. (1994b) 'Christian Democracy in Austria: the Austrian People's Party', in D. Hanley (ed.), *Christian Democracy in Europe*. London: Francis Pinter, pp. 87–100.

Neumann, S. (1956) 'Toward a comparative study of political parties', in S. Neumann (ed.), *Modern Political Parties*. Chicago: University of Chicago Press, pp. 395–421.

Nick, R. (1992) 'Vorwahlen in Österreich und der Bundesrepublik Deutschland', in H. Neisser and F. Plasser (eds), *Vorwahlen und Kandidatennominierung im internationalen Vergleich*. Vienna: Signum, pp. 75–103.

Plasser, F. (1987) *Parteien unter Stress*. Vienna: Böhlau.

Plasser, F. and Ulram, P.A. (eds) (1991) *Staatsbürger oder Untertanen?* Frankfurt: Lang.

Plasser, F., Ulram, P.A. and Grausgruber, A. (1992) 'The Decline of "*Lager* mentality" and the new model of electoral competition in Austria', *West European Politics*, 15 (1): 16–44.

Sickinger, H. and Nick, R. (1990) *Politisches Geld: Parteienfinanzierung in Österreich*. Thaur: Kulturverlag.

SPÖ (1987) *Materialien zum Organisationsbericht*. Vienna: SPÖ.

Stirnemann, A. (1989) 'Recruitment and recruitment strategies', in A. Pelinka and F. Plasser (eds), *The Austrian Party System*. Boulder: Westview Press, pp. 401–27.

Verba, S., Nie, N.H. and Kim, J.-O. (1978) *Participation and Political Equality*. Cambridge: Cambridge University Press.

4

The Decline of Consociationalism and the Reluctant Modernization of Belgian Mass Parties

Kris Deschouwer

Party structures under consociational rule

Until the early 1960s, Belgium was stable enough to puzzle authors linking political stability with cultural homogeneity (see especially Almond, 1956). In fact, Belgium is one of the typical examples of a consociational democracy (Lijphart, 1977), where potential instability turned out to be a self-denying prophecy, and where the prudence of the political elites led towards accommodation and power-sharing, rather than to system-destroying competition. Political parties play a very important role in such a democracy (Luther, 1992: 46). The parties are deeply rooted in society, and are much more than purely political organizations. They are the political centre of a densely organized subculture, of a world of their own. The parties can be seen at all levels of the society, and in almost all the spheres of life. Or, more precisely, the subcultural divisions can be seen, with the party which belongs to that subculture never being far away. When people in Belgium say (mostly complain) that something is becoming political, they really mean that the parties are becoming visible.

At the same time, the parties organize the search for consensus among the political elites, and it is the parties' elites that must be 'prudent leaders' in order to prevent subcultural divisions (organized and mobilized by themselves) from becoming the source of centrifugal drives. The political agreements then have to be implemented, which requires the parties to exert a firm control over parliament and public administration and this, in turn, brings us back to the idea that parties are almost everywhere.

The role played by parties under consociationalism explains a number of characteristics of their internal life. The most obvious is the need for a strong leadership. The elites must be able to make the most appropriate strategic choices without being constantly challenged about these choices. Too much elite-challenging behaviour would diminish the credibility of the leaders when negotiating with the other party leaders, and would therefore undermine the power and the weight of the party. Strong leaders are good for the party, and are needed to keep the consociational system going. The counterpart of strong leadership is, of course, a very low level of political participation, and passive citizens are an important precondition for the well-oiled functioning of consociational democracy (Huyse, 1969, 1971). The voters and the militants must be ready to follow the leaders, one day mobilizing to defend their subcultural values, the next accepting a compromise in which their own wishes (the wishes they were asked to defend) have only partially been met.

If the members of the subculture, and the voters of its party in particular, have to be loyal, their commitment to the party cannot be very ideological. Indeed, were the incentives on offer to participants to be mainly purposive (Clark and Wilson, 1961), then the party leadership could forfeit its strategic freedom. Thus the political and electoral stability in a consociational (and thus compromising) democracy serves as an indicator of the relative lack of ideological or purposive incentives in keeping the subgroups together. The incentives used instead are those of solidarity or association (participants are attracted by appealing to a sense of belonging to a social group or community), and material or selective (Clark and Wilson, 1961; Panebianco, 1988; Deschouwer, 1990). Moreover, solidaristic incentives are easily found by the parties in a consociational democracy with separated and closed societal subgroups. The parties sit in the centre of a societal segment, in which the members see and meet one other at all levels and in all spheres of social life, and the pillars then provide the parties with a reservoir of loyal members and voters (Steininger, 1977).

The societal segments in a consociational democracy are more than just subcultures, however. One of the consociational techniques is to delegate to them a series of state tasks so that they can distribute to their members the services of the welfare state. The Belgian 'Mutualities' (linked to the parties) reimburse patients for their medical costs, and the trade unions (linked to the parties) pay unemployment benefits. The parties thus also have a large reservoir of selective incentives. And since the pillarized organizations are also those recognized as the representative pressure groups in corporatist decision-making, the parties, by being almost everywhere, can offer almost everything. They are strong and safe, with loyal and elite-directed participants.

A final characteristic of the parties in a consociational system is the weakness of the parliament, the role of which is to reflect the procedures of decision-making. It is the party elites that agree on what has to be done, and parliament – being constitutionally the place where the rules should be made – must only approve the decisions that have already been taken. The parties must therefore be able to control their parliamentary fraktions. In this sense, it is not really important who actually sits in parliament; what matters is how many MPs belong to each party, and how well they are controlled. The Belgian parties under consociational rule are therefore very close to the prototypical mass party. They are the political wing of a societal group from which they originated, they have privileged links with the other organizations of that group, and they have a very formalized and centralized organization that allows them to use the weight of the masses whenever this is required.

Challenging the consensus

In 1960 the parties were more or less the same as those in the beginning of the century. The two-and-a-half party system was still in place, with two large parties, the Christian-Democrats and the Socialists, and a smaller Liberal Party. Each had its own pillar – two larger and one smaller. The Liberal Party, originally being a cadre party, was less 'societal' than the others, but was just as centralized and formally organized. This was also the last year in which everything was (or seemed to be) quiet and predictable. In 1961 the Liberal Party decided to transform itself. The principal novelty of the new 'Party of Freedom and Liberty' (PVV/PLP) was its explicit appeal to the Catholic electorate which, for a full century, had been well-secured within the Catholic pillar, serving as a stable and loyal electorate for the Catholic Party, and later for its successor, the CVP/ PSC. The 1961 elections were the last almost normal and predictable elections: the three traditional parties together polled almost 91 per cent of the votes, while the Communists won 3 per cent. The 1965 election, by contrast, is generally considered to mark the beginning of a new era, characterized by high volatility and increasingly high fractionalization. In 1965 the renewed Liberals almost doubled their vote, while Christian- Democrats and Socialists each lost about one-fifth of their support. The old and stable consociational system came under pressure. The main issues at that time were economic (with the Liberals being able to produce a clear opposition profile) and linguistic. The old and very complicated problem of the relationship between the Dutch-speaking north of the country, the French-speaking south, and bilingual (but originally Dutch-speaking, and surrounded by Dutch-speaking and also 'Frenchifying' territories) Brussels won a high place on the political agenda, and was to remain there for at least thirty years. This deeply affected the evolution of the parties and the party system.

In Flanders the *Volksunie* (VU) gained momentum in 1965, while in Brussels the *Front Démocratique des Francophones Bruxellois* (FDF) was created, winning three seats. The Brussels party became very strong within Brussels itself (increasing to 40 per cent in 1971), but was never strong at the national level (11 per cent in 1971 proved its absolute maximum). Being the largest party in Brussels, however, was enough to afford it a significant political role, and the party was in government from 1978 to 1980. In Wallonia a smaller and less successful *Rassemblement Wallon* (RW) was created in 1965, associating itself electorally with the Brussels FDF. These nationalist or regionalist parties constituted a double chal- lenge to the traditional system. In the first place, their electoral success obliged the other parties to give attention to the idea of granting more autonomy to the regions and linguistic communities. But autonomy was not the only value stressed by these new parties, for they also presented themselves as an alternative model for doing politics, and in this sense they challenged the system as such. They criticized pillarization, the power of the traditional pillarized parties, and the poor democratic quality of the system. This was of course connected with the linguistic problems, for both Flemings and Walloons felt that the way in which the system functioned made it impossible to take account of the real problems.

Two specific factors can be cited to explain the rapid success of these new parties. The first concerns the consociational system itself, which is indeed a very closed system, locking out those who at a certain moment might wish for more and better participation. The second is the nature of the traditional parties which, as real mass parties, lack the flexibility to adapt easily to new challenges, or to incorporate new questions and new movements. These then lead to the creation of new movements outside the existing parties (Deschouwer and Koole, 1992). As far as the first of these challenges was concerned, the reaction of the traditional parties was clear and coherent; as far as the second was concerned, however, the reaction proved much more erratic (and not so easy), and the attempt to take regionalist demands into account finally led to the split and death of the traditional parties. The Christian Democrats divorced in 1968 (creating the unilingual CVP and PSC), the Liberals in 1971 (creating the PVV and PLP), and the Socialists in 1978 (creating the SP and PS). Attempts to adapt to the participatory or anti-system challenge came later, within the newly created unilingual parties themselves. Understandably, however, they went in different and sometimes opposing directions. Moreover, while the successes of the new parties pushed the traditional parties towards change, they nevertheless also made the formation of governments more difficult by asking for more centralized and elite-directed structures. As a result, the parties seemed to be constantly looking for the ideal change, without really finding it, and then often just keeping things more or less the same.

The challenge to the traditional parties did not only come from the regionalist parties. In the first place, two new Green parties were also created, and developed and grew almost independently from each other. Towards the end of the 1980s, a party called *Vlaams Blok*, which was originally created as a radical Flemish Nationalist party in 1978 (protesting against the participation in government of the more moderate Volksunie), moved towards the extreme right of the political spectrum, stressing primarily the presumed damaging effects caused by the presence of foreigners. Competing only in Flanders, the party polled 1.9 per cent in 1987 and 6.6 per cent in 1991. Finally in 1991 a list called 'Rossem', led by the flamboyant ex-junkie, ex-stockbroker, and ex-formula 1 team manager, Jean-Pierre Van Rossem, polled 3.2 per cent, also mainly in Flanders.

In 1961 there were three major parties, with a tiny communist party and a very young and small Flemish nationalist party. In 1991, by contrast, no less than thirteen parties managed to have representatives elected to parliament. The three decades in between have been decades of change, both in the parties and in the party system. Moreover, after the three decades of volatility, fractionalization, dealignment and linguistic division, there is now no Belgian party system. Rather, there are now two party systems, with the Flemish parties presenting candidates only in the Dutch-speaking constituencies and in Brussels, and with the French-speaking parties presenting candidates only in the Walloon constituencies and in Brussels. Electoral results are never provided at the national level, but are always split up for the north and the south. Success or failure is measured only within the separate unilingual party systems. The two party systems come together only in the national government, and, up to now, all national coalitions have been 'symmetrical', which means that the two parties of the traditional party families – Christian Democrats, Socialists and Liberals – remain together either in government or out of government (although the termination of a coalition can often be the result of a conflict between the two parties of the same family).

The first reaction: internal separation

The changes in the Belgian parties can roughly be divided into two stages. The first stage is the internal split. The second stage is the further adaptation that then takes place within the newly created unilingual parties. This does not mean, of course, that the first stage shows only changes concerning the linguistic problems; rather it is simply that these problems clearly dominated the discussions of the parties' internal structure as well as the results of these discussions.

That said, the first party with which I am concerned, the *Communist Party*, is more or less an exception to the logic outlined above, in that in this case there is no second stage. The party has not been represented in parliament since 1985. In other words, it died completely, before even having to think of other kinds of adaptation and change. In 1971 the top organs of the party were divided, with the Central Committee having two autonomous language sections. The Central Committee of the Brussels constituency was given some autonomy, but required the approval of the national Central Committee, while decisions in that national Committee could be taken only with a majority from both language groups. In 1982 the party was almost completely divided. The regions (Flanders, Wallonia and Brussels) had separate Congresses, which elected three different executive bodies, or Councils, which, in turn, elected their own Political Bureaus. The national Political Bureau required a perfect 50/50 division, with half of its members being part of the regional Bureaus. The national Bureau elected the national president, and also a Flemish and Walloon president. The Belgian Communist Party is therefore a federation of at least two parties, with a smaller and still subordinate party in Brussels. In 1985, it won no seats, and in 1991 only the Walloon wing decided to present candidates, polling just 0.1 per cent of the votes.

When the old Catholic Party was recreated as a modern *Christian Democratic* party in 1945, it was presented as a 'unitary' party, which meant that the old '*standen*' were explicitly abolished, and that individual membership of the party as a whole became the rule. Yet the duality of the country was present within the party structures from the very beginning, in that two language wings were officially recognized with their own presidents, and with visibility in the Congress and the National Committee (the executive body). During the 1960s, there were no fundamental changes in the party structure, which consisted of local sections, united in federations at the constituency level. The federations sent delegates to the Congress, and the Congress elected the National Committee. There was also a party Council, a sort of smaller-size congress, that gave non-binding opinions to the National Committee, and presented the Congress the candidates for the National Committee and for the presidency. In 1965 the two wings of the National Committee became more autonomous, dealing with all the matters concerning their own part of the country, and electing their own executive bureau. The national president could be, but did not need to be, present at their meetings. The CVP/PSC then functioned as two different parties, with only the national president as the link between them. When the bilingual status of the University of Louvain (situated in Flanders) became a political problem in 1968, the two wings were so opposed that the two parts actually turned themselves into two parties simply by no longer inviting or recognizing the national president.

Unlike the Christian Democrats who accepted the existence of two wings after 1945, and had been organized in separate structures since the 1930s, the *Socialists* always presented themselves as a 'strong and unified' party, with the first acceptance of internal differences coming only in 1963. The second difference with the Christian Democrats was the number of wings into which the party is divided. The Christian Democrats were very strong in Flanders, and rather small in the French-speaking part of the country. The push towards autonomy came from the Flemish side, and led to a division according to language groups. The Socialist party, on the other hand, was weaker in Flanders, and very strong in the French-speaking electorate, which was itself divided into two regions, Wallonia and Brussels. Thus while the Christian Democrats divided according to the two major language communities, the Socialists began to divide between the three regions. This was to have important consequences for the way in which the French-speaking Socialists organized after the separation. In 1963 the statutes stated that half of the Bureau members, who were elected by the Congress, must be elected separately, that is, five by the Flemish constituencies, five by the Walloon constituencies and two by the Brussels constituency. These could also meet separately at a national congress, whenever this was felt to be necessary. The next change came in 1969, when all the Bureau members had to be elected this way. In 1973 the party created a double presidency (before there had been a president, with a vice-president of the other language group), and in 1977 it added the presidents of the 'Regional Committees' (regional congresses which had been recognized in the party rules since 1969) to the Bureau. By 1977, the only structure uniting the party was the presidency, and even that was divided. The Belgian Socialist Party was ready to die one year later.

Liberal strength was more evenly spread than that of its major rivals, being medium-sized in Flanders and Wallonia, and rather strong in Brussels. Separation was to prove a painful process. Unlike the other two parties, the Liberals did not formally recognize linguistic wings or regional structures, taking care only that the two language groups were more or less equally represented in its executive bodies. In 1972 the Dutch-speaking wing (including the Dutch-speaking Liberals of Brussels) went its own way, while the French-speaking section began a long process of further fractionalization. In Wallonia, the existing PLP carried on, and was reformed in 1977 into the PRLW. This was the result of a major split in the nationalist Rassemblement Wallon (RW). In 1979, one of the important men coming over from that party (Jean Gol) would finally create the new PRL (*Parti Libéral Réformateur*), reuniting the Walloon Liberals with the French-speaking Liberals in Brussels. The story of the latter is one of even more extreme fractionalization. Several small parties were created out of the Brussels part of the old national party, some of which were simply Liberal, while others wanted to be Liberal and Belgian, or Liberal and very francophone. Part of the Brussels Liberals was also swallowed up by the Brussels francophone party, the FDF.

The second reaction: adaptation and change

A further wave of change dealt with the secondary effects of the successes of the challengers, the first of which was to make the formation of government coalitions more difficult. Every coalition needs at least four parties to reach a majority, and every coalition has to find an agreement between the Dutch-speaking and the French-speaking parties. This means that, even more than before, the governing parties now needed structures allowing them to reach compromises. And while the regionalists push the traditional parties towards a more radical programme, they nevertheless do not govern themselves, and thus they oblige the traditional parties to be the ones who compromise. There is therefore pressure to maintain a strong leadership.

Another effect became visible when the regionalist challenge was partly replaced by the more explicit new-politics challenge of the Green parties, which gathered votes on the basis of a programme that also dealt with the way in which a party should be organized, and on the basis of a party structure that already reflected these new ideas. The formula directly criticized the elitism of the traditional parties, whose obvious response was to decentralize decision-making and to allow more possibilities for participation by members and activists. Yet there was still the pressure to have a party structure suited to coalition formation, and it was this which caused a major dilemma for the traditional parties. It might be said that this problem was 'solved' by taking over the rhetoric of internal democratization, while at the same time retaining the strength of the leadership. In any event, this strategic dilemma affords a useful starting point for a review of the major changes which did take place.

The Christian Democrats

When the national party split up in 1968, no structural changes were needed: the two new parties could continue with the rules of the old party, and this was done by the Dutch-speaking CVP until 1972, and by the French-speaking PSC until 1980. The new rules of the CVP introduced some changes at the top of the party. The old executive was divided in two parts: a *Partijbestuur* with members elected by the Congress and the party in parliament and in government, and a smaller Political Bureau, with a selection of *Partijbestuur* members. The creation of the Bureau, which meets weekly and is the real executive body of the party, has allowed the top of the party more autonomy. The Congress was also changed, and is no longer composed of representatives of the constituency level, but of representatives of the local sections plus the executives of the constituency branches. By going one level down, the party seems willing to give more say to the sections that are the closest to the members, but by allowing the executives of the constituency branches to take the place of representatives of this level, it nevertheless gives these executives more power. The party rules were completely rewritten in 1989. No important changes were introduced, but the creation of many permanent working groups and think-tanks suggests that there has been an increasing professionalization.

The French-speaking PSC used the old CVP/PSC rules until 1980. There had been a Congress in 1969, at which a document, which was presented and accepted, mentioned a long list of ideas for new party rules. These were intended to be 'effective and democratic' (both sides of the dilemma), and allow more opportunity for the participation of women and young people. While accepted in 1969, however, these rules were not really formally adopted until 1980. The most striking difference with the old CVP/PSC was the introduction of direct elections for the position of party president. In 1969 the delegates at the Congress elected their president, but from 1970 on all the members could cast a secret vote. Moreover, the 1980 statutes state that all the internal party mandates (including candidates on the electoral lists, and representatives at the constituency congresses up to the level of party president) have to be allocated after a general, free and secret election. The organizational structure was otherwise very conventional: local sections united at the constituency level, a

congress with representatives of these local sections and with the leaders of
the constituency sections (just like for the CVP), and an executive body,
the Comité Directeur, which is led by the directly-elected president.
Although no other member of the executive was directly elected by the
party members or by the Congress, it was nevertheless composed of
representatives of the executives of the constituency sections, and of
representatives of the party in parliament and in government, and was thus
fairly independent. In 1984 the executive structure was modified, and a
new body, the 'Committee for the Coordination of Action', was created,
composed of the party president, all the members of the party in
government, and the fraktion leaders. The new committee meets weekly,
while the Comité Directeur now meets monthly. This further reduces the
power of the members, who can now only choose their president.
Moreover, the president really is in control.

The Socialist Parties

One change that took place before the party split was that the Central
Committee lost its importance, while the Party Council became more
important. The Central Committee met once every two months in 1963,
once every three months in 1969 and once a year after 1973. From 1969 on,
the party fraktion was also represented in the Council (being then almost
the same as the Central Committee), and the Council explicitly became the
highest organ between congresses. This evolution had a logical outcome in
the new rules of the unilingual Socialist Parties. Both abolished the Central
Committee, and kept the Party Council as it was. The French-speaking
Parti Socialiste made its own new rules in 1978; the Dutch-speaking
Socialistische Partij did so in 1980. The former essentially retained the old
structures (except for the Central Committee), keeping even the idea of a
regional balance within the party: the Brussels and Walloon parts could
organize separate congresses and have their own presidents, and the
Brussels region had a guaranteed number of elected representatives in the
party Bureau.

The SP is much more homogeneous, in that the number of Dutch-
speakers in Brussels is too small to have any significant weight in the party,
and, in any case, consider themselves to belong to Flanders (conversely,
the French-speakers in Brussels do not consider themselves as Walloons).
The SP also largely reproduced the structures existing in 1977, without, of
course, the regional balance. The major change to be adopted was at the
top of the party, where the Bureau was split into an Administrative
Commission dealing with organization and a Bureau dealing with political
matters. The Bureau became the more important. The SP changed its rules
in 1992 in an attempt to become a more modern and democratic party. It
also introduced the idea that older people should have a reasonable
number (not specified) of intra-party positions. The main structural change
was the division of the Party Council into two new structures. The existing

Council (with delegates of the constituencies, the fraktions and the Bureau members) became a 'Cooption Council', and selects the coopted members of the Senate.[1] There is also a new 'Council of presidents and secretaries', consisting of the fraktions and the Bureau, with the presidents and secretaries of the local sections, which takes over the functions of the old Council. The idea was to democratize by giving a greater role to the basic units of the party; but whether it really means a decentralization of decision-making remains to be seen. Indeed, by going down one level, and by taking the local presidents and secretaries instead of elected representatives, the new Council might also prove to be a very docile structure.

The Liberal Parties

The Belgian Liberal Party is the only one which underwent important changes before the linguistic division, although these were not very visible at the level of the party's organizational structure. The old Liberals had been the party of the free market economy and the secular state, but, with the declining salience of the Church–State cleavage,[2] anti-clericalism came to be seen as detrimental to its appeal. In 1961, therefore, the party 'enlarged' itself into a modern liberal party, the Party for Freedom and Progress, and deliberately tried to attract liberal Catholics. This was also a successful strategy, in that the party was able to double its vote and now recruits support from among all religious and non-religious groups.

The party rules of 1961 were changed in 1963, in 1966 and in 1969, and with every new set of rules came both a change in the name and an expansion of the leading executive structures. Initially, a Permanent Committee composed of delegates of the constituencies, the party fraktions, the members of the government, the local mayors and lots of representatives of all the different liberal organizations (cultural, social, educational, etc.) was placed between the Congress and the executive bodies, with roughly the same function as the Party Council in the other parties. This was then abolished in 1966. The Bureau, which in 1960 consisted of the president, the party secretaries, representatives of the fraktions and the ministers, as well as representatives of the different liberal organizations, became larger: more representatives were brought in, with the executives of the constituencies joining in 1963, and representatives of the fraktions in the provincial councils in 1966. The Bureau also changed its name in 1966 and became the Political Committee. One level above the Bureau was the Executive Bureau (which became the Executive Committee in 1961, the Permanent Directorate in 1966, and the Permanent Bureau in 1969) which, in 1960, comprised the party president, vice-president and the party secretaries (the latter chosen by the president). The number of these officers (except for the president) increased in 1961, and in 1966 representatives of the fraktions were added, as were the representatives of a long list of liberal organizations in 1969. In fact, the Executive Bureau – then called the Permanent Bureau – became so large that a smaller executive body was created, the Direction Committee, comprising the party president, the secretaries and the fraktion leaders. In practice, then, the pattern is one of an expansion of the decision-making organs until they are so large that a newer and smaller body has to be created, which always includes the president, the fraktions and the party in government, and which then becomes the real locus of power in the party. In other words, attempts to open up the party have tended to create unwieldy structures which, in turn, undermine the capacity for strong leadership that was seen to be required in a party with an ambition to govern in coalition.

The Dutch-speaking Liberal party evolved in the same tradition as the national PVV/PLP, and changed mainly at the top. In 1972 the *Uitvoerend Comité* (executive committee) was a small group of ten members, meeting once a week. In 1977 it was then expanded to include representatives of the fraktions, of the party in government and of some other Liberal organizations. Though it still met weekly, a new executive body was also created, the *Dagelijks Bestuur* (daily direction), which included only the party leadership and representatives of the fraktions. In 1982, these merged once more and became the Bureau. In November 1992, however, the PVV itself was formally abolished, and a new party created in its place, the *Vlaamse Liberalen en Democraten* (VLD). The change was in response to the poor electoral result of November 1991, in which the party improved its vote only slightly, after four years of hard opposition, and failed to get into government. The change was also both organizational and ideological. The new VLD is more broadly liberal (actually mainly anti-state), and is closer to the ideas of Flemish nationalism. The former president of the VU has become one of the prominent leaders of the new VLD, and has also brought with him some friends and supporters. The new party wants to be absolutely independent from pressure groups, which means that their representatives have disappeared from the party structures. It also wants to be more open and democratic, and has introduced the direct election of the president and the bureau by the members. The new party rules were adopted in March 1993.

The most striking changes on the French-speaking side have also been at the top of the party, with the executive bodies being constantly reshuffled and having their names changed. In 1972 the Walloon PLP had a small Executive College at the top, and a larger Bureau. The Executive College was expanded in 1974, and in 1977 it merged with the Bureau. In 1979 the Bureau was expanded again, adding twenty-five members elected by the Permanent Committee (the intermediate Congress), and then, in 1989, was once more split again into a smaller Executive Committee and a Bureau. An interesting change also occurred at the level of the party presidency. Until 1989 the party president was elected by the Congress, and in order to avoid a continuing debate between two candidates, a system was introduced in which a team of president and vice-president would be directly elected by all the members on the same ticket. The double presidency – which the presence of two elected leaders actually involved – failed to work, however, and after the electoral defeat of 1991, former president Jean Gol announced that he wanted to lead the party again. The idea of a double election was dropped, but not the direct election itself, and the rules were changed in 1992 to elect Jean Gol. He was the only candidate.

The Flemish Nationalists

The Volksunie survived the three decades between 1960 and 1990, but it is not certain that it will continue to survive for many more years. The electoral result of 1991 was disastrous, and the more liberal and less nationalist wing of the party joined the new Liberal VLD, while the rump of the party now faces the direct threat of the much more militant Vlaams Blok.

The organization of the VU has always differed slightly from the other parties. In the first place, the party as such is an official and registered entity, in the form of a VZW/ASBL (non-profit organization). Standard rules exist for such organizations, and at the beginning of the 1960s these were in fact the only party rules. They were also fairly simple: all the members were to form a general assembly and elect their executive organs. In 1965, however, the VU doubled its vote, and began to work in a more 'classical' way, albeit still differently from the other parties, not least in that it provided much more space for participation. The rule-making structure in the party is the Council, which includes the leaders of the constituency branches, representatives of these branches, the members of parliament and some party professionals. This Council meets at least every month. It also elects the party president and the executive body, the *Partijbestuur*, which meets once a week, and is obliged to report to the Council. The party Congress is composed of the members of the Council, plus representatives of the local branches, meeting once a year to discuss general matters. Decision-making and strategic choices, however, are reserved to Council and Bestuur. In 1988 the Congress became the 'highest organ' in the party, winning the right to decide on all the fundamental matters, one of which is the explicit right of approval of the programme of a governmental coalition in which the VU has been asked to participate. The Council, meanwhile, continues to elect the president and the executive body. The overall pattern is thus very simple and smooth: virtually nothing changes, while the party itself slowly fades away.

The Green Parties

Even more so than the VU, the Green parties have been trying to create party structures that do not resemble those of the traditional parties. They have also more or less succeeded in doing so. Yet two different stories have to be told, in that the way in which the Greens were created in the north differed from that in the south, and both were created independently of one another. Both Green parties have a history of only one decade, but have already gone through important changes. They are very concerned with the way in which they are organized, and constantly seek to evaluate their party structures. The Dutch-speaking Greens (AGALEV) were formally created in 1982 as the political wing of a social movement with the same name: *Anders Gaan Leven* (for a different way of life). Their congress is simply a meeting of all the members, with a smaller group of 50 people forming the Steering Group. These are elected by constituency congresses, and represent the party between congresses. This structure comes fairly close to the position of the Council in the other parties, although in this case there are no members of parliament or professionals included. There is also no need for coherent strategic behaviour of all the top levels. The Steering Group is led by a 'debate leader', and there is no formal party president. The executive committee is a group of seven to ten people, elected by the Congress from among the members of the Steering Group. This is the political leadership of the party. The Steering Group then appoints the members of a Secretariat, which assumes the daily administrative leadership. Some tensions have occurred, however, especially as the professionals in the Secretariat became more powerful than the volunteers in the Steering Group and the Executive Committee. This led to a rule change in 1989, in which the Secretariat became 'the group that brings together all the professionals and volunteers that deal with the national party leadership'. The professionals are now appointed by the Executive Committee, whereas the others are selected and appointed by the Steering Group. The political secretary and the party secretary have the obligation to report to both the Steering Group and the Executive Committee. In this way, the professionals should lose some autonomy, and be subject to firmer political control. More generally, however, it is clear that AGALEV is under pressure to become more efficient, while at the same time wanting to remain democratic.

ECOLO – the French-speaking Green party – was formally created in 1980, and has a structure which is similar to that of AGALEV. All members can take part in the Congress, while a Federal Council, elected by the constituency branches, is the intermediate congress, and leads the party politically. The Congress elects a Federal Secretariat of five members as the administrative leadership of the party. ECOLO allows greater scope for a more or less permanent leadership than does AGALEV. Since 1988, the Federal Council elects a president and two vice-presidents of the Council, and one of these – together they form a Bureau – can be present at the meetings of the Federal Secretariat. The Federal Secretariat has also undergone some changes, which evidence an increasing need for some permanent leadership, and also the tension between the volunteers and the professionals. The Secretariat was expanded from five to nine members in 1983, and among its members the Council chooses three persons who can act during one year (and one possible extra year) as spokespersons for the party. In 1988 the rules stated that only two of these spokespersons could be professionals paid by the party, and the number of members of the Secretariat was again reduced to five members. That was also the case in 1989, when the rules stated that all the members of the Secretariat are spokespersons for the party. The strategic dilemma is clearly never far away.

The party leadership

The position of *party president* is very important in Belgian politics, and his remit very broad. He (and once in a while she) is the internal leader of the party. He is the chairman of the executive body and is in charge of the everyday leadership. He is the centre of the team of professionals that manage the party. He is the leader of all political negotiations. He will chair the delegation that negotiates on coalition formation and he speaks for the party during all the important discussions that are needed to keep the coalition going. The party president is also the most important selector when members of the government have to be appointed, and becomes – although not a part of the government himself – the leader of his party in government. Formally, each party in a coalition has a 'vice prime minister', who is the most important minister of the party, but who also needs the backing of the party – and this means mainly the president – for all important decisions. To be sure, the party fraktion in the parliament has its own leader, who is not the same person as the party president. In practice, however, the normal procedure is that the fraktion casts a block vote on all the important issues, and since these have been decided first among the government parties, this means that the party president either negotiated the decision, or explicitly backed it. In the media, the party president is also the most evident spokesman for the party. In many senses, the party president *is* the party, although, formally speaking, the party rules define his role only in a rather vague way, and limit it mainly to internal matters.

All the parties make provision for the formal election of the president, but the actual decision often comes closer to cooption. That said, there is some evolution towards more democracy in this respect, both in the party rules and in the political reality. All the parties, except the Volksunie and the Communist Party, elect the president at a meeting of the Congress,[3] although the PSC in 1970, the PRL in 1989 and the VLD in 1993 introduced direct election of the president by the members.

According to Maes (1990), who has analysed all elections of party presidents (including those in the Brussels FDF and the Walloon RW, but excluding the Communists), there has been an increase in the number of real elections, with a choice between several publicly known candidates, albeit only from 22.2 per cent in the period 1961–75 to 25.5 per cent in the period 1976–1990. If one looks at the party structure that makes the selection, one can see a sharp decline of the role of the Bureau (from 13.3 per cent of the decisions to just 2.0 per cent), and a clear increase in the role of the members (from 6.7 per cent to 21.6 per cent), again with the reservation that the members do not necessarily have a choice between a wide range of candidates. Since no party allows the president to be a member of the government or the president of one of the legislative houses, it is often necessary to replace a president who has resigned. When a president leaves, an interim president must be appointed. In this case, however, it is never the Congress or the members that decide, but rather the Council or the Bureau. The majority of the interim presidents easily become president later, and for most of the time they are then formally elected by the Congress or by the members, albeit without having to face a challenge from other candidates (Maes, 1990: 43).

The party executive

Although the names differ, all of the parties (except for the Greens) have a Political Bureau. This is a relatively small body (some thirty people on average), meeting weekly, and making all the decisions regarding the everyday leadership of the party, commenting on the current political issues, and eventually deciding on the strategy of the party in government. These meetings are led by the party president. While there is quite some variation in the composition of this Bureau, the general principle is that the membership comprises the president, the vice-president(s), the party secretary or secretaries, and a number of people elected by the Congress or by the Council. If the hypothesis of a growing centralization of the parties at the moment when compromise becomes more difficult is valid, there should then be changes in the party executives that reflect this concern with maintaining cohesion in all arenas. Moreover, these changes should be visible from 1960 on, and especially so following the separation of the two language wings.

Maintaining cohesion means in the first place that the party fraktions in both houses have to obey the party leadership. This has always been the case, but with the growing challenge to the consensus model, more control is needed and more subtle agreements are demanded. If there were any freedom of action for the fraktions, this obviously had to be reduced, and this is done by incorporating the members of parliament, or their representatives (for example, the fraktion leaders) in the party executive. At first sight this could be seen as evidence of the growing importance of the fraktions in decision-making. This is not the case, however, for while it does illustrate the importance of the fraktions, what is more relevant is that it illustrates the need to keep the fraktions under control. The fraktions are represented in the CVP/PSC executive from 1960 onwards (with no changes after separation), in the Liberal Party from 1966 and in the Socialist Party from 1963. Nor do the newer parties escape from this pressure to keep the fraktion under control. In the Volksunie, the fraktion was brought into the executive organ in 1966, and in both Green parties, the rules state explicitly that it is the party's executive organs that control the members of the fraktion. Moreover, in both the traditional and the new parties, votes in the parliament are almost always block votes, and it is a major event in Belgian politics when a member of a party fraktion does not vote along the lines desired by the fraktion, and thus by the party.

The party in government also has to be kept under the direct control of the party's central leadership. Government involves an ongoing negotiation between the parties, and the individual ministers must tell the party what they are doing, while the party will tell them what it expects. Yet control over the party in government is easier. The ministers are chosen by the parties themselves, and the party president has a very large say in these matters. One might say that the ministers owe their position to the party, where the party presidents are really in power. Indeed, at the end of the 1970s, political commentators coined the expression 'the junta of party presidents', to criticize the regular meetings of all the presidents of the coalition, which, in some matters, openly dictated to the government. This practice was then very visible, and while less evident today, remains valid in principle.

The party fraktions

The party fraktions are therefore not very autonomous, a conclusion which is confirmed by the rules regulating the way in which the fraktions work (Deschouwer, 1992: Tables III.D.7.a–j). In general, for example, the fraktion has to ask the permission of the party executive before taking important (legislative) initiatives. This control was already stated in the rules in 1960, and the subsequent incorporation of the fraktions into the party Bureau simply makes this control more easy and more direct. Although there might appear to be a problem in imposing this high degree of discipline on individuals who are in the first place controlled and sanctioned by the electorate, the Belgian electoral system, and especially the procedures for intra-party preference voting, does seem to be well adapted to the parties' need to reduce fraktion autonomy. The system was certainly not meant to have this effect, but since it does, there is no feeling that it should be rapidly changed. Only recently, the reformed Dutch-speaking Liberals began a real campaign against the system, advocating some kind of primary elections in order to give the voters real control over those elected. Moreover, although the electoral law allows for preference voting within a list, it is nevertheless the original list order that is really crucial. Indeed, since the introduction of the list-PR system, only twenty-nine candidates were elected because their number of preference votes was large enough to override the list order. Having the right place on the list is therefore the first condition for being elected, while the second condition is that the list itself receives enough votes. This system produces loyal candidates, who are easy to control because they can easily be sanctioned. Only the most popular candidates can claim more autonomy, but still risk being ousted the next time the lists are drafted.

The way in which the lists are produced is also quite important. The general rule used to involve the organization of an intra-party 'poll' in which all the members could participate, a practice which obviously gave considerable power to the individual members. This tradition of polling has gradually declined (De Winter, 1988), however, and today it is the central party executive, or eventually the leadership at the constituency level, which really decides. The members are sometimes, but not always, called together to approve the list proposed by the executive, and although changes might be made, it is the leadership which has the final word. The decline of the 'poll' nicely illustrates the growing need to maintain cohesion, and the need to know those who are in fact to be kept together.

The parties' formal rules can be very different in this respect, but the political reality is much more coherent than these rules might suggest. In the CVP/PSC, for instance, the poll was in the statutes in 1960, and the party executive needed a 75 per cent majority in order to change the list. In 1965 a rule was added which stated that the national executive decides on the list when the constituency level fails to do so. The Dutch-speaking CVP adopted this same rule in 1972, and two years later the statutes stated that only the candidates who have a real chance of being elected must be selected by a poll. For the rest of the list, any other procedure could be used. In 1989 the poll disappeared, and the constituency congresses are allowed to decide on the list. The national executive then ratifies the proposal, and can change it with a two-thirds majority.

While the CVP rules indicate a strong influence and ultimately almost decision-making power for the national executive, the new PSC adopted the rule that all the positions in the party, including placement on a list, must be the result of a general and secret vote. Yet reality is different, and is also foreseen in the rules, which state that a poll is not required when elections are premature, since there is then not enough time to go through the whole procedure. Since the creation of the independent PSC in 1969, however, only one election (1985) was not premature, and hence there was no real polling tradition in the PSC before 1985 (although some constituencies did organize real elections), with even the list formation in 1985 not being carried out according to the rules. Rather, the tradition of list formation with clear-cut proposals (so-called 'model-lists') coming from the executives at the constituency level, and eventually corrected by the national executive, was simply continued (De Winter, 1988).

In the Socialist parties, there were never any general rules dealing with candidate selection, and this meant that the constituency level was free to organize the formation of the list. In general, the rules at the constituency level envisaged a poll, albeit eventually with the right of the executive to reserve 'safe places' for some candidates. The national leadership had no power at all, except perhaps indirectly. In practice, many constituencies used the poll procedures in the early 1960s, but thereafter came a constant decline. This decline was sharper in the SP after 1980 than in the PS, and the most recent rules in the SP, adopted in 1992, for the first time give a formal role to the Bureau. All lists for elections at all levels must be submitted to the Bureau, which will judge whether the list respects the 'letter and spirit' of the statutes and the interests of the party. If there is a conflict, a special commission must decide, and if no agreement can be reached, the executive at the constituency level can decide.

The Liberal Party introduced rules on candidate selection in 1961 which gave the constituency branches the possibility (not obligation) to organize a poll, and which gave the national executive the right to approve the list, or to change it by a two-thirds majority. After 1963 the Bureau could also decide alone when no agreement could be reached at the constituency level. The Dutch-speaking PVV kept this rule after 1972, but from 1982 onwards the rules gave the final right of decision to the constituency branches, with the Bureau no longer having a role. In the constituencies themselves, the importance of the poll declined. The French-speaking PLP (later PRL) did not take over the old national rules, but simply gave full autonomy to the constituency level from 1972 on. In this case, the polling procedure is still used quite frequently (De Winter, 1988: 36), although the trend is also in decline. The recently reformed Dutch-speaking Liberals now want their lists to be approved by all of the members (and also by a new category of 'registered voters'), but the procedure will nevertheless begin with a list being proposed by the party executive. It remains to be seen whether the reform, as intended, will in practice give much power to the members.

The Volksunie had a quite centralized procedure of candidate selection after 1966 (before that there were no rules), in which the individual members had no role. The executive at the constituency level proposed a list to the Council at that level, and the Council then decided with a two-thirds majority (50 per cent in a second round) for every candidate. The national Council could then change the list with a simple majority. Five members of the constituency council could propose alternative names (since 1966), but since the 1970s they must first vote for the officially proposed candidates, and since 1973 new names can only be proposed when the list as a whole has been rejected.

Finally, the two Green parties are also different in this respect. ECOLO gives the decision power to the congresses at the different levels (this means to all the members), with a constituency congress (with a minimum presence of fifteen members) first voting on a list. In 1980 the rules allowed a national congress the right to approve the list for those constituencies where there is a chance for somebody actually to be elected, although this rule disappeared again in 1983. The national Congress still decides when fewer than fifteen members can be brought together at the constituency or the provincial level. Since 1988 the rules state that 20 per cent of the members (or at least fifteen members) must be present. The procedure is thus fairly open, with real power for the individual members. AGALEV operates in a more centralized way, in which the constituency branch organizes a vote, and then submits the list to the *Stuurgroep* (the national executive). This national executive also sets the rules for the elections at the constituency level. The general trend in all these changes is therefore a downgrading of the role of the individual member. At the same time, however, the central leadership is not necessarily in control of the whole procedure. The constituency level has considerable autonomy – which is understandable, since the elections are fought on that level – but it is the executive at that level which decides how to proceed. Finally, it must be recalled that almost all national elections in Belgium are premature, which reduces the time available to draft the lists, and which promotes a more centralized and less democratic procedure. At the local level, where the election date is fixed every six years, the polling tradition is still present (or has not declined very sharply).

The entire House of Representatives is directly elected from candidates chosen in the manner described above, while the Belgian Senate has 106 directly elected members who are also nominated in this way. In addition, however, there are also 'provincial senators', who are chosen by the legislative bodies at the provincial level, and co-opted senators, who are chosen by the elected and provincial senators. The election of both of these groups is based on a proportional system, and the party rules seldom say anything about the way in which they are chosen; where the rules do say something, it is to give the power to the national executive. Both of these types of non-elected members of parliament offer a useful way for the leadership to adjust for the decisions of the voters. Important candidates who failed to get elected can be resurrected, and the balance between the different party factions can be restored. The newly reformed Senate that will come into being with the next legislative elections will no longer offer such a corrective possibility, however. Forty senators will be directly elected (25 Dutch-speaking and 15 French-speaking), 21 will be appointed by the Community Councils (10 Dutch, 10 French and 1 German), and only 10 (6 Dutch, 4 French) will be coopted.

Election campaigns also evidence a slow process of centralization. To begin with, the party rules say almost nothing about campaigning, as if it were not an activity to be carried out by political parties. Only the new rules of the CVP in 1989 explicitly give the national executive the right to organize electoral campaigns at all levels. Of course, these rules simply make official what had for a long time been the normal procedure: campaigns are led by the party leadership. Moreover, this is not only the case for the CVP, but is also true for all the parties. In general, the party Council will meet to approve the electoral programme, which will have been drafted by the leadership. The exact origin of the programme is not easy to trace, however. Ad hoc groups, with of course the party president, the party secretary and some people from the study centre (thus professionals rather than the official executive) form a de facto campaign team that leads the campaign, although the party Bureau will certainly discuss the main campaign themes and the slogans to be used.

Parties have also been reluctant to accept help from outside experts for their campaigns. The 1960s witnessed the beginning of a new style of campaigning, in which the role of individual candidates increased, and in which the parties focused much more on mass communication techniques in order to reach as many voters as possible. While the parties had previously relied primarily on their own channels of communication in order to mobilize the vote of their own traditional electorates, they had now begun to look at the floating voter. At the same time, television began to find its place within a growing number of living rooms, and in 1965 the first programme on elections was broadcast on the French-speaking channel. Since 1974, the Dutch-speaking channel has also followed the campaign with a series of debates, and for all these reasons the parties began to feel the need for some professional advice. In 1968 the CVP was the first party to put its campaign production in the hands of a private marketing organization. The content of the messages still came from the party, but the professionals used their skills to communicate and sell the ideas. That said, when these professionals also pushed for a say in deciding the character of the product they would have to sell, not wanting to market something which could not be sold, the party expressed its unease, and there was a very visible conflict of this kind between the CVP and its marketing bureau in 1978. In the 1980s, however, the use of outside expertise became the rule, and campaign strategies are now set up in close cooperation between parties and marketing bureaus. The Liberals have tended to go further in allowing professional control over the whole campaign, while the other parties tend to keep more control themselves. The marketing specialists are seen as being particularly useful because they can rent the correct number of advertising sites at the most strategic places in the country, because they take care of buying space in the newspapers and magazines (political commercials on radio and television are not allowed), and because they produce drawings and photographs that translate the party's ideas into persuasive images. The Greens are an exception here because they do everything themselves.

But while there is certainly a process of centralization of the campaign at the top of the party, and a process of accepting outside help in devising campaigns, there has also been a tendency towards decentralization, which goes together with the growing importance of individuals in politics. Belgian elections are a rather local phenomenon, since they take place in thirty different constituencies. The parties have a list in each constituency, taking care to have at least one important 'head of list' in each. These candidates will avail themselves of the general campaign decided by the central party, but also have the freedom to lead their own local campaigns, and at this level a growing number of politicians tend to have their own individual agreements with marketing professionals. The hit parade of individual votes is one of the 'important' results of the election, and can make or break careers within the parties.

The Congress and the Council

Because of the importance of the party executive as the organ which has to keep the other party structures under control, rule changes deal with executive bodies more often than with other levels in the parties. There are rarely changes at the level of the Congress, for example, and when changes do occur, they tend to reveal an evolution towards more opportunities for participation and for setting the agenda. These adaptations correspond to the general idea that parties should become more democratic, and are in response to the challenge of the new parties. Thus while adaptation at the executive level is oriented toward keeping things under control, adaptation at the level of the Congress is oriented towards showing readiness to accept the idea of democratization. Moreover, when changes occur, they are often the result of pressures from below.

To be sure, nothing really spectacular can be seen at this level. But the idea that local or constituency branches must receive documents several weeks before the Congress and that these branches can add items to the agenda and propose motions, are either maintained or reinforced. There is no evidence here of the (formal) reduction of democratic participation. Yet these changes are also mainly symbolic, since the Congress is not the body that decides on the really important matters. Its role concerns the general ideology and policy of the party, rather than the concrete way in which this is translated into political decisions (always through agreements with other parties). It can also decide on who will be the party president, but seldom has a real choice. The only really important decision for which a Congress is normally convened concerns the participation of the party in a governmental coalition. The Congress is then asked to approve the coalition programme that was negotiated, but changes cannot be made since this would disturb the delicate balance of the agreement itself. That said, the representatives at the Congress do use their power, and much more criticism could be heard at the most recent congresses of this type, with a decline in the proportion of votes in favour of the leadership proposals. This might well signal the beginning of a reduction in this role of the Congress, although this would prove very difficult to sell to the grassroots.

Between party Bureau and party Congress, the Belgian parties also have a body called the Council, which can be considered as an intermediate Congress. It is smaller than Congress and meets more often (several times a year), and is composed of representatives of the constituency or local branches, but in smaller numbers than is the case for Congress. The major difference with the Congress is that the party Bureau is also present in the Council, as are also the fraktions, the party in government and a number of party professionals. The Council formally controls the Bureau in the periods between Congress meetings, and is used to receive approval of the militants on some major decisions. More so than Congress, the Council is controlled by the Bureau, and there is less time to prepare the meetings, and fewer opportunities for the lower levels to introduce items. This does not mean, of course, that the Council members simply accept everything that is proposed or carried out by the Bureau. Council meetings are often held behind closed doors (especially to avoid the presence of the media), and can be an opportunity for lively debates. For the leadership, they also provide a means of seeing and feeling what is really happening among the party activists. As is the case for Congresses, more recent Council meetings increasingly tend to show signs of greater discontent emanating from the lower ranks. This is again an illustration of the dilemma facing the parties of how to be more democratic while at the same time remaining effective in a coalition.

Membership and branches

The basic units of the Belgian parties are local sections organized at the lowest electoral level, which is the municipality. Until 1976, there were more than 2500 local municipalities, and no party is able to give a precise count of its number of local sections before that date. That is very understandable, since the local elections were in fact extremely local, and since the national parties presented lists which often used different names in different places. There are not even reliable composite results for local elections before 1976; rather, there are simply more than 2500 separate results.

This changed after 1976, when a fusion reduced the number of municipalities to 588. Furthermore, each party now receives a national number, which is to be used in every municipality where it is present under its national name. That number is the order in which the parties appear on the ballot paper, and now not only the number, but also the name of the party appears on the ballot paper. These changes in the electoral law, together with the fusion, have led to a higher degree of 'nationalization' of local politics (Dewachter, 1982; Deschouwer, 1991), and have also obliged the parties to keep an eye on their local sections, since these have to define themselves clearly as belonging to the party if they are to use the party's name and number. Again, then, there is evidence of increasing centralization. Yet the story is still not complete, since some local sections still use a special name, adapted to some local events in the local elections, but are claimed by the national party as being one of their lists. The indicator for the number of local sections is therefore the number of municipalities where the party is present at the local elections.

In Flanders the CVP and the SP cover more or less the whole region, with a section in almost every municipality (the section can also present candidates on a so-called 'cartel list' with other parties, which happens frequently). Moreover, both not only have party sections everywhere, but they also have a whole range of other organizations around the party. The

Table 4.1 *Party membership levels as a percentage of the total electorate*

	CP	CVP	PSC	BSP	PSB	PVV	PLP	VU	ECO	AGA	Total
1961	0.2	3.6		3.4		0.8		0.0			8.0
1965	0.2	2.3		3.5		1.5		0.2			7.7
1968	0.2	2.0	0.5	3.5		1.7		0.4			8.3
1971	0.2	1.7	0.8	4.0		1.1		0.7			8.4
1974	0.2	1.9	0.8	4.2		0.6	0.7	0.8			9.4
1977	0.2	2.0	1.0	4.0		0.9	0.6	0.8			9.6
1978	0.2	1.9	0.9	1.7	2.3	0.9	0.7	0.8			9.7
1981	0.2	1.8	0.8	1.7	2.4	0.9	0.7	0.7			9.4
1985	0.1	1.7	0.6	1.5	2.0	1.0	1.0	0.7	0.0	0.0	8.9
1987	0.1	2.0	0.6	1.5	2.1	1.1	1.1	0.7	0.0	0.0	9.3
1991[a]	–	1.8	0.6	1.4	2.2	1.0	0.7	0.6	0.0	0.0	8.6

[a] The figures for 1991 are the latest membership figures (1989 or 1990) as a proportion of the electorate in 1991.

Liberal Party, on the other hand, is not so 'societal' as the other two and, being originally a cadre party, is also less pillarized. The Volksunie covers more or less half of the region. While they claim to have more local sections, these nevertheless often use other names, and accept 'independent' candidates on their lists. Finally, there are also many local lists that cannot be labelled, and which can be either completely local, or combinations (cartels) of other lists. Local lists (or local combinations) are more important in Wallonia, which has more small and rural municipalities, where local elections are indeed less nationalized. Again, it is the Socialists and the Christian Democrats that have the largest number of lists, while the Liberals do not even reach 50 per cent of the Walloon municipalities. ECOLO, like its counterpart in Flanders, is growing, but not very spectacularly.

Membership figures

Belgium tends to be an exception to an otherwise quite general decline in party membership, with membership levels remaining both quite high and quite stable. Membership as a proportion of the electorate has fluctuated only slightly between 7.7 per cent in 1965 and 9.7 per cent in 1987, which makes it difficult to say whether there has been growth or decline, and why. Moreover, a number of the smaller parties offer only very few and very vague indications of their membership levels, and this may account for errors which can account for differences from year to year. The safest conclusion, then, is that membership numbers have not moved significantly in any direction (see Table 4.1).

One reason for the lack of a decline in party membership in the Belgian case might well be the lowering of the minimum age for membership. Before 1970, all the parties had reduced this minimum to at least 18 years (16 for Socialists and VU and 17 for Christian Democrats), even though the minimum voting age was then 21. The voting age was itself reduced to

18 in 1981, but, even now, some of the parties continue to have members who are too young to vote. A second possible reason is connected to the incentives that parties can offer to their members. It is certainly well known (De Winter and Janssens, 1988) that parties in Belgium offer many services to their members or to their potential members. At the very least, this clientelistic process provides votes for the parties; but it also means that the easiest way to give some 'payment' in return for the services provided is to buy, or renew, a membership card. In this regard, it is perhaps indicative that the membership levels of the two major political families, the Christian Democrats and the Socialists, have declined much more slowly than has their electoral support. Both party families are very frequently in power, and both the CVP and the PS are also quite strong at the local level, and thus have a large reservoir of selective incentives to offer. Conversely, the membership levels of their linguistic counterparts, the SP and the PSC, tend to drop much more quickly. Finally, the Liberal parties have tended to win both voters and members, but proportionally more of the former than of the latter. These parties are also not in power so often.

Party finance and professionalization

Belgian parties are under no obligation to publicize anything about their financial situation; it is an absence of obligation which they all take very seriously. Party income derives from a variety of sources. The parties collect membership dues, and receive gifts from individuals and from private organizations. Some receive gifts or logistical and material help from organizations belonging to their pillarized network, and the members of the parliament also have to give part of their salaries to their party. Expenditures involve the payment of all kinds of personnel, administrative and leadership travel expenses, support (albeit now no longer) for party newspapers and election campaigning. But questions about precisely who gets what from whom, and who gives what to whom, remain unanswered.

The recent 1989 law on public financing, however, does include the obligation to account for what has been done with the money received from the state. Yet this money is paid to a specially created institution, rather than to the party itself, and it is this institution that must publicize its accounts. Indeed, the parties (except for the Greens and Volksunie) do not legally exist. That said, some of the parties have decided to reveal more than is strictly required, and this means that from 1990 onwards, some sense of party finances might be obtained. But since there is no clear-cut framework within which the accounts have to be published, nor a clear obligation to do so, the picture remains obscure. The only exception is in the case of the Greens, which publish their complete accounts, and which therefore might allow researchers some basis on which to estimate the situation of the other parties. At the same time, however, the Greens are very atypical, having almost no members, and having a structure and an organizational philosophy that is completely different from that of the other parties.

Since nothing, or almost nothing, is known about income and expenditure of the Belgian parties, the same goes for the numbers of paid staff. We know one thing for sure, however: since 1971 a fairly large amount of state money is paid annually to the parties' parliamentary fraktions, and these fraktions can use this money without any control by the parliament. The fraktions also get help in the way of personnel who are paid directly by the parliament, and who work for the party. This means that there must have been a sharp increase in the number of people working for the party since 1971. The new state subsidy, which has been paid since 1989, constitutes another source from which personnel can be paid. Thus even if we assume that other sources of income have declined (which is at least not the case for membership dues), we nevertheless know for sure that the parties have a much greater capacity than before to employ paid personnel. Certainly, and even without exact numbers, it is easy to see that the parties' study centres are well-staffed. It is also well-known that some members of the 'cabinets' of national and regional ministers really work for the party of the minister rather than for the government. This works in two ways. A person can be a member of that cabinet and, for example, look after the clientelistic work of the minister. This can undoubtedly be considered as work for the party. Or somebody can be on the payroll of a cabinet while, for example, being in practice a member of the party's study centre.

Conclusion: the reluctant modernization of the mass parties

This story began in 1960 with three traditional parties controlling the quite stable Belgian democracy. Two of these traditional parties could be labelled mass parties, in that they were externally created, were fairly centralized, and had close links with a whole pillar of other organizations. The Liberal Party was smaller, originally a cadre party, but also (albeit less tightly) locked within a liberal pillar. The two larger parties felt little real need to change. The Liberal Party, on the other hand, which wanted to play a more important role, sought to improve its electoral position by attracting Catholic liberals in particular. The Liberal Party changed in 1961, and doubled its vote. The Socialists and the Christian Democrats faced a defeat, although they remained the larger parties and continued to govern together.

Since 1965 we see the two larger parties gradually decline, while the Liberals manage to grow slowly (with many ups and downs), and while several new parties emerge. Regionalist parties are the first new successes, followed by the Greens, and then by the right-wing extremist parties. All add to the pressure on the traditional parties, whose first reaction is clear and obvious: they follow the regionalists by dividing themselves into separate unilingual parties. The second kind of reaction is not so clear at first sight. While the parties effect lots of minor changes at all levels, it is nevertheless not easy to see the direction in which these go. Indeed, they sometimes appear very contradictory: one time decentralizing, another time centralizing. In fact, the adaptation of the traditional parties to the challenge of the new parties goes in both directions because it must go in both directions. There is the pressure to be more centralized and disciplined in order to be able to remain in power, for this has to be done by concluding delicate and difficult compromises with at least four partners. These kinds of change can be seen at the top of the party, with the president becoming even more powerful, with the fraktions being kept under control and with the selection of candidates becoming centralized. At the same time, there is the pressure to be more open and democratic, and this leads to changes at the level of the Congress, with local branches getting more involved, and with the opening of more opportunities for agenda-setting. This second kind of adaptation is less important, and very much symbolic, since the power of the Congress is small. The party Council is more powerful, and this is then much more controlled from the top.

Looking at the changes in the parties, one does not see any really spectacular or deep changes. One might even say that the parties fail to adapt. They fail because the system – especially the obligation to go through delicate processes of coalition formation – confronts them with a dilemma that cannot be solved. And they also fail to change because they are not built to change. Rather, they are real mass parties, with structures that were built in order to defend the interests of well-delimited and internally well-organized segments of the population, and that implies a heavy and inflexible structure, the organization of which might well outlast the subculture or the social community that it used to mobilize.

One might even argue that the fact that the traditional Belgian parties are real mass parties enforces their vulnerability. They are easily challenged by new parties, and because they fail to react properly, they provide extra arguments for those parties and movements which are precisely trying to prove that the old parties are unable to deal with the new problems of modern society. Protest against the system has been present since the 1960s, but has recently become much more radical (being picked up by the extreme right). And then again the traditional parties are those that are obliged to govern – even if they would prefer not to do so – and that will probably lose again next time, because governing in a four-party coalition seldom pays.

The old parties are thus still very much mass parties. They still have their privileged links with the other pillarized organizations, and these remain the privileged partners of the government in corporatist decision-making. The parties still have a reasonable number of members, and do not lose them in any spectacular way. Yet, at the same time, the parties are also modernizing. They now make greater use of external professional advice for their campaigns; they rely less heavily on their own media (if they still have them), but use the electronic media instead; and they receive large amounts of money from the state, which they use to pay for advice and to employ their own professionals. They have become modern and wealthy mass parties, albeit still mass parties.

Two kinds of parties escape this logic. The first, of course, are the new parties, which were different from the beginning, both ideologically and organizationally. Yet it is important to emphasize that their success is very relative. At their lowest point in 1991, the three traditional families (six parties) still together polled 70 per cent of the votes. The Volksunie reached 11 per cent (18 per cent in Flanders) in 1971, but is now down to 6 per cent, and will probably decline even further. The Brussels FDF and the Walloon RW together polled 11.3 per cent in 1971 (31 per cent of the French-speaking votes), but today the RW has disappeared, and the FDF is down to 1.5 per cent. The growth of AGALEV is also slowing down, and the party lost votes in 1991 to the extreme right and to the new 'libertarian' formation, Rossem. Today it is the extreme right that seems to be able to gather the votes of the discontented in Flanders, while ECOLO does so in Wallonia. The new parties are certainly different, but it is difficult to say that they are really more successful or less vulnerable than their traditional opponents. Moreover, new parties begin to lose as soon as they are perceived as being part of the 'traditional game', which certainly happens when they accept an offer to join the government.

The story is also slightly different for the Liberal parties. From the beginning, they were closer to a cadre party than to a mass party, and were smaller and less tightly integrated into a pillar. They were also more flexible, and could change in a more spectacular way. The change of 1961 in particular was ideologically important. In 1992 the PVV was radically changed into the VLD, and has produced completely new rules. It wants to be a modern and open party, and by doing so, it has furthered the old critique of the two other traditional parties. It remains to be seen how this new party will function. The change is mainly the result of the ideas of the party president, and the way in which he was able to realize his ideas provides a rather neat illustration of how strong a party president can be. He was also elected – by the members – as the first president of the new party, and is now even stronger than before.

The interesting thing about this Liberal reform is that the party wants Belgian democracy to behave in a more classical way, meaning a more Anglo-Saxon way. In saying this, of course, they aim at the heart of the old consociational logic. They want the pillars and their representatives in politics and in neo-corporatism to be destroyed, and they favour the introduction of referenda and primary elections. Yet even if they win voters with this programme, they will still have to govern with at least three other parties, and it is then they might rediscover the pressure to be effective in the first place. These are hard times for parties in a particracy.

Notes

1 This is a very unimportant function, and the decision has to be taken only after every national election. In the reformed Federal Senate there will be only six Dutch-speaking coopted senators, and this means that the SP will be able to select one of them. This effectively destroys the role of the old Council.

2 A general 'School Pact' was agreed on in 1958, ending the last school war in which Catholics and non-Catholics had confronted each other.

3 The VU elects its president in the Council. The Communists had no rules on the presidency before 1963; since then, the rules state that the Central Committee elects the president.

References

Almond, G. (1956) 'Comparative political systems', *Journal of Politics*, 18: 391–409.

Clark, P. and Wilson, J.Q. (1961) 'Incentive systems: a theory of organizations', *Administrative Science Quarterly*, 6: 129–66.

Deschouwer, K. (1987) *Politieke Partijen in België*. Antwerp: Kluwer.

Deschouwer, K. (1989) 'Belgium: the "Ecologists" and "Agalev" ', in F. Müller-Rommel (ed.), *New Politics in Western Europe*. Boulder: Westview, pp. 39–54.

Deschouwer, K. (1990) 'Patterns of participation and competition in Belgium', in P. Mair and G. Smith (eds), *Understanding Party System Change in Western Europe*. London: Cass, pp. 28–41.

Deschouwer, K. (1991) 'Small parties in a small country: the Belgian case', in F. Müller-Rommel and G. Pridham (eds), *Small Parties in Western Europe*. London: Sage, pp. 135–51.

Deschouwer, K. (1992) 'Belgium', in R.S. Katz and P. Mair (eds), *Party Organizations: A Data Handbook on Party Organizations in Western Democracies*, 1960–90. London: Sage, pp. 121–98.

Deschouwer, K. and Koole, R. (1992) 'De Ontwikkeling van Partij-Organisaties in België en Nederland, 1960–1990', *Sociologische Gids*, 39: 324–45.

Dewachter, W. (1982) 'Het Effect van de Samenvoeging van Gemeenten op Gemeenteraadsverkiezingen', *Res Publica*, 24: 445–60.

De Winter, L. (1980) 'Twintig jaar polls, of de teloorgang van een vorm van interne partijdemocratie', *Res Publica*, 22: 563–85.

De Winter, L. (1988) 'Belgium: Democracy or Oligarchy?' in M. Gallagher and M. Marsh (eds), *Candidate Selection in Comparative Perspective*. London: Sage, pp. 20–46.

De Winter, L. and Janssens, P. (1988) 'De stemmotivaties van de Belgische kiezer', *Dimarso-Gallup*.

Gerard, E. and Van Den Wijngaert, M. (1985) *In het teken van de regenboog. Geschiedenis van de Katholieke Partij en van de Christelijke Volkspartij*. Antwerp/Brussels: DNB/IPOVO.

Huyse, L. (1969) *De Niet-Aanwezige Staatsburger*. Antwerp: Standaard Wetenschaappelijke Uitgeverij.

Huyse, L. (1971) *Passiviteit, Pacificatie en Verzuiling in de Belgische Politiek*. Antwerp: Standaard Wetenschaappelijke Uitgeverij.

Huyse, L. (1987) *De verzuiling voorbij*. Leuven: Kritak.

Janssens, P., Fiers, S. and Vos, M. (1993) 'Morfologie van de Vlaamse Politieke Partijen in 1991 en 1992', *Res Publica*, 35: 503–59.

Lijphart, A. (1977) *Democracy in Plural Societies*. New Haven: Yale University Press.

Luther, K.R. (1992) 'Consociationalism parties and the party system in Austria', *West European Politics*, 15 (1): 45–98.

Maes M. (1990) 'De formele aanstelling van de partijvoorzitters in België, 1944–1990', *Res Publica*, 27: 3–62.

Panebianco, A. (1988) *Political Parties: Organization and Power*, Cambridge: Cambridge University Press.

Steininger, R. (1977) 'Pillarization and political parties', *Sociologische Gids*, 24: 242–57.

5

Party Organizational Change in Britain: The Iron Law of Centralization?

Paul D. Webb

The essence of the argument which will be examined in this chapter can be anticipated briefly: the major parties in Britain find themselves under increasing pressure in the 1990s, assailed by such phenomena as partisan dealignment, the progress (albeit often faltering) of minor parties and the diffuse sense of weakening legitimacy in the wake of the failure of governmental policies to counteract the widespread perception of Britain's continuing national decline. The response of Labour and the Conservatives to this pressure has occurred partly at the level of party organization. These are parties which always tended to be dominated by their parliamentary leaderships, as the classic study of McKenzie (1956) emphasized, and in many ways party leaderships were relatively uninterested in the participatory ambitions of their rank and file memberships. Even now, almost four decades after McKenzie, it can be argued that this has not really changed, despite some appearances to the contrary (for example, a long-standing campaign for the democratization of the Labour Party which has borne fruit in a number of constitutional changes since 1980). The tensions between leaders and members continue, and the response of the former to the growing pressures which they face in the competition for power and legitimacy has been largely seen in a further centralization of their parties and in the enhancement of their own autonomy and their capacity for strategic flexibility.

The organizational structures of British parties: an overview

Formally speaking, there are some notable differences in the organizational structures of the parties. Labour's constitution clearly asserts the sovereignty of conference and is self-consciously democratic. The notion of an active mass membership was for many decades an official party myth that Labour sought to sustain. In reality, however, the individual party members have always had to face the fact of a numerically far greater (and therefore, politically more influential) corporate membership (see p. 112). This membership is chiefly associated with the affiliated trade unions, although various socialist societies also affiliate members on the same basis, with each corporate body tending to affiliate for the number of members that happens to suit it rather than for the number it actually has, and paying an appropriate affiliation fee to the party. Conference votes are accorded to each affiliating organization (that is, union, constituency party or socialist society) on the basis of the number of members paid for, and since the unions have far more members than the local constituency parties, this has secured their potential domination.

Unlike some other European left-wing parties (see, for example, Wellhofer, 1979), the British Labour Party never really attempted to mobilize the indigenous working class by encapsulating it within an extensive network of interlinking social, economic and political organizations, and this has clearly affected the role of the membership both inside and outside the party. This is a point not necessarily lost upon the radical left in Britain, who have long lamented the failure of Labour to become a 'hegemonic' party and to provide an all-embracing ideological and cultural home for the domestic working class (Anderson, 1965; Miliband, 1972). Rather, the British Labour Party has been content to allow the affiliated trade unions effectively to become its organization. This has also meant that, unlike other parties of mass integration, it has not really needed to become an authentic mass membership party. In reality, coalitions of parliamentary and union elites have dominated the party, and even when delegates of the individual membership have succeeded in getting conference to adopt policies disapproved of by the leadership, the latter has been inclined to overlook such policies when drafting election manifestos (Hatfield, 1978; Kogan and Kogan, 1982).

The Conservative Party, by contrast, has never even made any pretence of running a democratic organization. The party developed out of a cadre-type organization based initially around parliamentary elites and, rather like the British state itself, is instinctively hierarchical and secretive. Formally, all authority and policy emanates from the leader, and the organization exists primarily to recruit and to aid the leadership. The membership is formally separated from both the parliamentary party and the extra-parliamentary party's organizational headquarters. Conservative Central Office is entirely the creature of the leader, whereas the National Union of Conservative and Unionist Associations federates the local constituency associations to which individual members belong. The National Union has its own standing rules and annual conference which the party leader is invited to address, with local area organizations (Constituency Central Associations) being represented at conference according to the number of constituencies they cover. The basic goals of the National Union include the selection and support of Conservative candidates for public office, but although it endeavours to 'work closely in coordination with Conservative Central Office' (National Union, 1988: 1), it is not subject to the authority of the latter, nor can it subject the latter to its own authority.

Since McKenzie's classic work, however, it has become commonplace to assert that formal differences such as these actually conceal a strong degree of convergence in the organizational workings of the two major parties. McKenzie's view, reiterated frequently ever since, was that power tended to reside with the elites in both organizations, notwithstanding the formally democratic form of Labour's written constitution (McKenzie, 1956).

There are three pertinent features to note with regard to the organizational structures of the Liberal/Liberal Democrat parties. First, they have (had) federal structures, in which the national parties in Scotland and Wales (and in England since the merger with the Social Democratic Party [SDP] in 1988) have been essentially autonomous. In the second place, the Liberal Democrat leader is elected directly by rank and file individual members. This idea was adopted from the SDP at the time of the merger; previously, Liberal leaders were elected by the parliamentary party. The third feature which distinguishes it from the major parties also originated with the SDP, and involves the Federal Policy Committee, which plays an important role in the development of party policy. Overall, the Liberal Democratic organization can be regarded as officially more democratic than the old Liberal Party since the members now have a potentially more influential role to play. Not only can they elect their leader, but they can now send representatives to a conference which is sovereign in defining party policy. The old Liberal Assembly had no such formal power. Formally speaking then, the Liberal Democrats are a more membership-oriented phenomenon than the Liberals were. This is perhaps an inevitable development for a party which has few members of parliament and relatively little corporate or state financial backing; its members are its lifeblood and need to be offered incentives to maintain their enthusiasm.

Despite this shift in the organizational style of the Liberals, however, and despite some recent movement towards greater membership orientation in the Labour party, British parties still tend to be dominated by national – or more specifically, parliamentary – elites. In general, moreover, the national party headquarters are also essentially subordinate to the parliamentary parties. Though the role of the headquarters' research and policy departments should not be overlooked, the overall objective is to serve the parliamentary elites in their search for electoral success. The coordination of local campaign efforts is therefore a central task of the national headquarters. What is more, British parties are in no meaningful sense mass membership parties, as we shall see in more detail in the next section. In Labour's case, as noted above, this may partially reflect the decision to eschew a strategy of encapsulation.

More broadly, this tendency may also reflect the determination of the British state to regulate election campaign spending in the locality from the onset of the democratic era, a practice which goes back to the Corrupt and Illegal Practices Act 1883, which first defined the limits of a candidate's spending in any given constituency (Pinto-Duschinsky, 1980: 26). What is striking here, however, is that expenditure by central party organizations is not similarly constrained, and this has meant that resources are inevitably

Table 5.1   *Estimated general election campaign expenditure, 1964–92*
(£'000)

	Conservative		Labour		Liberal[a]	
	National party	Candidates	National party	Candidates	National party	Candidates
1964	1233	497.7	538	471.6	–	211.3
1966	350	481.8	196	451.6	–	155.8
1970	630	596	526	517.5	–	221.4
1974 Feb.	680	794.3	440	702.1	–	423.2
1974 Oct.	950	745.7	524	724.5	127.8	411.8
1979	2333	1362.2	1566	1181.8	–	584.5
1983	3800	2101.6	2258	1852.8	1000	1598.3
1987	9000	2785.2	4200	2468.7	1100	2152.2
1992	14290	3766.8	7650	3227.1	1312.8	2002.8

[a] Official details of central Liberal election spending are largely unavailable. The 1983 and 1987 figures for the Liberals are in fact figures for the Liberal–SDP Alliance as a whole.

Sources: Labour Party *Annual Reports*; *Election Expenses* (HMSO, 1988, 1993); Pinto-Duschinsky, 1980; Pinto-Duschinsky, 1989a; Butler, 1989; Conservative Party *Annual Reports* and *Accounts*; Liberal Democrats' *Reports to Conference*

concentrated at the centre rather than in the locality (see Table 5.1). Again, there is relatively little incentive for local memberships to become mobilized and active. It is perhaps not too great an exaggeration to say that, at least for Labour and the Conservatives, individual members are simply not crucial to the parties, in either an electoral or in a financial sense. This impression is also reinforced by the fact that the only state financial subventions so far made available to British political parties (introduced in 1975), are directed exclusively towards (opposition) *parliamentary* parties. Furthermore, British political parties tend to make few demands of their members; typically, prospective members are obliged to declare a broad allegiance to the stated principles of the party and to make some kind of modest financial contribution. The Conservatives and the old Liberals never even set any minimum on this contribution. In short, little seems to be expected in terms of active commitment by the party membership.

The limits of the membership organizations

Changes in British political party membership since 1960 are summarized in Table 5.2. Members can, of course, be broken up into different (and sometimes overlapping) categories. Only the Labour Party maintains a 'corporate' membership – that is, those who are only indirectly members by virtue of their membership of affiliated unions or socialist societies, and who have paid a voluntary 'political levy' to that corporate organization.[1] All parties have ancillary categories of membership for women, trade

Table 5.2 *Party membership, selected years*

Year	Labour			Conservative	Liberal	SDP
				Individual	Individual	Individual
	Individual	Corporate	Total	(= total)	(= total)	(= total)
1960	790,192	5,538,138	6,328,330	2,800,000[a]	243,600[b]	–
1974	691,889	5,826,568	6,518,457	1,500,000	190,000	–
1983	295,344	6,160,393	6,455,737	1,200,000[c]	N/A	45,258
1987	288,829	5,619,320	5,908,149	1,000,000[d]	79,500	58,000
1992	279,530	4,644,000	4,923,530	500,000	100,000	–

[a] This figure is for 1953, the nearest available indicator of membership in 1960.
[b] 1961 figure.
[c] 1982 figure.
[d] 1988 figure.

Sources: Webb, 1992c, Table XII.B.1, which shows the complete figures available, and which is drawn from: *Labour NEC Annual Reports* and information office; National Union of Conservative and Unionist Associations; Liberal Democrats' information office; SDP Chief Whip's office; SDP Archive, University of Essex; HMSO, 1976; Butler and Butler, 1987; Finer, 1980; Rasmussen, 1965; *The Times* 14 Sept. 1987 and 11 Sept. 1989

unionists and youth/students, and local councillors. The Liberal Democrats alone also include a separate category for parliamentary candidates and constituency agents, and the Conservatives for teachers. In all cases it is a prerequisite that one is already a party member. Little information is available on the actual membership levels of these ancillary bodies, however, although the Conservative Trade Unionists did claim a three-fold increase in membership during the mid-1970s (from some 20,000 to some 60,000). Conversely, in the case of Labour, recorded figures regarding the numbers of branches tend to indicate a decline in both the Young Socialist (LPYS) and Women's sections. Thus, in 1960 there were 578 LPYS branches and 1564 Women's sections; by 1988 there were just 170 LPYS branches and in 1979 (the last year for which a figure is reported) the number of Women's sections had fallen to 970. In the middle of the 1980s it was estimated that there were around 5000 Young Socialists.

Given the party's distinction between individual and corporate membership, it has now become almost a cliché to speak of the 'myth' of Labour's mass membership base. To be an individual member of the party it is necessary, first, to be a member of whatever affiliated organization one is eligible for and, second, actually to obtain membership directly from a Constituency Labour Party.[2] On the other hand, organizations affiliated to the Labour Party are also entitled to take a political levy off those of their members who are happy to pay it, regardless of whether they are also individual party members. This money can be passed on to the Labour Party in affiliation fees, and those paying the levy are then designated the 'affiliated membership'. While trade unions are not obliged to affiliate all of those who pay the levy it is nonetheless clear that the bulk of Labour's claimed national membership over the years has been comprised of this affiliated element rather than of the individual element. It is also quite clear that many of those who do pay the political levy do so out of apathy rather than out of conviction; that is, they pay the levy automatically unless they can be bothered specifically to 'contract out'.[3] In the case of Labour, therefore, the true indicator of committed membership must be taken to be the individual membership rather than the affiliated membership.

The significance of corporate membership for Labour is clearly illustrated in Table 5.2. Not only is trade union affiliated membership by far and away the greatest component of total party membership, but it is also evident that there has been little or no change over time, with the unions' affiliated members generally accounting for around 90 per cent of total party membership since 1960 (and, indeed, since the birth of the party itself at the turn of the century). In fact, the official figures even indicate that individual membership is now a smaller part of the total than before: in 1960, it formed 12.5 per cent of the total, falling to 10.9 per cent in 1970 and to just 5.7 per cent in 1992. This partly reflects an important change in party rules, however. Prior to 1980, no local constituency party had been able to affiliate to the national party for anything less than 1000 members, although it was widely recognized that many had far fewer members in reality. This requirement was then relaxed (largely in order to relieve the financial strain upon local parties of paying for members they might not actually have), which explains the virtual halving of the party's claimed individual membership between 1979 and 1980. Nevertheless, it is clear that the Labour Party remains as dependent as ever on the unions for its nominal membership and also, as we shall see, for its financing. This almost certainly explains Alan Ware's (1987: 146) justifiable assertion that of all the mass membership parties, the British Labour Party is perhaps the one where (individual) membership recruitment has been taken least seriously.

Overall, Labour has obviously suffered from membership loss (as, indeed, have all British parties). Thanks to the 1980 change, individual membership has fallen by two-thirds with respect to the 1960 levels, and corporate and total membership by 16 per cent and 22 per cent respectively. Since its peak in 1979, the decline has been even more dramatic: corporate membership fell 29.3 per cent between the election years of 1979 and 1992, and total membership by 32.0 per cent. However, this largely reflects a huge drop in trade union membership over the period, which in turn reflects the impact on employment (especially in the manufacturing sector) of the economic slump of the 1980s. At the peak of union density within the workforce in 1979, there were 112 trade unions affiliated to the TUC (the major national union federation) and 59 affiliated to the Labour Party. These unions represented memberships of more than 12 million and 6.5 million respectively. By 1992 there were just 69 unions in the TUC and 29 affiliated to the party, representing 7.3 million and 4.6 million members respectively.

There are signs that the Labour Party is increasingly uncomfortable with its continuing dependence on the affiliated union membership. From the party's process of strategic and marketing renewal which commenced in the mid-1980s there emerged a conviction that the connection with the trade unions had to be reformed. This conviction only seemed to be strengthened by the stunning electoral defeat of April 1992, though it must be said that it is a view that has been contended bitterly in certain sections of the labour movement. As a first step towards diminishing the public perception that Labour was dependent upon (and therefore beholden to) the unions, it was suggested that the traditional reliance on the corporate mass membership, which effectively served to place power in the hands of an elite of parliamentary leaders and union barons, needed to be reduced. Thus, in 1990 the party voted to reduce the maximum proportion of votes that the unions could control at the annual conference (Webb, 1992a: 33–5). Moreover, in 1993 further reforms were endorsed that will enhance the voting power of both individual and affiliated members, but reduce that of union elites in three areas: conference, leadership elections and parliamentary candidate selection (Labour Party, 1993a, 1993b; Webb, 1993).

That said, however, such moves create a further problem for Labour's strategic renovators. Taking a long-term historical view, most observers agree that the parliamentary leadership has usually been able to rely upon the major union elites for support within the party. The downgrading of the unions' role, therefore, threatens to leave the constituency party activists – traditionally the home of the committed left – in a relatively stronger position at the party conference. This would undoubtedly be regarded as disadvantageous by the new wave of party reformers, and provides one explanation of the individual membership recruitment drive that Labour embarked upon in the late 1980s. As I have noted elsewhere, the mass membership drive is something of a paradox, in that the hoped-for influx of 'ordinary' new members can be seen as an attempt to weaken, rather than to reassert, the influence of the committed active party member (Webb, 1992b: 283).

In addition to this precisely defined tactical objective, Labour has also been prompted to push for a greater individual membership as a result of the incontrovertible evidence of organizational weakness at the grassroots. In Britain as a whole, a declining proportion of voters are actually individual members of the parties they support at the polls, although the Conservatives and (more especially) the Liberals/Liberal Democrats might claim that this is to some extent a natural corollary of their own increasing electoral support since 1964. This is clearly not the explanation in Labour's case, however, in that the 'people's party' has lost both voters and members. Hence that party's stated goal to generate a genuine mass membership of a million or more individuals.

In order to boost the membership drive, Labour reformed the process of joining the Party, with trade unionists becoming entitled to a temporary discount on subscription rates. Hitherto, prospective members could join only in the locality, but there is now the option of contacting the central party headquarters directly and joining via a computerized national register of members. (Central applications nevertheless continue to be referred to an appropriate CLP). Annual subscription rates for individual members increased from 30 pence a year in 1960 to £10 a year in 1989, and to £15 by 1993, but a special introductory £5 rate for the first three years was introduced in the case of new members recruited via the unions in the late 1980s. Moreover, proposals endorsed by the party conference in 1993 will effectively create a new category of 'registered' members from the unions who will have full individual membership rights but who will pay a reduced subscription.

In the end, however, it is hard to be convinced that there is now a strong prospect of converting the Labour Party into that which it has never really been – a classic individual mass membership party. There is no doubt that the party would like to reduce its financial, organizational and perhaps even political dependence on the unions, but this seems a forlorn hope given the twin circumstances of a general decline in British party member- ship, on the one hand and, on the other, the enduring refusal of those controlling the state (currently the Conservative Party) to increase substan- tially the public subvention available to political parties. Moreover, present indications of the progress of the membership drive are not encouraging for Labour. Despite a modest increase in individual member- ship to 311,000 in 1990, the computerized national membership scheme actually exacerbated the problems of collecting subscriptions. Nearly one- third of the estimated membership were not asked for their dues during the first complete year of the scheme (Wintour, 1991: 24), and by 1991 the individual membership total had slipped to around 260,000. At best, as Seyd and Whiteley (1992: 201) suggest, the party seems only to have stemmed the 1980s haemorrhage in individual membership. Perhaps it cannot even do that. Equally notable is what Seyd and Whiteley refer to as the phenomenon of a 'de-energized' party, with a number of indicators of a decline in activism even amongst those who do join Labour, including the increased number of inquorate branch meetings and the falling number of constituency resolutions tabled at annual conference (Seyd and Whiteley, 1992: 202). There is a distinct feeling of too little, too late, with the attempt to create a mass party based on an active membership in the context of modern British politics being surely an anachronistic flight of fancy.

Neither the Conservatives nor the Liberals have regularly reported their membership levels; indeed, they have not necessarily even known what their overall national membership levels are at any given time. The federalism of the Liberals/Liberal Democrats and the largely decentralized structure of the National Union have hampered the flow of this sort of information to the centre. In the case of the Conservatives, for example, neither the National Union nor Central Office even know precisely how many branches there are in each constituency association, let alone the precise number of members. This in itself seems to indicate the relative unimportance of an active membership for these parties (although the new Liberal Democrats, heavily influenced by the organizational and political efforts of the SDP to 'break the mould' of British politics, may see things rather differently from the old Liberal Party, which was essentially a modified cadre party). While some Conservative branch and constituency secretaries maintain formal membership lists, not all do so, and while national membership figures do emerge from time to time, they are usually little more than informed estimates. In 1953, the party claimed some 2.8 million members nationally; in 1974, the Houghton Commission on party finance estimated that this had fallen to 1.5 million. In the 1980s, the National Union conducted occasional surveys of constituency associations, the most recent of which puts the national figure at approximately 750,000. By 1993, media sources suggested that this had fallen further to some 500,000 (Wintour, 1993). Although the Conservative Party remains the closest thing to a genuine individual mass membership party in Britain, it is evident that it has suffered as much from membership decline as has Labour (indeed, perhaps even more in real terms, given the habitual overestimation of the latter's individual membership until 1980). Indeed, even if we disregard Labour's unreliable figures, it emerges from both Conservative and Liberal figures that party membership has broadly halved since 1974. For the SDP, the consequences of the traumatic merger of the Alliance parties are plain enough; the party lost 81 per cent of its members between 1987 and 1989.

The financial importance of membership

Consideration of the relevant data also reveals the relative unimportance of the members for the major British parties in terms of their financial role (Webb, 1992c: 867–8). The Conservative Party has not always been as forthcoming about its financial sources as the other parties; accounts were not published at all until the late 1960s, nor were they for a brief period during the early 1980s when (like Labour) the party was passing through a time of some financial embarrassment. Official party statements now merely distinguish between constituency income and donations, which leaves much unclear. Nevertheless, it is evident enough from the available information that the constituencies do not really figure prominently as a source of income. The most spectacular instance is provided by the election year of 1987, when it was estimated that the party brought in a total of nearly £15 million of which little more than £1 million came from the constituencies. Where did the rest come from? £4 million can be identified as deriving from the public limited companies that are quoted on the London stock exchange, and it is estimated that nearly as much again came from private companies.[4] This leaves more than £6 million unaccounted for, which must be assumed to have derived largely from contributions by private individuals and from interest on investments (BBC, 1990).

It is interesting to note that as the Conservatives' finances recover, so the degree to which they depend upon income from the local branches declines. In real terms the party's greatest expenditures since 1960 were on the elections of 1964 and 1987 (Pinto-Duschinsky, 1989b: 42), and these both coincide with periods in which financial dependence on the constituencies has been lowest,[5] which suggests that the Conservative Party is organizationally strongest when it is successful in soliciting heavy external funding. (By implication also, the party's most substantial election campaigns are those in which the centre is relatively independent of the constituencies.) Following its somewhat unexpected victory in the 1992 election, the Conservative government experienced a politically traumatic year which, together with suggestions of uncomfortably close associations with corrupt financial backers, undermined the potential for corporate donations. The result was a serious financial crisis for the party, with a reported overdraft of some £19 million (Conservative Party, 1993; Wintour, 1993), which may well force the Conservatives back to a greater reliance on individual members. For Labour it has been somewhat different, in that throughout the 1980s there has been a steady increase in the proportion of its income coming from the constituency parties, with the elimination of its financial deficits. And since this has occurred in a period of declining individual membership, it suggests that the key variable has been the level of the individual subscription. In the Conservative case the contribution depends entirely upon the individual, but in the case of the Labour Party there is central control of the membership fee, with an increase from £1.20 to £10.00 in the decade following the 1979 election.

Given their lack of major corporate backers, we might expect to find that the individual members are financially more important in the case of the minor parties. This was very evidently the case for the SDP, which derived roughly between a half and three-quarters of all income from its members. In the case of the Liberals/Liberal Democrats, this appears to be true only in the 1980s, with membership income now accounting for more than half of the party's income (Liberal Democrats, 1993a, 1993b). That said, however, there is some doubt about the reliability of the old Liberal Party figures in that they refer only to the Liberal Party Organization (LPO) which represented the extra-parliamentary body in England. Liberal Central Association (LCA) accounts, which cover the parliamentary organization, were rarely published. The decentralized nature of the party means that much of its real wealth really lay in the locality, and the central party organization remained skeletal.

The role of party members inside the party

The limits on the internal relevance of the membership are further underlined by the role played by party members within the party apparatus and internal procedures. Within the annual conference of the National Union, individual members are entitled to be represented at both constituency and ancillary levels of party organization. However, the annual conference itself is merely a (highly stage-managed) consultation process, as well as a morale-boosting exercise for the activists. Its decisions do not bind the parliamentary leadership, and it is only exceptionally that controversial subjects are debated.[6]

The same cannot be said of Labour's annual conference, however, at least on the surface. The party constitution avers the sovereignty of conference, yet the reality has generally been one of domination by a loose coalition of major union leaderships and parliamentary elites. Even where such coalitions have broken down temporarily, as they did towards the end of the 1970s, the parliamentary leadership has shown that it is quite prepared to overlook parts of the conference-made programme in drafting election manifestos. There has been some pressure for change during the past two decades but it is not yet clear that this has produced any decisive reform of the policy process in favour of the individual membership. Since 1981 representatives of the constituency membership have been able to take part in the process of electing the leader and deputy leader of the party, a task hitherto restricted to the parliamentary party; though a significant change, numeric preponderance within the electoral college remained with the unions, with 40 per cent of the votes, as against 30 per cent each for the CLPs and the PLP. Towards the end of the 1980s, however, as noted above, it became clear that the party was seriously considering the reform of the system of block voting at conference in an effort to remove the constraints on an active membership even within the trade unions themselves. As Hughes and Wintour (1989: 190) note, for example,

> the party's own internal surveys showed that very few active trade unionists devoted much time to the Party. Out of 6 million union members and 10,000 union branches affiliated to the party, possibly no more than 4,000 trade union activists were similarly active in the Party. The trade unions with the busiest Labour Party members were white collar professional unions which were not affiliated. . . . The manual unions, the life-blood of the party, had relatively few members in the party.

Accordingly, conference endorsed changes in 1993 that now allow union delegations to split their votes internally and which reapportion electoral college voting equally between CLPs, affiliated organization members and MPs/MEPs.

Reform has been much more apparent in the case of the Liberal Democrats, however, who have increased the potential policy involvement of members by making the new federal conference the sovereign policy-making forum of the new party; formally speaking, the old Liberal Assembly was simply consultative. The Liberal Democrats are also the only party which gives individual conference participants the right to propose motions; elsewhere this is a privilege extended only to party organs or bodies, such as constituency parties or the affiliated and ancillary organizations.

With regard to the national executive bodies, it is doubtful that individual memberships have much scope for influence. The General Purposes Committee of the National Union does not in any case have great policy significance, although in this case the members are represented through the chairs of ancillary organizations or through special representatives if they belong to areas having more than ninety constituency associations. For Labour, the NEC is an altogether more significant policy actor, and 7 of its 29 places are reserved for representatives of the local party membership who are directly elected by CLP delegates to annual conference. That said, this power is used primarily to elect prominent members of the parliamentary party. In the case of the Liberals, the individual membership was represented on the old Liberal National Executive in a manner similar to that in the Conservative General Purposes Committee, but the Liberal Democrat Federal Executive now has 14 places reserved (out of a full complement of 32–5) for those elected directly by the federal conference. Up to now, it has only been the SDP which ever made provision for executive members to be elected directly by the entire national membership (8/40 places).

The area of party activity in which the individual membership have greatest scope for influence is almost certainly that of candidate selection. In the major parties, the process of selecting candidates for national parliamentary contests has traditionally been dominated by local party elites rather than individual members as such, although individual members of the Conservative Party may attend a general meeting of the constituency association at which a ratification vote takes place. Moreover, in the case of Labour, the powers of constituency members have actually increased over the past decade or more. Since 1981 all Labour candidates have been subject to mandatory re-selection between general elections, and in 1993 the party conference decided that 'local electoral colleges' would be replaced by a system of direct balloting among individual members and 'registered' members from the unions on the question of whom to adopt. In both the Conservative and Labour cases, however, the central party apparatus can effectively veto a local choice. It can also be argued that Labour's shift towards a 'one-member-one-vote' (OMOV) selection procedure is actually part of a wider 'democratization as emasculation' strategy on the part of the leadership. It was certainly the case that former leader Neil Kinnock and his team of electorally sensitive modernizers were intent upon reducing the power of small elites of local party activists, fearing that such activists were often unrepresentative of mainstream citizens, as were those whom they tended to select as parliamentary candidates.

The smaller parties were historically quicker to give their members in the locality a direct vote in the selection process. For the Liberals and Liberal Democrats, the crucial choice is made by members attending a general meeting of the constituency party; in the modern party, the centre has even lost its right of veto.[7] The SDP central organization took care to retain the right to veto local short-lists, but the decision itself was made by a ballot of local members.

All of this therefore clearly points to a situation in which it would be misleading to speak of full mass membership parties. Though clearly not cadre parties, no British party has ever relied chiefly upon its membership as its prime resource and font of activity. Labour's 'mass membership' was always something of a myth, and the unions have tended to act as the chief organizational backbone in lieu of such a membership. Such mass membership as the Conservatives cultivated was only partially a political phenomenon; the bulk of the party's members have traditionally been motivated by primarily social factors (for example, to gain access to the local Conservative Club's leisure facilities). Much the same can be said of the Liberal Party's members. But while there is no sense in which the SDP or the new Liberal Democrats could ever be described as mass membership parties, nevertheless it is at least true of these parties that they are more conscious of the worth of the individual membership – necessarily, perhaps, given that they have had small parliamentary parties and relatively weak corporate financial support. In this sense, the members are relatively more important to the smaller parties, and hence it is not surprising that they are offered greater incentives to participate than are their counterparts in the major parties. Indeed, the SDP even went so far as to establish a separate extra-parliamentary leadership (the party president) for the membership (a feature retained by the Liberal Democrats), something quite innovative in the context of British party organizations. And while Labour has recently engaged in a drive for individual members, has enhanced membership powers, and has emphasized the growing financial significance of the individual membership, it nevertheless cannot yet be called a truly 'membership-oriented' party. The dominance of the parliamentary–union elite still continues and, if anything, changes in election campaign organization within the party may even have served to increase the autonomy of the parliamentary leadership (Webb, 1992b). Moreover, for the major parties at least, in the age of national media campaigning, members are not regarded as particularly important conduits of political communication,[8] whatever the veneer of legitimacy which they provide.

The parliamentary party and the party leadership

The degree of autonomy of the parliamentary groups and leaderships of the parties largely mirrors the patterns evident in the role of the memberships. Thus membership orientation tends to be weaker in the major parties and parliamentary leadership autonomy greater, whereas in the minor parties the parliamentary groups are much smaller in absolute terms and the memberships constrain the leaders to a greater extent. This applied less, perhaps, to the old Liberal Party than to the modern Liberal Democrats.

Prior to 1965, Conservative leaders 'emerged' from a series of secret negotiations among senior party figures; since then, however, Edward Heath, Margaret Thatcher and John Major have all been elected by their parliamentary colleagues. It should be said that Conservative MPs are expected to consider the views of party activists in the constituencies when deciding who to vote for in a leadership election; in practice, however, it is clear that the leader primarily owes his/her legitimacy to the support of parliamentary colleagues. In the case of Labour, as noted above, the party leader owed his legitimacy to the parliamentary party alone until 1981, but since that date he has depended on the confidence of a broader electoral college composed of the PLP, the unions and constituency delegates.[9] In policy terms too, there is no doubt that conference and the NEC have traditionally represented a very real constraint upon the parliamentary leadership, while the leadership has also needed to sustain a working relationship with certain key union elites in order to control a consistent majority in the key party arenas.

That said, however, and notwithstanding the apparent pressure for internal democratization of party procedures since the 1970s, the parliamentary leadership has been able to enhance its strategic control through certain innovations since 1983. In that year Neil Kinnock formed the Campaign Strategy Committee (CSC) to oversee the process of developing election strategy; later he supplemented this with the formation of the Campaign Management Team, a body responsible to him and charged with overseeing the day-to-day management of campaigns which was sometimes known simply as 'the leader's committee'. It has been suggested that, among other things, the CSC fulfilled the important task of enabling Kinnock to by-pass a hostile NEC during the early years of his leadership (Butler and Kavanagh, 1988: 50). Together, these bodies became significant devices of leadership direction within the party, and they were complemented by the supply of (largely free) professional marketing, media and advertising consultancy that Kinnock was able to call upon after the birth of the Shadow Communications Agency in 1985 (see p. 125). The leader now has an institutionalized battery of resources upon which he can draw to enhance his grip over the process of developing party policy and strategy.

The old Liberal Party stuck to the pattern of election by parliamentary party until the 1970s, even though the parliamentary group was probably too small for the legitimacy of such a process to continue unquestioned. In 1976 the new leader, David Steel, was elected by a special convention of constituency representatives, the composition of which was determined according to their support among voters (Finer, 1980: 83). However, the new Liberal Democrats have now followed the example of the SDP (which was the first British party to offer its membership the chance of directly electing the leadership), and the current leader, Paddy Ashdown, was elected directly by the membership in 1988. The leadership of the Liberal Democrats (as was also true of the former SDP) is also bound by the policy decisions of the conference, though in reality the deliberations of special policy committees considerably influence the conference agenda and debates.

Since the 1960s, then, we can note a certain trend 'from peer review of

Table 5.3 *State subvention to opposition parliamentary parties, 1975–89 (£)*

	Conservative	Labour	Liberal	Social Democratic
1975	150,000	–	33,234	–
1976	150,000	–	33,234	–
1977	153,750	–	33,234	–
1978	165,000	–	36,558	–
1979	143,335	139,698	29,457	–
1980	–	227,500	40,942	–
1981	–	290,000	52,108	–
1982	–	290,000	52,108	–
1983	–	296,497	57,150	25,299
1984	–	317,056	63,820	45,045
1985	–	440,355	88,641	62,562
1986	–	440,355	88,641	62,562
1987	–	436,669	75,238	44,494
1988	–	883,136	170,751[a]	72,634
1989	–	839,709	187,176	56,114
1990	–	839,709	187,176	56,114
1991	–	839,709	187,176	56,114
1992	–	946,250	199,420	14,029

[a] This figure incorporates both Liberal and Liberal Democrat subsidies, merger having formally taken place in March 1988.

Sources: *Hansard* parliamentary reports, parliamentary party chief whips' offices, House of Commons Fees Office

prospective nominees toward more popular decision making' (Epstein, 1986: 89) within the British parties. That said, however, the process remains very limited, and even in the case of the Liberal Democrats, the *nomination* process is dominated by the parliamentary party, and candidates can only be drawn from among the MPs. Hence, despite all the changes, the elitist nature of the leadership selection process still continues. As Punnett (1992: 160) notes, for example,

> leadership contests are infrequent, candidature is confined to MPs, the nominating process is controlled by MPs and the franchise is confined to a few hundred in the case of Labour and the Conservatives, and a few thousand in the case of the Liberals, rather than the millions who vote for each party. The procedures have become more participatory but the limits of the change are clear.

It must also be emphasized that, since the 1960s, the parliamentary parties have tended to become more financially independent of their extra-parliamentary organizations. MPs have long since received a certain amount of financial aid in order to employ secretarial/research assistance, and the party in office has traditionally benefited from aid to the Cabinet Office. Since 1975, however, official state subventions have been paid to opposition parliamentary parties. This so-called 'Short Money' is paid on the basis of a given amount for seats and votes won, but it is fair to say that it does not amount to a very substantial figure – from 1987 to 1992, for example, Labour received an average of just over £1900 per MP (see Table 5.3).

Party staffing and professional support

The principal theme of this chapter is that, if anything, the political parties
have tended to centralize power and resources as far as possible, notwithstanding certain pressures to the contrary. This trend may also be
discerned in patterns of party staffing, where both the Liberals/Liberal
Democrats and the Conservatives appear to have undergone a similar
pattern of change, albeit at very different levels (Webb, 1992c: Tables
XII.c.1.a–d). While there has been little apparent change in the number of
central party staff employed (although the Liberals did suffer a dip around
the middle of the thirty-year cycle, and a very brief surge following the
merger with the SDP), the number of sub-national staff has nevertheless
been radically reduced. The Conservatives have lost almost exactly half of
their sub-national staff, whilst the Liberal Democrats now maintain only
some 11 per cent of the number employed by the Liberal Party in 1960.
Indeed, the sharp decline in the number of sub-national personnel is a
phenomenon common to all the parties, with Labour losing over 60 per
cent of the number it employed in 1960. That said, however, these figures
fail to make a distinction between regional and local party staff. This is
important since regional personnel are actually appointed and employed
by the central parties, and in some respects they represent the eyes and
ears of the centre in the locality. Full-time constituency agents, on the
other hand, while being generally trained, 'certificated' and promoted
centrally, are nevertheless appointed and paid locally. When this is taken
into account, it is notable that Labour has maintained a fairly constant
number of regional employees, even though constituency agents have
shrunk in number. Thus in 1963, the party had 38 regional staff, as against
36 in 1989. By contrast, it had only 62 full time constituency agents at the
end of the 1980s, as against 208 in 1963. The Conservatives and the
Liberals have shed both regional and local staff: the former had 60 regional
employees in 1963, 41 in 1974 and just 26 in 1989, while for the Liberals/
Liberal Democrats the respective figures are 10, 6 and 8.

The Labour Party, in contrast to the Liberals and the Conservatives, has
managed to increase its complement of central party staff since 1960 (by
more than 40 per cent). However, none of this alters the fact that, even
after the sharp reductions which followed the 1992 election, the Conservative Party remains comfortably the best staffed, numerically speaking
(when one takes account of clerical staff, Labour's full complement at
Walworth Road in December 1993 was around 90, whereas the Conservatives in the same month maintained 148 at Central Office). Nevertheless,
taken together with the sharp drop in the number of constituency agents
we referred to earlier, this does rather suggest that Labour has become a
more centralized party: it has slightly closed the gap with the Conservatives
in terms of central staffing, though not local staffing, and the only sub-
national staffing levels it has maintained are at the regional level (where
appointments are made by the centre).

The parties appear to maintain only a minimal staff at the parliamentary level. Indeed, the Conservatives claim not to actually employ any at all, although in government they do benefit from the assistance afforded by the Cabinet Office. Moreover, the major parties receive the benefit of civil servants who are seconded to work in the parliamentary chief whips' offices, and all MPs receive a secretarial/research assistance allowance. It is difficult to make statements about change over time in parliamentary staffing levels given the difficulty of obtaining anything other than the most recent parliamentary staff data for the parties, but it is not unreasonable to surmise that the advent of Short Money has helped to develop parliamentary party organization in Britain.[10]

These staffing levels are of course supplemented by outside expertise. Since the 1960s, all of the parties have drawn on the talent and advice of marketing and advertising professionals, mainly in the context of election campaigns as, for instance, could be seen in the Conservative reliance upon the advertising skills of Saatchi and Saatchi during the 1979 and 1983 campaigns. In the Labour case, and notwithstanding the habitual reservations of some on the left, Neil Kinnock decided in the mid-1980s that policy reform had to be complemented by a more professional approach to marketing if the message of the party was to get across. In 1985 a new, high-profile director of communications and campaigning was appointed, Peter Mandelson, who oversaw the introduction of the Shadow Communications Agency (SCA), a largely voluntary group of professional experts from the world of marketing, broadcasting and advertising. The SCA is an umbrella organization with greater permanence and influence than its comparable predecessors in the party. The only paid consultants of the SCA were originally its coordinator, Philip Gould, whose brainchild the SCA was, and his professional partner, Deborah Mattinson. By 1987, however, it was estimated that around 200 such people were working on the party's election campaign free of charge, at a saving of around half a million pounds (Gould et al., 1989: 72). While these volunteers are usually sub-divided into professional groups, such as writers, art directors, journalists and broadcasters, it is probably fair to suggest that the work of the SCA also has implications for party strategy and policy. For instance, after the 1987 election the SCA undertook a thorough review of Labour's electoral appeal via a package of integrated market research initiatives, the results of which were fed into a major policy review. In addition, the Labour Party continues to retain the paid professional services of Robert Worcester's Market and Opinion Research International (MORI), which has conducted quantitative market research on the party's behalf since 1970. Following Mandelson's appointment Worcester insisted that his own organization be more closely and continuously integrated into Labour's campaign planning if it was to be effective. Thus while in 1983 the party's election campaign was largely in the hands of politicians and established party and union functionaries, with the NEC, the Campaign Committee and the long-standing press and publicity officers providing the hub of campaign organization, by 1987 the dominant elements were characteristic of what Panebianco (1988) has identified as the 'new professionalism'.[11]

In terms of organizational professionalization, the Conservative Party is at least as advanced as the Labour Party. Indeed, having recognized the value of propaganda during the First World War, senior party officials first employed the services of an advertising agency during the 1929 general election campaign, and Pinto-Duschinsky (1980: 101) estimates that its expenditure on campaign advertising actually reached an all-time high in real terms as early as 1935. Even at that stage it was already prepared to fund a non-party publicity organization from which it could benefit (the National Publicity Bureau). Given this early appreciation of the benefits of professional marketing assistance and the traditional financial advantage over Labour, it is therefore not surprising that the Conservatives outspent their main rivals in terms of advertising at the 1987 and 1992 elections. Some £6.7 million was spent on advertising and broadcasting production in 1987, and a further £219,000 on opinion research; in 1992, total spending in this area approached £10 million. The Alliance parties spent well under £2 million *in total* in 1987 and were therefore considerably behind the major parties. Advertising consultants were appointed only late in the day, and generally failed to distinguish themselves in the eyes of commentators either inside or outside the Alliance (Butler and Kavanagh, 1988: 80–1, 157; Wilson, 1987: 234–7, 252). The Liberals did no private polling, but the SDP did manage to commission a dozen MARPLAN polls of marginal constituencies during the campaign, and a few during the run-up period. In 1992 the Federal Liberal Democratic Organization spent £1.3 million on the general election campaign (total Liberal Democratic campaign spending was boosted by the separate contributions of the English, Scottish and Welsh parties). Nevertheless, to an even greater extent than Labour – but in a less coordinated way – the smaller parties were and are dependent upon the voluntary and gratis efforts of sympathetic professionals who may be mobilized at election times.

In addition to these external services, the parties are also in a position to avail themselves of professional research and policy assistance from independent policy institutes. None of these institutes is formally linked to any of the parties and none is represented within party structures. On the other hand, it is recognized that there are partisan and ideological sympathies as well as overlaps of personnel which act to tie the parties to particular research bodies. Both the Policy Studies Institute (PSI) and the Institute for Economic Affairs (IEA), for example, are essentially right-wing think-tanks, and David Willetts, formerly of the PSI, became an honorary director of the Conservative Research Department and then an MP for the party. Similarly, Patricia Hewitt, formerly Neil Kinnock's press secretary, later became director of the Institute for Public Policy Research. Nonetheless, while it rarely if ever happens that any of these bodies are directly employed by the parties, they can play a significant role and, in some areas at least, the PSI, the IEA and the radical right Adam Smith Institute have had a direct impact on government legislation during the 1980s (Whitehead, 1993).

It is all too easy to be seduced by the impression of growing professionalization, however. Certainly the Conservatives seem to have long been aware of the need to develop a professional attitude towards training personnel and building contacts with outside expertise, and even in 1929 the party chairman was talking of the need to circumvent the 'dead hand' of the local party bureaucrats by making greater use of advertising consultancies (Pinto-Duschinsky, 1980: 98). It is probably more accurate, therefore, to suggest that it has long been a habit to seek to adapt to modern conditions of political communication – subject, that is, to the constraints of financial viability. There is perhaps a stronger case for emphasizing more recent professionalization in the Labour Party, although in this case it must be emphasized that not all post-1960 election campaigns have necessarily been as incompetent as that in 1983, which is almost universally regarded as representing a nadir for the party. Nor did Labour totally eschew marketing expertise prior to the middle of the 1980s, and MORI has been employed by the party consistently since 1970. That said, it does seem that both Labour and the Liberal Democrats have been slower to adapt to the possibilities of the television age. General election campaign spending actually dropped in real terms after the elections of 1959 and 1964, for both major parties, and this may partially have reflected the growing importance of television, which was free. The Conservatives used advertising agents in the 1960s to coordinate their campaign but Labour did not (Rose, 1974: 87); in Labour's case there seemed to be greater willingness to continue to rely principally upon the army of what Panebianco (1988) calls the 'traditional party bureaucrats', among whom must be included the numerous trade union officials who campaigned for Labour at election time. In the case of the minor parties, on the other hand, it has been simply money which has placed the greatest constraint upon the advance of professionalization.

The parties, the citizenry and the state

If political parties have, as suggested, increasingly found themselves under pressure since 1970 or thereabouts, then it may well be that this is because they do not effectively fulfil important democratic functions of the type once identified by Samuel Finer – for instance, those of representation, participation and social integration (see Finer, 1980). While this is not the place in which to elaborate this theme in great detail, it is worthwhile observing that such shortcomings threaten the overall legitimacy of the parties and, indeed, of the political system itself. Therefore before concluding it is interesting to consider, if only briefly, the extent to which political parties in Britain continue to penetrate state and society.

There is of course little doubt that political parties have been, and continue to be, integral to the functioning of Britain's own peculiar brand of liberal democracy. I have argued elsewhere that Britain comes close to fulfilling Katz's criteria for 'party government', with the state bureaucracy being the only serious constraint on the governmental power that is wielded by the parties (Katz, 1986; Webb, 1992c). That said, of course, it is also clear that their declining membership does to some extent indicate a shallower penetration of society. This is also backed up by evidence of partisan dealignment, and especially falling electoral turn-out and the erosion of party identification. Turn-out at national elections fell from 85 per cent in 1959 to 75.3 per cent in 1987, and although there was some recovery to 77.3 per cent in 1992, this is still a striking decline in the context of the increasing media coverage and the rising number of candidates (Finer, 1980: 59). Turn-out at local elections has always been far lower, averaging well under 50 per cent, while survey evidence suggests that the proportion of electors having a 'very strong' partisan affinity fell from 47 per cent in 1964 to just 16 per cent in 1987. Further evidence of the declining 'partyness' of society might be found in the increasing take-up of non-partisan forms of mass media output, and higher participation in non-partisan interest groups. However, even though it is true that the number of television viewers has increased dramatically since the 1960s, and that the proportion of electors claiming TV to be their main source of political information is also high (Dunleavy and Husbands, 1985: 111), we should be careful of reading too much into these patterns. This does not necessarily mean that the parties are being supplanted by a new set of political communicators, for example; rather, it seems that the parties have worked hard to adapt to the reality of communicating principally through the medium of television, as witnessed by their willingness to professionalize their campaign approaches. Thus, while television may be formally independent of party penetration, the parties are nevertheless becoming increasingly adept at its use. In this sense, we should not underestimate the continuing capacity for party penetration of society.

It can also be argued that the parties may manage to adapt to the increased orientation of participation towards interest groups by establishing links with such groups, and this, in turn, may provide a form of continuing, though indirect, connection between party and society. Labour's organizational links with the unions are obviously well known and, despite speculation to the contrary, have not really been significantly eroded since the 1960s (Webb, 1992a: Ch. 2), even though the party–union link has yet again moved to the forefront of Labour's own internal agenda. This aside, less formal links have also been forged, especially between Labour and a host of single-issue groups concerned with nuclear disarmament, the environment, housing and social welfare. What this suggests, then, is not so much that parties have substantially less penetration into society than hitherto, but rather, and more simply, that this penetration may now be less directly evident.

Either way, of course, the degree of penetration does seem more shallow than before. There are two developments which are of particular relevance here: rapid social change since the 1960s, on the one hand, and growing disillusion with (established) parties, on the other. Given their aversion to (expensive) strategies of mass mobilization and political education, it would seem that the major parties have proved quite vulnerable to the disruption in the patterns of partisan loyalty brought about by the increasing levels of occupational and geographic mobility and by the dispersion of class-typical patterns of work and residence. On top of this, rising social aspirations and demands inevitably brought a sense of frustration on the part of many electors in the 1970s and 1980s, raising problems which were once discussed within the context of the problem of 'ungovernability'.

Nevertheless, the parties have sought to adapt and survive. Reference has already been made to their growing sophistication vis-à-vis the mass media and their new links with single-issue groups, but it also should be emphasized that parties with access to state resources and power have a clear advantage in maintaining their own position and denying such power to others. This applies particularly to the major parties; indeed, it calls to mind the question of possible collusion between a 'cartel' of major parties bent on retaining their primacy within the system, and adapting the resources of the state in order to provide an 'institutionalized structure of support, sustaining insiders while excluding outsiders' (Katz and Mair, 1992: 21–2).

There are indeed some indications that it may well be appropriate to apply the concept of a party cartel to the British case. The perennial debate about electoral reform (favoured by the Liberal Democrats) is inspired partly by a growing perception of the first-past-the-post system as a device well suited to the task of entrenching major party control of national government at a time when Labour and the Conservatives are threatened by the rise of minor parties. Similarly, until recently the enduring official resistance shown by the major parties to the introduction of widespread state funding of parties (also favoured by the Liberals) may well have been designed to protect their position within the state. So long as British parties are forced to rely on non-state sources of finance, then it is likely that Labour and the Conservatives will maintain their advantage over minor parties. The extension of state aid to a degree that goes significantly beyond the current limitations of 'Short Money' would release corporate donors from their present responsibilities and might well reduce the gap between the major and minor parties. Again, access to TV and radio for party political broadcasting is linked closely to the relative strengths of competitors in the House of Commons – and thus reflects the distorting impact of the electoral system, of course.

Yet there are also signs that pressure on this peculiarly British type of 'cartel' is developing – from both *within* and without. While the adversarial nature of the party system in Britain has tended to obscure the impression of excessively cosy collusion, the Westminster system in reality has been based on an implicit understanding of alternation in power by the major competitors. So long as this system worked, and despite the best efforts of the minor parties, there was little incentive for Labour or the Conservatives to modify the rules of the game; each was guaranteed its respective turn in office through the swing of the two-party pendulum. More recently, however, there are signs that this model is becoming obsolete (see, for example, King, 1993; Rose, 1992), and following a fourth consecutive Conservative general election victory in April 1992, majoritarian alternation now seems to be giving way to one-party dominance. Consequently, Labour – worried about being perennially condemned to opposition – is showing every sign of seriously reassessing the basis of its 'collusion' with the Conservative Party and, significantly, recently established its own internal commission to examine the question of electoral reform (Mair, 1994). Labour has also now joined the Liberal Democrats in urging the substantial extension of state subventions for political parties. In short, one element of the 'cartel' has been excluded from power and the resources of the state for too long, and may well join the other 'outsiders' in proposing the reform of a key foundation of that cartel.

In the end, however, we are left with the image of both major parties struggling to adapt to the changing political and behavioural environment by centralizing and standardizing organizationally, and of the political elites within the big parties – who continue, by and large, to be parliamentary elites – seeking to maintain their grip on state power by enhancing their own internal party power. There are no guarantees that such adaptation can be smoothly achieved in the context of a society which is increasingly prone to generate pressure for the democratization of its institutions.

Notes

1 Note that while, in keeping with the conventions of this comparative study, we refer to union block membership as 'corporate', the British labour movement habitually speaks of its 'affiliated' membership.

2 Note that some constituency parties tend to relax the requirement for individual members also to be members of affiliated unions for which they are eligible.

3 Between 1927 and 1945, when it was necessary specifically to 'contract in' in order to pay this levy, affiliated membership income declined significantly (Pinto-Duschinsky, 1980: 76).

4 Although it is a legal requirement that all corporations making political donations state so in their annual accounts, there are over one million private companies registered in Britain. Since it would not be feasible to scrutinize the accounts of all these companies, one is forced to rely upon estimates which derive from an examination of samples of the accounts maintained by the Registrar of Companies.

5 Expenditure in the 1992 campaign came to some £15 million. Total party income in that year was around £23.4 million, of which only £1.3 million derived from the constituencies; income in 1993 fell to £11.5 million, of which nearly £1.1 million came from the constituencies.

6 Although see Kelly (1989), who argues that the National Union Conference has more influence than is commonly understood to be the case. Certainly at a formal level, however,

the powers and rights of individual members are more limited than in the other major British parties.

7 Note, however, that all potential candidates have to be approved prior to selection by the Joint States Candidates Committee, a central body. Moreover, postal ballots are available on request to local party members unable to attend a selection meeting in person.

8 It is worth emphasizing that although the parties seem increasingly conscious of the need to develop a professional and coordinated strategy when election campaigning, a number of commentators have recently taken pains to stress the potential impact of campaigning in the locality – which relies predominantly on the voluntary work of individual party members. For instance, having emphasized that Labour and the Liberal Democrats were especially 'ruthless in concentrating their resources' and adopting a 'centrally planned strategy' in 1992, Denver and Hands marshal a variety of arguments to suggest that 'local campaigning does not appear to be a meaningless ritual' (Denver and Hands, 1992: 542–4). Whiteley and Seyd conducted a separate study of Labour's campaign in which they reached a similar conclusion, arguing that the party's modernization strategy had 'ignored an important component of party renewal, the grassroots members. If much more attention is paid to the issue of the recruitment, retention and energizing of local party members, our evidence suggests that this can bring significant electoral benefits to the Labour Party' (Whiteley and Seyd, 1992: 594).

9 Reforms endorsed in 1993 mean that leaders (and deputy leaders) are now elected by a new college in which the votes of unions and constituency delegates have been replaced by those of corporate and individual members. Labour MEPs now also enjoy the right to vote as part of the PLP section of the college.

10 State subsidies now make a significant contribution to parliamentary party resources; for example, although the Parliamentary Labour Party only actually employs 10 executive and 3 clerical staff in the House of Commons, it also enjoys the benefit of 4 civil servants appointed to help in the Opposition Chief Whip's office, not to mention 20 shadow cabinet research staff and 3 Labour peers' researchers paid for by the Short Money. Similarly, the Liberal Democrats in 1993 actually claim to have 15 parliamentary staff at their disposal, when all those provided for by state subvention of one kind or another are allowed for. In addition, there is a supply of purely voluntary research assistants from which parliamentary parties benefit.

11 The extent of Labour's commitment to the use of professional marketing was also underlined by its financial investment in the 1987 and 1992 election campaigns. Though heavily outspent by the Tories, Labour invested far more in marketing and advertising in 1987 than in 1983 – without even allowing for the benefit it derived from the free services of the SCA. In all, the party spent nearly £2.2 million on advertising, while the MORI consultancy cost £148,000 and Party Election Broadcasts (PEBs) a further £143,000 (Pinto-Duschinsky, 1989a: 19; see also the discussion in Webb, 1992b). In 1992 the party spent £3.3 million on media and advertising services (Labour Party, 1993c: 17).

References

Anderson, P. (1965) 'Problems of socialist strategy', in P. Anderson and R. Blackburn (eds), *Towards Socialism*. London: Collins.

British Broadcasting Corporation (1990) 'Paying for the party', *Panorama*, October.

Butler, D. (1989) *British General Elections since 1945*. Oxford: Blackwell.

Butler, D. and Butler, G. (1987) *British Political Facts, 1900–1985*. London: Macmillan.

Butler, D. and Kavanagh, D. (1988) *The British General Election of 1987*. London: Macmillan.

Conservative Party (1993) *Annual Reports and Accounts, 31 March 1993*. London: Conservative Party.

Denver, D. and Hands, G. (1992) 'Constituency campaigning', *Parliamentary Affairs*, 45: 528–44.

Dunleavy, P. and Husbands, C. (1985) *British Democracy at the Crossroads*. London: Allen & Unwin.

Epstein, L. (1986) *Political Parties in the American Mold*. New York: Madison.

Finer, S. (1980) *The Changing British Party System, 1945–1979*. Washington, DC: American Enterprise Institute.

Gould, P., Herd, P. and Powell, C. (1989) 'The Labour Party's campaign communications', in I. Crewe and M. Harrop (eds), *Political Communications: The General Election Campaign of 1987*. Cambridge: Cambridge University Press.

Hatfield, M. (1978) *The House the Left Built: Inside Labour Policy Making, 1970–1975*. London: Victor Gollancz.

HMSO (1976) *Report of (Houghton) Committee on Financial Aid to Parties*. London: HMSO.

Hughes, C. and Wintour, P. (1989) *Labour Rebuilt: The New Model Party*. London: Fourth Estate.

Katz, R.S. (1986) 'Party government: a rationalistic conception', in F.G. Castles and R. Wildenmann (eds), *Visions and Realities of Party Government*. Berlin: de Gruyter.

Katz, R. and Mair, P. (1992) 'Changing models of party organization: the emergence of the cartel party', paper presented to ECPR Workshop on Democracies and the Organization of Political Parties, Limerick, March–April.

Kelly, R.N. (1989) *Conservative Party Conferences: The Hidden System*. Manchester: Manchester University Press.

King, A. (1993) 'The implications of one-party government', in A. King, I. Crewe, D. Denver, K. Newton, P. Norton, D. Sanders and P. Seyd (eds), *Britain at the Polls 1992*. New Jersey: Chatham House.

Kogan, M. and Kogan, D. (1982) *The Battle for the Labour Party*. London: Fontana.

Labour Party (1993a) *Trade Unions and the Labour Party: Final Report of the Review Group on Party–Union Links*. London: Labour Party.

Labour Party (1993b) *Conference Arrangements Committee Report*. London: Labour Party, pp. 35–6.

Labour Party (1993c) *National Executive Committee Report*. London: Labour Party.

Liberal Democrats (1993a) *Reports to the Autumn Conference of the Federal Party*. London: Liberal Democrats.

Liberal Democrats (1993b) *Reports to the Autumn Conference of the Party in England*. London: Liberal Democrats.

Mair, P. (1994) 'Britain: Labour and Electoral Reform', in P. Anderson and P. Camiller (eds), *Mapping Europe's Left*. London: Verso.

McKenzie, R.T. (1956) *British Political Parties*. London: Heinemann.

Miliband, R. (1972) *Parliamentary Socialism: A Study in the Politics of Labour*. London: Merlin.

National Union (1988) *Rules and Standing Orders of the National Union of Conservative and Unionist Associations*. London: NUCUA.

Panebianco, A. (1988) *Political Parties: Organization and Power*. Cambridge: Cambridge University Press.

Pinto-Duschinsky, M. (1980) *British Political Finance, 1832–1980*. Washington, DC: American Enterprise Institute.

Pinto-Duschinsky, M. (1989a) 'Financing the British general election of 1987', in I. Crewe and M. Harrop (eds), *Political Communications: The General Election Campaign of 1987*. Cambridge: Cambridge University Press.

Pinto-Duschinsky, M. (1989b) 'Trends in British political funding, 1979–84', in H. Alexander (ed.), *Comparative Political Finance in the 1980s*. Cambridge: Cambridge University Press.

Punnett, R.M. (1992) *Selecting the Party Leader: Britain in Comparative Perspective*. Hemel Hempstead: Harvester Wheatsheaf.

Rasmussen, J. (1965) *The Liberal Party*. London: Constable.

Rose, R. (1974) *The Problem of Party Government* London: Macmillan.

Rose, R. (1992) 'Long-term Structural change or cyclical fluctuation?' *Parliamentary Affairs*, 45: 451–65.

Seyd, P. and Whiteley, P. (1992) *Labour's Grassroots: The Politics of Party Membership*. Oxford: Clarendon.

Ware, A. (1987) *Citizens, Parties and the State*. Oxford: Polity Press.

Webb, P.D. (1992a) *Trade Unions and the British Electorate*. Aldershot: Dartmouth.

Webb, P.D. (1992b) 'Election campaigning, organizational transformation and the professionalization of the British Labour Party', *European Journal of Political Research*, 21: 267–88.

Webb, P.D. (1992c) 'The United Kingdom', in R.S. Katz and P. Mair (eds), *Party Organizations: A Data Handbook on Party Organizations in Western Democracies, 1960–90*, London: Sage, pp. 837–70.

Webb, P.D. (1993) 'The debate about Labour Party–Trade Union relations', paper presented to the annual conference on Elections, Public Opinion and Parties, Lancaster, September.

Wellhofer, E.S. (1979) 'Strategies for party organization and voter mobilization: Britain, Norway and Argentina', *Comparative Political Studies*, 12: 169–204.

Whitehead, A. (1993) 'Planning in an unplanned environment', paper presented to the colloquium on Choice and Competition in National and International Transport, London, Guildhall University, July.

Whiteley, P. and Seyd, P. (1992) 'The Labour's vote and local activism: the impact of local constituency campaigns', *Parliamentary Affairs*, 45: 582–95.

Wilson, D. (1987) *Battle for Power: The Inside Story of the Alliance and the 1987 General Election*. London: Sphere Books.

Wintour, P. (1991) 'Labour in cash crisis over subscriptions', *The Guardian*, 26 November.

Wintour, P. (1993) 'Dissidents attack party fund deficit', *The Guardian*, 5 September.

6

Denmark: The Decline of the Membership Party?

Lars Bille

The Danish conception of party organization

Despite its categorical formulation, few scholars will disagree with the essence of Panebianco's (1988: 50) statement that 'a party's organizational characteristics depend more upon its history, i.e. on how the organization originated and how it consolidated, than upon any other factor'. Certainly in Denmark, the specific circumstances behind the founding of the party organizations and the traditions, procedures and practice that gradually developed during their formative decades, and especially from the mid-nineteenth century to around 1920, are essential for a proper understanding of the modern party organizations.

Two sets of rules have had an important impact on the organization of Danish political parties: first, the constitution and the overall governmental and administrative structure, and second, the electoral laws. In the first Danish Constitution of 1849 – as well as in the revisions in 1866, 1915, 1920 and 1953 – there is no mention of political parties. Indeed, it was explicitly stated in the constitutions prior to 1953 and retained in section 56 of the present (1953) constitution that MPs shall be guided by their personal convictions only and that they must not in any way be bound by any instructions given by their voters. This constitutional provision was taken very seriously by the MPs in the first decades after 1849, and no formal party organizations were established in parliament. With time, however, informal parliamentary groups of like-minded MPs were gradually formed around prominent political personalities, leading to the emergence of de facto parliamentary party organizations. In 1870, already existing liberal groups in parliament founded *Det forenede Venstre* (later renamed *Venstre* [V]), and during the second half of the 1870s the other main political faction in parliament, *Højre* (since 1916 *Det konservative Folkeparti* [KF]) also formed a more permanent parliamentary organization.

At the same time, closer links between the parliamentarians and their constituencies also began to be established. The initiative to create and strengthen this link came both from the parliamentarians themselves and from the different associations of voters. The parallel course of this process meant that the distinction between 'internally' and 'externally' created parties is only partly relevant here, although it did make sense to speak of a distinction between a parliamentary party and a membership party. Both Det forenede Venstre and Højre maintained and guarded that distinction in the construction and further development of their formal organizational structure.

This was also true of the founding of *Socialdemokratiet* (SD), which was established in 1871 as a section of the First International, and whose organization originally encompassed both the political party and the trade unions. A formal separation between the two occurred in 1878, when an independent party responsible for the political organization and mobilization of the workers was established (gaining its first representation in parliament in 1884), leaving the trade unions to take care of their professional organization. The Social Democrats, then, were founded as a membership organization independent of parliament. Once having won representation, however, and largely as a result of the provisions in the constitution, they created an organizational structure that included both a parliamentary party and a membership party, albeit with each working in close cooperation with the other as well as with the rest of the labour movement.

The founding of *Det radikale Venstre* (RV) in 1905 illustrates the influence that the distinction between a parliamentary party and a membership party exercised at that time. A prolonged disagreement in Venstre ended in 1905 with the expulsion of twelve MPs who then founded a new parliamentary party. At the same time a circle of voters who sympathized with the expelled politicians summoned a founding convention for a new party. Only after this meeting had agreed on a platform for the new party did the twelve parliamentarians attend the meeting and announce their support for the programme and for the founding of the new party.

All four of the old Danish parties, then, created organizational structures that involved a formal distinction between the parliamentary party and the membership party, and a similar basic structure was also adopted by the four new parties that were founded in the period from 1959 to 1973 (*Socialistisk Folkeparti* [SF] in 1959; *Kristeligt Folkeparti* [KRF] in 1971; *Fremskridtspartiet* [FRP] in 1972, and the *Centrum-Demokraterne* [CD] in 1973). In other words, this formal distinction constitutes an essential part of the Danish conception of party organization.

The electoral laws make up the other set of formal rules that have influenced the Danish mode of party organization. Before 1915 the electoral system was a traditional plurality system with single-member constituencies, which implied that the parties made a great effort to create at least one local organization in each of the (since 1895) 113 constituencies. In 1915 and 1920, however, a list system of proportional representation was adopted, the basic characteristics of which remain in force today (for details see Elklit and Pade, 1991), and which consists of a national level which is relevant for the allocation of forty compensatory seats, and a regional/county level with seventeen multi-member districts, where 135 seats are distributed. The original 113 constituencies from the old plurality system were by and large preserved as 103 nomination districts (constituency level), since it was generally agreed that this arrangement could help to maintain close ties between the elected and the electors. Most nomination districts cover more than one of the 225 municipalities that constitute the local level of government, with the polling district in the municipality operating as the lowest administrative level in the hierarchy of the electoral law.

All eight Danish political parties have adopted a basic organizational structure that is adjusted to the administrative structure of the electoral law, that is, they have all created national, regional, constituency and local organs. In addition to the formal distinction between the parliamentary party and the membership party, the second basic characteristic of the Danish conception of party organization is therefore a territorially defined hierarchial structure.

It must be emphasized, however, that this relatively high degree of uniformity in basic organizational structure has not been forced upon the parties. To be sure, they have adapted to the provisions of the constitution and the electoral law; nevertheless, the uniformity is not the result of any other direct state regulation, and a distinct party law which might, for example, require a specific organizational structure or specific rules for representation, or which might otherwise regulate the internal affairs of political parties, has never actually been proposed in Denmark. From both the general and the legal points of view (Vesterdorf, 1990), as well as from their perspectives, the parties are regarded as voluntary and private associations. This voluntary element is also reflected in the virtual absence of any obligations for party members beyond requiring them not to be members of any other parties and insisting that they remain loyal to their own party platform and policies. That said, members of the SD are expected to join an appropriate trade union and elected party officers must subscribe to the affiliated newspaper.

Another essential element of the national conception of party organization is that all parties emphasize the need to be membership-oriented and representative. Historically, the explicitly stated purpose in creating and maintaining membership organs was, and still is, to establish a means by which the voters could communicate their interests to party representatives in national, regional and local governments and, perhaps more importantly, to mobilize and encapsulate the voters and to create a stable source of party income. During the first half of the twentieth century the legitimacy of the parties and the assessment of their representativeness came to rest more and more upon their ability to form and maintain large membership organizations. The four old parties all succeeded in this respect in the decades preceding 1960, and despite a drastic decline in membership since then, these parties still perceive themselves as the prime representative organs for the people.

In general, then, the organizational similarities of the eight Danish parties are more significant than the differences, with the four old parties establishing the standard which was then followed by the new parties, despite some attempts (by the CD and the FRP) to deviate. And while there have been relatively frequent minor shifts and adjustments of the rules, reflecting a process of flexible adaptation to a changing environment, the basic structures have nevertheless remained essentially unaltered since 1960. All eight parties still make a formal distinction between the parliamentary party and the membership party. The latter is made up of local branches, constituency organizations, regional organizations, a national conference and national executives, that is, of a mainly pyramidal structure which, with some variations, stipulates a relatively high degree of regional/local autonomy. All eight parties also still perceive themselves as representative parties, and all attach a lot of importance to political mobilization and to having the individual party members (either directly or indirectly) represented in the leading party bodies. These basic characteristics are common to the eight Danish parties whether old or young, left or right, secular or Christian, or large or small, and, being essentially unchanged over the past decades, they also provide the organizational system of the parties with a relatively high degree of stability.

The membership party

The basic unit of all Danish political parties is a territorially defined local branch. Party membership is direct and individual. To become a member of a political party one must join a local branch, and the local branches register the members, periodically reporting their numbers to the party's central office. Thus, the precision and reliability of the figures reported depend on the efficiency and honesty with which each local branch conducts its affairs. Central registration of members at the party headquarters has traditionally been opposed by the local branches, which, apart from reflecting a general opposition to political registration as such, see it as a means of reducing their local autonomy. During the 1980s, however, all of the Danish parties introduced central membership registration, partly to overcome drawbacks in the traditional system, and partly because of the advantages which it offered to headquarters, including the possibility of direct communication with the individual members.

The trend in membership is clear and unambiguous. The traditional Danish mass party organizations have all experienced a drastic reduction in the number of individual members, a reduction which begins in the early 1960s, accelerates in the 1970s and stabilizes in the 1980s, albeit still with a downward trend.[1] The raw figures are certainly quite dramatic: from a total of around 600,000 members in 1960, the four old parties had fallen to just about 220,000 by the end of 1990. Moreover, it must be emphasized that this decline has not been compensated for by any major increase in the membership of the new parties which, despite having adopted an organizational structure which is very similar to that of the traditional mass party, and despite explicitly hoping to organize as large a proportion of the electorate as possible, have not succeeded in persuading their voters to join in any significant numbers. Indeed, none of the new parties has organized more than around 10,000 members, and in 1990 all four had a combined membership of only some 28,000 (Bille, 1992).

The declining ability of the eight parties to maintain their position as the prime organizing political force in Denmark is even more apparent when we look at the steady decline of party membership as a percentage of the electorate – from around 20 per cent in 1960 to around 6 per cent at the end of the 1980s[2] – with none of the parties being able to evade this downward trend. And while the two old class parties in Denmark (the SD and V) have experienced the sharpest decline, it is also worth noting that the combined membership of the four new parties (SF, KRF, FRP, CD) has never exceeded 0.7 per cent of the electorate, with the weakest of these, the CD, organizing less than 0.05 per cent of the electorate – and this is despite their relatively major electoral successes (the four new parties together polled 33.7 per cent of the votes in 1973 and 22.1 per cent in 1990).

The sharp decline in party membership is also reflected in the reduction in the number of local branches. Although some data from the beginning of the 1960s are unobtainable, reasonably accurate estimates suggest that there was a total of some 3800 local branches in 1960. By 1989, however, this number had fallen to just 2813. The municipal reform of 1970, which reduced the number of municipalities from around 1000 to 225, may of course account for some of this change, in that it encouraged the parties to adapt to the new structures by merging several local branches; since then, however, the further decline in local branches is likely to have resulted from the shrinking membership levels. Moreover, none of the new parties has been able to create the sort of fine-meshed local network which characterized that of some of the old parties (and especially the SD and V) up to the end of the 1950s. Within the old parties themselves, the average size of local branches has declined by about 25 to 35 per cent, and is now steadily approaching 40 to 100 members per branch, which is the relatively stable level characteristic of the new parties. The one exception here is the CD, which averages between 11 and 18 members per branch, indicating that some at least of the party's branches must barely have enough members to fill the posts of chairman, secretary and treasurer.

Except in the case of the SD, affiliated membership in Denmark is concentrated in the parties' youth organizations – in 1960, for instance, the V youth organization (VU) had around 53,000 members and the SD youth organization (DSU) had around 22,000 members, as against 4,000 and 15,000 respectively at the end of the 1980s. In 1991, however, a police investigation of the figures reported by the organizations to the authorities revealed widespread fraud, with exaggerated membership levels and fictional members being designated to ensure increased state subsidies, and with the youth membership lists of only the V and the KRF emerging with a clean bill of health. Nevertheless, even allowing for widespread inaccu-racies and misreporting, it is clear that the youth organizations have experienced an even more dramatic membership decline than is the case for their 'mother' parties, a decline which presents the parties with a serious recruitment problem.

In the case of the SD, affiliated membership is also important with respect to the various sections of the labour movement, the most important of which is the Federation of Danish Trade Unions, where membership has grown from almost 800,000 in 1960 to more than 1,400,000 in 1989. However, since this growth reflects the sheer growth in the size of the labour force, the strong tradition of union membership in Denmark (some 80 per cent of wage-earners are organized in trade unions), and the fact that labour market legislation and the regulation of unemployment insurance often require workers to take up membership of a trade union, it should not be read as reflecting an increase in support for the SD as such. Indeed, for many Danish wage-earners, membership of a trade union is seen more as an obligation than as a manifestation of party politics, and within the trade union movement itself there has been quite a marked growth in the number of members who oppose the provision of union financial support for the SD. Partly as a result of this, and partly also as a result of strong pressure from the bourgeois parties, especially the RV, a new law was passed in 1990 which emphasized the voluntary character of the relationship between party, union and member, and which introduced a contracting-out mechanism. Under this new legislation, members of an organization are given the right to be exempted from collective donations to parties, and thus individual trade union members may now simply sign a written statement which exempts them from any political subscription (Pedersen and Bille, 1991). While the SD's affiliated membership may therefore have grown, this does not necessarily indicate a strengthening of the party's position on the ground.

The role of the individual party members

The dramatic erosion of the membership organizations in Denmark clearly also raises the question of whether individual membership has become marginalized or perhaps even obsolete within the internal decision-making processes of the parties, as, for example, might be seen in changes in the patterns of representation in the leading bodies of the parties, such as the national conference, the party congress, and the national executive. Here again a useful distinction can be made between the four old parties (SD, RV, V, KF), on the one hand, and the four new parties (SF, KRF, FRP, CD), on the other, a distinction which allows us to see whether the latter have created, or at least have tried to create, modes of representation and functions that differ in any substantial way from the style established by the former.

The highest authority in the membership parties of the RV, V and KF is the annual national conference. In the RV, representation of the individual members at the conference in terms of voting rights is based purely on the number of party members in the constituency organization, with higher numbers guaranteeing more delegates, although in 1970 all members of the party were given the right to attend and to speak at conference. The number of party members in the constituency organization also determines the allocation of delegates in the V (the chairmen of the board of the constituency organizations are ex-officio delegates). In the case of both parties, however, the decline in the overall numbers of members has forced a reduction in the limits for sending delegates: from one delegate for every 75 members in 1962 to one for every 50 members in 1966 (RV), and from one for every 500 members in 1965 to one for every 300 members in 1980 (V). In both parties the delegates are elected by the party members at constituency meetings. A different principle is applied in the case of the KF, where each local branch is entitled to send one delegate for every 1000 votes cast for the party in the local district in the last general election. The delegates are elected by the members at a local branch meeting. In all three parties the members are represented in the party decision-making bodies as individuals and also vote as individuals.

The highest authority in the SD is the party congress, convened every four years. In 1961 each constituency organization could send one delegate for every 1000 party members in the constituency organization, the delegates being elected at a constituency meeting of delegates from the local branches. This was changed in 1977, when the local branch (one step down in the hierarchy) was given the right to send its own delegates: local branches with more than 1000 members were allocated three delegates, those with more than 500 members were allocated two delegates and those with more than 100 members were allocated one delegate – local branches with less than 100 members being allowed to pool their numbers and gain the right to send delegates according to the same formula. Constituencies with only one local branch were entitled to send two delegates, who were elected at general meetings in the local branches. All delegates vote as individuals in the party's decision-making organs.

As far as the representation of the individual members in the highest organ of the four old parties is concerned, the changes of the party rules all point in the direction of either maintaining or even increasing the level of representation. All four parties have adjusted their rules to take account of smaller membership levels as well as to ensure that all regions of the country are entitled to send at least one delegate regardless of how small the regional/local organization might be. This adaptation to the changing membership situation can be seen as a deliberate, but seemingly fruitless, effort to maintain the image and the position of the parties as representative bodies.

Since there is no corporate membership in Denmark and since ancillary membership has not been particularly widespread since the 1950s, the only remaining question in this regard concerns the representation of affiliated organizations. In general, however, representation of such organizations is highly marginal with respect to the number of delegates elected by the individual members. The party with the largest representation of affiliated organizations at the level of the national conference is the SD, while the RV has never actually maintained this sort of representation, being always proud to claim its independence of any organized interests. The SD, on the other hand, has always emphasized the need to have representation from the various branches of the labour movement, such as the trade unions, the cooperative federations, the cultural associations and so on.

The importance of the affiliated organizations in the SD increases markedly when we move from the party congress to the level of the party's national executive. The members of the executive bodies (national committee [*hovedbestyrelse*] and national executive [*forretningsudvalg*]) are partly elected by lower party bodies and are partly appointed ex officio by the affiliated organizations, with the proportion of representatives from the affiliated organizations being originally much higher in these bodies than was the case in the party congress. Since 1960, however, the representation of the affiliated organizations has been reduced and that of the individual members has been increased. In 1961, for example, the composition of the national executive was balanced between the two types of membership on a roughly fifty–fifty basis; in 1990, by contrast, affiliated representation had been reduced to about one-third. The remaining three old parties (RV, V, KF) afford hardly any formal role to affiliated organizations. Each provides for the representation of their respective youth organization, and the KF also provides for separate representation of Conservative Women in the national committee and the national council (but not in the national conference), while the V abolished such representation in the mid-1960s. Moreover, while there are no formal links between these parties and any occupational or professional organizations, there has nevertheless always been a close connection between the V and the various powerful agricultural and farmers' organizations, as well as between the KF and the employers' and business organizations. If we take the overall picture, then, we clearly cannot see any real evidence of these parties marginalizing their individual members. Indeed, in terms of the rules adopted by the four old parties, any changes actually point more in the opposite direction.

The modes of representation in the four new parties (SF, KRF, FRP, CD) are by and large similar to those of the old parties. In both the SF and the CD, the number of delegates to the national conference has been based on the number of members of the local branches throughout the period. In the KRF and the FRP, the number of delegates has been based on the number of votes cast for the party in the regional and local districts respectively. While the SF and the KRF have built a traditional 'Danish' organizational structure, that is, a relatively simple, territorially-defined, pyramidal organization, the CD and the FRP have in some respects deviated from this model. The basic territorial structure of the CD is similar to the other Danish parties, but the party has laid more stress on the separation of the membership party and the parliamentary party, and the rules explicitly state that the members have no say whatsoever regarding the policy of the parliamentary party. The MPs are free to consult the members, but the MPs alone make the decisions. There is no such explicit formal stipulation in the rules of the other parties.

The organizational build-up of the FRP has been heavily influenced by the party founder, Mogens Glistrup. It was not his original intention to form a traditional political party, but instead to create what he labelled a 'Progress Movement'. The overwhelming majority of the delegates to the inaugural conference of the party were invited by Glistrup personally, and there was some internal dispute and organizational confusion in the following years before the party finally adopted a basic structure similar to the other Danish parties. Since 1976 the rules stipulate that the number of delegates to the national conference is based on the number of votes cast for the party in the local district. But the rules also allowed Glistrup to maintain full control over the conference due to the (in a Danish context unique) prerogative enjoyed by the National Committee (*Hovedbestyrek-sen*) – of which Glistrup became a lifetime honorary voting member (this is also unique) and which he controlled completely – to fill any vacant delegate post from the regional or local branches. After some years of constant internal dispute Glistrup was expelled from the party in 1991, and apart from the continuing strong position of the National Committee, the FRP now no longer differs in any substantial way from other Danish parties regarding the representation of the individual members in the leading party bodies.

Other than through their respective youth organizations, which are small, none of the four new parties has any formal connections to affiliated organizations. Representation of the individual members in the leading party bodies, on the other hand, proved very important at the time of their foundation, and has remained so ever since. In this sense also, there is no (formal) evidence to suggest that individual membership has become marginalized.

A similar conclusion can be reached regarding the *functions* of the leading bodies. The national conference (the party congress in the SD) of the parties is and has always been the highest authority, and this means that it decides on changes of the party rules; it adopts the party manifesto; it determines the membership subscription (or the proportion of the dues to be sent from the local branches to the central party); and it elects the party chairman and a number of representatives to the various national executive bodies. None of these functions has been withdrawn or limited over the past thirty years.

That said, we can note one interesting change in procedures when we take a closer look at the *issuing of a new manifesto*. Up to the beginning of the 1960s, the normal procedure was that the national conference appointed a manifesto committee which prepared a proposal to be presented to the conference. This committee more or less worked out the proposal on its own. By the end of the 1960s, however, the procedure had changed to one in which the committee prepared a proposal, and this first draft was then sent to the local branches for discussion among the members and for possible amendment. On the basis of these responses, the committee then decided on a final proposal, which was circulated once more among the members before the final presentation and decision at the national conference. In this sense, the potential influence of the individual members had been increased.

The real influence of the national conference is somewhat more difficult to determine when it comes to *the election of the party chairman*. Formally speaking, the position is clear: the national conference elects the chairman of the national party organization. The question, however, is whether there is a real choice, and in general there is not. The normal procedure has been that the inner circle of the party conducts informal negotiations with various influential persons and party bodies with the purpose of finding one and only one candidate to be presented to the national conference. This leaves very little room for the representatives of the individual party members to exercise any influence. That said, there are nevertheless substantial examples to the contrary. In 1965, following strong opposition among the chairmen of the local and regional party branches to his proposal to merge with the KF, the chairman of the V retired. A similar example of the influence of quite a number of leading party members can be seen in the final outcome of the conflict in the KF in the first half of the 1970s concerning the election of a new party chairman. In 1991, the election of a new chairman of the SF took place at the national conference as an open contest between two candidates. The most recent and indeed historical example was the contested election of the new chairman of the SD at an extraordinary party congress in 1992. On this occasion, the influence of the delegates of the individual party members, contrary to what is traditionally the case in such matters in the SD, proved very strong, in that a majority of the local branch elected their delegates precisely on the basis of the support pledged to a particular candidate.

The real influence of the individual members on the election of the party chairman has never been marked, however. Despite the prerogative of the national conference to elect the chairman, the decision traditionally has been made by a narrow party circle. But since the rules have not changed in this respect, and since very recent developments in two of the parties (the SF and the SD) indicate an increasing influence on the election of the party chairman, it would be wrong to conclude that the individual members have been marginalized. Indeed, it is possible to argue that a trend in the opposite direction is actually apparent.

The *selection of candidates for national elections* is of crucial importance to any party (Sjöblom, 1968: 126). Given the importance of this process, and the obvious and numerous possibilities for internal conflicts, it seems reasonable to assume that it will be regulated explicitly and in detail. The question of who controls this process is therefore a central criterion in characterizing the party organization and in evaluating the importance of the individual party members (Bille, 1993).

Generally speaking, the individual member has always played an important and decisive role in the selection of candidates. At the beginning of the 1960s, their influence was exercised mainly at general local and regional meetings which were open to all members with the right to vote. The boards of the local/regional branches have always defended this prerogative from direct interference or orders from the central party, with candidate selection being considered as an indicator of their autonomy. Indirectly, however, the central and local levels have always collaborated in the nomination of leading or promising politicians in safe constituencies, not least because of an obvious mutual interest in ensuring that a candidate be elected and that a 'local' person win through to parliament. It is therefore difficult to distinguish situations in which the local organization has more or less been forced by the central party to nominate a specific candidate from those in which it sees its own interest in accepting a candidate proposed by the central office. Moreover, controversies of this kind rarely emerge before the public gaze.

By 1990, three of the parties (the SD in 1969, the CD in 1974 and the SF in 1976) had introduced a membership ballot for those situations in which more than one person would be proposed at the nomination meeting. In 1973, one party, the V, had also introduced an optional ballot. All of these changes have clearly increased the role played by individual members in the nomination process, especially insofar as these ballots may be cast without necessarily requiring attendance at a party meeting. In addition, none of the parties has adopted measures which might increase the formal role of the central party in the nomination process. Indeed, the role of the central party has remained effectively unchanged over the past thirty years, which means that in four parties (SF, SD, KRF, FRP) the national committee has to approve the list of nominees or the candidates actually nominated. In the remaining parties, the national bodies have no direct role, but do have the right to comment on the list, to propose changes or to be present at a nomination meeting in the local/regional organization.

The selection of candidates for national elections has always been largely a matter for the party members at the constituency/regional level and has increasingly become so, a development which is particularly interesting given the tremendous decline in membership levels. This decline was especially marked in the period from the mid-1960s to the mid-1970s, and it was precisely in this period that some of the parties changed their rules from a process of nomination at a membership meeting to a process of nomination via a membership ballot. It is therefore tempting to suggest that the increased role assigned to the individual member can be seen as an attempt to counteract the decline in membership levels per se. If this was the case, however, then it proved unsuccessful, in that the decline has continued, albeit on a much smaller scale.

The financial importance of the party members and the role of
state subventions

One of the main incentives for the development of mass membership party organizations was of course the need to have a stable source of income in the form of the membership subscriptions. As such, we can anticipate that the marked fall in the membership of the four old parties and the low level of membership of the new parties have had an impact on the structure of their revenues. The parties must either adjust their activities to the falling level of income, raise the dues to compensate for the shrinking number of members or seek other sources of income, with the latter being tantamount to saying that the role of the membership in financing the party has been reduced.

The decentralized structure of the Danish party organizations is reflected in the modes of collecting the membership subscription. In the FRP, the KF, the RV and the V, the level of fees paid by the members to the local branch is fixed locally, and therefore varies from area to area, while the national conference determines the amount to be paid by the local branches to the central party. This latter transfer depends on the number of members in the local branch. In the CD, the KRF and the SF, the subscription, fixed by the national conference, is the same for all members and is paid directly to the central party by each member. The central party then refunds a fraction of the sum to the local branches. This is also the case for the SD, except that the payment by the members is to the local branch, which then transfers a fixed amount per member to the central party. The level of the subscription also varies from party to party, and even from branch to branch within the same party, but in general is very modest. At the beginning of the 1960s the annual subscription in the SF was DKR 30 and in the SD DKR 14, and the amount to be paid (per member) by the local branch to the central party was DKR 2 in the V and just DKR 1 in the KF. In 1989 the annual dues had been increased to DKR 180–540 (depending on the income of the individual member) in the SF, DKR 248 in the SD, DKR 55 in the V and DKR 36 in the KF. Given the length of the period, this was a very moderate increase, and certainly any increasing economic strain on the family budget caused by the party fee cannot be cited as the explanation for declining membership levels. Indeed, one of the reasons for the modest rise of the subscriptions was the fear that a drastic increase might accelerate the exodus from the parties and thereby create a vicious circle. The shrinking income of the party organizations therefore had to be compensated for by creating a new source of income, which took the form of state subventions.

The Danish parties have always considered themselves as private, and financially autonomous, organizations, fully independent of the state. As a result, they were long-term opponents of direct public subsidies. Over time, however, this attitude has changed. In 1965 a law was passed granting a modest amount of money (a total of DKR 60,000) to the parliamentary parties in order to hire consultants and expert assistance. The sum was allocated to the parties according to their relative size in parliament. Formally, the grants were provided only for use by the members of parliament, but in real terms the grant was a supplement to party finances taken as a whole. The amounts involved were constantly augmented over the next decades and the rules were gradually changed, as, for example, when MPs were allowed to employ their own secretaries.

A law granting state subvention to the political parties' organizations as such was passed only in 1986. The law imposes no organizational requirements whatsoever; rather, it is simply the number of votes that counts, and nothing else, and even a single person participating on his or her own in a national, regional (county) or local (municipal) election is entitled to receive an annual sum of money from the state, the size of which depends on the number of votes received at the specific election. The rules regulating the state subvention are indeed very simple. Every year, the national organization of the party receives DKR 5 for each vote cast for the party in the last general election; the regional organizations receive DKR 2 for each vote received in the last regional election; and the local organizations receive DKR 3 for each vote received in the last local election. It is worth noting that by granting separate subventions to the national, regional and local organizations, the law may sustain a development towards an increasing decentralization of the entire party organization. Given that the rules have been in effect only from the fiscal year of 1987 onwards, however, it is too early to draw any hard and fast conclusions. What is clear, nevertheless, is that the Danish parties have granted themselves an enormous increase in their annual incomes. The amount of direct public subsidy to the parliamentary parties plus the national party organizations has increased from a total of DKR 57,262 in 1965, to DKR 8.3 million in 1980, and to DKR 72.4 million in 1990, and it is difficult, if not impossible, to find other parts of the Danish public sector which have experienced a similar growth in the 1980s. This does not imply that the parties have become 'wealthy' organizations, however. Indeed, compared to many of the Danish interest organizations, for example, the parties are still financial dwarfs, with the total 1990 'peacetime' budget of the KF (around DKR 8 million) being no bigger than the Federation of the Danish Industries' travel budget alone.[3]

To be sure, the introduction of public subvention has had an impact on the relative distribution of the income sources of the individual parties. It is difficult to establish the exact income profile of the Danish parties, however; party finance is an extremely complex and intricate area to investigate, and the Danish case is by no means an exception. Moreover, because of the traditional conception of parties as private organizations, contributions to the parties have been regarded as of no concern to the general public, and for a long time no rules were enacted to force the publication of party accounts. Thus, for example, neither the KF nor the V has ever published its accounts; in addition, there are wide variations in the accounting principles and periods used by those parties that do publish their accounts. The result is that any attempt to make comparisons between the parties or over time even in the same party is highly problematic. Indeed, it was only in late 1989, following prolonged pressure, especially from the RV, that a law was passed forcing the parties to publish their accounts. The new rules came into effect on 1 January 1991, and required all parties nominating candidates for general or European Parliament elections to deliver to the authorities an annual account of their finances, in which they provide information about various types of income: public subvention, membership subscription, private donations, interest and contributions from international organizations, collective private organizations, trade unions, occupational organizations, private enterprises, foundations and associations in general (Pedersen and Bille, 1991: 165).

Because of these difficulties, the discussion which follows should be taken primarily as illustrative of a trend, which takes the income profiles of the SD and the CD as examples representing two extremes: the SD with the largest organization, the CD with by far the smallest. Even with this qualification, however, the trend is clear and unambiguous. The financial importance of the individual members has decreased drastically and the importance of direct state subvention has increased correspondingly. The heavy dependence of the SD on transfers from the trade unions, especially in election years (between 41 and 67 per cent), cannot be taken as income generated from the membership because far from all the members of the trade unions are members of the party or even vote for the party. Yet even this party, with the largest organization and the highest membership figures, collects well over 40 per cent of its income from the public purse and barely 20 per cent from its members. The rest stems from the continuous willingness of the trade unions to transfer money to the party, and with the introduction of a contracting-out mechanism, the SD risks becoming even more dependent on state subsidies. This is hardly the prospect of the CD, on the other hand, since around 90 per cent of the party's income already originates from the state, and certainly from a financial point of view, the members of the CD are of no importance whatsoever.

Together with the dramatic decline in the number of party members, this particular development in the pattern of party financing (which is of course closely connected to the declining membership levels) is definitely the most impressive and decisive change which has occurred on the membership side of the Danish political parties since 1960. But while this suggests that members have indeed become marginalized, and perhaps even superfluous, any such conclusion would be far too exaggerated. Indeed, as has been seen, the rule changes adopted by the parties actually point in the opposite direction, with a strengthening of the position of the individual members in the leading party bodies. Nor have the functions of these bodies been altered. The opportunities available to individual members to influence the drafting of the party manifesto have increased, as has apparently their influence on the election of the party chairman. And, most importantly, their influence on and control over the process of candidate selection has been markedly increased.

This leaves us with a split conclusion, which in itself is illustrative of the painful dilemma facing the Danish parties. What is most important to the party: members, who imply representativeness and legitimacy, or voters, who mean money and seats? Without members there is no crew to run the machinery; without money there is no fuel to run the machinery. The actual development indicates that the parties have arrived at, or, more correctly, have been forced by circumstances to arrive at the conclusion that, in the end, votes count more than members.

The parliamentary party and the party leadership

The formal separation of the membership party and the parliamentary party, deriving from provisions in the Constitution, has the effect that the membership party is not formally represented in the executive bodies of the parliamentary party. Each parliamentary party elects a board at the beginning of each parliamentary session. This board chairs the political discussion at the group meetings, decides on the allocation of spokesmen for the various issues, appoints MPs as members of the standing committees of the parliament, and takes care of the financial resources of the group as well as the daily red tape.

The linkage between the parliamentary party and the membership party takes place through the representation of the former in the executive bodies of the latter and in most of the more or less permanent committees set up by the party. The degree of formal representation of the parliamentary party in the bodies of the membership party varies greatly from party to party, however. The RV is at one end of the spectrum, with a set of rules which have been in effect since 1966 and which do not stipulate any representation of the MPs in the national conference. All delegates are elected by the members. Moreover, only five of around 100 members in the party's national committee can be MPs, and these are elected by the National Conference, rather than by the parliamentary group. Finally, there has been no representation of MPs in the thirteen-member national executive since 1981. At the other end of the spectrum is the V, in which all MPs are included with the right to vote in the national conference and in which the chairman and vice-chairman of the parliamentary party plus an additional three MPs elected by the parliamentary group are members of the *c.* 75-member national committee. From a formal point of view, then, the representation of the parliamentary party in the executive organs of the membership party is relatively modest compared to that of the individual members. Indeed, the rule changes put in motion during the past thirty years even indicate a minor reduction in the number of the MPs in the membership party.

It follows, therefore, that the position of primacy which the parliamentary parties have always enjoyed within the Danish parties is not the result of any formalized pattern of representation. There are, in fact, several reasons for this. One is that the national organizations were primarily created as instruments for the mobilization of supporters and as means of raising money, while the obligations of the parliamentary party were to voice the interests of supporters and voters in parliament and in government. Moreover, because no single party has had a majority in parliament since the beginning of the century, agreements have always required ongoing negotiations and compromise, and in this daily political process it proved impossible for the parliamentary parties to take orders from, or even to consult, the national organizations. The MPs had to act autonomously, albeit, one assumes, on the basis of the principles of the party manifesto and within the broad guidelines set up by the national organization. Indeed, it soon became the rule that the national committee was given a briefing after an agreement was reached rather than being consulted on a prior basis. Normally, it was only in times of cabinet formation or cabinet crisis that the national executives were convened before a decision was reached. The leading role of the parliamentary party was further sustained by the increased fractionalization of *Folketinget* in the wake of the 1973 election. It then became even less possible for the national party organization to catch up with the volatile situation in which some eight to eleven parties were represented in parliament, in which a general election was held almost every two years, and in which there existed a very complex and turbulent pattern of inter-party cooperation, requiring the support of several parties to form a majority, and so on.

National politics, then, has always been carried out by the parliamentary parties without any significant interference from the national party organizations, and this has increasingly been the case during the last few decades. The constant focus by the mass media on the activities of the leading politicians in parliament has further fostered this development. But it is not only the demands of daily politics and the attention of the mass media that have promoted the leading position of the parliamentary party. Rather, there are also two additional components which must be taken into account: finance and staffing.

The financial autonomy and strength of the parliamentary party has improved considerably since 1965. Prior to 1965 no financial resources were at the disposal of the MPs, who had to rely on the bureaucracy of *Folketinget* and on the manpower of the national party organization. In 1965, however, as noted above, the principle of state subsidy to the parliamentary groups, distributed among the groups according to their relative size, was introduced, and in 1981 the scheme was enlarged to encompass secretarial assistance for individual MPs. Together with the extensive increase in the amount actually involved in the schemes during the 1980s, the state subsidy to the parliamentary party has become a major and indeed decisive financial resource to the party as a whole. For despite the fact that this subsidy was designed only for the use of MPs, in practice it is considered, and used, as income for the party as such. The central party headquarters of the SF, the FRP and the RV, for example, are located in *Folketinget*, and it is quite impossible to distinguish between money spent by the headquarters and money spent by the parliamentary groups, or to know whether the work done by the staff is for the benefit of the parliamentary group or the national party. Finally, when we also consider that the more recent and increasingly significant direct state subsidy to the central party organization depends on the number of votes cast for the party, and when we take account of the decisive role played by the parliamentary party in winning support from the electorate, it then becomes abundantly clear that the position of the parliamentary party has been considerably enhanced.

This situation is further reflected in the staffing of the parties. The staff often work for both sections of the party, so it is very difficult to give a precise estimate of the manpower engaged by the central party and by the parliamentary party respectively. Nonetheless, practically the entire increase of staff that has taken place has occurred within the organization of the parliamentary party. The main part of that increase resulted from the 1986 increase in the state subsidy which enabled each individual MP to employ a (part-time) personal secretary. At the same time, however, the larger parliamentary parties at least have also spent quite a substantial share of the subsidy in order to build up professional political-economic departments and press agencies. The most conspicuous example of this is the expansion of the secretariat of the SD group. As late as 1980 only five persons, purely clerical staff, were employed in the SD secretariat. In 1989, however, the staff had grown to twenty-three, of whom four were journalists and three were academics (Buksti, 1989). The functions of the secretariat also shifted during the 1980s, growing from an ordinary clerical service for the group to encompass a more analytical and policy role, an important purpose of which was to improve the quality as well as the quantity of party information communicated to the mass media and to the public in general. Moreover, the leadership of this secretariat has also played an increasingly important role in internal party decision-making. A development along the same line has taken place in the other parties' parliamentary groups, albeit not on the same scale as within the SD, and albeit definitely most modest in the small parties. Nonetheless, the trend towards increasing professionalization of the parliamentary parties is unmistakable, and stands in sharp contrast to the stagnation or in some cases even decrease in the staff of the membership organization.

Given these developments, it is hardly surprising to find that the real political leadership of the parties has always rested with the parliamentary party, and that this is even more the case in 1990 than it was in 1960. This situation is also a result of the way in which the leadership of the party is elected. In three of the four old parties (SD, KF and V), the same person traditionally has been chairman of the national party organization and party leader in parliament. His or her legitimacy then rested both on election by the party members and election by the MPs (who owed their legitimacy to the party voters). The position of the party leader in these three parties was, and remains, a strong one. This is also largely the case in the RV, even though the two posts are held by different persons. Real conflicts between the two levels have nevertheless been rare; while discussions and disputes have occurred more often, it is the opinion of the parliamentary party which has prevailed.

This was certainly not the case in the SF in the mid-1960s. One intention in founding the party in 1959 was to create a party characterized by extensive internal party democracy, which would allow a comprehensive influence by the members regarding the policy to be pursued by the party. In 1967 a majority in the national organization attempted to dictate the policy of the parliamentary group, and a severe conflict developed, involving, among many other issues, the fundamental question as to who had the right to determine party policy: the members of the national committee, who were elected by 8000 party members, or the parliamentary group, which was elected by 300,000 voters. The conflict ended with a split and the left wing of the SF founded a new party, the Left Socialists. Meanwhile, the SF adopted a provision in the party rules which stipulates that the parliamentary group may not enter into any major compromise with other parties in parliament without the prior consent of the national committee. This provision is unique in Denmark and gives the national organization a greater influence than is normally the case in the other parties. Even allowing for this, however, no major controversies have arisen between the two levels in the past decade, mainly because a stable understanding has been established between the chairman of the national party organization, also an MP and the de facto leader of the party, and the chairman of the parliamentary group. In the SF also, then, it appears that the trend has gone in the direction of a strengthening of the position of the parliamentary party, although it is not yet a stable trend.

In one of the other new parties, the KRF, founded in 1971, there also developed a situation which was similar in some respects to that of the SF, although in this case the national organization has never possessed the same formal power as in the SF. Following some turbulence in its formative years, the party eventually settled into a relatively traditional arrangement in which the leader of the national organization, elected by the national conference, was also the party leader in parliament. In the late 1980s, however, the national organization gained some ground, ending with a separation of the posts of chairman of the national party and parliamentary leader. And while it is premature to assess the consequences of this arrangement, it nevertheless might be symptomatic that the party experienced a serious rift over what it should recommend to the voters prior to the Danish referendum on the Maastricht Treaty in June 1992.

The case is more clear-cut in the two youngest parties, the CD and the FRP. Regardless of any formal rules, the undisputed leader of the FRP was its founder, Mogens Glistrup, and although the party gradually built a national organization headed by an elected chairman, and although the parliamentary party elected its own chairman, the true leader nevertheless remained the charismatic 'campaign leader', a title Glistrup had created for himself. During his three years' imprisonment for tax fraud, a new charismatic leader took over. Apart from being spokesman for the parliamentary group, her leadership was similarly unattached to any formal position in the party organization. Constant turmoil and conflict of a personal character has plagued the party for most of its lifetime, but with the final expulsion of Mogens Glistrup in 1991 the party seems to have settled with a weak national organization, a powerful national committee and a clearly predominant parliamentary party. Right from the founding of the CD in 1973 it was determined that the parliamentary party should play the leading role, and it was explicitly stipulated in the party rules that the MPs should be completely independent of the national organization. The party's organization is relatively complex, having for example a chairman of the national party, another chairman of the parliamentary group, and yet another chairman of the party per se. The last, elected by the national conference on the recommendation of the parliamentary party, is the de facto leader of the party. The overwhelming predominance of the parliamentary party has never been disputed, partly thanks to the authority of yet another charismatic 'founding father', Erhard Jacobsen, as well as that of his daughter, Mimi Jacobsen, who succeeded him as party leader in 1989.

In the end, then, while the 'official story' may tell us that there exists a formal separation of the membership party and the parliamentary party, the reality is that the two sub-systems are politically intertwined. The decisive influence of the parliamentary party on the policies of the party as well as on the major internal party issues was already evident in 1960. The predominance by the parliamentary party has increased even more since then, especially during the 1980s, due to the increased fractionalization in parliament, the complex pattern of inter-party cooperation, and the constant focus of the mass media on the activities of the MPs. Most crucial of all, however, has been the impact of the constantly increasing state subsidy, which has given the parliamentary party financial autonomy and the opportunity to expand and to professionalize its staff.

From partyness of society to partyness of state?

The formation of the four old political parties must be viewed in close connection with the general development of society during the second half of the nineteenth century. The various liberal elements merged into the Venstre, which became the leading party in the struggle for a democratic constitution, for equal and universal suffrage, and for parliamentary democracy. Simultaneously, the farmers emerged as an independent and strong social class, and through the founding of cooperative societies, and the education provided by the newly established popular high schools, they gradually obtained economic strength and organizational experience as well as political and cultural self-confidence. This also manifested itself in the growth of the Venstre. Venstre was the party of the farmers, and an almost complete overlap existed between the officials of the various agricultural organizations, the private associations formed in the country-side, and the party organization. In the period before the Second World War, Venstre had a clearly dominating position in the countryside. The splinter party from Venstre, on the other hand, Det radikale Venstre, was the party of the smallholders (together with intellectuals and minor tradesmen in the cities – indeed a peculiar mix) and in some local areas it held as strong a position as Venstre. In the cities the Social Democrats became the predominant party of the workers. At the same time, the workers also founded trade unions and cooperative firms, and thus the labour movement in Denmark was composed of the party, the trade union and the cooperative organization, all of which were organizationally connected. With time, the social democratic movement created a huge organizational network that was able to meet almost every human need from birth to death (Pedersen, 1989: 271). The conservatives, which began as Højre, were initially dominated by the landowners, but as a conse-quence of the increasing industrialization and urbanization this group lost its influence in the party to the new class of entrepreneurs. In 1915 the party issued a new programme, stressing general conservative attitudes appealing to business interests, middle-class values and national defence.

Prior to 1960, therefore, the situation was one in which the four old parties had more or less 'divided' the electorate between them. All were based on relatively distinct segments of society, and the parties played an important role in the various activities of society. This situation began to change around the end of the 1950s, however, when extensive social-structural changes resulted from the economic boom of the 1960s and the formation of the welfare state. The number of farmers decreased rapidly, the number of blue-collar workers stagnated and even decreased slightly, while the number of employees in the service sector increased, as did, most crucially, the number of civil servants. Living conditions for the average voter also improved considerably, and these almost revolutionary changes gradually loosened the traditional bond between party and social group. The electorate became more volatile and schisms between the parties and their 'friendly' interest groups occurred more often, most conspicuously within the labour movement. The result was that the four old parties lost their firm grip on their traditional constituencies. None of the new parties has been able to take their place. Nor has any managed to create any stable associations with specific organizations or groups in society in any way comparable to the comprehensive networks which had been formed by the old parties. Rather, there flourished a variety of single-issue movements and grassroots organizations, many of which had a left-wing orientation but rarely a definite party affiliation. In this sense, there was a gradual decline in the 'partyness' of Danish society.

Developments in the mass media reinforced this process. Prior to the 1960s, each region or major city had four daily newspapers, each of which was either owned by or affiliated to one of the four old parties. As Pedersen (1987: 38) has noted:

> Ties with the local party organizations were mostly close, and the existence of syndicates and other channels of centre–periphery dissemination of policy views and news made it possible for each party to bring out in public its specific message. So they did; party activists, members, and partisan loyals tended to read 'their own' paper which provided them with the local as well as the national party line . . . In many cases the editor was serving as member of parliament or of the municipal council.

Furthermore, the editors of the party press were formally represented in the executive organs of the parties. After the Second World War, and especially after 1960, this 'four-paper system' gradually disappeared, and a process of attrition and amalgamation has reduced the number of newspapers from 123 in 1945 to only 44 at present (Thomsen, 1987). Moreover, the remaining newspapers are no longer 'party papers': their readers vote for different parties, and the newspapers simply cannot afford to annoy their customers by promoting specific party messages. This has left the parties without one of their important channels of communication and hence without the ability to inform the electorate on their own terms.

The introduction of television in Denmark, which took place at the end of the 1950s, failed to compensate for the loss of the control over the newspapers. Until the beginning of the 1980s, Danmarks Radio had enjoyed a legal monopoly to broadcast radio and television in Denmark, and the station was headed by a board on which the parties were represented in proportion to their seats in parliament. Since then, however, the establishment of local radio and television stations has been permitted, and in 1988–89 a second nationwide television channel was set up on a semi-commercial basis. The present broadcasting law stipulates that commercials containing political propaganda are forbidden and that the programme policy of the nationwide television networks shall be characterized by comprehensiveness and fairness (Siune, 1982). A special set of rules is now adopted by Danmarks Radio at the outset of every general election. Any programme with even the slightest affiliation to politics is cancelled, and no politicians can participate in any programme other than those directly connected to the election campaign or to the broadcasting of news. Each party participating in the election – new or old, small or big, incumbent or in opposition – gets exactly the same amount of time to present its platform, and each party produces its own programme of a maximum of 10 minutes' duration. These programmes are subsidized by Danmarks Radio, with the same amount of money being given to all parties, but with the individual party being free to spend more should it choose to do so. The programme is shown in prime time and is immediately followed by a 30-minute programme in which three politicians chosen by the party are 'cross-examined' by two station journalists. Two days before the election, the campaign on Danmarks Radio ends with a debate among the leaders of all the competing parties (Bille, 1991). From the perspective of the political parties, television offers an important and much used channel of communication to the wider public; as against this, however, they do not control the medium and their messages are selected and edited by the journalists. Thus it is only during an election campaign that the parties have the opportunity to communicate on their own terms via television, and even then only to a very limited extent.

More generally, the planning, strategy, control and implementation of election campaigns is taken care of by a narrow circle of leading politicians and party officials. These decide on the party's main campaign themes, on nationwide advertising in the newspapers, and on the general strategy to be pursued. They sanction the material produced by headquarters as background information for the candidates, including information on the party's standpoints and 'results'. They also decide who will represent the party at the daily press conferences, and in the radio and television broadcasts. The campaign is therefore quite centralized, and this group constitutes its key element. The formal influence of the national executive bodies of the party is mainly confined to a confirmation of the plans prepared by the party leadership. The use of 'outside' expertise is modest; with a general election every two years, the party bureaucrats consider themselves to be the real experts. But there is also a decentralized element, with the individual candidate being free to choose the type or style of campaign that he or she thinks best for local conditions. Indeed, within the general and rather broad framework of the party's centrally determined campaign strategy and themes, there is a high degree of local self-determination and local variation, with much depending on the activity and commitment of local activists. The voluntary work carried out by the rank and file of the party organization therefore still constitutes a very important element in election campaigns.

Finally, while there is substantial evidence to suggest that the partyness of society has declined since 1960, there are also equally good reasons to claim that the partyness of the state has remained unchanged, or even increased. The parties continue to have a de facto monopoly on the election of candidates for parliament, and no independent candidate has been elected to parliament in the past thirty years. Recruitment to the political elite also continues to operate through the party organizations, although examples of rapid political careers on the part of, say, popular media personalities, have become more frequent. Moreover, it is still the parties that are held accountable for public policy. They still form and control the government and the state bureaucracy, although alarm bells are sometimes sounded concerning the inability of the parties to supervise and check the huge apparatus of the welfare state, and concerning the increased influence of powerful interest organizations on public decision-making. Even the existence of a large public sector could be read as indicating a growth in the partyness of the state, in that it is the parties which make the final decisions, and in that these decisions affect a larger proportion of society than ever before. In the end, then, while assessments of the degree of the partyness of society and the partyness of state are often somewhat impressionistic (Sjöblom, 1987), the evidence here suggests an image of parties which have tended to become rather less part of society, and rather more part of the state.

Concluding remarks

The parties in Denmark have been obliged to deal with strong demographic and socio-economic trends, and in the process they have lost their relatively undisputed position as the prime organizing political force in society. In 1990, only 6 per cent of the electorate were party members, and this implies that only some 2 or 3 per cent of the electorate is deciding on such vital issues as candidate selection, party programmes, the election of party leaders and executive bodies, and so on. When only such a minimal fraction of the population participates in the internal party political process, then there is clearly a deterioration of the parties' traditional linkage function. This further implies that the parties face serious problems in maintaining their representativeness and even their legitimacy. Concurrently, there is a decline in the capacity of the membership organization both to grasp and express popular sentiment, and hence the 'hold' of the parties on the electorate has also been eroded. Thus although the parties have tried to adapt to changing conditions without giving up their mass party structures, current trends suggest that, with time, they will be financed entirely by the state and will effectively be run only by the leadership of the parliamentary fraktions. Communication with the electorate and with society as a whole will take place through the mass media and, with voters counting for more than members, the internal party channels will eventually be downgraded.

Notes

1 Although the KF was exceptional in registering a membership increase in the 1960s, it also witnessed the sharpest decrease of all the parties in the 1970s.

2 This overall ratio of 6 per cent is somewhat smaller than that reported in the findings of electoral surveys (see Togeby, 1992).

3 Information given by the general secretary of KF, John Wagner.

References

Bille, Lars (1991) 'The 1988 election campaign in Denmark', *Scandinavian Political Studies*, 14 (3): 250–18.

Bille, Lars (1992) 'Denmark', in Richard S. Katz and Peter Mair (eds), *Party Organizations: A Data Handbook on Party Organizations in Western Democracies, 1960–90*. London: Sage, pp. 199–272.

Bille, Lars (1993) 'Candidate selection for national parliament in Denmark 1960–1990: an analysis of party rules', in Tom Bryder (ed.), *Party Systems, Party Behaviour and Democracy*. Copenhagen: Copenhagen Political Studies Press, pp. 190–204.

Buksti, Jacob A. (1989) 'Partiapparaternes rolle og udvikling', *Politica*, 3: 000–00.

Elklit, Jørgen and Pade, Anne Birte (1991) *Election Administration in Denmark*. Copenhagen, Ministry of Interior.

Panebianco, Angelo (1988) *Political Parties: Organization and Power*. Cambridge: Cambridge University Press.

Pedersen, Mogens N. (1987) 'The Danish "working multiparty system": breakdown or adaptation?' in Hans Daalder (ed.), *Party Systems in Denmark, Austria, Switzerland, The Netherlands and Belgium*. London: Francis Pinter, pp.1–60.

Pedersen, Mogens N. (1989) 'En kortfattet oversigt over det danske partisystems udvikling', *Politica* 3.

Pedersen, Mogens N. and Bille, Lars (1991) 'Public financing and public control of political parties in Denmark', in Matti Wiberg (ed.), *The Public Purse and Political Parties. Public Financing of Political Parties in Nordic Countries*. Helsinki: The Finnish Political Association.

Siune, Karen (1982) *Valgkampe i TV og radio. Politiske partiers anvendelse af TV og radio herunder samspillet med journalister*. Århus: Politica.

Sjöblom, Gunnar (1968) *Party Strategies in a Multiparty System*. Lund: Studentlitteratur.

Sjöblom, Gunnar (1987) 'The role of political parties in Denmark and Sweden, 1970–1984', in Richard S. Katz (ed.), *Party Governments: European and American Experiences* (The Future of Party Government, vol. 2). Berlin: Walter de Gruyter, pp.155–201.

Thomsen, Niels (1987) 'Politisk kommunikation, massemedier og opinion', in *Dansk politik under forandring 1945–1985. Et forskningsinitiativ under Statens humanistiske Forskningsråd*. Copenhagen: Forskningssekretariatet.

Togeby, Lise (1992) 'The nature of declining party membership in Denmark. Causes and consequences', *Scandinavian Political Studies*, 15: 1–19.

Vesterdorf, Peter L. (1990) 'Die Institution der politischen Partei in Dänemark', in Dimitris Th. Tsatsos et al. (eds) *Parteienrecht im europäischen Vergleich. Die Parteien in den demokratischen Ordnungen der Staaten der Europäischen Gemeinschaft*. Baden-Baden: Nomos Verlagsgesellschaft.

7

Finland: Nationalized Parties, Professionalized Organizations

Jan Sundberg

The five party organizations which are considered in this chapter were all established in the early years of this century, building on a heritage which goes back to the 1800s. This chapter focuses on how they have organized themselves, especially with regard to leadership, membership activity and the role of the staff during the period from the early 1960s to the beginning of the 1990s. This was a period of heavy urbanization, of strong public service expansion and of radical improvements in the economic standard of living, and in response to these major social changes, parties have been under pressure to find a new political role. The most visible signs of change, however, are those relating to elections and the holding of public office. From 1944 to 1991 there were fourteen parliamentary elections and thirty-six different cabinets. Indeed, prior to the early 1970s, party fragmentation in the Finnish parliament was greater than that in any other Scandinavian country and, until the early 1980s, cabinet instability was the rule rather than the exception.

Parties in Finland were originally organized around social and cultural cleavages. The Labour Party (founded in 1899, and in 1903 renamed the Social Democratic Party) was the first and only mass organized party until the end of the Second World War, with the short-lived exception of organized communist activities. The Communist Party itself was founded in 1918 and banned the following year. Shortly after this, the communist-influenced Socialist Workers' Party was organized on a mass basis, until it too was banned in 1930. The labour parties had grown out of a movement organized around the working class, which aimed at the improvement of their economic, social and political conditions, and when the movement was formally divided into a political organization and a labour union, these aims became more specialized and more suited to the two power centres in society.

Mass organization gave the members collective strength to change society, first by non-parliamentary, and later by parliamentary means, and the strong social democratic belief in pursuing their aims through public institutions is of central importance in understanding their organizational development (Sundberg, 1991: 109–38). Active participation was the most effective school for educating the members in running the organization, especially in that many of the pioneers had no or very poor formal education. After years of socialist pressure, municipal government was reformed when, for the first time, the social democrats won a majority of seats in parliament in 1916. Universal suffrage for municipal elections was introduced in 1917, and after the 1918 election all parties were free to nominate candidates. The social democrats were the first party to take the advantage of this reform and nominated their members in local council elections throughout the country. In contrast to the non-socialist parties, the socialist mass membership organization was well equipped to formulate local programmes, to nominate candidates and to mobilize the electorate, and social democratic branches were established in nearly all municipalities long before the introduction of universal suffrage in local elections and also before the first free parliamentary election in 1907. This was particularly important at the local level, in that the candidates were required by law to live in the commune from which they were selected.

Thousands of ordinary party members became municipal councillors and/or members of the numerous local functional boards. In practice, and in order to fill all the boards, every candidate managed to get a seat, and even active members who had not been candidates were given positions, a process which changed the focus of their activity from the private to the public sphere. Prior to this, the bulk of membership activity was concentrated on internal party activities; now it became concentrated mainly on public office. Originally, only the most active and qualified members were offered public offices (Kettunen, 1986: 195–7; Soikkanen, 1966: 483–92); later, however, recruitment was extended to cover most members, with less emphasis on qualifications.

Formal membership in the non-socialist parties was unknown before universal suffrage, and prior to the Second World War organizational activities were run by adherents rather than by formally defined members. The core of the adherents were activated for parliamentary elections, with the need for a defence against the socialist threat in local elections overshadowing internal party rivalries in the non-socialist bloc. This defence took the form of a non-political profile, which proved to be a very effective strategy during the inter-war period, and the various non-political groups were filled with a wide variety of locally known anti-socialist volunteers who successfully participated in the elections.

Largely in response to the growing communist threat, the non-socialist parties developed into mass organizations relatively soon after the Second World War. The communists had been strengthened by active support from their eastern neighbour, and they could no longer be fought on the same basis as before. Indeed, the anti-communist line had to be dramatically softened in respect of Soviet–Finnish relations. A strong organization therefore proved an effective instrument to compete against the communists in elections throughout the country, and in contrast to the self-confident reaction of the 1920s, when the non-socialist parties used the state machinery to repress the communists, they responded this time by establishing a strong organizational platform from which to combat communist influence. The social democrats maintained their traditional approach of competing with the communists in the factories and in the working-class estates, while the agrarian Centre Party adopted a new approach to competing with the communists in the countryside. Competition for votes and for the recruitment of members were extended to practically every village and street, requiring comprehensive organizational assistance. Moreover, the Centre Party was threatened not only by parties on the left, but also by its own shrinking electoral appeal, and the party attempted to respond by embracing voters from all social classes. The result was a transformation from a typical agrarian party to a party for all those rural voters who felt marginalized by the tremendous pace of post-war urbanization, but even this transformation would not have been possible without a growing organization and membership. This strategy proved to be the most effective method of influencing voters in the rural areas, where the pressure towards uniformity and solidarity is higher than in urban areas (Sundberg, 1985a: 299–317, 1989a, 1990: 209–38). The local elections were now no longer a competition between the socialist parties, on the one hand, and, on the other, a bloc of non-socialist groups which lacked organized partisan networks. While the agrarian Centre Party was the first in the non-socialist bloc to enter local elections on a mass basis, its success had forced the other non-socialist parties also to nominate candidates and to participate in elections, with the result that local politics became wholly 'partified'.

The mass political organizations in Finland were therefore created in two waves: the first among parties on the left, and the second among those on the right, with the first wave beginning as an offensive socialist movement in the early part of the century, and with the second wave reflecting organizational mobilization against the socialist threat after the Second World War. The two waves were followed by an attempt to integrate new categories of voters into the organizational network, and these different types of mobilization resulted in strong political membership organizations which closely resembled one another in organizational terms. That said, their mission to transform and protect is no longer on the agenda. The class-based move to change the economic and political order declined, beginning with the serious conflicts between the Euro-communist and the orthodox Moscow factions in the Communist Party in the late 1960s. Similarly, the second wave of mobilization declined with the incipient collapse of the Communist Party and with Centre Party dominance in foreign and domestic politics from the early 1960s onwards. In addition, the 1960s and 1970s witnessed the Christian League reacting against the erosion of Christian values in the Conservative Party, as well as the Rural Party's successful reaction to the Centre Party's large-scale agrarian policy, which had left the 'forgotten' smallholders no alternative but to give up and migrate to the urban centres.

The party organizations ceased to grow. Moreover, they changed from strong popular organizations, each with a common task, into state-regulated and highly institutionalized political parties. And whereas the earlier political strength of parties had been sustained by mass membership, the party organizations since the late 1960s would probably have declined were it not for the subsidies received from the state. The first step in this process was the introduction of public party financing in 1967, and the second step came immediately after, with the regulation of parties through the Act of Parties and the Act of Parliamentary Elections in 1969. Finally, in 1972, with the Act of Local Elections, the position of parties was cemented by making them legally necessary to nominate candidates, to run campaigns and to govern at the presidential, parliamentary and local levels.

In sum, the political parties in Finland have undergone a deep change in their role. Activity had formerly been spontaneous and members had been mobilized to either defend or change the prevailing society. Now, by contrast, activity is standardized by state regulations and the bulk of membership activity is undertaken outside the party organization, mainly in municipal boards and committees. Nominations and campaigns are the very essence of internal membership activity, but the continuous work which takes place is that of representing the party in different governmental bodies. The change of membership involvement from internal party activities to campaigning and governing in other institutions stems from the enlargement of party activity in the late 1960s, beginning with municipal government, and then extending through the Lutheran Church parishes, the governmental assemblies of cooperatives such as banks, insurance companies, slaughter-houses, wholesale trade, retail trade, water distribution, electricity and telephone services. The process of politicization began in the cooperatives owned by the labour movement and later spread to the big cooperatives and the church. All of these politicized institutions are now run by representative bodies elected by proportional voting between two or more competing lists of candidates.

Parties as membership organizations

The five parties discussed here are all hierarchically organized, and all start from the local party branch, with members being formally registered both here and at the central level. According to the 1969 Act of Parties, all political organizations which qualify as parties (which requires 5000 signatures, a political programme and rules which guarantee a democratic organization) are registered in the Party Register. Local branches, on the other hand, are registered in the public Association Register, which is a legacy of pre-1917 Russian rule. The branches are organized territorially, although both the communists and the social democrats formerly maintained some workplace branches. As a general rule, the activity of a minimum of three local associations is coordinated in a municipal association, which nominates candidates and contests the municipal council elections, and coordinates party activity in the municipal government. All local branches and municipal associations are members of a party district, and district boundaries usually coincide with those of parliamentary constituencies (a large constituency may be divided into two districts, and small parties may have districts that cover more than one constituency). The main function of these districts is to nominate candidates and contest parliamentary elections. Between elections, the districts coordinate party activities initiated both in the district and in the central party office. All branches have the right to send delegates to the council meetings of the party district, and it is the latter which chooses the executive members. The branches also are represented in the party congress. Finally, all sub-national organizations are represented in the party council.

The parties differ as to whether the local ancillary organizations enjoy the same right to send delegates to the party congress as the local party branches. The conservative National Coalition (NCP) gave party status to the local women's and youth organizations in the early 1950s, and a similar process of membership integration was effected in the Centre Party in the mid-1970s, when the affiliated status of the women's and youth organizations was raised to that of ancillary organizations. The Swedish People's Party (SPP), the Social Democratic Party (SDP), and the communist People's Democratic League have maintained the affiliate status of their women's and youth organizations, and neither these affiliated local organizations nor the affiliated members are therefore included in the party membership figures. Only the People's Democratic League maintains a corporate membership, of which the majority are members of the Communist Party. Indeed, the People's Democratic League was never intended to be other than an electoral umbrella organization and a political camouflage for the Communist Party, and most of the direct members were in fact members of the Communist Party.

In the beginning of the post-war period, the parties in the socialist bloc were the best organized, although the ban on the communists was lifted only in late 1944. A remarkable build-up of the non-socialist organizations began in the late 1940s, however, and the Centre Party quickly grew to be the strongest of all the party organizations (see Table 7.1). At its peak, the Centre Party averaged almost nine local associations per municipality, as against just three in the case of the communists, the social democrats and the conservatives (Sundberg, 1989a: 39). The small number of Swedish People's Party associations is due to its regionally based support in the Swedish-speaking coastal areas in the south and west. Nowadays, however, there is no systematic difference between socialist and non-socialist parties in terms of organizational presence, and while there is also no sign of a comprehensive organizational decline, it is nevertheless obvious that the

Table 7.1 *Growth in the number of local party associations, selected years*

	Com.	SDP	Swedish PP	Centre P	Nat. Coal.
1945	976	1115	–	453	186
1954	1647	1570	83	1561	586
1966	1867	1369	88	2807	638
1975	1764	1466	85	3362	1123
1989	1207	1436	151	3628	1041

Source: Sundberg and Gylling, 1992: Tables V.B.1.a–e

peak of organizational growth lies in the past. Of all voluntary organiz-ations registered in the period from 1965 to 1979, a full 27 per cent were party organizations (branches, ancillary and affiliated organizations), whereas in the period from 1980 to 1984 the party share had declined to 16 per cent, and to just below 9 per cent in the period from 1985 to 1989 (Siisiäinen, 1990: 74–5). Should this decline continue, it will probably indicate a stagnation in the network of party branches, with different voluntary organizations strengthening their position in the contest for members.

The membership figures of the parties are sometimes difficult to compare, especially insofar as the ancillary members of the Centre Party and National Coalition are not separately counted in the party registers and hence are included in the available records (for details, see Sundberg and Gylling, 1992: Tables V.B.1.a–e); in fact, ancillary membership in both parties has been declining for many years. More importantly, the non-socialist parties have gone through a fundamental transition from having relatively weak structures to having the sort of large networks of branches which resemble the socialist mass organizations. Although it is evident that the socialists are relatively good record-keepers, the strong expansion in Centre Party membership cannot be explained by poor registration techniques, and the Centre Party has undoubtedly been the superior mass organization since the early 1950s. Even the conservatives, who for long periods resisted all attempts at local party politicization, now maintain an organization which is almost as strong as that of the social democrats, and hence there is now no longer any reason to differentiate between socialist mass parties and non-socialist cadre parties (Duverger, 1954). That said, it is also clear that the period of rapid membership growth has now definitely come to an end. Indeed, the members are now ageing, and the parties have trouble recruiting younger cohorts. According to survey data, slightly more than 12 per cent of those eligible to vote in 1986 were party members (Sundberg, 1989a: 47). Of these, pensioners (28 per cent) and farmers (18 per cent) are clearly over-represented, as are rural residents (55 per cent), who make up only 38 per cent of voters. The representation of women has steadily increased, and in 1986 they counted for 45 per cent of the total membership reported in the survey (Sundberg, 1989a: 106–7).

Table 7.2   *An estimate of the percentage of members enrolled as branch board members, selected years*

	Com.	SDP	Swedish PP	Centre P	Nat. Coal
1945	14	13	–	12	–
1954	20	19	1	7	5
1966	22	20	1	7	6
1975	23	11	1	8	11
1989	27	13	2	9	12

Membership activity

Although there are differences in membership activity between parties, legal regulations have ensured that the functions are very similar. Every local branch has a board elected by the members, usually composed of between five and ten persons. If we assume that the average board membership is 7.5, then more than 56,800 members hold a position of trust in the party, with board members being responsible, among other things, for administering party activities, convening membership meetings and running the local campaigns in presidential, parliamentary, municipal and other elections. They therefore can be considered as party activists, in contrast to those members who only pay their fee.

Defined in this way, the proportion of activists varies considerably among the parties (see Table 7.2). Given the above assumption of the number of board members, the estimated share of activists is higher on the left and lowest in the Swedish People's Party. This difference can be explained only partly by membership decline in the socialist parties. What are more important are the organizational strategies which lie behind the figures. Socialist membership activity is traditionally explained by reference to strong ideological commitment, but since activity pursued through ideological devotion is capricious, it was very quickly institutionalized in a large network of local branches. With a high motivation to participate, it was relatively easy to build a network of branches and to fill the boards with volunteers. Nowadays, by contrast, the ideological devotion along the traditional left–right dimension has waned.

All in all, the branch delegates to higher levels of the party are selected first from among the board members. Others may also be delegates, however, and many more party members are involved than is suggested by the estimates in Table 7.2. Many of the members are also involved as delegates in affiliated or ancillary organizations, and the bulk of the continuous activity is undertaken by these people. In times of elections, both parliamentary and local, the membership is activated to a much larger extent, with the Act of Parliamentary Elections (1969) and the Act of Local Elections (1972) giving the party members a legal right to select and nominate candidates. Thus the members living in the constituency select the parliamentary candidates through the district organization and the municipal candidates through the municipal organization (if existing) or through the branches. Compared to the voters, who can only choose between candidates on a list, party members therefore have a considerable advantage in influencing the result. Moreover, the Parliamentary Elections Act also required that primary elections be held among party members living in the constituency. And while the national executive enjoys some formal rights to replace a quarter of the candidates selected in parliamentary elections, experience nevertheless shows that interference from the national executive is met with strong resistance from the sub-national party executives, and all formal attempts to move in this direction have been blocked. The national executive can, of course, avail itself of many informal channels in order to influence the selection of candidates, but even then they are careful to avoid open conflict with the sub-national party. In practice it is only when a party is divided into rival factions (for example, the communists in the 1970s and 1980s) that the party executive and the sub-national party cannot come to terms.

There are no detailed legislative rules regulating relations between the party executive and the municipal party in local elections. According to the law, candidate lists from party branches or municipal organizations can win official status only by proxy from the national party. In local conflicts between the branches or between factions in the municipal organization, the party executive is thus forced to take sides. Alternatively, the party executive can allocate the proxy to someone not involved in the local party conflicts. As a rule, however, the proxies are routinely written to local party leaders. The process of candidate selection and nominations is otherwise outside the control of the party executive, which is assumed not to know all the potential candidates.

In addition, although strategic policy decisions are made by the party leader alone, or in concert with the party congress, the party council, the party executive or the parliamentary party, the sub-national organization has power to determine the tactics involving electoral alliances. Because the distribution of seats in Finnish elections is based on the largest remainder method for separate parties as well as for those entering an electoral alliance, small parties are keen to share electoral alliances with other parties. Indeed, larger parties may also gain from an electoral alliance. According to party rules, the decision on whether to join an electoral alliance and with which party (or parties) is taken by the sub-national party under the supervision of the national party.

Mass membership in its original missionary sense seems, at least partly, to have outlived itself, and most of the membership activity now takes place within the formal structure discussed above. An exception is electoral campaigns, which partly activate passive members into voluntary work. But while the bulk of these volunteers are engaged in distributing campaign material and other less qualified tasks, they nevertheless involve only a small part of the total membership. Moreover, given the system of supporter groups organized around individual candidates, the amount of voluntary work carried on *outside* the party has increased considerably. It is easier to mobilize volunteers around an individual candidate than around a party programme, and hence non-members easily become active supporters. As far as the party members are concerned, this development is viewed somewhat equivocally, in that they welcome the help of supporters but are themselves left with the daily routines, the financial burdens and the responsibility to the party organization itself. As a result, the membership function is yet further reduced, and the members have become a problem for the leaders. All party offices are now debating how to motivate the members to remain in the organization, and the sort of inducements which can be offered to them. As against this, however, a large membership is no longer automatically seen as a resource, but rather as a growing economic burden.

The corporative party: standing on two feet

Interest organizations are not formally connected to parties in Finland, although they were not separated in the early days of the working-class movement, and it was only with the introduction of universal suffrage in 1907 that the division of labour between the two was manifested in the creation of a separate political party and labour union. Since then there has been an overlap between the memberships of both organizations, and the same thing was later to occur in the agrarian movement with respect to the producers' organization and the agrarian party. The interest organizations played the role of pressure groups over a long period, but the introduction of centralized incomes policy agreements in 1968 institutionalized cooperation between labour market organizations and the state, and since then corporatism has been a key element of central government in Finland (Alestalo and Uusitalo, 1988: 258–9; Anckar and Helander, 1985: 124–37; Heiskanen, 1977; Helander and Anckar, 1983; Huuska, 1968). Indeed, since 1968, and with the active consent of the parties, the interest organizations have usurped legislative power, a process which is indicated by the comprehensive nature of incomes policy agreements and the increased participation of these organizations in the work of committees preparing future policy and legislation.

As both types of organizations have successfully pursued their political and economic aims, it has become extremely important to maintain the ties (the overlapping membership) between them, and only through close cooperation can the party and the interest organization maximize power and influence in national politics. Maximization of power through overlapping membership with an interest organization has three clear implications for the party: first, it maintains the original social class base; second, it maintains a strong interest articulation; and third, it becomes extensively dependent on the interest organization itself.

The labour union is much more homogeneously working class than is the membership of the two socialist parties and, in contrast to Centre Party members, the members of the producers' organizations are all farmers.

The National Coalition Party has no legacy of close linkage to any interest organization, but informal ties were established through the official recognition of incomes policy agreements between the major participants in the labour market, and here too each of the three employers' organizations (Private Entrepreneurs, Employers' Confederation, and Confederation of Commercial Employers) has an homogeneous membership when compared to their close political associate (Alestalo and Uusitalo, 1988: 254–5; Alestalo et al., 1985, 188–210; Uusitalo, 1985: 169–75). Thus, the shared members almost exclusively represent the very core of the social base around which the party originally organized.

Second, overlapping membership means that the party gives greater weight to interest articulation in practical rather than ideological terms. Interest organizations pursue their economic and social goals in incomes policy negotiations, silently blessed by their allies in parliament and the cabinet. Party membership, per se, still has a function, as the cooperation between the political party and the interest organization helps to bring collective goods to the working class, or to the farmers, or to the upper class. This is especially true in the socialist bloc, where mass membership is the very essence of power and influence. Thus it is fundamentally important for organizational credibility that the party as well as the labour union maintains its membership.

Third, the interest organizations have been extremely successful in enlarging their membership density since 1968. In 1980 more than 80 per cent of all employees and about 75 per cent of the farmers were organized, as compared with 46 and 67 per cent respectively in 1960 (Alestalo and Uusitalo, 1988: 258–9), and at the beginning of the 1990s, membership density had increased to approximately 90 per cent (Kauppinen, 1992: 77–84). Except for the Union of Agricultural Producers, whose membership has declined slightly since 1970, all employees' organizations have increased their membership during the same period. This has been most marked in the case of the Workers' Central Union, which maintained a membership of less than 300,000 in 1968, and which increased to slightly more than 1 million in 1979, remaining at that level throughout the 1980s. This labour union thus became the largest and most influential interest organization in Finland, with more members than all the other organizations combined (Borg, 1980; Kauppinen, 1992: 77–84; Komulainen, 1988). Moreover, as is noted below, its resources are counted not only in members, but also in staffing and finances.

Compared to the two parties in the labour movement, the labour union is an extremely strong mass organization which the Social Democratic Party cannot afford to offend without risking the loss of human as well as economic resources. Similarly if the party fails dramatically in elections, as the communists did, the flow of resources from the union will also be reduced. Although the relative size of the Centre Party and the producers' organization is opposite to this, the flow of resources has the same direction and importance. For while the party and the related interest organization are mutually dependent in Finland, it is the party which always falls short in terms of organizational resources. Thus the Centre Party, with its extremely large membership base, is dependent on the much smaller producers' organization, which provides the party with a core of active members, economic support and staffing assistance.

Electoral parties: standing on one foot

Finally, the remaining eighteen parties presently registered in Finland (as at October 1991) are either weakly or not at all connected to interest organizations. Their social base is undefined or does not fit into an organized category of economic interests and, in contrast to the corporative parties, they did not develop from a movement knitted together by a common class interest or divided into mutually dependent political and corporatist divisions. The relevance of interest organizations to their activities is therefore either small or non-existent. Similarly, when pursuing their political aims, these parties lack corporatist support and are therefore obliged to resort exclusively to the electoral channel.

Corporatism is alien to classic theories of parliamentarism and also to the Finnish constitution, and this means that the electoral parties are exemplary in following the rules, whether choosing to do so or not. This brings little pay-off, however, as the electoral parties are weakly organized and lack personnel and economic resources. In addition, they have but a small role in government, and even this will probably decline with the abolition in September 1992 of the rule allowing a third of MPs to delay the passage of a Bill to the next parliament (Anckar, 1990a: 149–52, 1990b: 26–50; Jansson, 1992: 242–68).

Party persistence is at least partly a function of the party's social base, for without a defined constituency, wild electoral swings are likely and the risk of disappearance is high (Rose and Mackie, 1988: 533–58). During the past three decades the number of parties contesting elections has fluctuated between nine and twelve, of which between eight and ten won at least one seat in parliament. In this sense, the 1991 election was an exception, or alternatively the beginning of a new political pattern, in that seventeen parties contested the election and nine parties managed to win at least one seat in parliament. However, of the small parties in parliament, it is only the Liberal People's Party, the Christian League, the Rural Party and the Greens which have persisted, and none of these has a corporatist connection, while their social bases have either eroded (the Rural Party) or are diffuse. They articulate a non-socialist ideology with a strongly shifting pattern of success. In 1990 the Liberal Party had 2000 members, the Christian League 16,700, the Rural Party about 9000 and the Greens about 1000, and only the Christian League and the Rural Party can claim to have a national network of local associations.

Because of their lack of corporatist connections, no resources are transferred to the party from other organizations and electoral success provides their only channel for access to power and money. Electoral losses therefore spell disaster. Party work, on the other hand, is more voluntary and the party aims more idealistic, especially because these parties are rarely if ever in a responsible cabinet position. In this respect electoral parties also follow the traditional model, that is, they are voluntary organizations pursuing a common political ideology.

The conservative National Coalition and the Swedish People's Party are typical of a middle way, maintaining a much broader platform than the electoral parties due to their social base and their close ties to a wide network of cultural organizations and interest organizations. Both also carry legacy deriving from the language conflict between Finns and Swedes. When the Finns secured dominance in all central state functions, the National Coalition transformed itself into a class party for the rapidly growing sector of middle- and high-ranking white-collar workers (Alestalo and Kuhnle, 1987: 29–38; Kivinen, 1989: 109–14; Martikainen and Yrjö-nen, 1991: 55–65; Sänkiaho, 1991: 37–45; Uusitalo, 1975). At the same time, however, the party retained many organizational links to nationalist Finnish organizations and later to the white-collar interest organizations which surrounded the party with an infrastructure of support groups resembling that of the corporativist parties. In contrast to the National Coalition, the Swedish People's Party has maintained its original profile as the defender of the Swedish-speaking minority, although the party has strong ties to the Swedish Producers' Organization in Finland and some weak links to the employers' organizations. More important, however, is the network of ties between the party and the large number of Swedish voluntary organizations. The party was originally created out of the Swedish mobilization movement in the beginning of the 1900s, and the party remains the 'organic' head of a pyramid of Swedish organizations ranging from charitable associations to yacht clubs (Jansson, 1964: 292–94; Allardt and Starck, 1981; Sundberg, 1984: 91–108, 1985b). But while the party cannot sustain itself without support from this infrastructure of voluntary organizations, it nevertheless contrasts to the corporativist parties in always privileging the parliamentary channel.

The party leadership and the parliamentary party

Although according to the Party Act the formal government of parties has been highly standardized since 1969, the principles of democratic representative rule reflect an older legacy in the five main parties, with all of the representative units at different levels in the party hierarchy being filled by people with a mandate from the ordinary members. The composition of these units and the selection of members does vary, however, both over time as well as among the different parties.

The party leader in all five parties is both the leader of the party as a whole and the chairman of the party executive, and in some cases is also chairman of the party council and the working committee. The leadership mandate period runs for two to three years, with no formal obstacle to re-election. Since 1969, the party congress has selected the leader in all the parties, and thus it is in the largest membership unit, with representation from all parts of the country, where leadership selection takes place. Prior to the Party Act in 1969, the Centre Party leader was selected by the much more narrowly based party council.

In order to become a party leader nowadays, a candidate must enjoy support from among the rank-and-file members. Election is also character-ized by uncertainty, even though the problems of controlling mass congresses means that any nomination is well prepared in advance. The congress is more easily controlled on questions relating to changes in the party programme or policy, and the means of control are many and are now more refined than was the case in the early 1960s. Modern congresses are also much more formalized and well prepared than before. The participants receive a lot of information which is planned and produced in advance by the party staff. Issues are therefore well worked through and evaluated prior to being processed at the congress itself. In the early 1960s, by contrast, all documents were handled exclusively by the party secretary and no printed information was sent in advance to the congress partici-pants. Today, with a much larger party staff, the secretary and the party leader can no longer directly monopolize written communications, and hence the techniques of leadership and control have become more sophisticated. Moreover, while voluntary members are unwilling to accept subordination to authority unless it is connected with a strong ideological commitment and passion, the process of deradicalization in these five parties has nevertheless meant that authoritarian leadership action is no longer legitimized by reference to ideology. At the same time, radicalism has legitimized authoritarian rule in the formally democratic but orthodox communist Democratic Alternative; and, in the same vein, a passion for charismatic leadership has also legitimized authoritarian rule in the populist Rural Party. These cases are exceptional, however, and could not be duplicated in the five established parties without a fundamental change of party culture.

Older party congresses were also characterized by discussions on the political situation, with the annual party report having to be accepted by the participants (Fagerholm, 1977: 29). Delegates rarely submitted motions of their own. Nowadays, however, with growing consciousness of equality and democratic rights, the number of motions has multiplied. Indeed, when the number of motions in the Social Democratic Party, for example, has increased to over 400, of which approximately 60 per cent come from the local associations (Ramstedt-Silén, 1990: 95–129), it is hardly surprising to find that the party leadership have problems in dealing with them all. That said, coordinated membership pressure against the leaders can rarely be seen, in that the views and interests of the members reflect more of a mosaic than a unified position. Much of the work of leadership is therefore devoted to balancing different interests and to forming common policies among the unstructured wills in the organization. The more structured the wills, the more complicated it is to run the party.

Segmentation as a channel of influence

As this discussion indicates, the aspirations of the rank-and-file members to influence politics have grown substantially during the past decades, even though many of the attempts are weakly anchored in the membership and many of the issues are of minor importance. When these interests are pursued by one of the ancillary or affiliated organizations, on the other hand, or by the parliamentary party or a party committee, or a closely connected labour union or sub-national party, they carry much more weight, and hence must be balanced against other sectoral or regional interests. In addition, the attempt to pursue sectoral interests has been encouraged by the increasing segmentation of the party organization. In the first place, and in an effort to recruit new members and to maintain the old, the parties have increasingly appealed to people according to their gender, age and occupation. By so doing, the parties have tried to integrate people by adapting the organization to concerns shared by either young people, women, students, pensioners, different occupational groups and so on. The youth, women's and students' organizations have tended to strengthen their position within the party by raising their status from affiliated to ancillary linkages, but their members then become less motivated to become members of party branches as such, in that they already enjoy the same rights as ordinary party members.

Segmented interest articulation is most prominent during elections and party congresses, when all the organized interests tied to the party actively compete to get their people either nominated as candidates or elected to important party committees, to the party council, and to the party executive. This is, of course, also beneficial to the party leadership, who want candidates who can appeal to as broad a range of voters as possible, and who also want access to the specialist knowledge available in the organized segments. All this also requires an efficient party staff. Increasing segmentation is also a response to the expanding corporatist state and municipal government. To pursue the aims of the party effectively in the state committees where laws and decrees are prepared and planned, parties tend to follow a sectoral division similar to that of the state administration itself, and to enrol members with special qualifications. These are often state civil servants with inside knowledge about how the system is run, and the party uses committees of such experts to influence the form and content of laws and decrees long before the government bill is submitted to parliament. These highly professionalized party committees work in relative isolation from the party congress.

The modern party no longer pursues one common ideology in parliament. Rather it is an organizational umbrella sheltering a wide range of internal actors, each pursuing different goals in a variety of sectors of public decision-making. Indeed, ordinary members representing the same special interest often have more in common with members sharing the same special interest in other parties. Cooperation takes different forms. The women's organizations have institutionalized their cooperation through the establishment of a common platform for formal meetings. More informal party groups, such as environmentalists, cooperate in non-political environmental organizations. Regardless of form, however, inter-party cooperation promotes loyalties across parties and furthers internal party diversification, and it is only in election campaigns that the party must present a common programme to the voters.

The parliamentary party: an independent power authority

According to the constitution, parliament is the highest authority in Finnish society, and the parliamentary party therefore also holds the key position of power in the party organization. Compared to the other organizations, the parliamentary party is also effectively independent. According to the Parliament Act, for example, the MPs are responsible exclusively to their voters and not to their party, and neither the parliamentary party nor the party organization is mentioned in the Act (*Riksdagsordning*, 1928/7). Nonetheless, the party organization of today is linked to the parliamentary party both formally and informally.

Starting with the formal link, members of the parliamentary party are supposed to be party members and are elected to office from the party list. This requirement of membership is relatively new in the non-socialist parties, and prior to 1967, for example, it was only suggested that the approved parliamentary party members of the National Coalition should follow the party programme. MPs are nevertheless formally controlled by the party leadership through their membership in the branch, even though this link represents an inadequate means of control. In addition, the parliamentary candidates are chosen with a minimum of control from the party leadership, and the electoral system itself does not favour candidates with long experience in the party organization, but rather encourages people with qualifications from civil life to seek nomination. As a result, parliamentary elections involve a lot of uncertainty for the leadership. The socialist parties have traditionally seen their parliamentary parties as dependent on the party organization and, as a result, most socialist MPs tend to have had a long party career prior to being nominated. The non-socialist parliamentary parties, on the other hand, have traditionally been very independent, and in the most extreme cases from the past, it was the parliamentary party that led the entire party rather than the other way around. Correspondingly, non-socialist MPs have much shorter party careers prior to being nominated and elected to parliament (Borg, 1982: 457–546; Noponen, 1964: 255–63; Nousiainen, 1989: 180–3; Oksanen, 1972: 203–21; Oksanen and Pitkänen, 1989: 247–50).

Since the 1960s, however, the ties between the parliamentary party and the party as such have been formalized, and the independence of the parliamentary party has diminished. The parliamentary party has few formal channels to pursue its aims in the leading party units, with its members' right to vote in party bodies being replaced by a right to speak, and with its number of ex-officio participants being reduced or totally eliminated. In essence, the party secretary participates in the parliamentary party meetings and constitutes the visible link between the two units. And although this is not always formalized in the rules, it is the case in all parties.

Informally, the parliamentary party is effectively controlled by the chairman of the party who, as a rule, is an MP. In addition, the degree of independence from the party organization is not exclusively regulated by formal rules and informal ties, but also depends on whether the party is in government. When in opposition, the parliamentary party has a relatively free hand. Since the number of bills to be debated in the sittings has grown continuously, and since decisions are made quickly, it is both practically impossible and often of little political interest for the party executive always to intervene. Nevertheless, the MPs are assisted by party officials and party committees on important issues. The role of the party executive changes radically when the party takes office, however. According to the formal rules, participation in government is preceded by a joint decision of some leading party unit and the parliamentary party, and although the work of the cabinet group is not formally regulated, the party executive is a central focus of information for the parliamentary party. It is here that information about the planning and preparation of future bills are transmitted from the cabinet group to the parliamentary party. But while the cabinet group must of course consider the demands from the parliamentary party and the party executive, it is nevertheless problematic to determine which unit is influenced by the other and to what extent, since the actors are often the same individuals in three different roles.

The party staff

Most organizational work in the parties used to be undertaken by volunteers. It is of course possible to argue that the total amount of work was smaller in the past, and that the need for party employees was therefore less. Moreover, it is clear that the need for administrators is much greater in large organizations, and membership increases should therefore be accompanied by a growth in the number of party officials. The growth is not completely linear, however, and even though membership growth has now ceased or begun to decline, the number of party officials has continued to increase. An important factor here is the public subsidies which were introduced in 1967 for all parties with representation in parliament, and between 1960 and 1989 the biggest increase in the number party officials coincides with the introduction of public subventions. These were offered to the national parties rather than at the district or local level and, in accordance with the public rules of payment, the national party offices have used this money to build up their staffing. Conversely, the figures that are available from the sub-national level clearly show that these were given no new resources to recruit officials. The number of secretaries serving the parliamentary party, on the other hand, has increased across the period as a whole, and in particular in those parties which have been most successful in winning new seats.

Developments during the past thirty years seem to have strengthened the central party offices and the parliamentary parties, whereas the sub-national party districts continue to work with only one party official, sometimes assisted by one or two secretaries. In March 1991, for instance, the Social Democratic Party maintained 43 paid staff members working in their central office, of whom 18 could be categorized as support staff and the remaining 25 as party officials. In addition, each of the five main parties has its own educational institute and newspapers, and some also run temperance organizations, consumers' organizations, leisure organizations and so on, all of which (in addition to the ancillary and affiliated organizations) have their central offices closely connected to the party office. Because most of these offices are located in the same building, they form a common workplace where the different functions are mutually supportive. All this considerably augments and further strengthens the central party, although many of the connected functions also have at least part-time officials at the sub-national level. More peripherally, but extremely important for the Social Democrats and the Centre Party respectively, are the central offices of the labour union and the producers' interest organization. Most of the approximately 1500 officials employed by the labour union are social democrats (Sundberg, 1989a: 108), and the list of external offices somehow connected to the party offices could further be enlarged to include banks, insurance companies, construction companies, printing-works and so forth. All of these institutions support the party either financially or by providing services to the party and its members.

In general, the larger the number and the size of institutions linked to a party, the more professional are the potential resources available to it for use in political work. This statement also implies that the parties are supported by different types of institutions, which differ in the degree to which they are linked to the party and in how effectively their staffs can be used by the party. In the first place, the party office and the officials working in the ancillary organizations constitute the core of party professionals, in that their work is formally controlled by the party executive. Second, there are the officials employed by the affiliated organizations and the non-membership organizations (educational institutes, temperance organizations and so on) which were founded by the party and which support party interests, but which are also more or less autonomous in a formal sense. These people are very important for the party because they either undertake work for a specific target group or perform functions that often require specialized skills not available in the core party staff. Third, the interest organizations, which may have official representation in the party executives but which formally remain totally independent from the party, have a paid staff that constitutes a large resource for the party, even though the function of this staff is to look after their own members' economic interests. The greater the overlap in membership in the two organizations, the more inclined is the interest organization to serve the party with professional assistance. This also means that the interest organization is a spokesman for the party to its members on political issues.

The professionalization of party work

Parties with strong links to an interest organization tend to be more professional than those with weak or non-existent links, which remain totally dependent for financial support on their members and on state subsidies. Indeed, electoral losses have forced these parties to reduce their staff, since public subsidies are paid according to the number of seats in parliament. Thus elections are not only a competition for power, but are also a hidden pursuit for money. Parties with support from an interest organization that can guarantee some economic stability are therefore much less vulnerable to the organizational costs of electoral losses. Moreover, such links also give parties a much better platform from which to build supportive institutions that can bring in public money budgeted for youth activities, cultural work, sports, temperance work, educational work, press support and so on, and that can transform this money into staffing and service controlled by the party. Although indirect, these particular subsidies constitute a major part of all subventions given to parties. They also tend to favour the larger parties, leaving the smaller organizations almost entirely exposed to the uncertainty of winning parliamentary seats.

The parties with the largest professional staff are also the most influential, in that the pursuit of influence and the maintenance of power as a continuous process can hardly be undertaken in the absence of a professional staff. In preparing for elections, however, special skills not available in the party organization are needed, and therefore the service must be purchased at a price determined by the market. Four of the five parties (the Swedish People's Party is the exception) have for many years contracted the Finnish Gallup agency to undertake opinion polls for their internal use, and party electoral propaganda is now increasingly transmitted through external means. In some cases, as for example in the case of the Social Democratic Party, the parties plan their campaign and formulate the written campaign material with the assistance of a firm of consultants, and the visualization and the technical details of the party electoral propaganda is generally undertaken by advertising bureaus (Sundberg and Högnabba, 1992: 82–99). Moreover, the content of newspaper advertising is often decided by the party or candidate in cooperation with professional consultants, and the same is true for the production of propaganda tapes for the rapidly expanding local commercial radio stations and, since 1992, for TV advertising. However, some of the parties, such as the Left-Wing Alliance and the small parties, cannot afford to buy this kind of service.

The process of professionalization which has transformed the party central offices has nevertheless left the sub-national level relatively untouched, and the organizations at the sub-national level have become increasingly dependent on professional help from the central party office. This is particularly true for campaigning, in that all the party posters, leaflets and other propaganda material are planned and distributed from the central office. Moreover, the professionalization of the party leadership has increased the tendency towards uniformity and dependence at lower levels in the organization. In this sense, the party organizations have developed towards the classical type of bureaucracy conceptualized by Max Weber (1978: 956–8), with organizational routines becoming more effective and rational than before, but also more formalized and hierarchical. There is also little sign of membership opposition to this development; on the contrary, the active members actually tend to increase their demands for the services the party can provide. Meanwhile, voluntary party activity is more and more reduced to participation in meetings, with the preparation of meetings and the execution of decisions being undertaken by the party officials.

The role of the party staff is two-sided: to be the executive, on one hand, and the leader, on the other, and which role is taken is determined in the first place by the position of the staff members in the professional hierarchy. Those in lower positions are predominantly executives and those in higher positions have leading roles in the party. The party secretary is the most prominent by virtue of his/her ex-officio presence in all important units in the party, including the parliamentary party. Moreover, the leading staff positions are divided according to fields of responsibility. Each of these officials usually serves as a secretary in some of the large number of sectoral committees appointed and controlled by the party executive (Djupsund, 1990: 167–85). Furthermore, their influence over these committees is not restricted to formulating decisions, but also involves the selection of the issues on the agenda, either alone or with the chairman. These committees are particularly important because their work serves as an outline for party policy in cabinet and parliament. Many of the committees also deal with internal organizational problems which have repercussions for the running of the organization as such.

While support work by party secretaries has grown in importance, the voluntary members are now less inclined to carry out routine tasks for the party. On the other hand, increased support staff has made it possible to extend a professional service to the rank-and-file members as well as to the leaders. Services (including what information is spread, who gets a ticket for a boat seminar to Sweden or who is backed for top positions in the public administration) are not value-free, and much of what is offered to the rank-and-file members mirrors the political view of the staff. In addition, the leading staff members have increased their influence in line with the decline in membership activity, and the more passive the members the greater is the likelihood that the initiative passes to the professional staff. This tendency is reinforced by the technical assistance that is available at the party bureau, which gives the staff a huge advantage over the ordinary members.

The party and society

Although the general tendency of professionalization is prominent in the party organizations, there remain other factors which support the influence by party members on external spheres of activity. Thus while membership activity has declined in the socialist parties, the members nevertheless remain active in other contexts, and most notably in local government, in church parishes, in cooperative company councils, in interest organization councils, and through patronage in the public administration.

In candidate selection and nominations to state and municipal elections, the members are legally guaranteed formal rights, and given the legislative framework, rank-and-file members have the best means of influencing politics either indirectly (by participating in the nominations and working for the candidate), or directly (by becoming candidates themselves and winning election). The first option is most common in parliamentary elections, since very few of the members are nominated. In the 1991 election, for example, a total of 1875 candidates were nominated by seventeen parties, together with twenty-six candidates nominated by non-party lists. In municipal elections, on the other hand, the number of party candidates may exceed 60,000, which implies that at least 10 per cent of all members are candidates in elections (Sundberg, 1989a: 73–5, 1990: 89–117).

The local government council seats are filled with elected candidates in general elections. There are between 12,000 and 13,000 elected councillors in all, and each of these has two deputies. In addition, every sector of administration is led by a board and filled with party people according to their share of seats in the council. All in all, there are about thirty compulsory boards (which can be amalgamated) and, together with the voluntary boards, committees, inter-municipal councils and local state boards, the number rapidly increases, and the number of party people involved as ordinary and deputy members is counted in the hundreds of thousands. According to a survey undertaken in 1982 in a sample of 107 municipalities, for example, approximately 9 per cent of all eligible voters have a position of trust in the local administration (Sundberg, 1989a: 97–103, 1989b: 288–311). And since most of these are party members, candidates not elected are the first to be recruited to these positions, supplemented by members who have participated in campaign work, with other rank-and-file members and sometimes even party adherents recruited if required.

Those elected to municipal councils are regulated by rules and are formally controlled by the municipal party organization. Although the council group rules are a far cry from the parliamentary party rules, the idea is the same, that is, to govern in concert and in accordance with the party programme. However, when the issues on the agenda are dominated by pragmatic matters, it is difficult to act according to the party programme in local politics. Rather, since the issues are usually discussed and decided in advance in the council group, it is easier simply to fulfil the demands of group coherence. The municipal council and government constitute the leading local government bodies, whereas the boards have less political importance. Nevertheless, the boards are ranked according to the sector they govern, and the most important positions are filled by councillors, followed by campaign workers and then other members. Since 1988 the boards must be filled with men and women according to the Act of Equality, which shakes up the ranking order at least to some extent. In addition, party control over those members who have a position on a board but not in the council is extremely problematic, for even when compared to the issues discussed in the municipal council, the agenda in the boards is yet more concerned with practical issues. There are also no 'board groups' to guide members, and since many of these members are relatively passive participants in internal party work, their sense of independence is reinforced. In contrast, all members of the municipal council have participated as candidates in general elections, which increasingly serve as a party poll between parliamentary elections. Moreover, given the nationalized character of local elections, the candidates will by their participation have become aware of the party programme, whereas the relatively passive rank-and-file members chosen for the boards will often lack knowledge of even the most elementary matters that unite the party.

The modern party activist: more free entrepreneur than loyal party subject

The form and content of party membership activity has changed, in the sense that the bulk of that activity no longer takes place within the party organization as such. The modern party activists are now more akin to free entrepreneurs who need the party as a means of fulfilling their personal goals in society, whereas the party activists of before (at least in socialist parties) were supposed to take orders and work for the party as personified in its leadership. Even then, of course, personal rewards were offered, but these were mainly distributed within the organization, whereas the rewards of today, whether distributed by the party alone or in agreement between competing parties, are mainly found outside the organization. This is mainly the result of the politicization of local government, which has led non-socialist party members in particular to become more active than ever. Party politicization has not just been limited to local government, of course, and when the proportional system of election to parish councils was introduced in 1970, the socialist parties nominated candidates and the non-socialist parties followed their example. Of the approximately 10,900 parish councillors elected in 1986, for example, some 66 per cent were chosen from party lists among a total of 31,200 candidates in 426 parishes (Kauppinen, 1987). The parties have also extended their activity to the biggest cooperative council elections, whereas political competition has been long established in the labour union and in its twenty-seven member organizations.

What is both more problematic and more novel is the patronage system which was unofficially established around 1966 when the socialist majority in parliament brought a socialist-dominated cabinet to power. In reaction to the 'bourgeois hegemony' in public administration, this socialist majority began a campaign to implement a system of patronage based on parliamentary shares of power (Heiskanen, 1977: 245–53; Ståhlberg, 1979: 206–19, 1984: 237–47). Two tendencies are prominent in this Finnish variant of patronage. First, those who get offices generally enjoy permanent tenure; and second, patronage is not limited to the highest posts in the state bureaucracy, but also includes offices in the local administration and, depending on the supply and demand of work in the municipality, sometimes even basic service employment. In fact, the distribution of patronage jobs between the competing parties is now one of the most politicized issues for the municipal councillors.

In sum, as parties have extended their activity and control to large societal areas, the mass membership has become necessary for the filling of all the relevant positions with party members. For those with a personal career in mind, party membership offers a good basis from which to pursue their aims. As a rule, involvement is many times higher in the small rural municipalities than in the big cities, largely because the number of available positions and seats is proportionally much higher. Indeed, in the very smallest municipalities, virtually all the local inhabitants would be involved in government were it not for the fact that several positions are held by one person. That said, not all positions of trust are prestigious, and the parties have a growing problem in finding a sufficient number of motivated members, especially in these small municipalities, and some of the positions are increasingly seen not as a reward, but rather as an obligation to the party. Perhaps as a result of this, there is also an emerging process of professionalization with respect to the leading local positions. In a similar vein, sectoral boards are sometimes suspended and/or amalgamated, resulting in an increased concentration and aggregation of decision-making. Even in the 1980s, the participatory model of party politics dominated over the efficiency model, affording the big parties an advantage over their small competitors, who lack sufficient organizational

Linkages to interest organizations

		Weak	**Strong**
Degree of party involvement in local government and societal institutions	**High**	Mass organizations: National Coalition, Swedish People's Party	Large mass organizations: Centre Party, Social Democrats, Communists
	Low	Small electoral parties: Greens, Rural Party, Christian League	Small communist and left-wing parties: Democratic Alternative, Socialist Workers' Party

Figure 7.1   *The mass organization formula of political influence*

resources to nominate candidates in all municipalities, parishes and cooperative organizations. In addition, although the efficiency model is becoming more prominent in the 1990s, it nevertheless affords no better chances to the small parties, since they lack the political strength necessary to compete for the diminishing number of positions.

The large membership involvement in external functions has formally extended party control to nominations, elections and government across a wide range of public and private institutions. As far as the first two functions are concerned, the candidates are nominated and backed by the party. Party control is extremely problematic to achieve in government, however, with party members more or less acting as free agents until the time of the next elections. In these circumstances, the ideological profile of the parties has diminished and they have developed more as professional experts on elections. Moreover, parties exercise little control over their members in government, because often they do not know what to control other than attempting to limit open conflicts between members in office.

Conclusion

It seems evident that the mass political organization in Finland still continues to fulfil some of its functions, at least under certain conditions. There are two variables that explain the role of the mass membership organization as a means of achieving political influence. The first is the extent to which the party is linked to an interest organization (degree of overlapping membership), for when strong links exist, political aims can be pursued through both the parliamentary and the corporatist channels of influence. The second is the extent to which the members are involved in running local government and other societal institutions.

Both variables suggest the typology in Figure 7.1, in which the three parties listed in the upper right quadrant enjoy strong ties to the labour union and the producers' organization respectively, which have been the most effective and influential interest organizations in Finland since the introduction of incomes policy agreements (prior to then, they had been pressure groups acting closely with the connected party). Neither of the two parties in the upper left quadrant has strong ties to one dominating interest organization. In the case of National Coalition, the ties increasingly go to different influential organizations such as the employers' associations and the association of senior white-collar employees. The party also has a legacy of defending Finnish nationalism and maintains ties to these organizations. The Swedish People's Party, on the other hand, is the focus of most Swedish organizations in Finland. In contrast to the parties in the upper right quadrant, these two parties have used their organization defensively to protect their regular access to power. For long periods after the Second World War, the National Coalition lacked any direct vertical channel of influence, but due to its strong position in parliament, the parties in cabinet could not rule without its passive support. Horizontally, both of these parties are latecomers promoted by their conservative unwillingness to politicize local government and institutions such as the church parishes, and their modern mass organizations were developed quite smoothly after the Second World War in order to meet the challenge from the Social Democrats and Centre Party.

The small communist and socialist parties that split away from either of the two leading workers' parties are located in the lower right quadrant. Through their members these parties enjoy strong ties to the labour union, but they share no power in the organization and they lack any other effective channels of vertical influence. Because of their weak organization, they also lack resources to build horizontal channels of influence. Finally, in the lower left quadrant are the non-socialist parties that depend almost entirely on success in parliamentary elections. They lack natural links to any interest organization and they also lack the resources to build competitive horizontal channels of influence. Although some of these parties have been included in cabinet coalitions, their position has always been weak in relation to the big parties in office. As a rule, their vertical channel of influence is also therefore weak.

Taking all of this together, it is possible to conclude that the more a party seeks influence in society, the more it will require a mass membership. The complex Finnish society of today is highly centralized and sectorized, even though many aspects are administered at a local level. In order to optimize their influence, parties have to penetrate all of the hierarchical levels and the different sectors, and this can be done most effectively with a large party membership. It is also possible to see the factors that allow parties to become big and powerful. First of all, it is exclusively those parties with a social class base or ties to an ethnic group that have managed to build up a large membership and to win strong electoral support. The pursuit of the collective will of a large category of voters through a vertical channel of influence is therefore the basis for an early mass organization. The strategy is able to avail itself of the help of a closely-linked interest organization to pursue political aims following the introduction of the state-regulated incomes policy agreements.

Although a large and overlapping membership is important for parties wishing to achieve a strong vertical and horizontal political influence, it has also many other implications. One of the most important of these is that political power brings resources to the organization in terms of money and professional staff. This occurs not only through public subventions, but also through the links to an interest organization which allow parties with scarce resources the opportunity to build an infrastructure of affiliated and ancillary organizations. The larger the infrastructure of organizations around the party, the more financial and personal resources become available to it. In this sense, Figure 7.1 not only reflects a matrix of political influence, but also a matrix of the accumulation of organizational resources, and indicates how extremely difficult it is for challenging parties to break the dominance of those which are already established.

The large dominant parties have built complex cartels of supporting organizations and institutions. However, although these cartels accumulate power and influence, they are not run authoritatively by a leader and are not legitimized by a shared ideology. Within the cartel, the need for equilibrium requires that different views must be balanced, a process which is a necessity for effective leadership but which, at the same time, reduces the manoeuvrability of the party leadership. Within the party organization itself, on the other hand, essential functions are regulated by laws which also reduce leadership manoeuvrability. As against this, the professional-ization of the organization tends to strengthen the party leadership in contrast to the ordinary members. Indeed, the most prominent staff members are included in the leadership and have an advantage over the relatively passive party members in terms of skills, time and economic resources. Nevertheless, such control is restricted to internal party life, and members representing the party in different societal institutions are effectively free from leadership control.

In sum, the more the party organization and its membership are nationalized in terms of state regulations and financial support, or by membership involvement in public administration, the more restricted are the formal means through which party leaders may control the member-ship. Conversely, the more nationalized the party, the more formal rights are available through which the members may act independently of the leadership. In addition, public financing and party involvement in public administration support a growth in the numbers of skilled staff members, and the more professionalized the party, the better are the means to govern the organization without active support from the members. In this sense, the only effective way of managing both the staff and the leadership is to promote membership participation by utilizing the formal methods of democratic control.

Finland 183

References

Alestalo, M. and Kuhnle, S. (1987) 'The Scandinavian route: economic, social, and political developments in Denmark, Finland, Norway, and Sweden', in R. Erikson, E.J. Hansen, S. Ringen, H. Uusitalo (eds), *The Scandinavian Model*. New York: M.E. Sharpe.
Alestalo, M. and Uusitalo, H. (1988) 'Finland', in P. Flora (ed.), *Growth to Limits*. New York: de Gruyter.
Alestalo, M., Flora, P. and Uusitalo, H. (1985) 'Structure and politics in the making of the welfare state', in R. Alapuro, M. Alestalo, E. Haavio-Mannila, and R. Väyrynen (eds), *Small States in a Comparative Perspective*. Oslo: Norwegian University Press, pp. 188–210.
Allardt, E. and Starck, C. (1981) *Språkgränser och samhällsstruktur*. Stockholm: Almqvist & Wiksell.
Anckar, D. (1990a) 'Finland: dualism och konsensus', in E. Damgaard (ed.), *Parlamentarisk forandring i Norden*. Oslo: Universitetsforlaget.
Anckar, D. (1990b) 'Democracy in Finland: the constitutional framework', in J. Sundberg and S. Berglund. (eds), *Finnish Democracy*. Helsinki: The Finnish Political Science Association.
Anckar, D. and Helander, V. (1985) 'Corporatism and representative government in the Nordic countries', in R. Alapuro et al. (eds), *Small States in a Comparative Perspective*. Oslo: Norwegian University Press, pp. 124–37.
Borg, O. (1980) *Palkansaajien järjestövoiman kasvu 1945–80*. University of Tampere, Institute of Political Science.
Borg, O. (1982) 'Puolueiden ja eduskuntaryhmien suhteet', *Suomen kansanedustuslaitoksen historia XII*. Helsinki: Eduskunnan historiakomitea.
Djupsund, G. (1990) 'Kommitté-väsendet i finlandska Partiorganisationer', in G. Djupsund and L. Svåsand (eds), *Partiorganisasjoner: studier i strukturer och processer i finske, norske og svenske partier*. Åbo: Åbo Akademy Press, pp. 167–85.
Duverger, M. (1954) *Political Parties*. London: Methuen.
Fagerholm, K.-A. (1977) *Talmannens röst*. Helsingfors: Söderström & Co.
Heiskanen, I. (1977) *Julkinen, kollektiivinen ja markkinaperusteinen*, University of Helsinki, Department of Political Science.
Helander, V. and Anckar, D. (1983) *Consultation and Political Culture*. Helsinki: Finnish Society of Sciences and Letters.
Huuska, V. (1968) *Etujärjestöjen painostuspolitiikka Suomessa*. Porvoo: WSOY.
Jansson, J.-M. (1964) 'Finlandssvenska problem', *Nya Argus*, 20: 292–4.
Jansson, J.-M. (1992) *Från splittring till samverkan*. Helsingfors: Söderström & Co.
Kauppinen, J. (1987) *Seurakuntavaalit 1986*. Kirkon tutkimuskeskus, Sarja B No. 51, Tampere.
Kauppinen, T. (1992) *Suomen työmarkkinamallin muutos*. Helsinki: Ministry of Labour.
Kettunen, P. (1986) *Poliittinen liike ja sosiaalinen kollektiivisuus*. Helsinki: Societas Historica Finlandiae.
Kivinen, M. (1989) *The New Middle Class and the Labour Process*. University of Helsinki, Department of Sociology, Research Reports No. 223.
Komulainen, S. (1988) *Järjestösiirtymä työmarkkinoiden kasvu-ja kehitystekijänä*. University of Tampere, Institute of Political Science.
Martikainen, T. and Yrjönen, R. (1991) *Voting, Parties and Social Change in Finland*. Helsinki: Statistics Finland.
Noponen, M. (1964) *Kansanedustajien sosiaalinen tausta Suomessa*. Helsinki: Valtiotieteelli-nen yhdistys.
Nousiainen, J. (1989) *Suomen poliittinen järjestelmä*. Helsinki: WSOY.
Oksanen, M. (1972) *Kansanedustajan rooli*. Helsinki: Gaudeamus.
Oksanen, M. and Pitkänen, W. (1989) 'Kansanedustajan rooli', in M. Noponen (ed.), *Suomen kansanedustusjärjestelmä*, Helsinki: WSOY.
Ramstedt-Silén, V. (1990) 'Högt till tak och brett mellan väggarna!' in G. Djupsund and

184   *How Parties Organize*

L. Svåsand (eds), *Partiorganisasjoner: studier i strukturer och processer i finske, norske og svenske partier*. Åbo: Åbo Akademy Press, pp. 95–129.

Rose, R. and Mackie, T. (1988) 'Do parties persist or fail? The big trade-off facing organizations', in K. Lawson and P. Merkl (eds), *When Parties Fail*. Princeton: Princeton University Press, pp. 533–58.

Sänkiaho, R. (1991) 'Puolueiden kannattajakunnan rakenne', in *Statistics Finland, Parliamentary Elections*.

Siisiäinen, M. (1990) *Suomalainen protesti ja yhdistykset*. Helsinki: Tutkijaliitto.

Soikkanen, H. (1966) *Kunnallinen itsehallinto kansanvallan perusta*. Helsinki: Maalaiskuntien liitto.

Ståhlberg, K. (1979) 'Den partipolitiska förvaltningen', *Finsk Tidskrift*, H. 4–5.

Ståhlberg, K. (1984) 'Diskriminerande drag i utnämningspolitiken', *Förvaltningsforskning Årsbok*, del 2.

Sundberg, J. (1984) 'Ethnic maintenance in an integrated mass democracy', *West European Politics*, 7: 91–108.

Sundberg, J. (1985a) 'Demassified mass parties or overloaded cadre parties? The impact of parties on electoral outcome in Finland', *Scandinavian Political Studies*, 8: 299–313.

Sundberg, J. (1985b) *Svenskhetens dilemma i Finland*. Helsinki: Finnish Society of Sciences and Letters.

Sundberg, J. (1989a) *Lokala partiorganisationer i kommunala och nationella val*. Helsinki: Finnish Society of Sciences and Letters.

Sundberg, J. (1989b) 'Premisser för politiskt massmedlemskap: partierna i Danmark i en nordisk jämförelse', *Politica*, 21: 288–311.

Sundberg, J. (1990) 'Lokala partiavdelningar och medlemsinsatser i valarbetet', in G. Djupsund and L. Svåsand (eds), *Partiorganisasjoner: studier i strukturer och processer i finske, norske og svenske partier*. Åbo: Åbo Akademy Press, pp. 209–38.

Sundberg, J. (1991) 'Participation in local government: a source of social democratic deradicalization in Scandinavia?' in L. Karvonen and J. Sundberg (eds), *Social Democracy in Transition*. Aldershot: Dartmouth, pp. 109–38.

Sundberg, J. and Gylling, C. (1992) 'Finland', in R. Katz and P. Mair (eds), *Party Organizations: A Data Handbook on Party Organizations in Western Democracies, 1960–90*. London: Sage, pp. 273–316.

Sundberg, J. and Högnabba, S. (1992) 'Finland: the 1991 campaign', in S. Bowler and D. Farrell (eds), *Electoral Strategies and Political Marketing*. London: Macmillan, pp. 82–99.

Uusitalo, H. (1975) *Class Structure and Party Choice: A Scandinavian Comparison*. Research Group for Comparative Sociology, University of Helsinki, Research Reports No. 8: 169–75.

Uusitalo, H. (1985) 'Luokkarakenne ja intressien organisoituminen', *Sosiologia*, 3.

Weber, M. (1978) *Economy and Society*, Vol. II. Berkeley: University of California Press.

8

Parties in a Legalistic Culture: The Case of Germany[1]

Thomas Poguntke

Political parties are curious objects of analysis. They are located somewhere between the orderly realm of the state and the fluid and sometimes chaotic sphere of society. And, by trying to provide what is arguably the most important linkage between state and society, they extend into both arenas. At the same time, parties have substantial influence on the legal fabric to which they are subject, and their accomplishments and failures mould the society of which they are part. Portraying parties as organizations, and attempting to identify the most important changes and continuities over time, therefore, confronts us with the problem of selecting the appropriate point of departure. Nevertheless, given that the primary interest here is with organizational characteristics, I have chosen to move from arenas which are external, and which are relatively aloof from direct interference of individual parties, to arenas, which, within certain limits, can be autonomously designed and regulated by the parties. In concrete terms, this means first looking at parties and their environments, which includes looking at the legal and constitutional framework and their relation with society. Although all of these arenas are continuously subject to party political moulding, they are, to varying degrees, external to parties. The internal distribution of power, on the other hand, is characterized by the highest degree of self-determination. Whereas a party can individually change its statutes, it can at most expect to influence society, and it can change legal and constitutional parameters normally only in concert with its most important competitors.

The advantage of starting the analysis with factors which are relatively resistant to change is that it concentrates attention on aspects which come quite close to representing external constraints, and against this background, which is common to all parties, I will analyse commonalities and differences in organizational designs and strategies. That said, the relations between the different arenas remain relevant throughout the analysis, in that change in one arena will always have repercussions on all other arenas.

Rather than starting with a clearly formulated set of hypotheses on the organizational development of political parties in the Federal Republic, I will attempt to identify the most important trends and junctures in different arenas and attempt to summarize and integrate these findings in the concluding section. Nevertheless, attention should be drawn to one basic line of argument which relates to Panebianco's (1988: 12) proposition that, with regard to their environments, and depending on a range of conditions, parties may follow strategies of adaptation or domination. In principle, organizations have an interest in having stable and predictable relationships with their relevant environments, and this can be accomplished through either of these strategies. Parties are not free to choose, however, since it can be argued that their strategic options depend heavily on the kind of interaction involved. This argument relates to the proposition that it is analytically useful to distinguish between three separate faces of party, that is, the party in public office, the party on the ground and the party central office (Katz and Mair, 1994), each of which tends to look in different directions. Whereas the party in central office may mainly be inward looking, the party on the ground is likely to be confronted with growing difficulties when attempting to dominate segments of an increasingly differentiated society. As a result, parties in modern society have to live with a considerable degree of uncertainty about electoral results and membership figures which, from an organizational perspective, and at least in Germany, implies that they must also live with uncertainty about revenue.

These difficulties for the party on the ground clearly have repercussions upon the party in public office, which is, after all, dependent on electoral results. At the same time, however, the party in public office has fairly direct leverage over another important environment for the party as a whole, that is, the state. As long as it agrees with its main competitors, it can mould the relevant legal environment, which determines the framework for electoral competition and the flow of public subsidies. Such changes, of course, may not equally benefit all party arenas. Public subsidies, to use an obvious example, are likely to strengthen the central office and the party in public office, but may further weaken the party on the ground. It is in this sense that party change should be conceptualized as the result of different interactions of individual faces of party with their relevant environments.

Parties and state

The constitutional fabric of the Federal Republic sets a number of parameters which have an overriding impact on the mutual relationships of different party arenas. In addition, German federalism with its strong *Land* parliaments and governments makes for the territorial fragmentation of the main party structure, that is, the extra-parliamentary party organization. In a way, German parties have not only three faces, but they also have three faces in each *Land* party and on the federal level. Some of the most important characteristics relevant from this perspective are, according to the Basic Law, unchangeable, and hence beyond the influence of the parties.[2] Consequently, parties have to adapt to constitutional parameters which can legitimately be expected to have had a powerful effect in inducing convergence of formerly diverse organizational models and which include first, the federal structure of government; second, the constitutionally guaranteed complete legal independence of parliamentary parties from their extra-parliamentary organization (which is based on the principle of a free parliamentary mandate – Art. 38, Basic Law); and third, the constitutionally required limitation of public money for political parties.

As a result of the intricacies of German constitutional law and jurisdiction on party finance the cross-nationally familiar division of parties between parliamentary and extra-parliamentary arena is complemented by a third element, the party foundations. These are, more precisely, 'party-oriented political foundations' (*parteinahe politische Stiftungen*), in that their extremely generous state funding and hence their very existence rests on the somewhat questionable supposition that they are not part of a specific party. Formal independence, of course, does not preclude intensive and very substantial substantive linkages, as will be seen below in more detail.

Constitutional parameters have therefore led to the fragmentation of party organization into three principal arenas which are, at least formally, independent of each other. Legally speaking, the parliamentary party and the party foundations are completely autonomous. They are connected with the extra-parliamentary organization only through personnel overlap and ideological affinities, but not through any statutory co-determination rights of party bodies in the affairs of either foundations or parliamentary parties. Correspondingly, the constitutionally stipulated need for the extra-parliamentary party to be democratically organized (Art. 21, Basic Law) prevents domination by its parliamentary fraktion.

German parties are also federations of more or less independent and powerful *Land* organizations. Clearly, the mere fact that the old Federal Republic was governed by eleven *Land* governments[3] and one federal chancellor means that, from the outset, the distribution of power, resources and incentives has set clear limits to the centralization of intra-organizational power. It is hardly surprising that German parties have tended to adapt their territorial structure to the federal and administrative structure of the Federal Republic (Kaack, 1971: 372). Since parties field candidates for elections at local, district, regional, *Land* and federal levels, there have been obvious pragmatic arguments to organize along these lines. On the other hand, a brief glance at their organizational history corroborates Panebianco's (1988: 17) argument that history goes a long way to explain their contemporary structures: regions have remained the most powerful territorial unit of the Social Democratic Party, while the Christian Democrats founded a North Rhine-Westphalian *Land* party only in 1986 (Schmid, 1990: 104f; Schmitt, 1992: 164). However, since a detailed longitudinal analysis of the organizational map at *Land* level is beyond the scope of this study, the focus throughout the chapter will be mainly on the federal level of party organization, with the role of lower-level organizational units being addressed only when they are of direct relevance to the federal party.

The legal framework

Whereas the fundamental constitutional environment cannot be changed by German parties, there is nevertheless an array of legal regulations directly affecting their central interests (such as the flow of public money, the electoral law, and the party law) which are subject to change by the law-makers, and hence by parties. Their discretion is constrained by constitutional law, however, and it is a typical, and somewhat questionable, feature of the German political process that the constitutionality of legislation concerning these aspects is regularly contested and hence controlled by the Constitutional Court.

   This raises the question of the extent to which the Constitutional Court is subject to party influence. Were it under fairly direct political influence, it could be argued that the legal environment of parties would be an object of domination rather than requiring adaptation. The situation is more intricate than this, however, and underlines the notion that roles may have an existence independent of actors. Thus, while the process of selecting Constitutional Judges is controlled by parties, the requirement to elect candidates with a two-thirds majority necessitates the search for candidates with a moderate and consensual political background, and this inhibits partisan political jurisdiction. This would not preclude jurisdiction in the interests of a party cartel, of course, and it could be argued that there have been examples of this. Nevertheless, several arrangements have tended to counteract such temptations, including the fact that constitutional judges enjoy extraordinarily high status, with the office itself representing the culmination of a legal career. There is, therefore, a built-in incentive for all members of the court to strive for highest professional standards. In addition, the prohibition of re-election guarantees maximum independence, in that there is nothing which a member of the Constitutional Court would normally expect from parties after the expiration of his or her term of office.

The electoral law

The electoral law includes detailed regulations regarding the nomination of list and constituency candidates for national elections, and, as a result, this aspect is scarcely mentioned in the party statutes (Poguntke with Boll, 1992: 368–71). That said, the Social Democrats do envisage the 'consultation' of their national executive in the nomination of both constituency and list candidates, even though the electoral law allows a veto only for the former[4] (Poguntke with Boll, 1992: 368), while in 1968 the CSU removed a clause from its statute which allowed its *Land* executive (or *Land* chairman) to veto constituency candidates on political and not only on procedural grounds – something which was in accordance with the electoral law (Poguntke with Boll, 1992: 370–1). In practice, these veto powers have never played a conspicuous role in the process of candidate selection (Kaack, 1971: 595), which is primarily dominated by local and regional power centres. Constituency candidates normally need a secure and well-entrenched local power base (Hesse and Ellwein, 1992: 205f), and it is only in exceptional circumstances that *Land* or federal party leaderships can hope to impose candidates of their own choosing. Similarly, *Land* lists are usually the result of intricate bargaining between the relevant district or regional power brokers, and external interference tends to be strongly resented (Haungs, 1992: 195; Niedermayer, 1993: 241). It is therefore not surprising that the very limited influence of *Land* or national leaderships on the composition of their parliamentary parties has been sometimes bemoaned (Wildenmann, 1989: 106). The placing of external candidates tends to be easier for constituencies which offer very little prospect for a direct seat. Since German parties normally expect their list candidates to run also in a constituency, the typical pattern is that external candidates are allocated a hopeless seat somewhere in the diaspora and are simultaneously pushed by the party leadership for a safe position on the *Land* list. The SPD has consistently tended to send prominent renegades like Otto Schily and Günter Verheugen to Bavaria.

From the perspective of organizational change, the electoral law represents a factor of continuity that has been reflected by the virtual absence of relevant statutory changes by the parties. The direct effects of legislation on internal party rules is, however, exemplified by the impact of the 1967 party law reform, to which I will now turn.

The party law

The fact that political parties were not even mentioned as legitimate actors in the political process by the Weimar constitution does not seem to have enhanced their legitimacy in that period. Learning from this lesson, the Basic Law includes explicit mention of the role of parties in the process of the 'formation of the political will of the people', with Article 21 going on to demand that their internal life be organized democratically. The specification of this rather general stipulation is left to further legislation and, interestingly enough, it took the *Bundestag* almost two decades (until 1967) to comply with this constitutional requirement. This late codification can be explained partly by the parties' unwillingness to constrain their own freedom of action through legal regulations (Oberreuter, 1992: 32), and by their inability to agree on the regulation of public subsidies, a source of income which had become increasingly important after 1959 (Kaack, 1971: 367). The most important reason for the actual timing of the party law, however, was a decision by the Constitutional Court in July 1966, which outlawed direct public funding of political parties, and which effectively

compelled the law-makers, who had already been discussing party legislation for a long time, to devise a comprehensive party law. This not only
regulated the conditions of public subsidies for specific party activities, that
is, election campaigns, but also codified a number of basic principles of
intra-party democracy, which had thus far remained unspecified (Hesse
and Ellwein, 1992: 164ff).

As regards the internal organization of parties, the most relevant
innovation of the party law was a severe limitation on the number of ex-
officio memberships in party assemblies and executives,[5] stipulating that
these could no longer exceed 20 per cent of the total membership (§9,11
Party Law) and that all executive bodies had to be elected by the respective
assemblies or assemblies of delegates (§9 Party Law). This can be
interpreted as a reaction to the trend of including ever greater numbers of
such members in these bodies, with the result that the number of ex-officio
members in executives frequently exceeded the number of elected
members. Indeed, prior to the party law, the SPD was the only party with
an executive composed exclusively of elected members. The FDP, on the
other hand, elected only 18 of its 35 members to the *Bundesvorstand*, while
in 1962 the CDU elected only 7 of its 69 executive members with full voting
rights through the national party congress, with 16 being elected by the
Bundesausschuß, 3 being coopted by the executive, and with 43 being ex
officio (Kaack, 1971: 381). There could be little doubt that such practices
were constitutionally problematic. Article 21 of the Basic Law had always
required parties to be democratically organized, and as long as this
stipulation was not specified through ordinary law, this had been the legal
basis of party organization.

The Party Law of 1967 resulted in the most far-reaching statutory
reforms in the parties during the past three decades. The Christian parties
had to revise their statutes substantially. Before 1967, the CDU party
council, which included many ex-officio members and was not directly
representative of the membership, had elected the bulk of the elected
members of the national executive. With the adoption of the new statute in
1967, however, this right was transferred to the party congress. Simultaneously, a substantial number of ex-officio memberships to the national
executive were abolished (Poguntke with Boll, 1992: 351–4), cutting its
overall size by half. Previously, the chairmen of *Land* parties, affiliated and
special organizations, CDU members of the federal government and a
representative of the *Bundestag* fraktion had been ex-officio members of
the national executive. The CSU underwent a similar substantial adaptation. Before 1968, only the *Land* party chairman was elected by the *Land*
party congress, with the remaining members being either ex-officio or
elected by the *Land* council (Poguntke with Boll, 1992: 354). In conformity
with the new legislation, these voting rights were transferred to the
congress in 1968, although the number of additional members was raised
from 15 to 25 in an effort to 'rescue' a number of ex-officio memberships.
Even then, however, the size of this body was reduced almost by half. The

Liberals chose a somewhat different path. From the outset, they had had a smaller national executive, and in 1968 they simply substituted the 11 *Land* party chairmen, who had been ex-officio members in the national executive, with 11 more elected members (Poguntke with Boll, 1992: 357). The Social Democrats were only obliged to make a minor statutory adjustment: the new party law required the secret election of party executives and delegates to higher-level assemblies (§15 Party Law), and this was written into the statute in 1968 (Poguntke with Boll, 1992: 349).

The passing of the Party Law would seem to offer a good example of a situation in which non-decision represents the optimum for all actors involved, in that as long as Article 21 of the Basic Law remained unspecified, all parties had maximum freedom of action regarding the organization of their internal affairs. When external forces (that is, the Constitutional Court) forced them to comply with the requirement of the Basic Law and to draft specific legislation, however, they were confronted with pervasive democratic norms which they could hardly ignore, even if this required substantial and, arguably, unwelcome organizational change. On the other hand, the streamlining of the organizational structure did bring about the statutory weakening of collateral organizations (in the CDU/CSU), which might be interpreted as an indication of growing independence of central party elites from partial external control.

Party finance

The most important aspect of the party law has been the regulation of public subsidies for political parties; ever since, it has also been the most problematic. Whereas all other regulations remained intact without any major adjustment, the history of legislation on party finance has taken almost as many twists and turns as an average roller-coaster ride, with most of these turns being imposed upon law-makers by the Constitutional Court.[6] At bottom, this is due to the ambivalent role given to political parties by the constitution. According to the Basic Law they are not part of the state machinery and it follows from this that parties are entitled to public subsidies only for activities that are directly related to the sphere of the state, that is, to the process of government or, more precisely, to the selection of political personnel (Oberreuter, 1992: 27). Consequently, parties can legitimately claim compensation for their expenses during election campaigns but cannot claim support for general organizational maintenance. That said, the fact that parties are organizations geared to the overriding goal of contesting elections makes this distinction largely academic, and election reimbursement has in reality developed into the functional equivalent of a general state subsidy to parties, which is paid in proportion to their strength at the previous election day (Landfried, 1990: 67; Oberreuter, 1992: 38; for details, see Poguntke with Boll, 1992: 384). The separation of parties from the state also demands (and this has been emphasized by the Constitutional Court) that parties must not get their

revenue predominantly from public budgets which, following the jurisdiction of the Constitutional Court, means that they cannot get more than
50 per cent in this way (Hesse and Ellwein, 1992: 175; Landfried, 1990: 46;
Oberreuter, 1992: 37).

Several attempts by the German parties to stretch these boundaries have
been met with at most temporary success, with relevant decisions by the
Constitutional Court being regularly reflected, and frequently 'misinter-
preted', by subsequent legislation (with the inevitable need to be corrected
by yet another Constitutional Court decision). Indirect state subventions to
parties were introduced in 1954, when donations became tax-deductible.
Then, in reaction to the 1958 judgement by the Constitutional Court,
which outlawed tax-deductibility, parties invented direct subsidies, which
were declared unconstitutional in 1966. However, since the Court had
indicated that financial compensation for election-related activities was
acceptable, election reimbursements were introduced in 1967 and first paid
in 1968. At the same time, tight limits were set for the tax-deductibility of
donations (600 DM per person, 1200 DM for married couples), and these
regulations remained basically unchanged until the biggest scandal related
to illegal financing of parties, the so-called Flick affair, made a complete
revision inevitable.[7] At the beginning of the 1980s, it had become apparent
that large donors had channelled their party donations through *gemeinnüt-
zige Organisationen* (organizations with a charitable status) in order to
make them tax-deductible. These illegal practices sparked off a wave of
prosecutions against senior politicians and the upper echelons of German
industry and commerce and virtually dried up the formerly continuous flow
of private finance to all established parties (von Arnim, 1991: 312ff). It is
therefore unsurprising that the parties had to devise a new system of party
finance. And since their members could hardly be expected to compensate
for the evaporation of private and corporate donations, they turned instead
to the state budget.

In 1984, the levels of tax-deductibility of private donations to parties
were increased to 5 per cent of private incomes and, for corporate
purposes, to 0.2 per cent of the total company wage bill. Since this would
have entailed substantial hidden subsidies to those parties which stood
greater chances of attracting large private or corporate donations, the so-
called *Chancenausgleich* was introduced at the same time, which involved a
formula leading to direct state subsidies to those parties which had less
chance of (that is, less success in) attracting donations. The calculation of
the *Chancenausgleich* also took account of the income from membership
fees, since these were also tax-deductible (Landfried, 1990: 46ff). Yet
another decision by the Constitutional Court in 1986 (initiated by the
Green Party) led to a revision of these regulations in 1988, and, from 1989
onwards, tax-deductibility of both corporate and private donations was
limited to 60,000 DM per annum (120,000 DM per annum for married
couples). At the same time, another direct subsidy, the *Sockelbetrag* (flat
rate) was paid in addition to the election reimbursement to all parties

which gained more than 2 per cent of the second vote in federal elections (Landfried, 1990: 64ff; Mintzel and Oberreuter, 1992: 566).

The whole system of public finance came up for revision again in April 1992, when the Constitutional Court, after another appeal by the Greens, corrected an earlier decision of 1986, which had tolerated the introduction of direct subsidies to the party organization through the *Chancenausgleich* in 1984 (Landfried, 1990: 96; Hesse and Ellwein, 1992: 175). The new decision not only abolished the *Sockelbetrag*, but also the *Chancenausgleich* and the generous ceilings for tax deductions. Tax-deductibility of corporate donations was declared unconstitutional, and private donations were limited to 1200 DM per annum (2400 DM for married couples). Whereas the *Sockelbetrag* was outlawed immediately, parliament was obliged to change all other regulations by the end of 1993 (Mintzel and Oberreuter, 1992: 567; *Süddeutsche Zeitung*, 10 April 1992).

All of this, of course, serves to show how the parties have been constrained by the Basic Law throughout the post-war period. Nevertheless, within these limits, parties have still been able to shape their legal environment according to their most imminent needs. Thus, when looking at trends over time, there are three important points to be underlined. First, the relative proportions of public subsidies to the three party arenas have remained fairly stable. Only in the case of the CSU has there been a noticeable gain in the financial weight of the party foundation, because it was founded only in 1967 (von Vieregge, 1977: 47). At the same time, there has been a very substantial growth in absolute figures, and even compared to general economic indicators (GNP, rate of inflation, income from dependent labour), the growth has certainly been out of proportion (Landfried, 1990: 91ff; for a different interpretation see Naßmacher, 1990: 143). Nevertheless, salaries of party employees, memberships and electorates have also grown, and a special commission called by the President of the Republic has argued that state subventions have actually lagged behind the expansion of the costs of the parties' political work (Landfried, 1990: 93).

Second, even if we disregard the enormous sums that go to party foundations, national parties have become increasingly dependent on money from public budgets. While the raw figures fluctuate widely with election cycles (Poguntke with Boll, 1992: 384ff), there is nevertheless a clear tendency for public money to become more important: by the end of the 1980s, for example, the proportion of state subventions had reached between 60 and 80 per cent of total central office income.[8] Moreover, as a means of compensating for the severe constitutional limitations to the expansion of public funding of extra-parliamentary activities, parties have continuously increased revenues for their parliamentary parties in the *Bundestag* (Poguntke with Boll, 1992: 384–8). From 1949 onwards, part of this money was spent on employing staff for the parliamentary parties (see Table 8.1). In addition, publicly paid parliamentary assistants for individual MPs were introduced in 1969, which put an end to the so-called three

Table 8.1 *Numbers of fraktion staff paid by the state, by fraktion*

Parliament	Date	CDU/CSU	SPD	FDP	Greens	Total
1949–53	1953		1			
1953–57	1957		25			
1957–61	1961		40			
1961–65	1965		50			
1965–69	1966	33	67	15		115
	1968	37	78	16		131
	1969	40	99	21		160
1969–72	1970	99	104	23		226
	1971	113	99	27		239
1972–76[a]	1974	71	130	42		243
	1975	75	134	47		256
1976–80[a]	1977	74	141	50		265
	1979	78	154	50		282
1980–83	1981	175	159	59		393
1983–87	1983	192	190	51	75	508
1987–90	1987	227	252	54	86	619

[a] The CDU/CSU data are incomplete, as is therefore the overall total.

Sources: Schindler, 1984, 1988

classes of parliamentarians: those who could dispose of support from assistants employed by their parliamentary party because of their senior function, those who could employ assistants through external support (for example, interest organizations or large firms), and those who had nothing (Schindler, 1984: 983ff). Finally, although the data in Figure 8.1 are incomplete, a clear picture emerges. The number of publicly paid staff, either directly for MPs or for the parliamentary party as a whole, has continuously increased, despite the fact that the actual number of MPs for individual parties has at times shrunk quite substantially due to unfavourable election results (Poguntke with Boll, 1992: 338–40).

More specifically, however, there has been a faster growth in the number of personal assistants for MPs. Parliamentarians can select their personal aides individually and are allowed to use these funds for employing assistants in their home constituencies,[9] a factor which has tended to strengthen the position of individual MPs vis-à-vis their parliamentary leadership. At the same time, it goes without saying that much political work, which otherwise would have been carried out by the extra-parliamentary party, has been taken over by parliamentary parties or by MPs' assistants (Ismayr, 1992: 42). The somewhat unexpected lessons of the Greens following their accession to the *Bundestag* are witness to the normative power of financial realities (see p. 207; and Poguntke, 1987, 1993a: 136ff, 1993b; Raschke, 1993: 572), while the coincidental provision of public money for parliamentary assistance with the new regulations on party finance in the late 1960s was certainly not accidental.

Third, party-related foundations have been allocated phenomenal financial resources since 1965 (Poguntke with Boll, 1992: 384ff; von Arnim, 1991: 366). The very condition of their existence has always been the

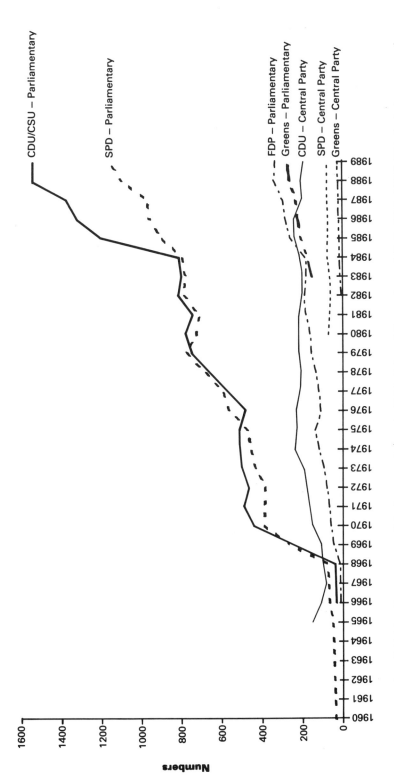

Figure 8.1 *Paid staff* ((a) Parliamentary staff is the sum of data in Table 8.1 and Poguntke and Boll, 1992: 338ff. This includes personal assistants and personnel of the parliamentary parties. Missing data have been estimated. (b) Central Party staff data from Poguntke with Boll, 1992: 338ff)

presumption that they are not part of political parties, and the party law of 1967 therefore prohibits the overlap of leading positions in parties and foundations (§11.2). This prohibition extends only to the positions of chairman and treasurer, however, and leading party politicians, including party chairmen, have always served on the boards of the respective party foundations (Landfried, 1990: 111f; von Arnim, 1991: 113; von Vieregge, 1977: 35ff). However, there is obviously a wide range of activities which are not directly relevant for the domestic political success of the 'mother' parties. Roughly two-thirds of the foundations' funds were predetermined for specific purposes, and frequently for Third World projects (Landfried, 1990: 110). The so-called foreign policy of party foundations and scholarship schemes for foreign and domestic students are also examples of how public money is administered through party foundations, although even these functions can strengthen the respective party. Scholarships for students, for example, serve as important incentives for the recruitment of junior politicians, and party foundations represent an important patronage arena (frequently after political careers have passed their peaks) (Landfried, 1990: 103ff; Schmidt, 1986: 625). The remaining one-third of public money has always been paid without detailed requirements for public accounting and was intended to help the foundations in their efforts to further 'political education'. Most of these activities are also of direct benefit to the 'mother' parties. Party foundations organize all sorts of seminars, which tend to attract mainly party members, and carry out or commission research that is directly relevant for party purposes (von Arnim, 1991: 133ff; von Vieregge, 1977). The Christian Democratic Konrad-Adenauer-Stiftung is particularly efficient in conducting longitudinal electoral studies which are certainly of interest to the party's planning staff (Landfried, 1990: 103ff; von Vieregge, 1977: 81ff). Another important activity, which otherwise would have to be paid for directly by the parties themselves, is the administration of the party archive and the documentation of party history. Last but not least, party foundations maintain contacts with relevant social segments of society, such as intellectuals, trades unions, religious groups and the like (von Vieregge, 1990: 168ff). Given that it is impossible to estimate the proportions of the foundations' budgets which directly benefit their 'mother' parties, public funds for foundations cannot simply be aggregated with other public subsidies for parties. Nevertheless, a brief look at the sheer amounts involved clearly shows that party foundations represent powerful and resourceful conglomerates which are, in effect, under party control.[10]

The one very unambiguous message that emerges from these data is that German parties are to a very substantial degree dependent on the continuous flow of public money. If we accept the somewhat questionable assumption that party foundations are not part of the party machine, dependency of *national* party headquarters on public money has tended to fluctuate between 50 and 70 per cent since the late 1960s, with a tendency to increase over time, whereas it has fluctuated around 40 per cent for the party as a whole (Landfried, 1990: 95, 115). If we add the income of party foundations and the subsidies to the parliamentary parties of the *Bundestag* (which excludes the salaries of MPs' assistants), the self-generated income of political parties on the *national level* becomes almost negligible,[11] falling from around 20 per cent to less than 10 per cent since 1970 in most cases. This is not to suggest, however, that membership contributions per se have become irrelevant to the extra-parliamentary party as such. The proportion which membership fees have contributed to party budgets has not changed dramatically since the end of the late 1960s, although it has fluctuated considerably. In general, the following picture emerges: the CDU and SPD *head offices* have obtained about 30 per cent of their incomes from membership fees, whereas the figure for the CSU budget is some 10 per cent. Both the FDP and the Greens are below even this margin. Similarly, both large parties could count more on the membership as far as their *total budgets* were concerned than could their smaller competitors. By and large, half of the SPD's total income has come from its members since the late 1960s, whereas the CDU raised this share from around 30 per cent to around 40 per cent, and the CSU from 20 per cent to about 25 per cent. The FDP has remained near the 20 per cent level, while the Greens have remained around the 10 per cent level.

In fact, even these figures underestimate the true financial dependence of parties on the state, in that the parliamentary deputies of the CDU/ CSU, the SPD and the FDP pay, on all levels, substantial shares of their incomes (which come from public budgets) to their parties. Between 1968 and 1983, these party taxes had to be listed separately in the parties' annual financial reports, and have contributed, on average, the following shares of total party incomes: CDU 9 per cent, CSU 7 per cent, SPD 9 per cent, and FDP 7 per cent (Landfried, 1990: 99). The Greens had a different system, which nevertheless strengthened the party indirectly by enhancing its social anchorage, in which MPs were expected to donate large sums to their eco-fund, which was used to support alternative projects (Poguntke, 1993a: 145f; Raschke, 1993: 505). As noted, generous tax deductions for party donations also represent indirect public funding.

Parties as systems of patronage

Patronage is another important resource for German parties, and includes preferential promotion within the civil service, appointment to positions in companies and corporations which are under political control, and favourable treatment of political friends in public contracts. The possibility to reward the party faithful represents an important incentive for recruiting active members and office holders, particularly on the local level, where political mandates are not in themselves very attractive financially. In addition, and politically more relevant, patronage is an important means of perpetuating political power beyond a specific party's governmental incumbency (Derlin, 1988: 60; Hesse and Ellwein, 1992: 349; von Arnim,

1980: 17). Widely cited examples include recruitment of school head-masters on party political grounds and politically guided promotion within the educational bureaucracy. The German administrative system also allows for the institution of a limited number of 'political civil servants' at the top of the bureaucratic hierarchy, who can be retired on political grounds. In addition, the differentiated vertical structure of the German governmental and administrative system provides wide scope for the politically motivated allocation of non-political jobs. German federalism means that all *Land* bureaucracies are also 'natural' targets for political parties who want to reward members or sympathizers within the civil service. In principle, local government, particularly in smaller communes, need not be dominated by party politics. Nevertheless, German parties have permeated the political process right down to the local level, albeit with certain competition from independent local lists (*Wählervereinigungen*), particularly in the south (Rudzio, 1991: 363ff). Since the top positions of local administrations are elective offices with up to twelve years of service, it is hardly surprising that political parties should have successfully attempted to attain control over these spoils.

Those parties with governmental relevance at either of the three principal levels of government (federal, *Land*, local), therefore, decide between them upon virtually all positions which are either directly political or located at the top of the respective bureaucracies. In addition, they influence promotion procedures in the administration and the allocation of positions in publicly controlled companies on all levels of the political system. It is an important feature of the German party system that all established parties have been in this comfortable position throughout the history of the Federal Republic. Even the Greens have been part of local governing arrangements from the very beginning of their existence.[12] Furthermore, it took the Greens only six years to enter the first *Land* government (Poguntke with Boll, 1992: 330).

The scope for patronage is also ample, ranging from directorships in the *Landesbanken* (the *Land* equivalents of the *Bundesbank*) and top positions in the publicly controlled electronic media, to managing positions in local or regional service companies for water, electricity, local transport or waste disposal. Many of these companies are organized as private firms, which means they are not subject to civil service regulations. This means that the respective political bodies which control these companies are legally unconstrained when it comes to deciding upon lavish annual incomes. Since the bulk of such companies are controlled by local politics, German town and city politics is more 'attractive' than appears to be the case at first sight.

As far as quantitative empirical evidence is concerned, patronage is, of course, just as hard to grasp as political corruption. In most cases, all the participants involved are beneficiaries, and there is virtually no incentive for anybody to testify that a specific appointment has been made on political grounds. That said, the existence of the phenomenon is beyond doubt and examples abound, and there is little dissent in the literature that long-lasting incumbency of one party or coalition regularly leads to a situation in which virtually all higher posts in the bureaucracy are occupied by party members or declared sympathizers. Moreover, since overall majorities are not the rule in local councils, parties have, at least in some cases, been tempted to use inter-party agreements in order to ensure that all relevant parties get their share of the spoils. It goes without saying that such deals tend to disregard smaller parties or even new entrants to the political game, and can therefore be regarded as a conspicuous example of cartel-like behaviour (Derlin, 1988: 61; Scheuch and Scheuch, 1992; von Alemann, 1992: 119, 129; von Arnim, 1980).

In general, then, the legal environment requires some adaptation but also offers itself to a certain degree of domination – as long as the central actors can muster the necessary parliamentary majorities. Since an absolute majority on the federal level has only occurred once in the history of the Federal Republic, parties have normally been confronted with the need for collective action,[13] thereby trying to anticipate the repercussions of such decisions upon their own organization. Of course, this involves substantial risks. Consequently, and not surprisingly, the rules of the game are hard to change by the players themselves. A good example was the abortive attempt during the Grand Coalition (1966–69) by the Christian Democrats and the Social Democrats to introduce a majoritarian electoral system in order to eliminate the FDP from federal politics (Kaack, 1971: 399). In the end, the Social Democrats shied away from the risk of getting stuck in an inexorable minority position and preferred to maintain the familiar situation (which gives the FDP a pivotal position).

There is also one important conclusion which emerges from the preceding analysis of party legislation. *Bundestag* parties have consistently tried to privilege themselves. When election reimbursements were introduced in 1967, the threshold for eligibility was 2.5 per cent of the second vote. Similarly, legislation has tended to privilege parties as opposed to independent candidates or non-party lists. Until 1979, for example, independent candidates could not claim election reimbursement. In addition, parties which are not represented in the *Bundestag* or a *Land* parliament need to collect signatures in order to be allowed to put up candidates (Poguntke with Boll, 1992: 331). Although established parties have repeatedly been forced by the Constitutional Court to correct such regulations, they nevertheless got away with substantial competitive advantages, the most conspicuous example of which is certainly the toleration of party foundations. The requirement formulated by the Court that all 'relevant and lasting' political forces should have access to public money for political foundations is operationalized through representation in the *Bundestag* or *Land* parliaments and is not available to new entrants to the political game (von Arnim, 1991: 114). The substantial growth of resources for parliamentary parties has a corresponding effect of strengthening those who have already arrived in the centres of power.

Parties and society

Parties and collateral organizations

Unlike the Social Democrats and the Liberals, which have always had unitary party structures, the Christian Democrats have an array of affiliated organizations with, in most cases, only partially overlapping memberships.[14] Before party legislation stipulated comparatively high standards of internal democracy for German parties in 1967, the Christian parties had substantial ex-officio representation of their affiliated organizations on their national executives, which were intended to be as representative as possible of all relevant social and regional groups within the party structure (Haungs, 1983: 69). After 1967, the Christian Democrats 'shifted' the representation of affiliated organizations primarily to the national council, whereas the composition of the national executive continued to be strongly influenced by regional aspects (Schmid, 1990: 158). Since the party council is a larger body, a larger number of ex-officio representatives is legally acceptable. The CSU has always had this kind of representation on its *Land* council, but limited it to the chairpersons of the *Vereinigungen* after 1968, whereas there had been representation according to the membership levels before 1968 (Poguntke with Boll, 1992, 350–61). Representation of affiliated organizations on party congresses played no role after the introduction of party legislation in 1967. Consequently, the CSU abolished the proportional representation of its affiliated organizations in the congress in the same year. This does not, of course, preclude the invitation of guests, which is sometimes (as in the FDP since 1974) laid down in the party statute.

Limiting the representation of affiliated organizations on party executives was also arguably in the interest of the Christian Democratic party elites who used external (that is, legal) constraints to move closer towards a unitary and more centralized party structure (Schönbohm, 1985: 69). Nevertheless, some affiliated organizations have remained important power bases for party careers (Haungs, 1992: 197; Höfling, 1980a: 145; von Winter, 1993: 66), even though the political power of leaders of such organizations does not depend primarily on statutory rights. Rather, it is directly related to their ability to control relevant power resources like money or strategically indispensable segments of the electorate. Experience has shown that this is fairly independent from the actual membership levels of affiliated organizations. The trade union wing of the Christian Democrats (CDA), for example, has always been a powerful internal force, because it controlled a segment of the electorate which was crucial both arithmetically and as evidence that the CDU and CSU were indeed *Volksparteien* (Pütz, 1985: 40ff). Correspondingly, Christian Democratic women's organizations have played minor roles – for most of the post-war period, female Christian Democrats have tended to be loyal and fairly deferential party members (Haungs, 1983: 53). Finally, the *Wirtschaftsrat der CDU*, a Christian Democratic business association, which has always been very powerful, never actually developed formalized links with the party, knowing that formalized linkages would not enhance their influence, which was based on their control of donations (Dittberner, 1973: 217ff). Indeed, a formal link could have made their activities more open to public and party scrutiny, and could have required (after 1967) a more democratic internal structure (Höfling, 1980a: 132). Generally speaking, however, and with these exceptions, the development of organizational linkages has tended to follow the real weight of the respective affiliated organizations, and the gradual reduction of representation rights of the 'special organizations' (*Exil-CDU, Landsverband Oder-Neiße*), which took care of the interests of refugees from the East, mirrors the declining relevance of these organizations.

The Liberals and the Social Democrats, on the other hand, have never had representatives from ancillary or affiliated organizations with voting rights on their leadership bodies. The FDP admits only advisory members of its youth and student organization. However, this is where similarity ends, for, with the exception of its formally independent youth[15] and student organizations, the FDP is a party without sub-organizations (Dittberner, 1987: 91; Vorländer, 1992: 303–4),[16] whereas the SPD organization is characterized by an array of ancillary organizations with complete membership overlap (Poguntke with Boll, 1992: 334f). As late as 1986, the SPD introduced the advisory representation of the trade union liaison council and the council for party seniors on the party council (Poguntke with Boll, 1992: 350), but has no formalized representation of the party's ancillary organizations. As regards organizational linkages to society, the immediate post-war period represents a crucial moment on two accounts: the trade unions reorganized independently from political parties, and it became apparent that the traditional subcultural network would not recover its former viability (Lehnert, 1983: 179; Schütz, 1955: 209f). In conjunction with the party's ideological reorientation, these developments culminated in the famous Godesberg Programme, which laid the foundation for the conversion of the SPD into a modern 'people's party' with a cross-class appeal and for its successful abandonment of the '30 per cent tower'.[17] Nevertheless, although Social Democratic ancillary organizations have no special representation rights in the main party structure, some have proved very powerful actors in their own right. Not surprisingly, this has always been the case for the trade union-oriented *Arbeitsgemeinschaft für Arbeitnehmerfragen* and, more recently, for the women's organization, the *Arbeitsgemeinschaft sozialdemokratischer Frauen*, which successfully fought for women's quotas within the party (Heimann, 1986: 2153ff; Poguntke with Boll, 1992: 373; Schmitt, 1992: 165). In the aftermath of the student rebellion, the 'march through the institutions' led many neo-Marxists into the Young Socialists, which became a powerful and sizeable focus for intra-party dissent. Tighter controls of the Young Socialists through the party leaderships on all organizational levels were introduced in 1975 and the conflict between the Young Socialists and the party leadership culminated in 1977, when the national executive successfully initiated the dismissal of the former's newly-elected chairman (Heimann, 1986: 2163). Ever since, the Young Socialists have played no major role in internal debates – not least because the Greens attracted most of the radical youth throughout the 1980s.

The Greens have no sub-organizations (the project of a Green youth organization was launched only in the early 1990s), even though working groups (*Bundesarbeitsgemeinschaften*) could be regarded as a functional equivalent to ancillary or affiliated organizations in other parties. These do not organize segmental interests, however, but are oriented along ideological and/or thematic lines. They also serve as an important linkage between the party and its subcultural environment, which is made up of the so-called social movement sector (Poguntke, 1993a: 161). In fact, the capacity of the Greens to influence the political agenda of the Federal Republic depends to a considerable degree on their relation with various social movements and the level of social movement mobilization. Corresponding to the functions traditional collateral organizations like trade unions, the Catholic Church and business associations perform for SPD, CDU/CSU and FDP (though obviously with declining importance), social movements represent an important societal anchorage for the Greens. That said, they are also much less constant, less reliable and less open to domination from above, that is, from party leaders (Kitschelt, 1989: 226ff; Raschke, 1993: 687ff).

Parties and party members

Contrary to developments in several other European democracies, membership levels of German parties have not decreased significantly throughout the 1980s (Poguntke with Boll, 1992: 332). When looking at the size of membership as a percentage of the total electorate, there has also been no dramatic decline, although it is evident that the year 1980 does mark the peak of party mobilization (Katz, Mair et al., 1992: 341). There has been some erosion in absolute numbers, however, and this trend has accelerated substantially in the early 1990s (see Table 8.2), arguably as a result of the growing popular disaffection with the performance of political parties in the wake of growing socio-economic problems following unification (Falter and Schumann, 1993; Niedermayer, 1993).

The development of party membership figures is witness to the conventional wisdom on post-war German history. The 1950s and 1960s were characterized by widespread political apathy, and then, in the aftermath of the student rebellion and the election of the first Social Democratic chancellor in 1969, German society underwent substantial political mobilization, which was reflected in an overall increase of party membership. The most conspicuous trend in the data is clearly the rapid membership growth of the CDU and the CSU in the 1970s, which was the result of the

Table 8.2   *Numbers of party members in the new Germany, 1990–92*

	31 Dec. 1990	31 Dec. 1991	31 Dec. 1992
CDU			
West Germany[a]	685,411	641,454	619,579
East Germany	134,409	109,709	94,267
Total[b]	777,767	751,163	713,846
CSU	186,198	184,513	181,758
SPD			
West Germany[a]	919,129	892,657	860,214
East Germany	30,421	27,214	25,744
Total[b]	949,550	919,871	885,958
FDP			
West Germany[a]	71,368	68,641	66,283
East Germany	106,966	68,916	36,904
Total[b]	168,217	140,031	103,505
Green Party			
West Germany[a]	40,049	37,533	36,399
East Germany	1,267	1,340	1,149
Total[b]	41,316	38,054	35,845
PDS			
East Germany	±200,000	172,578	146,742

[a] Includes Berlin (SPD 1990 only West Berlin).
[b] Breakdowns do not always sum to totals (see note on sources).

Sources: Totals are taken from financial reports of parties; *Bundestagsdrucksachen* 12/5575 and 12/6140. Due to the turmoil of the unification process, the figures for East Germany are (un)reliable estimates by party headquarters; for breakdowns, see Niedermayer and Stöss (1993); the figures for the Green Party are provided by party headquarters

combined effects of the intense political polarization over Willy Brandt's *Ostpolitik* in the early 1970s and the successful organizational moderniz-ation of the party machines following the loss of governmental power (Haungs: 1983: 28; Schönbohm, 1985: 84ff). After 1969, and cut off from the governmental resources they had been used to ever since the beginning of the Federal Republic, the CDU in particular realized that it needed a modern mass-based party as a means for recapturing power in Bonn (Kleinmann, 1993: 316f; Pütz, 1985: 58ff; Schönbohm, 1985: 99ff), and party elites saw party members as an indispensable device for getting their message across in a society that was then dominated by Social Democratic and Liberal ideas. This perception of the role of party members has arguably changed since then, although this is not easily substantiated. In any case, the growing importance of electronic media and the increased professionalization of election campaign techniques has tended to down-grade the external function of members. Indeed, there is now an ongoing debate, particularly in the CDU, about whether party organizations should be turned into modern service organizations (von Winter, 1993: 76). As noted above, however, party members remain important financial contributors, and, significantly, models for the reform of public party finance, which are currently debated, tend to take account of the amount of membership contributions when it comes to devising formulae for the allocation of public money (Bundestagsdrucksache 12/4425 (1993): 27). This indicates that the number of members is implicitly regarded as a yardstick for the legitimacy of certain political parties.

As regards the internal function of party members, their most important role has continued to be that of providing the virtually exclusive reservoir for party elites at all levels of the political system, and the recruitment of political personnel without a prolonged intra-party career has remained a rare exception. In internal decision-making, the rights of individual party members are guaranteed by the party law and yet are severely limited by the harsh realities of politics in large organizations. Formal rights of party members are nonetheless quite extensive and relatively uniform. All party executives have to be legitimated through secret elections, and even at party conferences ordinary delegates can try to influence proceedings with motions concerning points of order (*Geschäftsordnungsanträge*) or emergency motions (*Dringlichkeitsanträge*). The differential effects of these participation rights in different parties underlines the need to move beyond formal rules when analysing party organizations: whereas Green Party congress delegates have tended to obstruct and confuse proceedings through the excessive use of these participation rights (Raschke, 1991), CSU party conferences, to use an extreme example, have rarely been venues of lively and controversial discussion.

The real influence of ordinary party members is hard to assess without accounting for differential internal participatory cultures and informal processes. From this perspective, the CSU, at least until the early 1990s, has remained a party with a highly centralized and cohesive power elite which is capable of controlling all important decisions. Similarly, the CDU remains an example of an organization that is largely dominated by (sometimes competing) leadership groups (von Winter, 1993: 62). As a corollary of low membership levels, individual members of the FDP are in a position to exert a comparatively strong influence, but this virtually never happens in practice. The Social Democrats, on the other hand, have undergone substantial changes regarding their internal culture of debate. With the influx of New Politics-oriented members and party elites (Schmitt, 1987), the old dogma of *Geschlossenheit* (closed ranks), based on the central norm of solidarity, has given way to a more controversial style of internal debate – something Helmut Schmidt experienced with some bitterness during the later years of his incumbency. After a successful consultative membership ballot in the 1993 leadership contest, the party leadership successfully pushed for further *Basisdemokratie*. In November 1993, the party congress approved of the proposed opening up of party structures and party lists for general elections to non-members and the introduction of binding membership ballots (SPD-Parteivorstand, 1993a,

1993b). Ironically, the Greens have moved in the opposite direction. Following their defeat in the first all-German elections, they have not only abandoned some of the principles of grassroots democracy (Poguntke, 1993a: 167ff; Poguntke with Boll, 1992: 360f), but have also become increasingly willing to grant their elites some discretion in the management of the party in everyday politics and even, to an extent, in matters of fundamental ideological orientations.

The internal distribution of power

In attempting to draw a map of internal power relations in German parties, it is necessary not only to look to the three faces of party, that is the party in public office, the party on the ground and the central party office; but also to the effects of federalism and the role of party foundations. This also inevitably raises the question of an adequate conceptualization of power. First and foremost, there is formal power. Party statutes and the legal framework specify the competencies of individual intra-party positions or bodies, such as party leaders, party congresses, or general secretaries. However, the mere fact that the party congress has the formal right to denounce policies pursued by its own chancellor, for example, obviously does not mean that it can freely exercise this right without risking the electoral performance of the party, and hence its organizational stability, as a whole. The strained relationship between Helmut Schmidt and the SPD during the debate over the deployment of medium-range nuclear missiles offers a vivid example, and also indicates that it makes more sense to conceptualize power as the ability to dominate intra-party decision-making processes and exchange relations which are relevant for the organizational survival of the party (Duverger, 1964: 146ff; Panebianco, 1988: 22). Formal competences are, of course, always a very important resource in power games, and this justifies looking first at the distribution of formal power. There are also other resources, however, which may weigh more heavily at times. Such resources may even be located outside the actual party organization, as we have seen in the case of the *Wirtschaftsrat der CDU*. In fact, control over relevant resources may be more effective without formal linkages, because such a constellation leaves other party arenas without the possibility of using formal powers to gain at least partial control over these resources. Hence, the degree of autonomy of party arenas vis-à-vis one another should also be considered when attempting to assess their relative weight. Finally, external factors, such as access to mass media, and hence electoral appeal, are crucial when seeking to assess the location of political leadership.

Formal powers

From the perspective of democratic theory, the relation between parlia-mentary and extra-parliamentary party is of overriding interest, and in all

Western democracies, the liberal tradition of the free mandate collides with the aspirations of extra-parliamentary parties to dominate, guide or control 'their' parliamentarians. In the age of modern party-dominated politics and, particularly, in systems with proportional representation, parties view MPs as their own creatures and hence as subject to their command. Of course, traditions also differ substantially. It was only in the 1970s that the CDU/CSU and the FDP, coming from the tradition of the bourgeois cadre party (Duverger, 1964: 63ff), moved somewhat closer to the concept of political guidance through an extra-parliamentary party organization. The Social Democrats, on the other hand, have a long tradition of extra-parliamentary dominance, which was gradually relegated in the course of the party's movement towards a modern, ideologically moderate catch-all party. Ironically, the Greens rediscovered old Socialist principles and called for an 'imperative mandate' (Poguntke, 1993a: 146), albeit without noticeable success, since constitutional law prevents any serious attempts to put pressure on MPs. This also explains why German parliamentary parties are autonomously organized and why there are no formal links from external party organizations to parliamentary parties. In the opposite direction, however, the Christian parties and the Liberals have always ensured representation rights of their parliamentary fraktion in the national executive and the national council. The SPD, on the contrary, has never had any such linkages, whereas the Greens introduced them in 1991 (Poguntke with Boll, 1992: 361).

As regards the formal control of the national leadership over the party, there has been a moderate tendency towards more domination through the introduction of a general secretary in the CDU 1967 (Poguntke with Boll, 1992: 352) and in the FDP in 1971 (Poguntke with Boll, 1992: 355), and through the introduction of the right of the national executive to control ancillary organizations in the SPD (in 1971; Poguntke with Boll, 1992: 349). By and large, however, the formal distribution of power has remained fairly static over the past three decades, and the most important changes have already been discussed above in conjunction with the party law of 1967. The extensive legal regulation of internal democracy has in fact led to very similar formal party structures after 1967. In all parties, the democratic sovereign is the party congress which has to be convened at least biannually and has the right to elect the party leadership and decide upon the party programme and policy guidelines (Poguntke with Boll, 1992: 364ff). All parties have a party council as an intermediate body between party leadership and party congress, which is often called the 'little party congress' and, since it meets several times per year, this body tends to take over the political functions of party conferences on a more permanent basis (Poguntke with Boll, 1992: 350–61). The most noticeable change since 1967 has been the complete restructuring of the Green Party council, which was intended to improve coordination between *Land*, federal and parliamentary politics through personnel overlap. In addition, the new body lost its right to make binding decisions for the federal leadership – something which had led to much internal conflict in the Green Party throughout the 1980s (Poguntke, 1993a: 167ff; Poguntke with Boll, 1992: 360f).

All of these structures on the federal level are essentially mirrored in the organizational structures of the *Land* parties which, despite certain control rights of the federal leadership, enjoy considerable autonomy. Parties are voluntary organizations, and individual *Land* organizations could always choose the exit option. Party head offices, on the other hand, have the right to disown *Land* organizations which have defected from the common cause. The Greens were confronted with this problem when their rudimentary *Land* party organization in West Berlin had drifted to the far right in the mid-1980s.

The weight of resources

As has been indicated above, resources in internal power games can range from money and staff to more immaterial resources such as electoral appeal or media access. Let us first look at material resources, the distribution of which is arguably decisive when it comes to political preponderance in an everyday political process which is characterized by a high degree of specialization and dependency on legal and technical knowledge. Party arenas with good access to resources will clearly be in a stronger position when it comes to drafting specific legislation or writing detailed and specific policy proposals or action programmes. First of all, however, it needs to be emphasized that, despite their enormous budgets, the party foundations are practically of no importance in internal power games. Were this to be otherwise, the parties would risk the outlawing of their bonanzas by the Constitutional Court. This is not say that the foundations do not participate in the political debate of their respective political tendency; on the contrary, they organize research, workshops, and discussion groups on political problems. Nevertheless, they must refrain from getting involved in the actual policy formation process, and the parliamentary party and party head office are therefore the only relevant contenders for political power at the federal level.[18]

As far as the development of total incomes of party head offices and parliamentary parties is concerned, there has been no conspicuous shift in the balance (Poguntke with Boll, 1992: 378ff). Incomes do not tell the whole story, however, and how the money is spent is arguably more important. This makes all the difference, and the data support the argument that the bulk of public money going to parties is indeed, according to legal requirements, spent on campaigning (Poguntke with Boll, 1992: 381ff).[19] There is therefore a fairly limited permanent effect on the organization as such. Party headquarters certainly dominate the organization and execution of election campaigns, but they have little capacity to screen or even guide policy formation at the parliamentary level. The development of paid personnel at the disposal of head offices and Members of Parliament is an important indicator here, for while head offices have not succeeded in expanding their numbers of staff significantly over the past two decades, MPs have legislated for substantial increases in their own staff (see Figure 8.1). This effect of the parliamentary system, in conjunction with low membership figures, probably helps to explain the failure of the Greens to realize the intended dominance of extra-parliamentary politics (Poguntke, 1992, 1993b).

Political leadership

The most relevant aspect of power refers to the question of political leadership, that is, the power to dominate decisions over the 'great issues' and hence the capacity to determine the electoral performance, which is most relevant for a party's organizational stability. In modern mass media societies, such political leadership is inevitably based on formal power and media access, and on both counts parliamentary parties are structurally in a strong position. The logic of the media system is focused on the activities of the national government and, as a corollary, on the behaviour of parliamentary elites in relation to the government. Consequently, the performance of parliamentary parties has a considerable effect on electoral fortunes. In addition, their independence is constitutionally guaranteed. The method of candidate selection determines the power relations between parliamentary party and party organization more than any constitutional article or statutory rule, however, and we have already seen that party headquarters have relatively little influence over the nomination of parliamentary candidates. Parliamentarians know that their re-selection depends primarily on their personal reputation in their constituency or, in the case of list candidates, on their support in the regional party organization. And since their re-election, that is, their party's electoral performance, depends to a very considerable degree on the performance of their parliamentary party, MPs owe relatively little to the party head office.

Moreover, German federalism has tended to weaken national extra-parliamentary leaderships over the past decades. As a result of the increasing inter-weaving of federal and *Land* politics, the portion of federal legislation which needs approval of the *Bundesrat* has grown substantially. Depending on the constellation of majorities in the *Bundestag* and the *Bundesrat*, *Land* prime ministers have frequently, and arguably increasingly, followed their own *Land*-related interests. Since *Land* parties are primarily interested in their own electoral success, this is hardly surprising.

Finally, leadership depends considerably on the constellation of leading personalities and the position of the respective party in government or opposition. Hence, it can come as no surprise that the political dominance of party arenas has varied considerably over time. The CDU of the 1950s, for example, had little organizational life outside parliament and was almost entirely dominated by Konrad Adenauer. When the party was relegated to opposition in 1969, the extra-parliamentary party was strengthened organizationally and politically (Haungs, 1983: 70ff; Schönbohm, 1985: 99ff). After Helmut Kohl had also become chairman of the parliamentary party in 1976, leadership began to shift back to the *Bundestag* party, a process which culminated in the late 1980s and early 1990s, when Kohl had assumed almost *Alleinherrschaft* in the CDU and, to an extent, even over the CSU. Whereas the growing importance of the party head office in the early 1970s was accompanied by a corresponding growth of head office staff, later changes were not reflected in the respective weight of resources. Clearly, they were almost exclusively the result of political and personal constellations. The developments in the SPD are almost the mirror-image of the CDU developments, and culminated in the strong position of Helmut Schmidt which, of course, did not long remain unchallenged by the extra-parliamentary party. There can be little doubt that this was also a result of personal constellations, in that Willy Brandt remained party chairman after his resignation as chancellor in 1974. The Liberals have, throughout their history, remained in the tradition of a cadre party with parliamentary politics dominant. This has also been facilitated by their pivotal position in the party system and their virtually continuous presence in federal government.

German parties after unification

Not surprisingly, unification with their East German counterparts confronted West German parties with a unique organizational and financial burden. As regards organizational change, however, the experience of party politics has not differed significantly from that of unification per se: to put it bluntly, the West German model has been retained for the new Germany and, with the exception of the Greens, it is hard to find any noticeable features of East German organizational traditions. In most cases, party statutes were temporarily adapted to the needs of unification. The Christian Democrats, for example, reduced the number of deputy chairpersons to just one, which was then taken over by the former East German Prime Minister, Lothar de Maiziere, and later by Angela Merkel. As soon as 1992, however, the party had reverted to its old model, retaining no special representation rights for East Germans. The FDP, in its turn, enlarged its national executive until 1991 in order to create positions for East Germans (Vorländer, 1992: 302).

The Greens are in fact the only party that has changed significantly as a result of unification, undergoing a two-stage process of amalgamation with its East German allies. First, it united with the East German Green Party on the night after the 1990 election; second, after a prolonged negotiation process, the East German citizens' movements, which had set up their own party called *Bündnis 90*, signed a unification treaty with the Greens in

January 1993, which was then ratified by a postal ballot of the members of both parties, becoming operative in May 1993. Although the East German party was hardly an organizational heavyweight with its mere 2709 members in August 1992 (Wielgohs et al., 1992: 93ff), the fusion was considered essential for the long-term electoral consolidation of the Greens in the united Germany, in that *Bündnis 90* represented the only genuinely East German political force which was not, in one way or another, tainted by cooperation with the old regime.[20] In addition, the East German partner, which insisted that the new party would also retain its old name (it is now called *Bündnis 90/Grüne*, or, for short, Greens) could boast an impressive leadership which helped to bring down the old regime. Organizationally, the reluctance of the *Bündnis 90* to become a party is reflected in the institution of 'freelance party activists', in which everybody, even members of other parties, is invited to participate in the new party, albeit without voting rights. As a safeguard against infiltration, these 'freelance activists' must also accept the political and organizational principles of *Bündnis 90/Grüne*. In addition, the former *Bündnis 90* will be allowed to organize as an intra-party organization called *Bürgerbewegung* (Poguntke and Schmitt-Beck, 1994).

Before fusion with *Bündnis 90*, the shock of the totally unexpected election defeat of 1990 (Boll and Poguntke, 1992) had induced substantial organizational reform in the Green Party, and had resulted in the modification of some of the sacred principles of *Basisdemokratie*. The most important changes were the abolition of the strict separation of office and mandate for the newly created *Länderrat* and the rotation principle for members of the federal executive (Poguntke, 1993a: 167ff; Poguntke with Boll, 1992: 360). As regards the internal distribution of power, the effects of the statutory reform are hard to estimate, since the new party has only eight deputies in the Bonn parliament. Nevertheless, it soon became apparent that the abolition of the *Bundeshauptausschuß* and the instal-lation of the *Länderrat* has led to the intended reduction of internal conflict, and to the better integration and coordination of extra-parliamentary Green politics. Primarily, this can be attributed to the introduction of personnel overlap of the *Länderrat* with *Land* parliaments and *Land* executives.

Conclusions

Because the external conditions of the German political system have resulted in a process of horizontal and vertical fragmentation, the parties are closer to a stratarchic than to an oligarchic model. Moreover, as a result of the extensive legal regulation of party politics, they are also fairly similar as regards the main structure of their hierarchy of decision-making bodies. There is also, nonetheless, some conspicuous variation. Whereas the Liberals, Social Democrats and Greens have unitary party structures, the Christian parties are characterized by multiplicity of channels which reach into relevant segments of society, thereby obscuring the boundaries of the party organization.

Although formal party structures changed very little after 1967, there has nevertheless been substantial organizational change. After all, statutes define the rules of the game, but one set of players may follow different strategies and control more resources than another. Until the 1980s, German parties converged towards the catch-all model. The Christian parties imitated the Social Democratic model and created a strong external party organization based on mass membership and a professionalized central party office staffed with organizational and, to a lesser extent, political professionals. With the advent of the Greens, however, things became more complicated, for while the Greens were forced to adapt their model of grassroots democracy to the imperatives of the parliamentary system, they have also induced some change, particularly inside the SPD, towards a more participatory model. As yet, however, and with the exception of the quotas for women, this has not been reflected in statutory changes, but these are likely to come in the future.[21] Once again, the Liberals may follow a different course. Thus far, their pivotal position in the party system has ensured their electoral survival, and their ideological tradition would, in any case, discourage attempts to embark on a catch-all strategy. They can also therefore afford to remain relatively indifferent to their competitors' strategies of organizational adaptation.

The most conspicuous change over the past three decades has been a substantial loosening of ties between parties and society. The Greens clearly represent a partial aberration in this regard, although their claim to be the mouthpiece of the new social movements has always been closer to wishful thinking than to reality. They will also not remain unaffected by processes of social change and systemic adaptation, which, of course, in most cases, result from the party political decisions of their competitors.

Party members remain financially important for the parties, even though their external role as 'communicators' vis-à-vis society is in the process of being taken over by media and marketing specialists. There is also substantial evidence of professionalization in all party arenas, even though, when looking solely at the numbers of central office employees, this argument appears unjustified. The trend towards marketing methods in campaigning is nonetheless unmistakable, and even the Greens have relied on a PR agency in the lead-up to the 1994 campaign. Politics has thus become more capital intensive, and since the capacity of parties to attract private donations has been limited by the intricacies of tax and party finance legislation, they have turned instead to the state. This increasing dependency of the national parties on state budgets is partly self-induced, and partly a reaction to their declining societal anchorage.

Patronage reflects another important aspect of parties' movement towards the state, even though it is difficult to demonstrate this by means of hard empirical data. It can be deduced, however, from the structure of the political and administrative system of the Federal Republic, and within limits, it can also be substantiated empirically in the tendency towards the colonization of the state and the higher echelons of administration through parties, and in the role of party foundations, which have partially taken over classic functions of the state, such as foreign policy and developmental aid. This process has fundamentally altered the incentive structure for party members and party elites, one result of which is a pervasive professionalization of political careers.

In the end, however, we should be cautious in attributing parties too hastily to the sphere of the state. They rather resemble amphibians, who can still swim in society, but who may increasingly lose this ability as, through the course of evolution, they become increasingly adapted to the solid ground of the state.

Notes

1 The author would like to thank Matthias Zürn for his help with the data.

2 The *Ewigkeitscharakter* (guarantee of eternity) of these basic principles of the Basic Law could have been changed if a completely new constitution had been designed upon the unification of the two Germanies.

3 West Berlin, though not formally a West German *Land*, can be included from this perspective.

4 This was also clearly the reason for using the softer term 'consultation'.

5 See p. 191 for the rules on party finance.

6 Since the Court cannot act on its own initiative, these decisions have tended to be the result of appeals by those political parties which disapproved of the current regulations.

7 Minor adjustments were the lowering of the thresholds of eligibility (again as a result of decisions by the Constitutional Court) and an increase in the amount of money paid per voter (see Mintzel and Oberreuter 1992: 564ff; Poguntke with Boll, 1992: 384).

8 This is also at least partly due to the declining volume of donations as a result of the Flick scandal in the early 1980s (Poguntke with Boll, 1992: 378–81).

9 In 1989, roughly 60 per cent were not working in Bonn (Ismayr, 1992: 228).

10 As another example of the importance of systemic constraints, it is interesting to note that the Greens first tried to obstruct this indirect channel for public party financing through an appeal to the Constitutional Court. When their case was rejected, and after a prolonged and frequently bitter debate which gave vent to their own ideological reservations about *Staatsknete* (a pejorative slang term for public money), they decided to launch their own network of party foundations in order to avoid competitive disadvantages (Müller-Rommel and Poguntke, 1992: 345f; Raschke, 1993: 507ff).

11 It needs to be emphasized that this perspective excludes all similar state subsidies on the *Land* level. Hence, only federal subsidies to party foundations are included here (documentation of payments from *Land* budgets would require a research project in its own right). By and large, the inclusion of these funds under the heading 'national income' is justifiable, because the foundations are centralized (von Vieregge, 1977). The only exception is the Green foundation *Regenbogen*, which includes a federation of autonomous *Land* foundations.

12 Typically, this was done by tolerating Social Democratic minority governments in exchange for specific policy concessions (Frankland and Schoonmaker, 1992: 168; Scharf, 1989).

13 Constitutional changes, within the limits set by the unchangeable essentials, require a two-thirds majority.

14 For details see Pridham (1977: 291ff); Haungs (1983: 51ff); Höfling (1980a, 1980b); Schönbohm (1985: 218ff).

15 In 1983, the *Deutsche Jungdemokraten*, who had resisted the FDP's drift towards a coalition with the Christian Democrats, were replaced by the newly founded *Junge Liberalen* (Dittberner, 1987: 123; Poguntke with Boll, 1992: 335).

16 There is a 'working group of liberal local politicians' (*Bundesvereinigung Liberaler Kommunalpolitiker*) which had 3096 individual or corporate members in 1991, which can hardly be counted as reflecting an organizational linkage to society.

17 In the 1950s, this metaphor was used to refer to the apparent inability of the SPD to attract voters beyond its traditional working-class clientele.

18 In principle, this argument applies also to the distribution of power in *Land* parties.

19 These are only recent data, however, since, with the exception of the SPD, the parties did not begin publishing their expenditure accounts until 1984.

20 The East German Social Democrats were founded too late and were too short-lived to have legitimate claims in this respect.

21 The Baden-Württemberg CDU introduced proportional representation of women in party offices in November 1993.

References

Boll, Bernhard and Poguntke, Thomas (1992) 'The 1990 All-German Election Campaign', in David M. Farrell and Shaun Bowler (eds), *Electoral Strategies and Political Marketing*, London: Macmillan, pp. 121–43.

Bundestagsdrucksache 12/4425 (1993) *Empfehlung der Kommission unabhängiger Sachverständiger zur Parteienfinanzierung*, February.

Derlin, Hans-Ulrich (1988) 'Verwaltung zwischen Berufsbeamtentum und Parteipolitik: Personalrekrutierung und Personalpatronage im öffentlichen Dienst', *Politische Bildung*, 21 (2): 57–71.

Dittberner, Jürgen (1973) 'Der Wirtschaftsrat der CDU e.V.', in Jürgen Dittberner and Rudolf Ebbinghausen (eds), *Parteiensystem in der Legitimationskrise*. Opladen: Westdeutscher Verlag, pp. 200–28.

Dittberner, Jürgen (1987) *FDP – Partei der zweiten Wahl*. Opladen: Westdeutscher Verlag.

Duverger, Maurice (1964) *Political Parties*, 3rd edn. London: Methuen.

Falter, Jürgen W. and Schumann, Siegfried (1993) 'Nichtwahl und Protestwahl: Zwei Seiten einer Medaille', *Aus Politik und Zeitgeschichte*, 11: 36–49.

Frankland, E. Gene and Schoonmaker, Donald (1992) *Between Protest and Power. The Green Party in Germany*. Boulder, San Francisco, Oxford: Westview.

Haungs, Peter (1983) 'Die Christlich Demokratische Union Deutschlands (CDU) und die Christlich Soziale Union in Bayern (CSU)', in Hans-Joachim Veen (ed.), *Christlich-demokratische und konservative Parteien in Westeuropa*, Vol. I. Paderborn, München, Wien, Zürich: Schöningh, pp. 9–194.

Haungs, Peter (1992) 'Die CDU: Prototyp einer Volkspartei', in Alf Mintzel and Heinrich Oberreuter (eds), *Parteien in der Bundesrepublik Deutschland*, 2nd edn. Opladen: Leske & Budrich, pp. 172–216.

Heimann, Siegfried (1986) 'Die Sozialdemokratische Partei Deutschlands', in Richard Stöss (ed.), *Parteien-Handbuch (Sonderausgabe)*, Vol. 4. Opladen: Westdeutscher Verlag, pp. 2025–216.

Hesse, Joachim Jens and Ellwein, Thomas (1992) *Das Regierungssystem der Bundesrepublik Deutschland*, 7th. edn. Opladen: Westdeutscher Verlag.

Höfling, Wolfram (1980a) 'Die Vereinigungen der CDU. Eine Bestandsaufnahme zu Organisationsstruktur, Finanzen und personelle Repräsentanz', in Heino Kaack and Reinhold Roth (eds), *Handbuch des deutschen Parteiensystems*, Vol. 1. Opladen: Leske & Budrich, pp. 125–52.

Höfling, Wolfram (1980b) 'Funktionsprobleme des Vereinigungssystems der CDU', in Heino Kaack and Reinhold Roth (eds), *Handbuch des deutschen Parteiensystems*, Vol. 1. Opladen: Leske & Budrich, pp. 153–74.

Ismayr, Wolfgang (1992) *Der Deutsche Bundestag*. Opladen: Leske & Budrich.

Kaack, Heino (1971) *Geschichte und Struktur des deutschen Parteiensystems*. Opladen: Westdeutscher Verlag.

Katz, Richard S. and Mair, Peter (1994) 'The Evolution of Party Organization in Europe: The Three Faces of Party Organization', in William Crotty (ed.), *Parties in an Age of Change*, special issue of the *American Review of Politics*, 14: pp. 593–617.

Katz, Richard S., Mair, Peter and Bardi, Luciano, Bille, Lars, Deschouwer, Kris, Farrell, David, Koole, Ruud, Morlino, Leonardo, Müller, Wolfgang, Pierre, Jon, Poguntke, Thomas, Sundberg, Jan, Svåsand, Lars, van de Velde, Hella, Webb, Paul and Widfeldt, Anders (1992) 'The Membership of Political Parties in European Democracies, 1960–1990', *European Journal of Political Research*, 22 (3): 329–45.

Kitschelt, Herbert (1989) *The Logics of Party Formation*. Ithaca: Cornell University Press.

Kleinmann, Hans-Otto (1993) *Geschichte der CDU*. Stuttgart: DVA.

Landfried, Christine (1990) *Parteifinanzen und politische Macht*. Baden-Baden: Nomos.

Lehnert, Detlef (1983) *Sozialdemokratie zwischen Protestbewegung und Regierungspartei 1848–1983*. Frankfurt/Main: Suhrkamp.

Mintzel, Alf and Oberreuter, Heinrich (eds) (1992) *Parteien in der Bundesrepublik Deutschland*, 2nd edn. Opladen: Leske & Budrich.

Müller-Rommel, Ferdinand and Poguntke, Thomas (1992) 'Die Grünen', in Alf Mintzel and Heinrich Oberreuter (eds), *Parteien in der Bundesrepublik Deutschland*, 2nd edn. Opladen: Leske & Budrich, pp. 319–61.

Naßmacher, Karl-Heinz (1990) 'Parteienfinanzierung im Wandel', in Hans-Georg Wehling (ed.), *Parteien in der Bundesrepublik Deutschland*. Stuttgart, Berlin, Köln: Kohlhammer, pp. 136–60.

Niedermayer, Oskar (1993) 'Innerparteiliche Demokratie', in Oskar Niedermayer and Richard Stöss (eds), *Stand und Perspektiven der Parteienforschung in Deutschland*. Opladen: Westdeutscher Verlag, pp. 230–50.

Niedermayer, Oskar and Stöss, Richard (1993) 'DDR-Regimewandel, Bürgerorientierungen und die Entwicklung des gesamtdeutschen Parteiensystems', in Oskar Niedermayer and Richard Stöss (eds), *Wähler und Parteien im Umbruch*. Opladen: Westdeutscher Verlag.

Oberreuter, Heinrich (1992) 'Politische Parteien: Stellung und Funktion im Verfassungssystem der Bundesrepublik', in Alf Mintzel and Heinrich Oberreuter (eds), *Parteien in der Bundesrepublik Deutschland*, 2nd edn. Opladen: Leske & Budrich, pp. 15–40.

Panebianco, Angelo (1988) *Political Parties: Organization and Power*. Cambridge: Cambridge University Press.

Poguntke, Thomas (1987) 'The Organization of a Participatory Party – The German Greens', in *European Journal for Political Research*, 15: 609–33.

Poguntke, Thomas (1992) 'Unconventional Participation in Party Politics – The German Experience', *Political Studies*, 40 (2): 239–54.

Poguntke, Thomas (1993a) *Alternative Politics. The German Green Party*. Edinburgh: Edinburgh University Press.

Poguntke, Thomas (1993b) 'Goodbye to Movement Politics? Organizational Adaptation of the German Green Party', *Environmental Politics*, 2 (3): 379–404.

Poguntke, Thomas, with Boll, Bernhard (1992) 'Germany', in Richard S. Katz and Peter Mair (eds), *Party Organizations: A Data Handbook on Party Organizations in Western Democracies, 1960–90*. London: Sage, pp. 317–88.

Poguntke, Thomas and Schmitt-Beck, Rüdiger (1994) 'Still the Same with a New Name? Bündnis 90/Die Grünen after the Fusion', *German Politics*, 3 (1): 91–113.

Pridham, Geoffrey (1977) *Christian Democracy in West Germany: The CDU/CSU in Government and Opposition, 1945–76*. London: Croom Helm.

Pütz, Helmuth (1985) *Die CDU. Entwicklung, Organisation und Politik der Christlich Demokratischen Union Deutschlands*, 4th edn. Düsseldorf: Droste.

Raschke, Joachim (1991) 'Die Parteitage der Grünen', *Aus Politik und Zeitgeschichte*, 11/12: 46–54.

Raschke, Joachim (1993) *Die Grünen*. Köln: Bund Verlag.

Rudzio, Wolfgang (1991) *Das politische System der Bundesrepublik Deutschland*, 3rd edn. Opladen: Leske & Budrich.

Scharf, Thomas (1989) 'Red–Green Coalitions at Local Level in Hesse', in Eva Kolinsky (ed.), *The Greens in West Germany*. Oxford: Berg, pp. 159–88.

Scheuch, Erwin K. and Scheuch, Ute (1992) *Cliquen, Klüngel und Karrieren. Über den Verfall der politischen Parteien – eine Studie*. Reinbek: Rowohlt.

Schindler, Peter (1984) *Datenhandbuch zur Geschichte des Deutschen Bundestages 1949 bis 1982*, 3rd edn. Baden-Baden: Nomos.

Schindler, Peter (1988) *Datenhandbuch zur Geschichte des Deutschen Bundestages 1980–1987*. Baden–Baden: Nomos.

Schmid, Josef (1990) *Die CDU. Organisationsstrukturen, Politiken und Funktionsweisen einer Partei im Föderalismus*. Opladen: Leske & Budrich.

Schmidt, Ute (1986) 'Die Christlich Demokratische Union Deutschlands', in Richard Stöss (ed.), *Parteien-Handbuch (Sonderausgabe)*, Vol. 1. Opladen: Westdeutscher Verlag, pp. 490–660.

Schmitt, Hermann (1987) *Neue Politik in alten Parteien*. Opladen: Westdeutscher Verlag.

Schmitt, Hermann (1992) 'Die Sozialdemokratische Partei Deutschlands', in Alf Mintzel and Herbert Oberreuter (eds), *Parteien in der Bundesrepublik Deutschland*, 2nd edn. Opladen: Leske & Budrich, pp. 133–71.

Schönbohm, Wulf (1985) *Die CDU wird moderne Volkspartei: Selbstverständnis, Mitglieder, Organisation und Apparat 1950–1980*. Stuttgart: Klett-Cotta.

Schütz, Klaus (1955) 'Die Sozialdemokratie im Nachkriegsdeutschland', in Institut für Politische Wissenschaft e.v. (ed.), *Parteien in der Bundesrepublik*. Stuttgart, Düsseldorf: Ring-Verlag, pp. 157–271.

SPD-Parteivorstand (1993a) 'SPD 2000: Eine moderne Reformpartei (Stand 13.9.1993)', mimeo.

SPD-Parteivorstand (1993b) *Politik*. December 1993.

von Alemann, Ulrich (1992) 'Parteien und Gesellschaft in der Bundesrepublik', in Alf Mintzel and Heinrich Oberreuter (eds), *Parteien in der Bundesrepublik Deutschland*, 2nd edn. Opladen: Leske & Budrich, pp. 89–130.

von Arnim, Hans-Herbert (1980) *Ämterpatronage durch politische Parteien*. Wiesbaden: Karl-Breuer-Institut der Steuerzahler.

von Arnim, Hans-Herbert (1991) *Die Partei, der Abgeordnete und das Geld*. Mainz: v. Hase & Koehler.

von Vieregge, Henning (1977) *Parteistiftungen*. Baden-Baden: Nomos.

von Vieregge, Henning (1990) 'Die Partei-Stiftungen: Ihre Rolle im politischen System', in Göttrik Wewer (ed.), *Parteienfinanzierung und politischer Wettbewerb*. Opladen: Westdeutscher Verlag, pp. 164–94.

von Winter, Thomas (1993) 'Die Christdemokraten als Analyseobjekt oder: Wie modern ist die CDU-Forschung?' in Oskar Niedermayer and Richard Stöss (eds), *Stand und Perspektiven der Parteienforschung in Deutschland*. Opladen: Westdeutscher Verlag, pp. 57–80.

Vorländer, Hans (1992) 'Die Freie Demokratische Partei', in Alf Mintzel and Herbert Oberreuter (eds), *Parteien in der Bundesrepublik Deutschland*, 2nd edn. Opladen: Leske & Budrich, pp. 266–318.

Wielgohs, Jan, Schulz, Marianne and Müller-Enbergs, Helmut (1992) *Bündnis '90. Entstehung, Entwicklung, Perspektiven*. Berlin: GSFP.

Wildenmann, Rudolf (1989) *Volksparteien. Ratlose Riesen? Eine Studie unter Mitarbeit von Werner Kaltefleiter, Manfred Küchler, Alf Mintzel, Karl-Heinz Naßmacher, Hans-Martin Pawlowski, Thomas Poguntke, Gordon Smith, Ulrich Widmaier*. Baden-Baden: Nomos.

9

Ireland: Centralization, Professionalization and Competitive Pressures

David M. Farrell[1]

Irish electoral politics has changed dramatically over the past two decades. Twenty years ago, the Irish case could be summarized under three main headings. First, it was a two-and-a-half party system. Second, the dominant – if not predominant – party in this system was always Fianna Fáil, with electoral competition being structured around the opposition between Fianna Fáil and 'the rest' (that is, Fine Gael and Labour). Third, the system was inherently very stable, with governments tending to last for three- to four-year terms (including two periods when Fianna Fáil was in power for sixteen consecutive years, from 1932 to 1948 and then again from 1957 to 1973).

None of these points now apply in the early 1990s. The entry of three new parties (the Workers' Party/Democratic Left, the Progressive Democrats and even the Greens) – all gaining Dáil representation – has transformed the format of the party system.[2] Electoral politics has become more volatile, and more competitive, with elections occurring more frequently, and with each producing a change of government. Indeed, it is worth emphasizing that no incumbent government has been fully returned to power in the eight elections held between 1973 and 1992, a pattern which is in stark contrast to the mere four changes of government which occurred between 1932 and 1969. Moreover, this trend is also consistent with Eurobarometer evidence on Irish party attachment throughout the 1980s (Farrell, 1992: Table VII.A.4.i.b): in 1981, 24 per cent of Irish voters did not feel close to any party, a proportion which rose throughout the decade and which reached a startling 58 per cent in 1989. By the end of the decade, Fianna Fáil found itself forced to face the inevitable when, for the first time, it actually formed a coalition government, first with the PDs in 1989 and then, in 1992, with Labour. In so doing, the party seemed to abandon its long-standing predilection for single-party government, while at the same time putting itself into a position where it is likely 'to participate in [coalition] government under almost any election result that is likely to emerge in Ireland in the medium-term future' (Laver and Shepsle, 1992: 70).

Developments in the mass media have also contributed to these changed circumstances. In the first place, and as elsewhere, the introduction of television in the early 1960s – the first 'television election' was in 1965 – had a profound effect on Irish parties, particularly in their running of election campaigns. As early as 1961, for example, Fine Gael was in discussion with RTÉ television producers requesting negotiations concerning 'the conditions under which political viewpoints and political personalities will be featured'; by the end of the 1960s, it was sending its politicians on television training courses.[3] Second, the coverage of politics provided by the media more generally has itself been undergoing a substantial change which, while most visible during election campaigns, is nevertheless also equally relevant between elections. This is particularly evident in relation to what US researchers refer to as 'horserace' or 'game' coverage, in which the media are seen to be increasingly concerned with elections as games with winners and losers, and with assessments of form, strategies and tactics. In the Irish case, for example, a content analysis of coverage by two newspapers (the *Irish Independent* and the *Irish Times*) of the 1973 and 1989 elections indicates that the proportion of total election coverage which is devoted to this sort of 'game' coverage has increased from some 14 per cent to 37 per cent (Farrell, 1993).

The central theme of this chapter is that the changes which have been taking place inside Irish party organizations must be seen within the context of this general change in the electoral and competitive environment. At the same time, however, it must be emphasized that I do not attempt to establish any process of causality: certainly, the parties have been obliged to adapt to these new circumstances, but, as we shall see, they are also at least partially responsible for their creation. Either way, the fact that there have been such dramatic changes in Irish electoral politics – whether measured at the level of the party system, the electorate or the media – certainly does suggest that we should also find evidence of changes in the parties themselves, particularly with regard to their professionalization. To put this theme into its proper context, however, we must first look to the specifics of the Irish setting, most notably with regard to the differing organizational traditions of the main parties, on the one hand, and the role of the electoral system, on the other.

The organizational setting

Contrasting traditions of party organization

The predominant party model in Ireland has always been one of 'stratarchy', characterized in addition by the independence of the parliamentary party from the rest of the organization. All Irish parties share in common the fact that 'the party in public office' predominates, and that there is a weak central office organization. Indeed, the distinction between the 'party in public office' and the 'party central office' (Katz and Mair, 1994) is not strictly relevant to the Irish case. Members of the headquarters' staff (from the general secretary downwards) are answerable to the party leader, and while the national executive may have an influential role over internal organizational matters, this is by no means an exclusive role. Moreover, this does not include any influence over policy matters, and neither does it allow the national executive to scrutinize the activities of the parliamentary party (see Farrell, 1992: Tables VII.D.7.a–f). Finally, it is worth noting that the membership of the national executive always includes parliamentarians.[4]

While the main Irish parties share in common a strong 'party in public office', they nevertheless have tended to differ with regard to the 'party on the ground', especially in the past, when these differences could be traced back to the origins of the political system. Labour was always the weakest – organizationally as well as electorally – of the three main parties. Founded in 1912 as the political wing of the trade union movement, it never achieved the same degree of electoral success of the other two parties. The party is small and accordingly its organization is weak and its access to resources is limited. So while there is a branch structure it is not as dense as the other parties. Nor is there much of a hierarchical structure. Described generally as a 'loose coalition of like-minded but independent TDs [i.e. MPs]' (Manning, 1972: 80), Labour was also always the least cohesive of the main parties. For instance, the traditional Labour election campaign consisted of running single candidates in the individual multi-member constituencies, and even when headquarters wanted to field second candidates in these constituencies, there was little scope for them to force this decision on the local parties. Furthermore, the candidates themselves often tended to minimize their association with the party, in some cases failing even to mention it in their promotional literature (for example, Gallagher, 1982: 91). The weakness of Labour headquarters was revealed starkly in a report of the party's Financial Secretary on the 1965 election (cited in Mair, 1987: 125) which referred to infrequent and brief meetings of the campaign committee, poor media liaison, the lack of attention to marginal constituencies, shoddy fund-raising and the provision of only one, constantly engaged, telephone line at headquarters.

Fine Gael originated in the 'pro-Treaty' side of Sinn Féin which, as the Cumann na nGaedheal party (as it was known until the early 1930s), formed the first Free State governments from 1922–32. It was also a party which was established from inside the new parliament, with all the subsequent organizational weaknesses which that entailed. Due to the fact that the 'anti-Treaty' side abstained from active electoral politics throughout that period, the government faced little electoral competition in the early years of the state. Moreover, as Garvin (1981: 147) points out, that first generation of party leaders 'appear to have had a positive contempt for the whole business of grass-roots organization'. The organizational complacency which this spawned was also met by a lack of enthusiasm at the electoral level, and as a party which had compromised on the 'national question', it never achieved quite the same degree of committed support as that enjoyed by Fianna Fáil. In sum, then, the early leaders of Cumann na nGaedheal/Fine Gael, absorbed as they were with setting up a new political system, fighting a civil war, negotiating with the British and the Unionists, and so on, 'subconsciously came to define politics as government and government as administration' (Garvin, 1981: 147). Fine Gael began as a top-down cadre-style party, which was loosely organized, had an undeveloped branch structure and little internal democracy, and in which any mobilization which occurred was through the influence of local notables.

Fianna Fáil, by contrast, built its organization from the grassroots upwards, albeit with the backing and support of elected deputies.[5] Moreover, from the beginning, Fianna Fáil succeeded in attracting a strong community-wide response. There are at least two features of the early organization of Fianna Fáil which have a bearing here. First, from the beginning it was de Valera's (the party leader) intention that the party should be more than a *party*; rather, it was a *national movement*. This, of necessity, required an open and fluid membership – everyone could be a member. Second, as Garvin (1981: 156–7) shows, the party was built up almost directly on the basis of old Irish Republican Army companies, battalions and divisions, through which the basic unit was to become the branch (or *cumann*). With such a pedigree it was not to be expected that the party would attempt to keep accurate membership records. Rather, the issue of who was a branch member (each branch theoretically had at least ten members) was the exclusive concern of the branch. As far as the national party was concerned, all that mattered was the number of branches and the payment of registration fees. Hence, 'rather than emphasizing organizational centralization and, perhaps, organizational efficiency, the intention was to have a party presence in as many areas as possible, however small' (Mair, 1987: 116).

These were, of course, the traditional differences between the party styles, separating the comprehensive and densely organized network of Fianna Fáil, on the one hand, and the more loosely structured approach of Fine Gael, and especially Labour, on the other hand. Whether these differences have been maintained into the present day is more open to question, however, as is the extent to which they may have been challenged by, or eroded through, a process of organizational convergence. I shall return to these questions later in this chapter.

The single transferable vote and party organization

The Irish electoral system of proportional representation by the single transferable vote (STV) clearly feeds the localist emphasis in Irish political culture. STV is a candidate-based system operating within multi-member constituencies, in which voters are expected to rank the candidates in order of preference. Candidates from the same party are therefore often in open competition with one another, pressing their competing claims by emphasizing a focus on constituency work (Farrell, 1985). Together, these effects promote a 'tension' between the central parties and their constituency organizations.

In traditional party organizations, there is a tendency to view the local organization as having a dual purpose: both to promote the party's candidates and to market the (national) party in a 'corporate' sense. Under this scenario, the development of a more modern organization would seem likely to lead to a growing emphasis on centralized marketing with, for example, a greater use of mass media outlets and professional, centrally organized techniques, and with party funds increasingly being concentrated in the centre. Therefore, with the passage of time, we should expect to see a growing role for national media systems, centralized state support and so on, and, more importantly, a concomitant decline in the role of local activists. One of the consequences of STV is to complicate such a scenario, however (Katz, 1980). More precisely, it is not just the central party which needs members and supporters on the ground – for money, canvassing, etc. – it is also the individual TDs and candidates who need a local presence, not so much to help the party as a whole, but mainly to advance their own individual campaigns in competition with their fellow party candidates.[6] In this context, therefore, and unusually so, candidate appeal must often be asserted over and above party appeal, and hence growth at the centre need not necessarily imply decline at local level. Both may in fact be strengthened at one and the same time, with an emphasis on the centre deriving from the need to assert the party appeal per se, and with the emphasis at local level deriving from the need to assert the appeal of competing candidates within the party.

This STV-inspired 'tension' between centre and periphery has been exacerbated in recent years by vote-management strategies which, in turn, have become increasingly important as the overall political balance has become more competitive. Vote-management is a necessary part of a central party's efforts to increase the 'efficiency' of the vote (that is, to maximize seat-to-vote ratios), and, as we shall see below, requires a more activist role by the centre in candidate selection. It also often entails the selection of candidates from different parts of a given constituency in order to maximize the 'friends-and-neighbours' voting effect for the party as a whole and, in its most elaborate form, directs party supporters in different parts of the constituency to vote in a varying preferential order for the party's candidates. This clearly requires close coordination by the centre, using constituency polling to check voter trends (and calm candidate nerves), and canvassing literature to direct voters on how they should rank-order the party's candidates.[7] It also necessitates a great deal of co-operation from the individual candidates themselves, since each faces the risk of not being elected, and since the parcelling out of voter preferences may make some of them even more vulnerable to defeat than would normally be the case. It can therefore prove to be the source of considerable centre–periphery tensions inside the party.

In the following examination of party organizational development in Ireland, our analysis can be guided by two expectations. On one hand, despite the increased nationalization of campaigning, there is a recognition of the need to keep local parties alive. On the other hand, there is a need to reform the organization in order to limit the damaging effects of intra-party rivalries, to rein in the activities of local barons, and to increase the cohesion of the party across the country. As we shall see, these latter developments have been facilitated both by constitutional amendments and by the centre making greater use of already existing powers.

The professionalization of Irish electioneering

Thirty years ago it might have been correct to say of Irish parties that they were predominantly local, volunteer machines, lacking any kind of centralized structures (Chubb, 1959). Today, however, such a description would no longer be valid. The contemporary Irish party which campaigned in the most recent 1992 general election contrasts very sharply with the predecessor which campaigned in 1957. It has a far more developed organizational structure, it has more staff and resources, and it now makes substantial use of marketing specialists and their techniques in order to plan a national strategy. There are two levels at which this can be shown. First, we can see the growing professionalism of the parties through an examination of their campaign styles. Second, we can look more deeply at the underlying changes which facilitate more professional campaign practices through a study of the parties' organizations and how these have changed. This section will assess the parties' campaigns, and then go on to look at staffing. The following section will discuss the questions of organizational centralization and vote-management.

Campaigning

Prior to 1977, Irish electioneering could be summarized as consisting primarily of four elements: short-termism, localism, voluntarism and machine politics. There was little if any long-term planning, with campaign strategies usually being drawn up only after an election was called. Everything was decentralized, in the sense that there was really no national campaign, with all efforts being focused on the individual constituencies and the individual candidates. Propagandizing and canvassing for support relied on armies of volunteers, with some printing provided by overloaded, under-resourced headquarters.

The 1977 election, when Fianna Fáil, which had been out of office since 1973, unleashed a highly professional, nationalized campaign, and published its first ever election manifesto, proved to be the watershed in this regard (Farrell and Manning, 1978). Whether this can be credited with producing one of the best election results in Fianna Fáil's history is a moot point; what cannot be disputed, however, is that it set the pattern for electioneering ever since. Fine Gael mounted a similar marketing strategy in the subsequent 1981 election (Farrell, 1986), and by the mid-1980s 'political marketing' had fully taken root, with professional, national campaigns being mounted by all parties which could afford it. Contemporary election campaigning – particularly by the larger parties – is characterized by the following four features. First, the parties draw up long-term campaign plans involving the establishment of a central campaign committee, the commissioning of polls to test the market and the production of numerous policy documents. Second, there is a greater emphasis on centralization, with a major feature of the campaign being the centrally coordinated leader's country-wide tour, and with campaign literature and advertising being printed, or at least designed, in national headquarters. Themes and slogans are also now drawn up by headquarters for use by the local organizations, and there is much greater coordination of local campaigns, with particular attention being paid to candidate selection and local vote-management (see p. 226).

Third, greater use is now made of special consultants and agencies and of the new communications technologies. Headquarters' staff are supplemented for the duration of the campaign by marketing specialists and former journalists, and the parties employ the services of advertising agencies (often several), public relations specialists and marketing agencies. By the mid-1980s, these specialist consultants and agencies had begun to receive close attention from political journalists, and a new term had entered the Irish political lexicon: 'the national handlers'. Available estimates on campaign expenditure also reveal an increase in the amount spent by parties over the period,[8] not least as a result of the spiralling costs of these specialist services. In the 1969 general election, for example, Fine Gael spent, in 1989 prices, the equivalent of £126,600 on advertisements. In 1981 it budgeted for an expenditure of £327,200 (also in 1989 prices). This increased in 1987 to an equivalent of £365,700, and by 1989, the party was spending just less than £480,000. In that same election Fianna Fáil's advertising campaign cost a staggering £979,000.[9]

Fourth, closer attention is paid to the views of the voters through the use of increasingly sophisticated techniques of market research. Market research was initially used by one or two of the Irish parties at the end of the 1960s and early 1970s, with Fianna Fáil first employing these techniques in 1977. Since then there has been a heavy reliance by the two larger parties on market research in order to draw up campaign themes and slogans, to segment the electoral market and to facilitate constituency vote-management strategies.

Staffing

In a political system where localism prevails, and where presence and work in the constituency counts for a great deal, it may be expected that the scope for a large central apparatus will be relatively restricted. Throughout the 1960s, staffing in all the parties was in single figures (Farrell, 1992: Table VII.C.1). Typically, each party had a general secretary served by a number of administrative secretaries in head office and supplemented by a skeleton staff at Leinster House (the parliament).

In the 1970s and 1980s, however, staff numbers in the two larger parties gradually expanded to a maximum of about twenty-five or twenty-six employees, before falling back to about fifteen or sixteen employees in 1993, in the wake of severe financial cutbacks (see also p. 233). And while this is perhaps 'one of the most evident features of organizational growth' in this period (Mair, 1987: 108), it is even more significant to note the parties' reliance on state support in financing these new appointments, with much of this expansion resulting from a new scheme of administrative/ secretarial assistance paid for by the Department of Finance, which was introduced in late 1981 and made available to parties with at least seven TDs (Farrell, 1992: Table VII.E.4.ii). By 1989, according to the Department's figures, it was paying for thirty-two party staff, which represented some 50 per cent of the total number of staff employed by those parties which were eligible for the scheme (Farrell, 1992: Table VII.C.1).

While there has been a quantitative change in the area of staffing, there has not been an equivalent qualitative shift. The bulk of party-paid staff are clerical employees and, with the exception of press and research officers and a limited use of higher level professional specialists or administrators, the parties have not made any great strides towards bringing in more specialized personnel. On the one hand, this probably reflects a general reluctance to allow the professionals to take over the party; on the other, it reflects a tendency for Irish parties to buy in outside expertise as required, and most notably, as we have seen, during elections. It is also interesting to note that Fianna Fáil has always had the lowest pay bill of the three parties (Farrell, 1992: Tables VII.E.2.b–d). And while this is consistent with the expectation that smaller parties have to give over proportionately more to finance their administration and that there are economies of scale, it is also consistent with the fact that, as the party most regularly in government, Fianna Fáil has had greatest access to the services of state employees.

These increases in the staffing of party headquarters are dwarfed by those of the party in public office, as can be seen both in the growing numbers of employees serving the parliamentary party and in the increased use of political and personal advisers by government ministers. Up until the mid-1970s, while the parties in government did of course benefit greatly from access to civil service support, individual parliamentarians lacked any personal secretarial assistance, and the parliamentary parties were obliged to rely exclusively on the skeleton services provided by party headquarters. In 1975, however, a new scheme was introduced for non-office holding TDs. Initially the ratio was one secretarial assistant for each ten TDs. This figure was gradually increased, until by 1982 each TD had his/her own secretarial assistant. A similar scheme was introduced for Senators in 1981, and by 1985 the scheme had been extended so that three Senators shared a secretary between them. We can see just how dramatic was this development by looking at the ratio of parliamentary staff to total headquarters' staff (for the three established parties),[10] which increased from just 0.35:1 in 1975 to 2.3:1 in 1989 (Farrell, 1992: Table VII.C.1). Moreover, and to an ever-increasing extent, ministers have also begun to enjoy the resources of the civil service to help them in their constituency work as well as to guide their political decisions. By the end of the 1980s, for example, the average minister (and junior minister) had up to ten civil servants working on such tasks, all paid for by public funds (Gallagher and Komito, 1992: 146). This represented a total of more than 300 civil servants. The move towards personal ministerial *cabinets* went even further in early 1993, when the newly elected Fianna Fáil–Labour government appointed what was described by one leading journalist as 'the biggest political staff outside of the permanent civil service in the history of the State' (*Irish Times*, 20 February 1993), and which included a total of 135 programme managers, special advisers, personal secretaries and personal assistants.

Such developments are clearly consistent with the process of professionalization: the numbers of staff at headquarters have increased, there has been some move towards more senior level appointments, and greater use is now being made of specialized agencies and advisers during elections. But this is more than party professionalization per se. As we have seen, much of the expansion in staff has resulted from the administrative/secretarial scheme, first introduced in 1981, and it is no coincidence that a large proportion of these new appointments are to service the parties' press offices which, in all cases, are not based at party headquarters, but at the parliament. In other words, a significant factor behind the increase in party staff sizes has been the move by the parties to provide a more efficient press service for their parliamentarians, paid for out of state money. At the same time, the parliamentarians and government ministers have benefited from a considerable increase in the staff resources made available to them at an individual level.[11] The result is that the parliamentary party has become increasingly self-sufficient and autonomous from the central party office and, in this sense, it can be argued that the trends in staffing are actually leading to a situation where the central party organization becomes little more than a campaign organization, not unlike the situation which prevails in the United States (see Katz and Kolodny, Ch. 1, in this volume).

The increased role of the centre

As was noted above, one of the distinguishing features of Irish party organizations has been their decentralized character, something which suited the very localist political culture and which, to an extent, was also a by-product of the STV electoral system. Politicians enjoyed considerable autonomy in their constituencies, there was little if any central scrutiny of branch networks and candidate selection was always decided by the constituency organizations. From the 1970s onwards, however, in one of the more striking organizational developments in the past thirty years, each of the party headquarters has sought to enhance its control of local activities and to effect a greater coordination from the top.

Paper branches

All of the parties have always faced a problem of a large 'ghost' membership being affiliated to what are in effect 'paper' branches. Apart from the fact that the central headquarters may not receive all the subscriptions due to them and hence may suffer financially as a result of these paper branches, this system also allows sitting TDs, acting as local 'barons', to create small personal fiefdoms, thus preventing the emergence of new blood and reducing the opportunities for the party to win additional seats. Paper branches are, of course, to be expected in a system where localism prevails and where there are multi-seat constituencies. In the absence of centralized membership lists, it was impossible for the centre to know how many members – and therefore how many bona fide branches – it had, and hence there was nothing to stop a TD from establishing paper branches. Moreover, the individual politicians had much to gain from this practice. Parliamentarians do not enjoy the right of automatic re-selection as candidates, and since the selection process itself is determined by branch delegates, there is the always the potential for a parliamentarian to 'pack' the selection convention with 'ghost' members. In this way, the candidate could ensure her/his re-selection, while at the same time blocking the advancement of any potential rivals. Paper branches can also be used to send extra delegates to the national conference where, among other things, the delegates play an important role in electing the members of the national executives.[12] As far as the central party was concerned, on the other hand, paper branches brought virtually no benefits, apart from the very small income that could be generated by branch affiliation fees, which, in these situations, was often paid from the personal resources of the local baron. This hardly compensated, however, for the potential damage to party morale among the legitimate membership, nor for the potential limitations on an effective vote-management strategy.

From the mid-1970s onwards, within the context of an increasingly competitive electoral market, all of the parties have made some effort to deal with this problem, including the establishment of central registers of members (achieved both by Fine Gael and Labour in the latter half of the 1970s), and the amendment of party constitutions.[13] Other strategies were also attempted. Fianna Fáil, for instance, made several attempts to 'weed out' inactive branches by giving a mandate to the general secretary to carry out investigations of particular constituencies. In recent years this process has also been carried out by special party commissions, and in 1984 'Operation Dublin' was set up in order to rationalize the branch network in the Dublin area, with similar operations being carried out in the other regions. In 1985 this process was put on a firmer, more permanent, footing, with the establishment of the National Organization Committee.[14] Labour has also sought to clean up its branch structure, closing down some branches and merging others. In addition, there was one significant rule change in 1981 when minimum sizes were established for branch membership (at least five members in rural areas; ten in urban areas).

It is in the case of Fine Gael, however, that this problem has proved most acute, and certainly this party has gone far further than any other in changing its rules in an attempt to eliminate paper branches,[15] beginning in 1977 when Garret FitzGerald became the new party leader and set in train a major overhaul of the organization. A number of new rules were quickly put in place. In the first place, local officers (constituency organizers and public relations officers) were appointed in each constituency. Their role was to improve the communication between centre and the constituency, and so to reduce the reliance on the individual TDs. More importantly, they were to be answerable to headquarters and they were prohibited from putting themselves forward for candidature at the next general election.[16] Second, in 1978 the candidate selection rules were changed, with the introduction of new 'model rules' aimed at removing the incentive for paper branches. Under these rules, the number of delegates which a branch sends to the selection convention was to be based on the number of electors in the area, rather than on the (claimed) size of the branch membership (Farrell, 1992: Table VII.D.5.d).[17] Third, Fine Gael also changed the rules governing subscriptions, introducing a new clause in the 1978 constitution allowing the national executive to determine what proportion of membership subscriptions would be paid to national headquarters. At the same time branch subscriptions to headquarters were also increased, up from £5 in the late 1970s to £30 by 1988 (Farrell, 1992: Table VII.B.2.d).

Candidate selection

The process of candidate selection is of course of particular relevance to the issue of the distribution of power inside the parties, and over the years there have been developments in this area which are also indicative of a general trend towards increasing the power of the centre (Farrell, 1992: Tables VII.D.5.a–f). Moreover, they also show the increasing extent of party organizational convergence. These developments have occurred at two levels: reforms of the rules in some of the parties regarding candidate selection; and a growing tendency to make use of existing rules to strengthen the position of the leadership.

As far as rule changes are concerned, the principal exception has been Fianna Fáil which, over the years, has made no changes to its formal procedures. Indeed, and perhaps reflecting the party's long-term electoral dominance, the Fianna Fáil central organization has always had available to it all of the powers necessary to control the nomination process. Thus the party's 1953 constitution sets down five main roles for the *árd comhairle* in candidate selection, and these have remained unchanged ever since. The *árd comhairle* fixes the number of candidates per constituency; appoints the convention chairmen; ratifies or rejects the candidates nominated by the conventions; imposes any extra candidates it deems necessary; and enjoys the right to remove completely the decision-making role on candidate selection from the hands of a constituency organization.

Fine Gael, on the other hand, has made the most dramatic changes to its rules on candidate selection. In 1963, Fine Gael's national executive had the power only to determine the numbers of candidates to be fielded in each constituency. In order to provide the party's national executive with similar powers to those enjoyed by Fianna Fáil's *árd comhairle*, therefore, constitutional amendments were made in 1970 (to appoint convention chairs; to ratify candidates; to impose extra candidates), and again in 1978 (to make arrangements for alternative selection systems in some constituencies). In 1982 Fine Gael went one step further in giving its national executive the power to request that nominating conventions take geographical considerations into account, thereby reflecting the increased effort being given to vote-management strategies.

Curiously enough, the Labour party constitution has no provisions regarding candidate selection. The rules are instead listed in a note, which apparently dates from the early 1960s, and which indicates that Labour's general council has for some time enjoyed similar powers to those of the Fianna Fáil *árd comhairle*. The two major differences are that Labour's general council cannot fix the number of candidates, nor can it take overall control of the process away from a constituency organization. And while there are no records available of when Labour's rules on candidate selection have changed,[18] it is nevertheless important to note that this set of rules has been drawn up by the party's national executive and thus can be changed by it at will. In other words, there are basically no constitutional limits to the powers of Labour's general council over candidate selection.

The Workers' Party rules have remained unchanged since its 1973 constitution. On paper, the *árd comhairle* has the power only to ratify the choice of candidates made by the constituency organizations, although the constitution also has the additional requirement that a prospective candidate must be an active party member of two years' standing. However, in reality, the democratic centralist nature of the party organization has ensured a predominant role for the party leadership in the selection process. At the outset, the Green Party had no rules on candidate selection, reflecting both its emphasis on decentralization and the reality that, as a new party, it simply wanted to encourage candidates to come forward and therefore placed no obstacles in their path. In 1989, in the wake of the election of the first Green Party TD, the rules on candidate selection were changed giving the party's Council the right to reject proposed candidates. As far as the PDs are concerned, the powers granted to the party's national executive regarding candidate selection in the first (1986) constitution are, for the most part, very similar to those of Fine Gael's national executive.

Another way of examining developments in candidate selection is to look at the extent to which national executives actually make use of the powers which are already available to them. One rule which each of the national executives of the main parties shares (albeit only since 1970 in the case of Fine Gael and since 1984 in the case of Labour) is that which allows it to add candidates to the list of those selected at local level. This has important implications for vote-management, in which the number and type of candidates chosen may help to maximize the party's seat-to-vote ratio. Fianna Fáil has made ready use of this instrument since the 1977 election, when it added sixteen candidates to various constituency lists, intervening again in subsequent elections in order to add ten names in 1981, three in November 1982, and eight in 1987 (Gallagher, 1988; Mair, 1987: 132). In the 1989 election, four candidates were imposed on constituencies by Fianna Fáil's *árd comhairle*, while in 1992 candidates were added in ten constituencies (Farrell, 1990, 1993). This increased interest of the centre in the candidate selection process was underlined by the creation in the mid-1980s of the Constituencies Committee – chaired by the party leader – whose role was that of head-hunting prospective candidates, identifying and focusing resources on marginal constituencies, and liaising with the relevant constituency organizations. This committee plays a crucial role in the party's efforts at vote-management.

Fine Gael's national executive has gone even further than Fianna Fáil's in its involvement in candidate selection, which was a key issue in FitzGerald's organizational reforms in the late 1970s. Since then head office has played an active role both in adding candidates (eight in November 1982, four in 1989) and in targeting candidates for vote-management strategies. In the latter case, a key instrument used by headquarters to placate any constituency fears is constituency polling commissioned by the centre. Moreover, the Fine Gael national executive has been particularly active in attracting public figures into the party as prominent candidates in marginal constituencies. Labour Party head-quarters has also been playing a more active role in candidate selection. In the 1989 election, it interfered in four constituencies and, in its prep-arations for the 1992 campaign, it paid very close attention to the selection of 'appropriate' candidates (Farrell, 1993). The PDs' national executive made considerable use of its power to impose candidates in the party's first election of 1987. This was justified on the grounds that, as a new party, it was too early for good local candidates to have emerged. By contrast, in the 1989 and 1992 elections, there was relatively little interference by the centre in the selection of PD candidates.

In general, therefore, while it remains the case that the candidate selection process may be characterized as one of 'constituency-level selection, with national supervision and influence' (Gallagher, 1988: 125), the degree of central involvement has nevertheless increased. And when this is also associated with the attempts to rationalize branch structures and to weed out paper branches on the one hand, and with the staffing developments and the professionalization of campaign strategies on the other, then the image of organizational centralization clearly becomes very persuasive. The question remains, of course, as to the implications of these trends for both party membership and party finance.

Party membership

Reliable data on party membership levels across the entire Irish party system are virtually impossible to obtain, not least because Fianna Fáil, which is by far the largest party, has never even attempted to maintain membership records. What matters in Fianna Fáil is the number of branches, or *cumainn*, and the party has rarely if ever probed the extent to which these are underpinned by an active membership. Thus while crude estimates can be obtained from the party – the most recent suggesting a total membership of 75,000 (see Marsh et al., 1993: 202) – these are not regarded as reliable, even by the party itself.

Figures can be obtained for the other main parties, however, albeit only for recent years (Farrell, 1992: Tables VII.B.1.a–f), and these show that in the case of Fine Gael, the major period of growth occurred during the late 1970s, largely as a result of the organizational changes which were being pushed through by the new leader, Garret FitzGerald. Traditionally, a party seeking to breathe new life into its organization may often begin with a membership drive, and interestingly the Fine Gael peak in 1985–86 also coincides with the high point in membership for the Progressive Democrats. In both parties there is a sharp decline during the remainder of the period, with Fine Gael membership in 1990 falling back to the level of the mid-1970s. To some extent this drop in Fine Gael's membership reflected a fall in organizational morale as the coalition government became more and more unpopular, ultimately losing power in 1987. It may also have reflected a decline in the role available to an active membership in an increasingly professional organization, however, particularly since the party had developed other, more centralized forms of fund-raising, and since the organization in general was increasingly centralized (see p. 224).

It is also striking how Labour's membership continued to rise (albeit with a shallow trend) even though for much of the period the party's vote was in steady decline. Like its British counterpart, Labour has a corporate membership which today is made up of twelve of the most powerful unions in the country. Union members have the right to attend and vote (albeit without block-voting privileges) at the party's national conference, and they also provide financial support for the party.[19] In 1989, for instance, trade union contributions amounted to £26,829, representing just over 8 per cent of the party's total income.[20] While this affiliated membership clearly dwarfs the individual membership, and while it has continued to increase steadily over much of the recent period (Farrell, 1992: Table VII.B.i.b), it is nevertheless important to note that there has been a gradual decline in the overall proportion of union members relative to direct members, falling from a ratio of around thirty-eight to one in 1976 to twenty-seven to one in 1989.

In common with comparative European trends (Katz et al., 1992), however, the total number of members in Irish parties does appear to be in decline. For the most part (in Fianna Fáil and Labour), this downward trend appears to begin in the late 1980s; in Fine Gael there is a more distinct trend which starts in the early 1980s.[21] This overall pattern is echoed by the trends in the numbers of party branches, for which reasonably reliable Fianna Fáil data are available (but note also the gap in the Fine Gael data during the period 1967–76), and which are shown in Figure 9.1. Once again we see that Fine Gael's big growth period was in the late 1970s. Whereas in the 1960s its branch network was on a par with the much smaller Labour party, by the early 1980s, for a brief period, Fine Gael had almost managed to establish as many branches as Fianna Fáil. Since 1981 the trends for the two large parties have shown a divergence, with the number of Fine Gael branches going into decline. Initially this probably reflected the closure of paper branches: as noted above, head-quarters applied itself to this task with almost missionary zeal. By the end of the 1980s, however, this continued drop also included the loss of active branches. Fianna Fáil also had a slight drop in the numbers of *cumainn* at the end of the decade, again at least partially due to the rationalization of branches, while Labour's trend is very gradually downwards.[22] In the Fianna Fáil case, where the records include information on the numbers of *cumainn* per constituency, it is clear that the party continues to have a particularly strong presence in rural areas (see also Mair, 1987: 117), with almost four times as many electors and voters per *cumann* in Dublin in 1989 as against the overwhelmingly rural west. That said, the ratio of electors to *cumainn* has tended to increase over time, and in 1989 there were almost twice as many electors per *cumann* in Dublin as was the case in 1981.

What is perhaps most surprising in all of these figures is the fact that despite the evident importance of local branches and local party activities in the Irish case, Ireland is nevertheless characterized by one of the lowest levels of party membership in Western Europe, exceeding only Britain, the Netherlands and (West) Germany (Katz et al., 1992). Moreover, the overall decline in party membership since the latter half of the 1980s would also seem to run counter to what might be expected to occur within such a localist political culture, even though this most recent trend is consistent with the processes of professionalization and centralization.

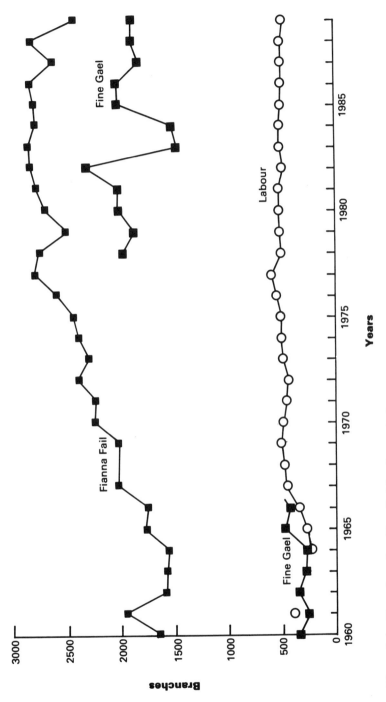

Figure 9.1   *Party branches* (Supplied by the parties)

What then do these patterns tell us about the parties' attitudes to their members? Do the parties value membership, or are they indifferent to it?

The evidence is ambiguous. There is certainly plenty of talk about the importance of party members, and the parties' annual reports regularly announce new membership drives. But, with only a few exceptions, there is little tangible evidence of anything being actually done to try and expand membership. These exceptions include, first, Fine Gael's very public revitalization at the end of the 1970s which did result in a dramatic expansion of membership (Figure 9.1), and, second, the launch of the PDs in the mid-1980s, which was deliberately intended to attract a lot of members, and which succeeded in signing up many who had never before joined a political party (Lyne, 1987). The parties have also apparently shown an interest in recruiting membership through ancillary organizations, a variety of which were established in the 1970s and 1980s with the aim of attracting certain categories of voters, including women, trade unionists, farmers and young people, the latter category of membership being developed in the context of the provision of state funding for party 'Youth Officers' in 1985. Internal democratization, on the other hand, which could give the members real powers and thereby make membership more appealing, is only beginning to be considered as a means of expanding membership. Thus in 1989 the Labour party decided to change the rules regarding the election of the party leader, giving an individual vote to all party members of at least two years' standing (Farrell, 1992: Table VII.D.2a.b.i). More recently, a wide-ranging internal report on programmatic and organizational renewal in Fine Gael recommended the abandonment of a delegate system in intra-party decision-making and the introduction of direct membership elections at all levels within the party. The report also proposed the introduction of an electoral college for leadership elections, which would give 50 per cent of the votes to members of the parliamentary party, 10 per cent to local councillors, and the remaining 40 per cent to the members on an individual basis (Fine Gael, 1993: 37–48).[23] In the other parties (apart from the Greens) the party leader is elected by the parliamentary party.[24]

In general, therefore, there is only limited evidence to suggest that the parties are serious about their declared aim to expand their memberships. Indeed, it can be argued that, if anything, the parties (with the exception of the PDs) have sought to include in their constitutions provisions which act to constrain, or control, their members' activities. The most common such provision is a form of loyalty clause which generally requires that members support only the party's own candidates, and that they do nothing which might be 'unbecoming for a member of the organization' (Fianna Fáil, 1953 Constitution). Fianna Fáil, Labour and the Workers' Party introduced this sort of provision in the 1950s, with more restrictive amendments being adopted in the 1970s and 1980s. Fine Gael first introduced such a rule in 1987. Other rules are clearly designed to prevent the practice of membership packing, as for instance would be the case were there to be a sudden accession of large numbers of new members which would decide a particular vote. In 1989 the Green Party introduced a six-month probation clause into its rules. Fianna Fáil has had a clause since 1980 which prevents a new member from voting immediately on joining; the individual has to wait until the subsequent meeting. Of all the parties, the Workers' Party has gone furthest in requiring new members to pass through a probationary initiation period before receiving full membership rights.[25] A third set of party rules requires an active role from party members. In other words it is not enough simply to pay membership dues; rather, the member must show a commitment through her/his voluntary work for the party. As might be expected, the Workers' Party stresses this function in a 1973 rule (updated in 1983), contributing to a problem in the late 1980s of 'membership burnout' (Dunphy and Hopkins, 1992).[26] Fianna Fáil is so far the only other party to have similar requirements (sometimes dating back to its foundation – see Mair, 1987: 115–16), including the need for members to help in such activities as the national collection and to attend some branch meetings (or else lose AGM voting rights).

Party finance

Organizational professionalization, a decreasing emphasis on party membership, and nationalized campaigning have all had their effects on the state of the parties' finances. Specifically, as we shall see, the parties are relying more on state funding as well as on new, alternative sources of private funding, matching an increasingly 'elite-oriented' organizational style with an equally 'elite-oriented' approach to raising revenues; or, to put it another way, parties that are becoming increasingly capital-intensive tend also to need increasing amounts of capital. This has also led to other problems, however, and the issue of party solvency has now become quite prominent, reflecting the growing financial difficulties of the parties, on the one hand, and the more intensive probing by journalists, on the other.[27] While estimates of the parties' levels of indebtedness do vary, sometimes quite wildly, it nevertheless seems that those with the greatest problems are Fianna Fáil, Fine Gael and the Workers' Party, with only Labour and the PDs appearing to have succeeded in controlling their debts (see Table 9.1).

While the response of both Fianna Fáil and Fine Gael to this financial crisis has been to cut back and reorganize, emphasizing the need to increase funding, reduce spending and attract new members, the long-term problem remains that, by the 1980s, party politics in Ireland had become very expensive. It is in this sense that the role of both state and (private) corporate party funding becomes very significant. As we have seen, there is now a greater tendency for parties to make use of external consultants and

Table 9.1   *Estimated party indebtedness in the 1990s*

Party	Estimated debt (IR£ '000)	N. members[a]	Debt per member (IR£)
Fianna Fáil	3,000	75,000	40
Fine Gael	1,000–1,300	25,000	40–52
Labour	60–70	7,400	8–10
PD	50–87	7,000	7–13
Workers' Party	300–500	2,800	107–179

[a] Membership figures/estimates provided by the parties for *Irish Political Studies*.

Sources: Farrell, 1993 (based on newspaper estimates); *Irish Political Studies*, 7: 163 (1992).

agencies, and this shift towards professionalization has also tended to coincide with a switch from a heavy reliance on membership dues towards alternative sources of finance, a trend which is easily apparent in the case of both Fine Gael and Labour from about the mid-1980s onwards.[28]

The question of the reliance of the parties (particularly those not on the left) on sources of revenue from the private sector is significant, but, given the absence of disclosure rules, it is also difficult to deal with in any comprehensive way. That said, some indication has recently emerged in evidence presented to a public enquiry concerning allegations of corruption which was held in the wake of the collapse of the Goodman beef empire in late 1991. During the course of these proceedings three of the parties provided information on the amount of money they had received from companies in the agricultural sector, including Fianna Fáil, which stated that between 1987–91 it was in receipt of £297,000, representing the equivalent of about 10 per cent of total party income during this period. In the same period, agricultural business contributions to Fine Gael totalled £138,550, representing an equivalent of about 7 per cent of total party income. The PDs gave figures for 1986–91, totalling £45,000, or the equivalent of about 3 per cent of total party income. Labour and the Workers' Party denied receiving any corporate finance from the agricultural sector.[29] It is worth emphasizing that, while these amounts are substantial, they refer to one economic sector only, and give no indication of any additional funding which may have been derived from other sectors of industry or services. Until such time as parties are obliged to disclose all of their sources of income, this sort of party funding is likely to remain secret.

Public funding of parties has also proved an essential requirement for the parties' modernization efforts. With the partial exception of the UK and Ireland, all of the other countries examined in this volume maintain some system of public subsidy for parties, candidates, and/or elections. Nassmacher (1989) has identified three overlapping stages in the implementation of public subsidies. The first of these is the stage of 'experimentation', in which governments make tentative steps towards introducing subsidies. In the second stage of 'enlargement', there is an extension in the scope and an increase in the amount of the subsidies, and this is usually then followed by the stage of 'adjustment', which mainly involves the institutionalization of the subsidy system to take account of trends in inflation.

Ireland is usually regarded as falling outside this system, in that there has been a general impression that parties are not subsidized at all by the state, and in recent years there has been much debate as to whether a scheme of state aid should be introduced as perhaps one means of introducing controls over company donations. In fact, however, Irish parties already receive substantial financial support from public funds, which are divided across five main categories of financial aid (Farrell, 1992: Tables VII.E.3–4): first, the travel and postal allowances which are given to members of the parliamentary parties; second, the money which is provided for the employment of a secretary for each non-office holding TD and each three non-office holding Senators; third, since 1981, the money which is given to the parties for the employment of assistants for administrative and research purposes; fourth, under the rules of the Oireachtas Grant, the state funding from the Department of Finance which is given to parties that have fielded candidates as a recognized party in a general election and that succeed in having at least seven deputies elected to the Dáil; and fifth, since 1985, the money which is provided to the parties in order to employ Youth Officers. Moreover, consideration is currently being given to the possible introduction of state funding of parties on a grander scale and to the introduction of rules on disclosure.

In 1989, for instance, the combined total incomes of all the political parties amounted to £2,721,306. In that same year, an additional (estimated) £4 million was provided by the state for parties and their representatives. More generally, the increasing trend in state transfers to the parties is shown in Figure 9.2, where the figures have been standardized (to 1989 prices) in order to take account of cost of living increases. These figures evidence a steady increase since the beginning of the 1960s, and then an acceleration as we move into the 1980s, suggesting that Ireland has, perhaps unwittingly, entered into Nassmacher's (1989) second stage of enlargement of public funding.

These overall developments in party finance are clearly in line with our expectations regarding the increasingly capital-intensive style of organization. First, the parties – to varying degrees – all face debt problems, reflecting the growing expense of politics in general, and campaigning in particular. Second, the parties (especially those on the centre-right) appear to rely increasingly on corporate contributions to fund their activities, a pattern which has tended to coincide with the general decline in the proportion of party income originating from membership dues. And third, contrary to the general view, Irish parties are in receipt of quite substantial public funding.

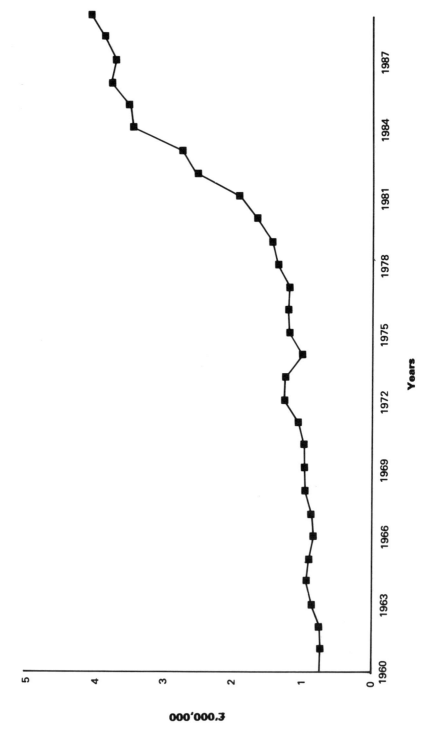

Figure 9.2   *State subventions to Irish parties, constant prices* (Central Statistics Office; Farrell, 1992: Table VII.E.4.ii)

Conclusion

The process of party adaptation in Ireland has also resulted in a process of organizational convergence. All parties have attempted to professionalize (especially the two larger parties) and all have tended to become more centralized. Party leaderships have been given greater coordination powers and have shown a greater willingness to resort to these powers, especially with regard to candidate selection and vote-management. There has also been a decline in the role of the party members as shown both by the decline in the number of members towards the end of the 1980s and by the shift away from a reliance on the income generated by membership dues. The parties have also taken steps to assert greater control over their memberships by weeding out paper branches, by rule changes regarding the obligations of members and (with the exceptions of Fianna Fáil and the Green party) by moving towards the central registering of members.

These developments also suggest a consolidation of the stratarchic model and the increasing autonomy of the parliamentary party, which is underpinned both by staffing developments and by the nature of state funding. The 'hold' of the parliamentary party over the organization as a whole has also clearly been consolidated over the past two or three decades, with the locus of power shifting firmly to the leadership in the Dáil. Staff at headquarters are controlled by the party leader, and staff appointments are her/his sole prerogative. Party policy is set by the frontbench. And while this process has been facilitated by the general willingness of the national executive to work in cooperation with the leadership, it must also be remembered that a large proportion of the membership of this executive is constituted by parliamentarians. In this sense, all moves towards an increase in the powers of the centre and towards a concomitant diminution in the powers of the local party and the local membership have ended up by consolidating parliamentary party control over the organization as a whole.[30] Taken to the extreme, this trend could presage a situation where the organization simply becomes an appendage of the parliamentary party, and certainly the developments in Irish party organizations over the past two decades or so are suggestive of just such a move.

Party organizations in Ireland have been changing at a time of considerable party system flux. The 1960s began with just three main parties while the 1980s ended with six (although the old three still continue to dominate). Party competition proved intense in the 1970s and 1980s and posed a threat to the long-term predominance of Fianna Fáil. By the end of the 1980s, Fianna Fáil had recognized the change and had finally accepted the need for coalition government, thereby possibly securing its place in all future governments for the foreseeable future. This could of course imply that the system has found a new equilibrium, shifting from a situation in which Fianna Fáil was dominant on its own to one in which it is dominant in coalition, with the period in between (the 1970s and 1980s) being a

competitive era of transition as well as a period of substantial organizational reform. The fact that organizational change, and particularly the
centralization and professionalization of party organizations, occurred
during this period of competitiveness was by no means coincidental; but
whether it was the new competitiveness which led to organizational
change, or vice versa, remains more open to question.

Notes

1 I am grateful to Enid Lakeman for comments on an earlier draft of this chapter. I also
wish to acknowledge the considerable assistance of Richard S. Katz and Peter Mair in
improving on earlier drafts. Any remaining mistakes are, of course, mine alone.

2 This chapter examines the Irish party system up to the end of the 1980s. It therefore deals
with the Workers' Party as it was, and ignores the newly-formed Democratic Left, which
emerged from a split in the Workers' Party in early 1992. In the subsequent 1992 election,
Democratic Left held on to four Dáil seats; the Workers' Party retained none.

3 The quote is from papers in the Fine Gael archives in University College Dublin (P39/
TC6/15(b)), which is also the only reasonably complete set of party archives which has been
maintained. Information on the negotiations between party whips and RTÉ is from a private
interview with a senior RTÉ executive. On the proposal for TV training of Fine Gael
politicians see the Fine Gael/UCD archives (P39/TC8/7(a)).

4 Depending on how it is calculated, about one quarter of Fianna Fáil's *árd comhairle* is
currently made up of parliamentary party members. In Labour the figure is close to a third;
while in Fine Gael it is approaching about one half (Farrell, 1992: Tables VII.D.2.b–d).

5 For a discussion of the close similarity between Fianna Fáil's organizational style and the
old branch structure of parties which dated back, before independence, to the 1880s, see
Garvin (1981: 156), who notes that the party 'found a ready-made foundation for its
organization, but its leaders had to work hard to weld it together'.

6 Between 1951 and 1977, for example, roughly one-third of the incumbent TDs who lost
their seats were displaced by running-mates from the same party, with a somewhat higher
proportion suffering the same fate in the 1980s (Carty, 1981: 114; Gallagher, 1990: 88).

7 Some real illustrations of this type of strategy are discussed in Mair (1987a: 124–7) and in
Gallagher (1990: 81–3).

8 For campaign expenditure from 1961–1989, see Farrell (1992: Table VII.E.6.i). In the
1992 election expenditure dropped sharply, reflecting the dire financial straits of the parties
(Farrell, 1993).

9 The early figures have been gleaned from the Fine Gael archives and from party
headquarters. The figures on advertising expenditure in 1987 and 1989 are from Farrell (1992:
Table VII.E.6.ii). All figures have been standardized using the average annual index of the
Central Statistics Office (CSO), based on the Consumer Price Index (series to base of August
1963 = 100).

10 Note that in this calculation, 'headquarters' staff' includes administrators paid for out of
state money: i.e. the administrative and secretarial assistants, appointed under the scheme
referred to above, who work for the party organizations rather than for the individual
parliamentarians.

11 It should also be noted in this context, that the Oireachtas Grant (see p. 235) – the
annual lump sum payment to the parties – is given to the parliamentary party leader. It is used
at her/his discretion; there is no requirement that this money should be handed over to the
party organization.

12 For an illuminating account of this practice in the context of recent developments in the
Labour Party, see Collins (1993).

13 The damaging effects of paper branches could also be dealt with by the centre playing a
more active role in candidate selection (see p. 226).

14 It is notable how the decline in the number of party branches, dealt with below, dates from around this time (Figure 9.1).

15 In stark contrast to Fine Gael, few if any rule changes have been made by Fianna Fáil or Labour regarding the selection of conference delegates or the role of the member in candidate selection.

16 These new constituency officers played a significant role throughout the 1980s in improving the coordination of the party. Inevitably, however, there tended to be quite a slow turnover in the posts and by the early 1990s there was an impression that perhaps some had been in office for too long. In 1992 there was an attempt to 'stand down' all constituency officers (*Irish Times*, 7 May 1992), but this was rejected by a subsequent *árd fheis* vote.

17 Furthermore, no more than one-third of the branch could be delegates and the membership must have been registered at least two months in advance of the convention.

18 Gallagher (1988) suggests that there was a change in 1984 giving the national executive the right to add candidates, although there is also evidence to suggest that the practice of adding names to local lists dates back to at least 1981 (Mair, 1987: 132).

19 To a large degree this is at the discretion of the union involved. It is the union which decides how many of its members it wishes to affiliate (determining how many individual votes it will have at national conference) and therefore how much money it is prepared to contribute to Labour funds.

20 Trade unions provide other means of support, such as sponsoring parliamentary candidates or running supportive newspaper advertisements during elections.

21 It is worth noting that the trend for both the Workers' Party and the Greens is steadily upwards, reflecting the gradual electoral inroads both parties made during the course of the 1980s (Farrell, 1992: Tables VII.B.1.a,e,f). Hidden in the global membership figures are changes in the nature and organization of the party membership which, of themselves, reflect a shift towards professionalization. Seeking to target selected groups more effectively, parties began to establish ancillary organizations from the late 1970s onwards, an important factor behind the overall rise in membership figures at that stage. The PDs did not establish any ancillary organizations until the early 1990s.

22 In his analysis of the evidence up until the mid-1980s, Mair (1987: 106) remarks on how '[i]t is . . . interesting to note the decline in the number of Labour branches . . . despite the reported increase in individual membership of the party'. An examination of the party's membership cards reveals that much of this is due to the closure of some branches (for non-payment of registration dues) and the merger of others. In other words, the organization was being gradually streamlined.

23 This section of the report, appropriately entitled 'A party that belongs to its members', also recommended the creation of specialist groups and single-issue groups which would be open to people outside the party. Fianna Fáil also recently commissioned a special report on organizational renewal, which ended up by placing more emphasis on the need to streamline the role of local and national officers in the party rather than on any major organizational restructuring per se (Fianna Fáil, 1993).

24 There is also mixed evidence regarding subscription fees for membership. Neither Fianna Fáil nor the Greens charge a membership fee, but all the others do. And whereas Fine Gael, the PDs and Labour expect subscriptions which amount to a maximum of the order of £4–6 per annum, the Workers' Party charges a maximum weekly rate of fifty pence (£26 p.a.).

25 According to the rules set originally in 1957 (updated in 1973), new members have a six-month period in which they have no voting rights. They have to attend special classes at the end of which they must show they have an understanding of party policy.

26 Since 1973 the Workers' Party also has another rule which is central to its democratic centralist form of organization: 'While accepting that differences of opinion can exist in relation to formulation of policy or in deciding on strategic or tactical activities, the existence of factions or individuals that oppose or refrain from engaging in activities decided upon by the movement shall not be allowed' (Workers' Party, 1973 Constitution).

27 With the singular exception of the Labour Party, the annual accounts published by the parties list only their annual revenue and expenses; no details are provided about the state of

the parties' balance sheets, about their surpluses or deficits (see Farrell, 1992: Tables VII.E.1–2).

28 Fianna Fáil does not publish any breakdown of its sources of income – for details on the other parties, see Farrell (1992: Tables VII.E.1.a–f).

29 Subsequently it was revealed that, for some time, Labour had been in receipt of corporate donations to fund election campaigning, amounting to £70,000 in 1992.

30 Discipline, and hence leadership control, also appears to have been enhanced *within* the parliamentary parties. In July 1993, for example, for the first time in its history, the Fianna Fáil parliamentary party drew up a set of eight regulations governing discipline, the conduct of meetings, leadership elections and motions of no confidence ('FF adopts rules to remove whip', *Irish Times*, 9 July 1993).

References

Carty, R.K. (1981) *Party and Parish Pump: Electoral Politics in Ireland*. Ontario: Wilfrid Laurier Press.

Chubb, B. (1959) 'Ireland, 1957', in D. Butler (ed.), *Elections Abroad*. London: Macmillan.

Collins, S. (1993) *Spring and the Labour Party*. Dublin: O'Brien Press, pp. 183–226.

Dunphy, R. and Hopkins, S. (1992) 'The Organizational and Political Evolution of the Workers' Party of Ireland', *Journal of Communist Studies*, 8: 91–118.

Farrell, B. (1985) 'Ireland: From Friends and Neighbours to Clients and Partisans', in V. Bogdanor (ed.), *Representatives of the People?* Aldershot: Gower, pp. 237–64.

Farrell, B. and Manning, M. (1978) 'The Election', in H.R. Penniman (ed.), *Ireland at the Polls: The Dáil Election of 1977*. Washington, DC: American Enterprise Institute, pp. 133–64.

Farrell, D. (1986) 'The Strategy to Market Fine Gael in 1981', *Irish Political Studies*, 1: 1–14.

Farrell, D. (1990) 'Campaign Strategies and Media Coverage', in M. Gallagher and R. Sinnott (eds), *How Ireland Voted 1989*. Galway: Centre for the Study of Irish Elections/PSAI Press, pp. 23–43.

Farrell, D. (1992) 'Ireland', in R.S. Katz and P. Mair (eds), *Party Organizations: A Data Handbook on Party Organizations in Western Democracies, 1960–90*. London: Sage Publications, pp. 389–457.

Farrell, D. (1993) 'Campaign Strategies', in M. Gallagher and M. Laver (eds), *How Ireland Voted 1992*. Dublin: PSAI Press/Folens.

Fianna Fáil (1993) *Commission on the Aims and Structures of Fianna Fáil: Final Report* Dublin: Fianna Fáil.

Fine Gael (1993) *Report of the Commission on Renewal of Fine Gael*. Dublin: Fine Gael.

Gallagher, M. (1982) *The Irish Labour Party in Transition, 1957–1982*. Manchester: Manchester University Press.

Gallagher, M. (1988) 'Ireland: The Increasing Role of the Centre', in M. Gallagher and M. Marsh (eds), *Candidate Selection in Comparative Perspective: The Secret Garden of Politics*. London: Sage, pp. 119–44.

Gallagher, M. (1990) 'The Election Results and the New Dáil', in Michael Gallagher and Richard Sinnott (eds), *How Ireland Voted 1989*. Galway: Centre for the Study of Irish Elections/PSAI Press, pp. 68–93.

Gallagher, M. and Komito, L. (1992) 'Dáil Deputies and their Constituency Work', in J. Coakley and M. Gallagher (eds), *Politics in the Republic of Ireland*. Galway: PSAI Press.

Garvin, T. (1981) *The Evolution of Irish Nationalist Politics*. Dublin: Gill & Macmillan.

Katz, R.S. (1980) *A Theory of Parties and Electoral Systems*. Baltimore, MD: Johns Hopkins University Press.

Katz, R.S. and Mair, P. (1994) 'The Evolution of Party Organizations in Europe: The Three Faces of Party Organization', in William Crotty (ed.), *Political Parties in a Changing Age*, special issue of the *American Review of Politics*, 14: 593–618.

Katz, R.S., Mair, P. and Bardi, L., Bille, L., Deschouwer, K., Farrell, D., Koole, R.,

Morlino, L., Müller, W., Pierre, J., Poguntke, T., Sundberg, J., Svåsand, L., van de Velde, H., Webb, P. and Widfeldt, A. (1992) 'The Membership of Political Parties in European Democracies', *European Journal of Political Research*, 22: 329–45.

Laver, M. and Shepsle, K.A. (1992) 'Election Results and Coalition Possibilities in Ireland', *Irish Political Studies*, 7: 57–72.

Lyne, T. (1987) 'The Progressive Democrats', *Irish Political Studies*, 2: 107–14.

Mair, P. (1987) *The Changing Irish Party System: Organization, Ideology and Electoral Competition*. London: Pinter.

Mair, P. (1987a) 'Party Organization, Vote Management, and Candidate Selection: Towards the Nationalization of Electoral Strategy in Ireland', in H. Penniman and B. Farrell (eds), *Ireland at the Polls 1981, 1982, and 1987*. Washington, DC: American Enterprise Institute/ Duke University Press, pp. 104–30.

Manning, M. (1972) *Irish Political Parties: An Introduction*. Dublin: Gill & Macmillan.

Marsh, M., Wilford, R., Arthur, P. and Fitzgerald, R. (1993) 'Irish Political Data, 1992', *Irish Political Studies*, 8: 169–214.

Nassmacher, K.-H. (1989) 'Structure and Impact of Public Subsidies to Political Parties in Europe: The Examples of Austria, Italy, Sweden and West Germany', in H. Alexander (ed.), *Comparative Political Finance in the 1980s*. Cambridge: Cambridge University Press.

10

Italy: Tracing the Roots of the Great Transformation

Luciano Bardi and Leonardo Morlino

The first half of the 1990s clearly marked a major turning point in post-war Italian politics, with a transformation of the electoral arrangements, the parties, and the relations between politics and civil society.[1] The electoral strength of the *Leghe* (Leagues) had already become clear in the regional elections in May 1990; in February 1991 the Communist party (PCI) dissolved itself and formed the Democratic Party of the Left (*Partito Democratico della Sinistra*, PDS); in June 1991, for the first time, the result of a referendum ran counter to the positions of the traditional parties; the general elections in April 1992 witnessed the establishment of a new dimension in the national political space represented by the opposition of a variety of new parties (for example, the *Leghe, Verdi, La Rete* and *Lista Pannella*) mobilizing against the traditional formations; in 1993, the complex relationship developed over the years between political parties, civil society and the economy virtually came to an end as a result of the decision by the government to privatize a large share of the Italian public sector; and finally, although falling outside the remit of this chapter, the March 1994 general elections resulted in a substantial victory for a right-wing electoral alliance which was led by Silvio Berlusconi's newly formed *Forza Italia*, and which included both the *Lega Nord* and the former *Movimento Sociale* (MSI), now renamed the *Alleanza Nationale* (NA). These elections also witnessed the creation of a new left-wing electoral alliance, led by the PDS, which became the second strongest group in the parliament, and further resulted in a major defeat for those new formations which had emerged from within the traditionally dominant Christian Democratic party (DC), including the DC's direct successor, the *Partito Popolare* (PPI), which managed to win just thirty-three seats. In all, slightly more than 70 per cent of those elected to the new parliament in 1994 were new MPs.

The most important watershed in this new process of transformation was probably the consolidation of an apparent commitment among all political actors (both traditional and new) to reform Italian political institutions with a view towards improving the effectiveness of government at all levels. This commitment had been preceded by a new law for local elections, providing for the direct election of mayors, and by a referendum in April 1993 which changed the electoral system for the Senate, and which later led to a new law for elections to the Chamber of Deputies, allocating 75 per cent of the seats to MPs elected by simple plurality system within single-member districts (D'Alimonte and Chiaramonte, 1993). In addition, albeit less directly so, it also effected the acceleration of the organizational transformation (and potential demise) of the remaining traditional political parties.

The demand for reform had increased significantly during 1992 and 1993, when investigations in many Italian cities revealed widespread corruption and evidence of illegal party financing. This effectively dismantled the 'alternative' party financing system, and thus forced through a process of party reform. All of the major parties admitted to having huge deficits, which led in turn to strong and recurring demands that they transform themselves, both organizationally and financially. However, the most important single event in this process event was the perceived need for a drastic reduction of the public sector and for the privatization of the major public corporations which had been the core of party control of civil society for almost half a century (Morlino, 1991).

But while some events of the early 1990s may have accelerated the process of party transformation, it is nevertheless possible to see evidence of a much longer trend towards party organizational change and decline, dating back to at least the late 1960s. Indeed, profound changes in Italian party organization were actually long overdue, with each party, in its own way, being anchored in a network of relationships which effectively slowed down the process of change, and which, once finally disrupted, proved to be the catalyst of transformation. From this perspective, the key problems to be addressed include, first, the question of how it was possible to build up such a widespread and articulated party organization; second, the question of how it was possible to maintain this organizational network for such a long period of time; and third, the question of what finally brought about the change. We will begin with the first of these questions.

Although the particular symptoms of organizational change and decline which have been seen since the 1960s were often party-specific, it is nevertheless clear that all of the parties experienced serious difficulties in adjusting to the momentous changes taking place in Italian society in this period. Growing demands from civil society prompted sometimes unsuccessful attempts to 'open up' party organizations to new, and/or emerging, and/or simply different, social groups. Our analysis, which starts in the beginning of the 1960s when the main phase of democratic consolidation had ended, and when the trend towards party change had not yet begun, explores four levels of change: first, the organization of the parties, with particular reference to party membership; second, the relationships between party organizations outside and inside parliament; third, party staff and finances; and fourth, the relationships between the parties, on the one hand, and both interest groups and the media, on the other, including, above all, the question of party penetration of state agencies as a means of controlling civil society.

The pre-1994 Italian party system, the now defunct party system, as it were, was highly complex, with a large number of cleavages,[2] on the one hand, and the then low-threshold proportional electoral formula, on the other, giving rise to a large number of parties. Moreover, during the course of its half-century duration, there occurred several waves of party formation, beginning with the traditional parties which were founded or refounded between 1942 and 1948, which were then followed by new parties which came out of the popular movements of the 1960s and early 1970s, such as the Radicals (PR), Verdi, *Democrazia Proletaria* (DP) and then, in the 1980s, by yet more new parties which were characterized by localist attitudes and anti-politics positions, such as the Leghe, La Rete, and the Pannella group, which replaced the Radicals.

Having at least three groups of parties created in different historical periods gave the system its third feature, which was the coexistence of different models of party organization. In fact, at least three different party models have coexisted even among the traditional parties since the foundation of the post-war party system, with two different types of mass party (DC vs. PCI and Socialists [PSI]), and also elite or opinion parties (the Liberals [PLI], the Republicans [PRI] and the Social Democrats [PSDI]). Indeed, precisely because of these differences, and because of contradictory developments even within individual organizations, the four levels of analysis mentioned above are not always relevant for each of the parties. Hence we will concentrate on the most important features and on the parties which are most relevant for these features, beginning with a picture of party organizations as they were in the early 1960s.

In general, however, it should be emphasized that the Italian party system was a complex system created through different kinds of parties and through a number of related ancillary organizations, which together advanced a strong and persistent appeal to civil society, and which succeeded in establishing very stable links with that society. This is also shown by the long-term stabilization of electoral behaviour. The main explanations of this organizational 'overdevelopment' (for which see, for example, Alberoni, 1968; Barnes 1967; Tarrow 1967) include the importance of the Fascist legacy at the mass level (Morlino, forthcoming), the role of Catholic structures, the pronounced ideological configuration, the size of the public sector and finally, but crucially, the overt bipolarization. Indeed, the development of this party organizational network is, in the final analysis, one of the most characteristic features of democratic consolidation in Italy.

The starting point: the early 1960s

The early 1960s represented the end of the main phase of consolidation, and also witnessed the crisis of the centrist government formula which combined the DC together with a number of junior partners (PLI, PSDI and PRI). The other relevant parties in this period included both the Socialists and the Communists, and the term 'great transformation' is one that basically applies to all of these parties. Organizational change proved just a minor problem for the parties formed during the 1970s or after, which were born in a new historical phase, and which, with the exceptions of the *Rifondazione Comunista* (RC) and the PDS, were either unwilling or unable to organize according to traditional mass party models. Nor did these new parties ever establish a developed and centralized non-parliamentary organization. In this sense, they were genuinely new, and were characterized by either the presence of a strong national leader and very little central or peripheral organization (for example, the PR, the Leghe, and La Rete);[3] or by coalitions of leaders with a poor organization which overlapped considerably with the parliamentary groups (the Verdi, the DP) and which derived mainly from the relatively weak institutionalization of the political movements of the 1970s and early 1980s. As far as the traditional parties were concerned, however, with the exception of the MSI, the problem of change and organizational decline proved paramount.

The three main parties represented at least two different mass-party models. The DC was a confessional or denominational party, already very close to the catch-all-party model (Kirchheimer, 1966); the PCI was a classic party of mass integration; and the PSI attempted to imitate the communist model, although with limited success. A similar mass-party idea was also predominant in the formation of the MSI, which had abandoned the more traditional fascist militia model (Ignazi, 1989: esp. Ch. 2). The PLI and PRI, on the other hand, were elite and opinion parties, and despite its recurring references to Socialist mass-party models, the PSDI lay in an intermediate position between being a mass party and being a party of notables (Vallauri, 1981). In general, the most important characteristic conditioning the limited organizational structures of the small traditional parties was their continuous participation in government as junior partners of the DC.

Organizations and membership

In spite of the structures provided for by the party statutes, the organization of the DC existed mainly on paper (Poggi, 1968), with Amintore Fanfani, party secretary between 1954 and 1959, having failed in his attempt to create a modern mass party with a large membership, a central organization and, above all, a diffuse peripheral structure. There was, to be sure, a steady growth of membership and of membership density, but the party's strength nevertheless lay in its support by Catholic organizations, thus making it both highly dependent and weakly institutionalized. Greater growth of membership in the south rather than in the north (Poggi, 1968; Rossi, 1979) suggests the importance of exchange relationships, and also indicates a second feature of the party: that is, the growing salience of clientelistic politics for a party that even by 1960 had been continuously in office for fifteen years. The third relevant aspect of the DC in the early 1960s was the internal organization of at least six factions, each with its own de facto structures, and even with supporting press agencies. The fourth, and closely related feature was a network of notables which was very relevant not only to the organization of the party and its factions, but also to recruitment, for, in addition to the Catholic organizations, it was the local leaders who often recruited the new political class or who controlled entry into the party.

The PCI in the early 1960s, that is after the 20th Conference of the Soviet Communist Party and the failed Hungarian revolution, presented a different picture. Members' rights had already been emphasized in the 1957 statutes, but the key Leninist-Gramscian characteristics were basically unchanged. And although rephrased, the conception of 'democratic centralism' remained basically the same. Moreover, the mechanism of appointment was cooption from above, and any activity aiming at the formation of autonomous factions within the party was strictly forbidden. As was the case in the DC, the main decision-making bodies at the central level were the secretary and the executive, with the top leaders being in reality the party managers. More so than in the DC, however, the greatest strength was provided by the 'activists', that is, by the most ideologized and active militants who were motivated only by their ideals, and who worked for the party, ran electoral campaigns at the local level and organized propaganda activities.

Unlike the DC, the Communists had a capillary organizational network at the local level, in which territorial sections came to be more important than functional cells (Poggi, 1968: 132ff). In other words, a Leninist party organized for the revolution or other forms of political action such as strikes, demonstrations or riots, was transformed by the period of peaceful democratic activities and became more and more a classic party of integration. This transformation was compounded by a steady decline in membership. By the early 1960s, the mobilization at the end of the war had become just a memory; indeed, it was clearly impossible to maintain such a high level of mobilization for any length of time. But, even in the early 1960s, there was also a clear perception that the moment of social and radical revolution had passed. Thus while membership density remained much higher than in the other two mass parties, it was less than half that in 1946 and was also clearly declining (it was 17.6 in 1968), in contrast to the lower but more stable membership levels in the other two parties. Finally, although the Catholic organizations supported the DC politically as well as electorally, they were also autonomous from the party. In contrast, and in addition to the women's or youth sections of the party and to their special relationships with the trade unions (CISL for DC and CGIL for PCI), the Communist Party was able to build a group of organizations that proved both very close and dependent. These proved very important in winning electoral support in the 1950s, and helped to prevent any possible social isolation during that period.

In the early 1960s, when its estrangement from the Communists was complete, and when the basic decision to enter a governmental coalition with the DC had been made, the third mass party, the PSI, was no longer characterized by the Leninist structure which Morandi had attempted to create in the late 1940s and early 1950s. In formal terms, the PSI was similar to the Communists; in practice, however, it was very different. The local units were territorial sections, and the NAS (*Nuclei di Aziendali Socialisti*), corresponding to the communist cells, had never really developed during the 1950s. Lower participation at the grassroots level gave more prominence to the provincial federations, which then became the basis for the power of local notables. This ostensible mass party was therefore also a party of notables which was managed by its leaders. Factions flourished after 1957, and in this sense the party, which had been so close to the Communists for many years, came to resemble the DC in organizational terms. The PSI maintained a fairly stable membership at the end of the 1950s, following a sharp decline between 1955 and 1957. Membership density was also stable, following a pronounced decline since the early 1950s. The most meaningful figure, however, is Cazzola's (1970: 41) cautious calculation of the ratio between PSI members and militants (50:1) in these years and its comparison with that of the DC (23:1) and the PCI (18:1). The contrast with the PCI was especially striking in relation to ancillary organizations, for even without considering the PSI relationships with the trade unions (see p. 251), the party was a minority in ARCI, in the *Alleanza Contadini*, in the UDI, and in the League of Cooperatives. It is therefore impossible to consider that these associations, which were virtually monopolized by the Communists and which were supported by the Communists, as Socialist ancillary organizations. Rather, they simply reflected the remnants of an earlier phase in which there had been an active unity between the Socialists and the Communists.

Staff and financing

Three other important features of party organization are also consistent with this picture. Within the DC, the PCI and the PSI, a more developed central and peripheral organization and a higher number of members were associated with greater staff numbers, with a more extensive financing of party activities, and with a weaker and more dependent role for the parliamentary party. Although no precise data are available regarding staffing levels and party financing in the early 1960s, Galli (1966: 167–8) has suggested that the staffs of both the PCI and the DC numbered in the thousands as against about 1000 for *all* other parties. Such figures fail to give an adequate idea of the situation, however, in that there also existed a large number of civil servants who worked for their own parties, and whose activities were substantially integrated within those of the formal party staff. Thus the DC and the PCI, but also the PSI, profited from their governmental positions in the communes and the provinces, as well as from a mutual tolerance in the local branches of central administration (for example, in the Postal Service, which was often staffed with large numbers of clientelistic appointees).

Given the absence of any law on state subvention and of any rules regarding campaign financing, it is not possible to determine the amount of money devoted to party activities. That said, some information which was available at the time and which has recently been confirmed by documents and witnesses suggests that the main sources of DC party financing were the 'black funds' which derived from the public sector and from the private contributions of entrepreneurs. The PCI, on the other hand, gained substantial financial support from import/export companies and from the USSR, sources which enabled the party to establish an enormous organizational apparatus. From the late 1940s until 1956–7 the Communists also generously financed the PSI, which was therefore committed to defend and maintain the parties' joint positions. However, once the balance among the various factions in the PSI began to change (especially at the Venice party conference in 1957), and once the power of Nenni's Autonomists clearly prevailed (the Naples conference in 1959), the PSI entered a serious financial crisis (Landolfi, 1968: esp. 119). Later, following its entry into the centre-left cabinets in the 1960s, the party's sources of financial support became more similar to those of the DC, deriving mainly from the public and industrial sectors.

Parties and parliamentary groups

There is no mention of the party MPs and the parliamentary groups as such in the 1957 statutes of the PCI; nor is there much concern for the role of the parliamentary groups in the PSI statutes, which simply specified that the presidents of the groups were allowed to participate in meetings of the Socialist *Comitato Centrale*, but without voting rights. In the DC, by contrast, MPs were designated as ex-officio participants in the party national conferences; a number of MPs were elected by the national conference as members of the *Consiglio Nazionale*, which also included other members chosen by the parliamentary groups themselves and by the presidents of the parliamentary groups, as well as all DC members of the cabinet (usually MPs); in addition, the presidents of parliamentary groups were also members of the *Direzione* (and ministers could be invited to attend its meetings). However, the dependency of the parliamentary groups on the party itself is evidenced by a DC statute which suggested that their rules would have to be approved by the *Consiglio Nazionale*.

In this case the reality is also basically consistent with the statutes. In the first place, a period of activity in the party (longest in the case of the PCI and shortest in that of the DC) was generally required before being elected to Parliament. Second, despite the growing presence of MPs in the

Socialist Conferences and party executives (see Cazzola 1970: 120), the overlap between party leadership and parliamentary members is greatest in the DC and lowest in the PCI. Third, in the case of the PCI, the leaders of the parliamentary groups had a basis of support in the party, were appointed by party bodies without any open competition from, or participation of, the parliamentary group, and, in becoming parliamentary leaders, they did not automatically acquire greater power inside the party as such. In the DC, by contrast, although parliamentary leaders also enjoyed a basis of support inside the party, the parliamentary groups did nevertheless play an autonomous role in the leadership selection process, and, given the kind of multi-leader party the DC had become, parliamentary leadership was also able to provide a source of strength in intraparty conflicts. This was also largely true for the PSI (see Cotta, 1979: 352–4).

The smaller parties

The most important distinction as far as the smaller parties were concerned was that between the neo-fascist MSI, on the one hand, and the governing parties (PLI, PRI, PSDI), on the other. The picture painted by the MSI statutes of 1952 and 1954 was that of a mass party rather than a fascist militia party, with the relationship to fascism existing in terms of ideology and leadership rather than organization. Although some members were associated with fascist, extremist and violent groups, the party's organizational model was more like that suggested by the socialist tradition, with the local section as the key unit, with a central role given to the provincial federations and the Central Committee, and with the greatest political importance attaching to the secretary and the national executive. The MSI also had its own ancillary organizations, and in this sense it simply paralleled the other Italian mass parties which have been sketched above, although in this case the provincial secretary had somewhat greater powers vis-à-vis the provincial federation and was also more dependent on the centre. Although there are no reliable membership data for the MSI, the party secretary claimed half a million members in 3700 sections in the mid-1950s, a level which clearly declined during the crisis of the early 1960s. The relationships between the party and the parliamentary groups were similar to those of the Socialists, and on all political issues the MPs had to rely on the positions put forward by the committees which were formed by the Central Committee and which paralleled the Parliamentary Committees.[4] In effect, therefore, the dependence of the parliamentary groups on the party leadership had become well established during the 1950s.

The PLI, the PRI and the PSDI were all opinion parties. All maintained youth organizations (sometimes in conflict with the party), university organizations, a mass tradition in a few areas (one-third of all PRI members were based in Romagna), newspapers and, in the case of the PSDI, a women's organization. At the same time, however, all had very limited numbers of members (for example: 170,000 PLI members in 1957; between 123,000 and 150,000 PSDI members in 1956–58; fewer than 50,000 PRI members in 1963), a provincial structure which existed on paper but which did not really constitute an intermediate organization, and no diffused mass presence. Moreover, the role of a small number of leaders and a fairly continuous governmental presence for almost the entire decade confirmed their elite or opinion status, and provided them with a distinct middle-class electoral appeal. Finally, as might be expected, the parliamentary groups were very influential in all three parties, albeit less so in the case of the PSDI, whose socialist model discouraged a strong parliamentary presence in the leading party bodies and promoted a strong sense of party discipline among the MPs.

Parties, civil society and state

The 1950s was clearly a period of party dominance vis-à-vis civil society. This was reflected in two ways: first, in the relationships between parties and more or less organized pressure groups, particularly business organizations and trade unions, and between parties and religious organizations, particularly between the DC and Catholic organizations; and second, in the particularistic relationships between the parties and non-organized social groups or individuals, especially with regard to the increasing party penetration and control of the state and public economic agencies, and to the clientelistic system which was established during this decade.

During the first phase of Italian democracy, Christian Democracy had been defined by its closeness to various religious organizations, to the hierarchy and to the Vatican. Indeed, the strong Catholic subculture constituted the core of DC electoral strength in many areas of northern Italy, with a similar linkage function being performed by Marxist ideology in the case of parties such as the PCI and the PSI. The clientelistic system that lay at the core of the ties between civil society and the parties (such as the DC, the PLI and the PSDI) in some southern areas of the country, on the other hand, was basically established in the 1950s with the creation and expansion of the public economy, as, for instance, in the case of the *Cassa per il Mezzogiorno* (see Graziano, 1980; Pasquino 1980: 95).

Despite some pioneering work by LaPalombara (1964), there has been little in the way of substantial research on the relationship between parties and interest associations in Italy, and it is only recently that some conclusions have proved possible (see Morlino, 1991). In the agricultural sector, for example, the most meaningful relationships concern the DC, as the main party in government, as well as some of the smaller parties of the right. Thus the association of land-owners, the *Confagricoltura*, which initially opted for neutrality and a multi-party appeal, ended up in the 1950s by approaching the DC, and at the same time sought to develop a privileged relationship with other rightist parties in an attempt to effect a dual strategy of internal and external management of the DC. The pattern was somewhat different in the case of the association of small landowners, the *Coldiretti*, for while there were some elements of symbiosis in their links with the DC, much as might be the case between a party and a trade union, the relationship can perhaps best be seen as one of domination by the party. Beginning in the early 1950s, the representation of the *Coldiretti* in the Ministry of Agriculture and in Parliament was paralleled by the presence of numerous party representatives in the provincial and local executives of the association itself. Moreover, land allocation during the implementation of the agrarian reform was clearly exploited politically, while crucial sectoral programmes were formulated inside the party, with subsequent decision-making taking place both in the government and parliament.

The situation in the industrial sector was not substantially different. Here too there was a dominance of the DC, which was effected through the penetration of public economic agencies, and through the marginalization and isolation of the organized groups of the left, and here too party control of access to the decision-making arena was contested by neither the industrial business association, *Confindustria*, nor the trade unions. Thus the DC gradually established its dominance vis-à-vis *Confindustria*, while the parties more widely came to dominate the trade unions (the DC in the case of the Catholic CISL; the PCI in the case of the largely communist CGIL; the PSI in the case of some sections of both the CGIL and the UIL; and the Republicans in the case of other sections of the UIL).

What was of crucial importance here was the expansion of the public sector. In agriculture, for example, the *Federconsorzi*, the agrarian reform agencies, public pension agencies and the *Cassa per il Mezzogiorno*, effectively determined the pattern of relations between the DC and the interest associations. The same applied in the industrial sector, where the basis of the relationships between the governmental parties, on the one hand, and business and the trade unions, on the other, was defined by the role of IRI in economic reconstruction, by the creation of ENI in 1953 and the Ministry for State Investments in 1956, by the laws on hydrocarbons in 1957, by the activity of the *Cassa per il Mezzogiorno* in the industrial sector, and by both the presence of public banks and the creation of a series of public agencies, all of which were controlled by the parties in government. To this can also be added the stance of the left as a whole, which supported the expansion of the public sector for ideological reasons, and which failed to appreciate the political side effects of such public intervention until it was too late (see also Maraffi, 1991: 222–3).

There were two phases in the relationship between the parties and the trade unions prior to 1960. In the first phase, party domination was both clear-cut and strong. With the split in the previously united trade union movement (1949–50), however, there came a second phase, in which party remained dominant, but in which the role of the trade unions themselves overlapped with that of the parties. There was thus some degree of penetration of the DC by the Catholic trade unions, for example, while the

CISL exerted pressure on the government to provoke the exit of public companies from *Confindustria*. Moreover, the parties offered their resources to sustain trade unions in a phase of demobilization and debility, and the fact that the trade unions never took a clearly autonomous position in the area of industrial relations during this period provides confirmation of party dominance. It was only in the early 1960s that there developed a clearer differentiation of roles, with the trade unions assuming somewhat more autonomy within the sphere of industrial relations.

There was, therefore, a well-defined network of relationships between parties and interest groups at the end of the 1950s and also, more generally, between parties and civil society. This also reflected the Italian style of party government, which was characterized not only by the colonization of the public sector of the economy and by the penetration/ control of civil society, but also by the 'occupation' of the bureaucracy and by the absence of any possibility of alternation in government (see Pasquino, 1987).

Party organization in Italy since 1960

The period between 1960 and the early 1990s witnessed profound changes in party organization in Italy. After the initial phase of democratic consolidation, the political system itself discovered a new equilibrium, and for most of this period cabinets were supported by three-, four- or five-party centre-left coalitions, based on the DC and, playing a crucial pivotal role, the PSI. With these centre-left cabinets there began a greater degree of competition within the governmental party system, one of the consequences of which was the greater demand for material and political resources. In order to maintain and strengthen their organizations, the party leaders (and the parties) were inevitably drawing resources from the public sector, which expanded enormously under two distinct stimuli: the 'natural' stimulus provided by the sharp economic growth of the 1960s, and the 'artificial' stimulus provided by the policies of the centre-left coalitions. These developments also had an impact on the parties' organizations. The growth of the public sector reinforced the dependence of civil society on the parties, while the implementation of regionalization from the 1970s contributed to the emergence of autonomous, regionally based, intra-party groups. The PSI in particular gained enormous advantage from these developments, while at the same time not detracting in absolute terms from the resources available to the DC. Finally, widespread and sustained consociational practices, which found their greatest expression in the 1976–79 period of national solidarity, blurred the distinction between government and opposition.

Throughout this period, social changes also posed demands which required organizational reforms. In this case, however, the most important transformations did not really bear fruit until the early 1990s, by which time the various party models described above had all but disappeared, at least on the surface. The PDS remained closest to its earlier tradition, and the preliminary party rules accepted in 1991 provided a formal structure which resembled the mass-party model, albeit in a context of emerging factionalism and stratarchy. All of the other traditional parties, by contrast, were caught up in self-reform processes which threatened to produce even more radical results. Moreover, there was also a widespread belief that representation should be developed through non-party organizations, with the idea of partyness being considered a thing of the past, and with 'party' itself becoming almost a dirty word. At least on the surface, the new 'party' model would be more 'open'. Finally, although the full effect of a lot of these changes is still impossible to ascertain, there were also other important processes of change which had already begun long before the revolution of the early 1990s, and it is to these that we will now turn.

The membership party

Formally speaking, there was little discernible change in the overall levels of party membership in the thirty years after 1960; in 1989, total party membership had declined by only some 3 per cent, to about 4,150,000 (Bardi and Morlino, 1992: Tables VIII.B.1.a–k). Even allowing for the considerable expansion of Italy's voting population (which grew by almost 28 per cent between 1963 and 1992), these data could be taken to reflect a remarkable capacity on the part of the parties to maintain their position in society. As against this, however, we need only look at the situation at the beginning of 1993, which was characterized by an apparent collapse in the memberships of the three most important parties, the DC, the PDS and the PSI, a collapse which was only partially compensated for by the expansion of the numbers belonging to their less traditional competitors. In some cities, such as Turin, for example, the Lega now has more members than the DC and the PDS, a shift which partly reflects the appeal of the Lega itself, and partly reflects the simple decline in membership of the other two parties.[5]

While the phenomenon of progressive de-alignment and the erosion of party roots within the important subcultures was characteristic of the entire period, it was only in recent years that it became overtly reflected in measures of party membership and other aspects of party organization. The main reason for this may have been the stagnation of the party system as a whole, and the stagnation of the all-party grip on the political system and on important parts of civil society in particular. Moreover, party membership never entailed any very strong commitment, but rather represented an expression of sympathy on the part of individual card-carriers (Galli, 1976), and this in itself probably allowed the parties to maintain a constant membership bedrock through the years. Indeed, formal membership required no more than the annual payment of fees, an obligation which was often met by the heads of families or even by local leaders in need of undemanding support.[6] Interviews with local cadres responsible for party organization confirm that by the 1970s, and even for the PCI, membership had become a family affair; and even a party like the MSI, which had extremely rigid formal rules for the admission of its members, tended to ignore these rules in an effort to build the widest possible membership (Ignazi, 1989).

Official conceptions of membership have not changed much for most parties over the years; in practice, however, and even in the case of those parties, such as the PDS or MSI, which continued to prescribe an active role for their members, membership became an extremely weak notion. On the other hand, membership is perhaps more important for the new actors in the party system, albeit in a different sense. Thus La Rete and the PR viewed membership as their main source of income (the most recent fees were 0.5 per cent of personal income in the case of La Rete, while the minimum fee in the case of the PR amounted to a stunning 300,000 lire). Moreover, the PR also saw members as sympathizing financial donors, who sometimes belong to other parties and who have no other obligations. The Verdi are also somewhat unusual, maintaining a system of collective membership in which relationships with individuals are determined by the single lists making up the federation, while the Lega maintains a more traditional, but rather undemanding view of membership (at least on paper), characterized by low admission requirements and generic member- ship obligations. In practice, however, Lega members are actually divided into four hierarchical categories: supporters, who have no voting rights and no obligations (in effect, their role is simply to provide financial support); militants, who have voting rights at local level and also 'active militancy' obligations; full members, who are appointed by the National Assembly after having 'demonstrated excellent militant commitment' and who enjoy voting rights at national level; and founding members, who enjoy lifetime voting rights at national level (Tarchi, forthcoming [b]).

The evolution of DC membership offers a clear illustration of the sheer suddenness of the Italian party crisis. Reflecting the party's uneven organizational fortunes, DC membership evolved in a see-saw fashion, with highs of over 1.8 million members in 1973 and 1988 and a low of just under 1.1 million members in 1977. After a further and unprecedented peak of more than 2 million members in 1990, membership dropped dramatically to less than 1.4 million members in 1991, with fourteen important provincial committees (including Milan, Rome, Naples and Palermo) not having yet reported their membership figures by the time (1 December 1992) party Secretary Mino Martinazzoli had announced his decision to 're-found' the party. Martinazzoli's decision included the complete renewal of party membership through the 'erasure' of old membership records and the request to all prospective members (old and new) to file new applications. The second important aspect of the projected reform was a proposed regionalization of the party's organization. The apparent collapse of *partitocrazia* in 1992 and 1993 affected the DC more than any other party; in complete contrast to the pattern of the past fifty years, the party's centrality was no longer an asset but a burdensome liability, and Martinazzoli's project was simply the latest attempt by a DC Secretary to 're-establish', 'revitalize' or 'reorganize' the party. And while earlier attempts to improve the party's machinery during the 1970s and the 1980s had proved disappointing, they nevertheless confirmed, at least for the DC, that organizational inadequacy pre-dated the crisis of the 1990s by at least two decades.

The progressive erosion of the party's privileged relationship with the Catholic subculture was paralleled by a process of self-confessed seculariz-ation, in which a party apparatus was to replace the Catholic organizations as the means of garnering electoral support. At least formally, the DC organizational structures had been considerably strengthened during the 1970s and early 1980s, even though factionalism and patronage never ceased to play a role, thus rendering the formal organization itself of little value in any attempt at centralization. Secularization found its principal expression in the creation of *sezioni ambiente*, that is, non-territorial branches which were intended to replace the Catholic organizations as the means of maintaining party contact with civil society. In 1991, these accounted for little more than 5 per cent of the DC's 13,700 branches, but for more than half (230 vs. 211) of those located in the major cities (D'Amore, forthcoming). However, research from the mid-1980s indicates that many DC branches were little more than empty shells, with no permanent offices, let alone telephones or other equipment. Many branches were also effectively inactive during inter-election periods (Rossi, 1987). This suggests that the formal organization itself was subject to the same artificial inflation that had always characterized its membership. For example, while National Congress delegates came to be allocated accord-ing to the party's share of the popular vote, they were nevertheless nominated and elected in regional congresses which were based on the registered membership, and this, in turn, continued to offer a powerful incentive to inflate such figures.

The notion of membership is very weak in the case of the DC, with ordinary members having very little contact with the party's organization and scarcely participating in any of its activities. As in the 1950s and 1960s, the burden continued to rest mainly on the party activists, of whom there were an average of about five or six in each of the 13,000 basic units. Many of these also held salaried public offices which allowed them to work almost full time for the party, thus greatly reducing the need for permanent staff. Indeed, the data on central party staff are contradictory and confused, with independent estimates or confidential sources fluctuating between 500 and 800 during the 1980s. Figures on regional party staff are even more difficult to obtain. Moreover, most DC senators and deputies were availed of a special indemnity which was intended to cover the costs incurred in the documentation needed for their offices and which enabled them to hire one or more personal assistants; in fact, in terms of both size and staffing, the personal 'secretariats' of some MPs came to rival the most important regional headquarters. By the early 1990s, however, the fiscal crisis had forced a reduction in the DC central staff from about 800 to about 500. At the same time, the declining share of the vote and the increasing judicial and public scrutiny of civil service appointments had reduced the opportunities available to all of the parties to use public office-holders (especially at the local level) and civil servants as party activists.

The most important change in the post-war organizational history of the PCI was perhaps the disappearance of the cell as the basic organizational unit (Bardi and Morlino, 1992: Table VIII.B.1.b). At the 1979 party congress, for example, there was representation from only some 2000 factory cells, with the *sezione* having become the basic territorial unit. The disappearance of the cell marked the transition to a much more pragmatic posture (from mass integration to catch-all party), with the notion of membership also undergoing a parallel evolution. In the 1940s every member had been a militant, and even by the mid-1950s at least 350,000 communists still held leadership functions (Ghini, 1981: 241); by the late 1960s, however, the bulk of party activities, including recruitment and campaigning, were carried out by a handful of members in each of the 12,000–13,000 branches (Galli, 1976), and a decade later the outer circle in the PCI's membership was described simply as the *iscritti* (literally, the enrolled), switching easily from that status to that of just 'sympathizers' or even 'voters' (Casciani, 1981). It is from this vantage point that the alternating fortunes and temporary membership expansion of the PCI can best be understood. Thus the rising red tide of the mid-1970s had probably attracted many 'exchange' voters (see Parisi and Pasquino, 1980) who sought personal advantages through membership, only to abandon it once more when the party lost its bid for power. There were also more fundamental reasons for the organizational and electoral decline of the PCI, however, not least of which was the decline and cultural transforma-tion of the Italian working class, historically the PCI's largest constituency, with which the party insisted on preserving a privileged relationship.[7] The party's ability to attract new members was substantially reduced, and the composition of the membership also changed drastically, with an almost complete disappearance of student members, with a decline in the num-bers of industrial and agricultural workers, and with an increase in the numbers of pensioners and housewives.

These trends also appear to be confirmed by the 1991 and 1992 PDS membership data,[8] and it is now widely accepted that most of the PCI/PDS misfortunes may be ascribed to the belated nature of the transition. But while organizational inadequacy and strategic ambiguity may have been responsible for at least some of the party's declining electoral fortunes and for its inability to redirect its links with civil society, the inadequacy of the territorial section had already been noted in the early 1980s. Thus it was argued that the territorial section could not 'grasp . . . the problems of modern urban sprawl', and strong doubts were cast on the ability of section-based activists to represent the membership at large, let alone the 11 million-strong party electorate. The result was an entrenchment of local interests and a subsequent and progressive pulverization of what had been an apparently monolithic structure (Hellmann, 1985: 59–60). And even if these conclusions tend to be rather extreme, the recorded evidence nevertheless confirms the decline of PCI sections (Galli, 1976; Ghini, 1981), with praise for the party's organizational superiority being justified only by comparisons with other parties (Rossi, 1987).

With the resignation of Bettino Craxi as PSI Party Secretary after almost seventeen years, 1993 also marked the formal end of what seemed one of Italy's most impressive political success stories. By then, however, the best available membership figures indicated that the strong positive trend (Bardi and Morlino, 1992: Table VIII.B.1.de) experienced by the party under Craxi had already come to a very abrupt end. Despite its change of status from the 1960s through to the mid-1970s (from opposition to government), and despite its subsequent problems (the split of the left wing as the PSIUP in 1963, the re-unification with the PSDI into the PSU in 1966, and the final separation from the PSDI in 1969) the basic organizational structure of the PSI did not change very much in this period. Power remained concentrated in the hands of faction leaders, although in this case the factions, unlike those in the DC, never represented links with selected sectors of civil society (Pasquino and Rossi, 1980: 78). Indeed, in some cases, these factions actually hindered the party's ability to expand its membership, with the faction leaders discouraging the recruitment of members who might lean towards their opponents (Mattana, 1981: 59; Merkel, 1987: 60). Moreover, the relative importance of the party's geographic (the industrial north) and functional (the working class) constituencies also continued to decline.

The apparently considerable changes under Craxi were mainly intended to consolidate his own leadership rather than to give the party a more efficient and flexible organization, and they proved unable to prevent the collapse of the 1990s. During a conference in late 1992, for example, it was interesting to note a prominent PSI leader, Valdo Spini, declaring that the party's 'crisis' had been unavoidable because the power it wielded for so many years was unjustified by its size. Although Spini was referring to the party's electoral weight, organizational deficiencies were also to be blamed, for despite the appearances maintained during Craxi's leadership, most of the party's defects persisted or even worsened. Thus the party's organization on the ground remained very weak and was active only at election time (Merkel, 1987; see also Rossi, 1987). Moreover, although factions had been neutralized, at least at the national level, the links between the members and the party had become even more personalized (Cazzola, 1982). Weak participation and personalism acted to strengthen the provincial federations and to favour the consolidation of locally based factions which, were it not for the impact of Craxi's strong leadership from the end of 1970s, might well have turned the party into a quasi-federal organization. The most important distortion, however, was the emergence of the so-called *rampanti* (the go-getters), who exploited the party's organizational permeability and the weakening of its roots in civil society in order to build very rapid careers and to take advantage of the party's disproportionate share of political and material resources.

In general, then, the main characteristics of the 'Craxi model' were those of a party which a more and more powerful leader sought to change and rebuild only in order to guarantee support for his person and his policies. At the roots of Craxi's success, and perhaps ironically, lay a strong leadership manoeuvrability, together with the continuous expectation of great success (also in the electoral arena) which derived from the decline of the Communists and from the possible defeat of the DC at both governmental and local levels. Such success never laid the basis for solid PSI growth, however, and the party was eventually stymied by its own organizational weaknesses, by the resistance and later temporary recovery of both major antagonists and, finally, by the intervention of the Milanese prosecutors who charged Craxi with corruption and other criminal violations of the law on party finance.

Party finance

The reality of Italian party organizations can be grasped only by exploring the complex, and often illegal, system of relationships between political parties and organized or even individual interests, a system which can perhaps best be illustrated by a discussion of party finance. For although official data are clearly inadequate, and although unofficial information is very difficult to obtain, with the official and the unofficial story diverging considerably in this regard, it is nevertheless reasonable to surmise that Italian party organizations were enormously expensive machines.

Official party finance data are practically impossible to obtain prior to 1974, when party budgets first became public and standardized according to the law on the public funding of political parties. Most importantly, this new law prohibited party (both the organization and the individual members) financing by public companies (that is, companies with at least 20 per cent of the capital being held by the state), and was also intended to discourage illegal contributions. In reality, by establishing strict and cumbersome regulations and procedures, the law also made it very difficult to provide for *legal* contributions.

The major aims of the 1974 law largely failed to materialize; indeed, political corruption as well as the involvement of public companies in illegal party financing not only failed to disappear, but actually seem to have increased. The law also had another serious defect: the amounts of the funds which it established could be changed only by law and were to be divided among all parties represented in Parliament (Bardi and Morlino, 1992: Table VIII.E.3.i). The result was that there were only very few and

Table 10.1A   *The official finances of Italian parties: incomes (I) and expenditures (E) of PCI, DC and PSI (in billions of lire – current prices)*

Year	PCI		DC		PSI	
	I	E	I	E	I	E
1974	23.9	23.8	24.7	20.2	8.6	8.7
1984	104.7	109.3	68.9	61.8	22.1	33.9
1989	113.7	117.1	77.8	72.0	53.6	53.6

Table 10.1B   *The official finances of Italian parties: incomes (I) and expenditures (E) of PCI, DC and PSI (in billions of lire – constant [1974] prices)*

Year	PCI		DC		PSI	
	I	E	I	E	I	E
1974	23.9	23.8	24.7	20.2	8.6	8.7
1984	25.5	26.7	16.8	15.1	5.4	8.3
1989	19.7	20.3	13.5	12.5	9.3	9.3

Table 10.1C   *Public financing of Italian parties: amounts of annual funds (in billions of lire – current prices)*

	Parliamentary groups	Election Campaign Funds			Total
		National	European	Local	
1974	45	15	na	na	60
1980	45	15	15	15	90
1981	72.6	15	15	20	109.6
1982	82.9	15	15	20	132.9
1985	82.9	30	30	40	182.9

Source: Bardi and Morlino, 1992

infrequent increases (from a theoretical maximum of 60 billion lire in 1974 to about 183 billion lire in 1985)[9] which, in periods of high inflation, such as in the years following the implementation of the law, led to a considerable decline in the officially recorded real incomes and expenditures of the parties (see Table 10.1). This is especially noticeable in the case of the DC, whose other sources of income failed to make up for the deficit. And while this might have resulted in a progressive scaling down of party activities, the general belief is that the cost of party politics in Italy has actually increased enormously, especially since the mid-1970s. Thus, for example, the 'media revolution', which allowed previously prohibited private broadcasts, pushed up the costs of information, propaganda and campaigns; the 'office revolution', which occurred in the same period, and which resulted from the spread of new technologies (personal computers, photocopying and fax machines), also required large investments to provide party headquarters and newspapers with new equipment; finally, although officially Italian parties are very sparsely staffed and salaries are very low, salary expenditures were the only expenditure item to reveal real increases in all three major parties' official budgets (between 1974 and 1989, the real increases in expenditure on salaries amounted to 170 per cent in the case of the PCI, 119 per cent in the case of the DC, and 153 per cent in the case of the PSI).

Parties could therefore hardly afford to give up funding from public companies, despite its becoming illegal; hence the explosion of the *tangenti* system since the 1970s. A first assessment of the importance of these *tangenti* for party financing is based on a study of 101 political corruption cases tried between 1945 and 1987 for which it was possible to obtain accurate figures concerning the actual amounts involved (out of a total of 272 considered in the study); according to these data, which represented only the tip of the iceberg, Italian parties received on average at least 60 billion lire a year (1986 lire) in illegal funding between 1979 and 1987, a figure equal to about 75 per cent of the total public fund for the subvention of parliamentary parties (Cazzola, 1988: 138–9). In the light of the *mani pulite* inquiry which began in January 1992, however, even these estimates appear to be too conservative, and Cazzola's own revised estimates, which are substantiated by other revelations suggesting that the major private and public companies have been funnelling enormous sums (up to 800 billion lire a year from one single company) into party coffers, recently placed the total amount illegally obtained by Italian political parties at some 3400 billion lire a year (*La Repubblica*, 20 February 1993: 7), at least ten times the total official income of *all* Italian political parties (including those, such as the PR, the Greens and the MSI, which were not part of the *tangenti* system). Subsequently, of course, it appears that the investigations of illegal party financing may have reduced these amounts to just a trickle, with the result that all of the traditional parties quickly approached bankruptcy.

The parliamentary party and the party leadership

The organizational bodies of the Italian parties at national level generally appeared rather similar to one another, with the national congress enjoying mainly representative functions, and with executive functions being shared between the *Comitato Centrale* (CC) or *Consiglio Nazionale*, and the *Direzione*. In the PCI the *Segreteria*, the body closest to the Party Secretary, was perhaps the most important body, being responsible for all major strategic innovations (Farneti, 1983: 176). In all cases, however, these bodies appeared to guarantee the predominance of the extra-parliamentary organizations.

Although the strong centralized control of parliamentary recruitment which prevailed during the first three decades of the post-war democratic system remained effective into the 1990s, as did the power of the national leadership to determine parliamentary behaviour, there have nevertheless been a number of important changes. Thus, for example, the composition of parliamentary parties tended to become less reflective of the parties' links with particular social classes, especially from the mid-1970s, and by the early 1990s more than half of all MPs were professionals, with farmers and blue-collar workers virtually disappearing even from the ranks of the PCI by the late 1980s. Intra-elite relationships also changed after 1960, at least in the case of the PCI/PDS and the PSI; and even without considering the turnovers of personnel which took place several times in all parties (including the DC) at the intermediate parliamentary level (but almost never at the top elite level), formal power structures also became radically different. Perhaps the greatest transformation was in the PCI, even prior to its rebirth as PDS. Although the PCI remained formally committed to democratic centralism until 1990, alterations in its elite structure had already manifested themselves at least six years earlier (Pasquino, 1991: 4). Up to that point, however, changes in the top power structure of the party, even if they had occurred, were almost unnoticeable.

The absolute dominance of the PCI's top executive bodies in the vertical organization of the party had also been reflected in the horizontal relationship with the parliamentary party. Although the PCI often declared parliament to be the central institution of the Italian political system (Baldassarre, 1981: 446), the parliamentary party remained in a subordinate position with respect to the extra-parliamentary party. This could be seen in a variety of ways. In the first place, there was a low level of 'parliamentarization' of the party's executive bodies, especially the *Direzione*, where at no time were more than 30 per cent of the members also members of parliament. Second, even if the reverse was also true, the presence of party executives in the parliamentary groups was always qualified by the presence of most members of the *Direzione* and the *Segreteria* (about 70 per cent), a circumstance which allowed for a 'qualitative' if not a quantitative encroachment of the executive over the parliamentary groups. Third, party leaders always enjoyed a monopoly of the parliamentary leadership. Fourth, national executive bodies remained solely responsible for the selection of parliamentary candidates (recruitment was always internal to the party). Fifth, there were always sharp seniority differences between backbenchers and frontbenchers, the latter being the only ones who were normally allowed to spend more than two terms in parliament (Baldassarre, 1981: 461, passim). Sixth, at any given time, at least until the 1980s, no less than 70 per cent of PCI members of parliament were professional politicians and therefore dependent on the party apparatus for their very livelihood. And seventh, even when there would develop a potential towards greater autonomy on the part of one of the two parliamentary groups, this would be nullified by Italy's perfect bicameralism, in which there was a total absence of coordination between the groups in the Senate and the Chamber of Deputies (Baldassarre, 1981: 471–2).

Following the emergence of new movements and demands seeking political expression after 1969, it appeared desirable that the party would begin to 'open up' to the representation of non-working-class social and cultural groups. In practice, however, the only response was a gradual increase in the number of independents elected as PCI candidates in parliamentary elections. This was especially relevant in the Senate where the electoral system made it easier to assign 'safe' seats even to candidates who were unknown to the party electorate. Thus although few independents were elected during the first four post-war legislative terms, the independents in the Senate were already strong enough in 1968 (eleven members and almost 11 per cent of the PCI delegation) to form their own parliamentary group, *Sinistra Indipendente* (Independent Left – a similar group was formed in the Chamber of Deputies in 1983 when twenty independents were elected). The number of independent PCI Senators grew to almost 20 per cent in 1976, a level equalled and even surpassed in 1983 and 1987, after a dip to less than 14 per cent in 1979 and, even though its candidates were dependent on the PCI organization for re-election, the group proved itself to be a relatively autonomous parliamentary party. Although the idea of the Independent Left had been intended to make the PCI the hegemonic force of the left by enlisting personalities who could not find a political space within their own original parties and groups (Baldassarre, 1981: 473), it nonetheless failed to allow for the expression of potentially dissenting views within the party. Indeed, if anything, it prevented the emergence of significant requests for more autonomy from the PCI parliamentary groups themselves, which exercised some discretion only on institutional matters (Baldassarre, 1981: 471–2). Nevertheless, by the late 1980s, and certainly during the transition to the PDS, the presence and example of the Independent Left proved an important element in promoting the increasing assertiveness of the parliamentary party and, ultimately, in promoting the factionalization of the party.

The PCI's monolithic structure remained unchanged at the top long after the Leninist model had been significantly altered at the grassroots. The next cracks in the structure manifested themselves at an intermediate level. Following the unprecedented victory in the 1975 administrative elections, the recruitment of a large number of new local and regional executives was required in order to replace those who had taken office in local and regional councils, a process which created tensions because of the diverse backgrounds of the newcomers (Ignazi, 1992: 93; Sebastiani, 1983: 99–105). Democratic centralism nevertheless managed to survive until 1984 or even 1987, when new procedures permitted the nomination of national congress delegations by groups of at least 20 per cent of the regional congress delegates (Pasquino, 1991: 4–5), thus putting a definitive end to the system of cooption and paving the way for the transformation of internal 'tendencies' into fully fledged factions (Ignazi, 1992: 95). In this sense the long-delayed change in the internal power structure did actually take place, even if the internal institutional balance was not formally altered. Moreover, the Central Committee (CC) kept expanding in order to give every (developing) faction adequate representation, thus weakening its executive role. The new representative character of the CC was also evident in the deliberate emphasis on gender representation. The body as a whole grew progressively to 357 members in 1990 (as opposed to 128 in 1960), of which about one-third were women (as opposed to less than 8 per cent in 1960 and less than 14 per cent even in 1979 – see Bardi and Morlino, 1992: Table VIII.D.9; Ignazi, 1992: 113). The need to accommodate the demands of the *correnti* was even more evident in the composition of the PDS 'executive' bodies. The 547 members of the *Consiglio Nazionale* (the PDS counterpart to the CC) and the 118 members of the *Direzione* (more than double the number in the PCI CC in 1946) were all openly elected as representatives of their *correnti* (Pasquino, 1991: 12). Stratarchic tendencies can also be detected in the PDS, with the growing importance of provincial federations and their secretaries, whose political ambitions often elude all central control.[10]

Stratarchic elements and factionalism were always present in the PSI, and were formalized in 1959 with the adoption of PR in internal party elections at all levels. However, the party's power structure was profoundly modified for at least fifteen years (between 1976 and the early 1990s) by Craxi's personal leadership (Massari, 1987: 403), and during this period the PSI changed into what has been described as a '(quasi)-monocratic' party (Di Virgilio, forthcoming). The 'quasi' was necessary because of the clear division of labour between the top and intermediate levels of party leadership, which was particularly important since the PSI lost its remaining character as a mass party with the virtual disappearance of a grassroots organization. Furthermore, the consolidation of Craxi's leadership was evident in the various modifications of the party statutes which formalized his successful attempt to control the disruptive factional fights which had characterized the party prior to 1976. These modifications included: the 1981 provision for the election of the party secretary directly by the national congress; the creation of a new body, the *Esecutivo ristretto* (six members including Craxi in 1983) as an inner cabinet making all important decisions; the transformation of the CC into the *Assemblea Nazionale*, a fully fledged party parliament including over 120 external members (out of a total of 473, as opposed to 141 in the pre-Craxi CC), and no longer an executive body;[11] and a parallel, although somewhat see-sawing, expansion of the *Direzione* (from 34 members in 1972 to 110 in 1993, with a dip to 26 in 1978), coupled with a progressive reduction in its powers (Merkel, 1987: 67).[12]

The disappearance of internal factions created a monocratic party structure at the top elite level, albeit paralleled by the growing autonomy of provincial federations. The party under Craxi became more and more electorally oriented, a tendency which was reflected in rule changes attributing equal importance to the provincial membership and to the share of the popular vote in determining delegate allocation for national congresses (Bettin, 1983: 92). Given the disproportionate amount of power derived from the party's pivotal position between the DC and the PCI in most local and regional councils, elective positions became increasingly important, especially at this local level. Moreover, PSI administrators became leaders at the local level, exercising power at their own discretion, a consolidation which was the price paid by the national leadership in return for the social pact at the national level and for electoral support.

Craxi's strategy aimed at developing a very tight and homogeneous national inner circle of leaders whose fortunes were clearly connected to his own. This implied an almost complete disappearance of internal factions and a stepping down of all 'old-guard' leaders. The success of this strategy at the national level was not matched by a parallel success at the regional level, however. Indeed, the two-level power structure in the Italian political system as a whole is paralleled by a similar two-level resource flow which, in the case of the PSI, allowed the periphery of the party almost complete autonomy from the centre in both political and financial terms. The national leadership had a free hand in making the major strategic decisions and even in drawing up the lists of parliamentary candidates, but it was seldom able to exercise any real influence on local government alliances or even on single decisions. Moreover, the fact that official financial transfers from the centre to the periphery declined dramatically between 1974 and 1987, from 38.1 per cent to 15.6 per cent of the total budget (Di Virgilio, forthcoming), did not appear to perturb the local groups. Rather, the ever-spreading and growing 'alternative' party-financing system proved able to funnel sufficient resources to pacify regional demands. The system also provided a number of high profile and often well-paid positions in local agencies and banks which were able to accommodate the personal ambitions of regional PSI leaders. In some cases, however, tensions did develop between the two levels. In at least one case a local leader was coopted into the national leadership, but more often party commissars were dispatched from Rome to take over provincial federations or regional committees (Di Virgilio, forthcoming). That said, such drastic actions did not have lasting effects, with local groups being able to rebuild their power bases very quickly and thus being able once more to erode the influence of the centre.[13]

The internal power structure of the PSI was finally changed dramatically only as a consequence of the *mani pulite* investigations. These had three major effects. First, they decapitated the party leadership: in addition to Craxi's resignation as party secretary, the investigations also led to the resignation of his deputy, Claudio Martelli, and eventually to those of many of the indicted PSI parliamentarians from their party leadership positions (Martelli resigned from the party altogether). Second, they dried up the main sources of party revenue which, besides forcing it to confront its enormous indebtedness, had immediate and profound consequences for the local organizations, with many local headquarters, especially in northern Italy, being either reduced in size or closed down. Third, they caused an unprecedented decline in electoral support. As a result, the post-Craxi PSI immediately lost its monocratic character, and the expansion of the *Esecutivo* to forty-nine members in early 1993 reflected a re-emerging demand for factional (and provincial) representation in a technically 'executive' body. The Secretariat also lost most of its authority, as demonstrated by Secretary Giorgio Benvenuto's resignation over a conflict with the parliamentary party.[14]

According to Paolo Farneti (1983: 202) the DC is the Italian party which most closely approaches the catch-all-party model, albeit while maintaining some mass party characteristics, with the growing importance of the parliamentary parties and the unquestionable relevance of internal factions (linking the party with selected sectors of society) reflecting its main electoral orientation. These characteristics were reinforced after 1960, especially following the adoption in 1964 of a proportional system of representation in elections to the *Consiglio Nazionale* (Bardi and Morlino, 1992: Table VIII.D.2.f.i), which completed the process by which factions had become institutionalized (Leonardi and Wertman, 1989: 109). As a consequence of the 1964 changes in rules, the growing importance of provincial federations in determining parliamentary nominations contributed to the further strengthening of the autonomy of the parliamentary groups. DC leaders have always experienced difficulty in winning the complete support of elected party officials, including those at the national level, and this has been clearly reflected in the actions of the *franchi tiratori* (literally, snipers), who have affected the stability and the efficiency of almost every post-war Italian government. This was not simply a manifestation of parliamentary party indiscipline or autonomy; rather, and at least until the mid-1970s, it could also be seen as an indicator of *faction discipline*. Following the 1976 parliamentary elections, which were characterized by turnover of 37 per cent, the DC parliamentary groups became even more autonomous, as, for example, could be seen in the strong opposition in early 1970 to the secretariat's strategy of favouring a formal alliance with the PCI (D'Amore, forthcoming).

The lack of internal discipline is one reason why DC leaders periodically attempted to strengthen the party organizational structure; in addition, the various attempts at reform could also be seen as a response to demands coming from disgruntled factions or even from frustrated younger cohorts. The latter were certainly influential in provoking the radical reshuffle that took place between 1975 and 1976 which, even then, failed to achieve a significant turnover in the party's representative and executive bodies (D'Amore, forthcoming). Indeed, the formal power structure of the party has never been significantly altered at leadership level, and here again the crucial elements in the DC elite's internal power relations appear to have been the dynamics within and among the factions.[15] The only noteworthy change which took place occurred in the mid- to late 1980s, when the then party secretary, Ciriaco de Mita, in a move reminiscent of developments in other Italian parties, attempted to redistribute internal power in favour of the regional level by increasing the powers and responsibilities of the regional secretaries.

As with the PSI, effective reform was eventually forced on the DC by external events. The DC leadership was closely identified with corruption and, in the south, had been accused of conniving with organized crime. The complex network of illicit relationships that engulfed the party was an integral part of the DC power base and could not be spontaneously eliminated. Thus although the secession of part of the Sicilian DC, led by the former mayor of Palermo, Leoluca Orlando, gave rise in the early 1990s to La Rete, an anti-mafia Catholic group, it had very little effect on the rest of the party. In 1992 a similar move by Mario Segni, who founded the *Popolari per la riforma* (Populars for reform) showed more promise, but its enhanced appeal probably owed more to the new climate in the country. By then, the anti-corruption and, even more dramatically, the anti-mafia investigations had shaken the DC organization to its foundations.[16]

The parties, the citizenry and the state

During the early years of the Italian Republic political parties had established very important links with organized interest groups and had set the stage for a full-fledged occupation of the state. This was to a large extent due to the intrinsic weakness of Italian civil society (Pasquino, 1985: 1, passim), the most important element of which was the absence of a hegemonic class, a role which the Italian bourgeoisie had never been able to acquire. The predominance of parties over society has continued after 1960, with all of the historic parties maintaining very well-developed roots in at least some parts of the country, even if, as in the case of the MSI, these were of quite limited extent. That said, it must also be emphasized that the nature of this relationship changed, especially after the end of the 1960s, when a 'growth' of civil society either caused or simply coincided with a decline of 'ideology' and a parallel growth of 'opinion' within the Italian electorate (Farneti, 1983: 156). Moreover, the frequent resort to referendums after 1974 tended to make the Italian electorate increasingly issue-oriented and, consequently, less ideological.[17] Thus, while it might be argued that Italian multi-party-ism had delayed the development of catch-all electoral orientations, it must at the same time be recognized that there have nevertheless been important changes in the relationships between party and the electorate.

Reliable time-series data on party identification are sorely lacking, and studies in this field are very rare. One exception, however, is the survey carried out by Renato Mannheimer (1989), which found that slightly fewer than 24 per cent of respondents fell within the two strongest identification categories of the 5-point scale which he employed, with an additional 23.6 per cent being classified as weak identifiers. These results are also consistent with those of a previous survey from 1985, which indicated that 'a portion of the electorate oscillating between 40% and 50% could be considered at least to some extent identified with a party' (Mannheimer and Sani, 1987: 116). Although these findings are not comparable with the situation which prevailed in the late 1950s, and although it is therefore difficult to draw any clear conclusions regarding changes over time, there are nonetheless other *qualitative* changes in Italian electoral behaviour which can be noted and which are loosely equivalent to changes in party identification. On the basis of Parisi and Pasquino's (1980) well-known typology, for example, Mannheimer and Sani (1987: 58) conclude that 'opinion' voters, who were practically non-existent during the 1950s, had become much more numerous than both 'exchange' and *appartenenza* ('belonging') voters. A more recent study, on the other hand, which was based on ecological analyses of election and referendum data, found that *appartenenza* voters still prevailed in the centre-north, that exchange voters remained dominant in the centre-south, and that opinion voters were only of marginal importance (Cartocci, 1990). But despite the contrary nature of these two sets of findings, it nevertheless remains clear that *appartenenza* and exchange relationships became modified over the past thirty years. Electoral stability, of which *appartenenza* voters are one of the cornerstones, was normally associated in Italy with the importance of political subcultures, which tended to 'freeze' electoral behaviour on the basis of the territorial roots, the organizational strength, and the other cultural and organizational links which the parties have maintained with civil society. Even by the early 1990s, however, it had become clear that some of these links had been transformed.

In response to growing popular demands for more assertive behaviour which, in turn, followed on from the often spontaneous actions undertaken in the immediate post-1968 period at the plant level (a sharp departure from the Italian practice to call general or at least sectoral strikes – see Regini, 1980: 49–50), industrial relations began to replace the political system as the more important arena for class action. This development afforded the unions a degree of autonomy which had a number of important consequences, including a greater independence from the political parties;[18] the near-unification of the three major confederations (CGIL, CISL, UIL), and the acquisition of an autonomous role in their relationships with the government and with the state at large.

Although these developments were seen by some at the time to reflect the establishment of successful PCI hegemony over the union movement as a whole, they nevertheless created the conditions for a gradual separation between unions and parties. At the same time, DC attempts to interfere in the nomination of the *Confindustria* president provoked a split within that organization which was hidden only by the decision of Gianni Agnelli to present his own prestigious candidacy (Martinelli, 1980: 83; Mattina, 1989).[19] This marked an important turning point in the policy of *Confindustria* and in its relationship with the parties. Agnelli and his successor, Guido Carli, often by-passed the government and the parties and negotiated directly with the unions. The most important product of this approach was the 1975 agreement on salary indexation, which was hailed as a success for the workers, but which actually created the conditions for a fragmentation of the workers' movement.[20] Based on this new autonomy and assertiveness, *Confindustria* then went on to establish a privileged link with another party, the PRI, which, unlike the DC, was convinced of the importance of the organization as a political actor and as an independent defender of 'efficiency and competition against the centralization and bureaucratization of the economy' (Martinelli, 1980: 83). In practice, PRI ministers adopted the role which had been previously held by their PLI counterparts, and represented the views of *Confindustria* in the government coalitions. The dominant position of the DC was not endangered, however, and even within the Agnelli family the pro-PRI position of Gianni Agnelli was counterbalanced by the election of his brother, Umberto, as a DC senator. Most importantly, the privileged relationship of the DC with the economy remained as the sum of individual links, sometimes established through party factions, with single firms or business associations, links which compensated for the decline of the agricultural sector and for the diminishing importance of the relationship with *Confindustria*.

On the left, PCI hegemony over the unified workers' movement was definitively broken during the 1980s. The unprecedented decision by Craxi, then prime minister, to modify by decree the cost of living adjustment mechanism known as the *scala mobile*, created a split in the union movement, and in the CGIL itself, between the Catholic and socialist components, on the one hand, and the communist component, on the other.[21] This division was exacerbated by the equally unprecedented PCI decision to call a referendum to repeal the decree, which had since been converted into a law, the rejection of which confirmed the end of PCI hegemony over the labour movement. The emergence in the late 1980s of powerful autonomous unions and COBAS (*comitati di base*, or grassroots committees), which mainly organized teachers, civil servants and railroad workers, eventually favoured a return to more unified action by the traditional confederations, even if by then they had lost most of their political importance.

The de-ideologization and secularization of the 1960s also strongly affected the relations between the parties and their collateral organizations. As the traditional organizations declined through the erosion of the subcultures, the parties tried to develop new structures or strategies in order to open themselves up to new social movements and actors in civil society as a whole. The DC all but lost its most important link with civil society, Catholic Action, membership of which had fallen from 3.3 million in the mid-1960s to just 550,000 twenty years later, and which had adopted positions in crucial circumstances, such as in the 1974 divorce and 1981 abortion referendums, that were not so strongly pro-DC as had been expected by the party. The party's relationships with ACLI followed a different pattern, but the results were not dissimilar. Although ACLI also suffered a serious membership drop, this was caused by left- and right-wing splits which took place in the early 1970s precisely because of a dispute about the ties the movement should have with the DC. The *Coldiretti*, on the other hand, did not change its supportive stance, although its importance declined with the shrinking of the agricultural sector (Leonardi and Wertman, 1989: 217). And while the relative position of the PSI and the PCI within the various organizations of the socialist subculture remained basically unchanged, the hegemonic influence of the PCI, which was preserved until the end of the 1970s, declined considerably during the 1980s.

For about twenty years, 'culture' was a magic word for the Italian parties. The year 1968 had been a catalyst for the manifestation of profound social, political (most of all in terms of representation) and cultural demands which had been repressed for at least a decade, and which all but shattered the rigid subculturally based organization of Italian society. All of the parties, but especially those on the left (the PCI, the PSI and also the PRI) and the DC therefore felt the need to 'open up' to potential members, but most of all to potential voters, who might otherwise have lain outside their respective subcultures – hence their need to make their presence felt in society at large, and hence also their relentless efforts to organize 'cultural events' with a potentially broad appeal. The first manifestation of this trend was the progressive de-politicization of the *Unità* Festivals, which had been originally intended to raise funds for the spread of communist propaganda, and which gradually turned into anonymous fairs where pop culture and ethnic foods did more to attract visitors than did communist ideals. Although not so popular, the festivals organized by the DC, PSI, PRI, PSDI and even by the MSI, have evolved along similar lines. In much the same vein, but equally illusory, especially for the left and for the PCI in particular, was the growing success of party-connected recreational and broadly cultural organizations, such as ARCI (PCI/PSI), ENDAS (PRI) and, in some respects, ACLI (DC). Rather than reflecting an expression of political sympathy for the sponsoring party, membership in these organizations was very often instrumental, in that members were usually entitled to discounts on the costs of cinema and theatre admissions. Moreover, in some cases the interests of the cultural organization or of one of its sections were diametrically opposed to the line adopted by the sponsoring party.[22] Young people in particular were resistant to regimentation in the organizational structures of the traditional parties, with the PCI again suffering more than its competitors. Membership of the FGCI fell dramatically in the twenty years following the 1968 protests, and a similar drop was registered among the MSI youth affiliates. And while more positive trends were observed for the DC and PSI (see Bardi and Morlino, 1992: Tables VIII B.I.b,d–f, i), the DC youth movement was nevertheless faced with a powerful challenger in Cl (*Comunione e liberazione*, Communion and Liberation), a 60,000-strong extremely militant Catholic youth organization, which contrasted sharply with the secular tendencies within the DC itself (Accattoli, 1988).

Italian parties were among the most important news publishers in Italy. During the 1950s, and in addition to their official newspapers, the larger parties had also acquired control of some important 'independent' titles, the moderate or even conservative line of which was guaranteed by the party-sponsored appointment of editors and journalists. Until recently, however, newspaper publishing was a loss-making enterprise, and during the 1960s large editorial conglomerates were created by industrialists such as Attilio Monti (oil) and Nino Ravelli (chemicals), who were motivated by a political strategy rather than by profit, and who used the press as a bargaining chip in negotiations with the government and the parties. A 1976 Constitutional Court ruling that put an end to state monopoly of radio and television broadcasts did not substantially change the relationship between political parties and the media (Giglioli and Mazzoleni, 1990: 205). The ruling permitted an overnight explosion of private local television stations which, by the mid-1980s, were concentrated into three national networks owned by media tycoon Silvio Berlusconi (later to be the founder and leader of Forza Italia). Berlusconi's successful attempt to go beyond the limits posed by the Constitutional Court was made possible by the personal support which he received from the PSI and Bettino Craxi, and in this way Craxi redressed the television media balance which at the time was heavily pro-DC (Marletti, 1987). The DC controlled the presidency of RAI (the state-owned broadcasting network) and RAI 1, the most popular channel, while the PSI controlled RAI 2. This partition was also effected with the approval of the PCI, which obtained control of RAI 3, the most recently created and least popular state channel.

The consolidation of *partitocrazia* continued at least through the 1960s and the 1970s. In fact, there was a considerable expansion of party control of large sectors of the Italian economy during this period, albeit without effecting any major qualitative changes. The institutional and organizational bases for the complex network of holding companies and their subsidiaries, banks, and social security and welfare agencies (including a National Health System created in 1978), which came under more or less direct party control, had actually been created during the Fascist era, and it was not until the mid-1950s that the dominant position of the DC allowed Amintore Fanfani to acquire for his party direct control of the public sector of the economy. Through this control the DC obtained an autonomous power base, the continuous expansion of which created enough resources to allow it to be shared with other coalition parties and even, albeit to a very limited extent, with the PCI. In the mid-1980s, public companies accounted for about 30 per cent of Italian sales and 50 per cent of Italian investments, with state-controlled banks and savings banks accounting for at least three-quarters of Italian banking; and it was not until very recently that the frequent initiatives to reform and extensively privatize the public sectors of Italian industry and finance yielded other than very meagre results.

Conclusion: the long-term pressure for change

The momentous changes in the party system and in the party organizations themselves, which were triggered off by the *mani pulite* investigations in 1992–93, can only partially be explained as the simple consequence of these investigations. In fact, as we have seen, the pressure for extensive reform had been building up for almost thirty years, with the investigations serving largely as a catalyst for changes which the party leaderships had been trying, successfully up to then, to postpone indefinitely. In other words, while the discovery of *tangentopoli* and the consequent public outcry against the political parties and 'their system' may well explain the *timing* of the transformation, they nevertheless shed only limited light on the reasons why it occurred. In this sense it is important to note the evidence of the inadequacies of the Italian party organizations which can be seen in the important changes that took place *prior* to 1992. These include the 1991 reform and split of the PCI (Ignazi, 1992), as well as the emergence of new actors, such as the PR, the Verdi and La Rete, all of which organized according to non-traditional models, as well as the Lega Nord, with its overtly anti-system goals. Each of these new actors (and later again, Forza Italia) seemed better able than many of their traditional counterparts to respond to the emerging needs of certain sectors of civil society.

During the years which had elapsed since democratic consolidation, and during the extended period in which the parties had consolidated their organizations, there had also occurred important changes in civil society and in the economy, as well as in the institutional framework and the international context. Thus traditional classes and subcultures were profoundly eroded; there was a considerable decline in the agricultural and industrial sectors, to the advantage of the service sector; and, even more importantly, groups based in both sectors gradually lost their sense of cultural identity. Other societal trends included a stabilization of internal population flows and a pronounced ageing of the population. In practice, however, the party response to these changes failed to match their extent.

The completion of the process of industrial development and the enormous expansion of the public sector were the most important economic developments in this period, which also witnessed the final implementation of the constitutional framework, which, in turn, led to important institutional and political consequences (Bartolini, 1982). These latter changes included the establishment and increasing assertiveness of the Constitutional Court; the politicization but also the growing independence of the Judiciary; new labour and family laws; the frequent resort to referendums on high-profile issues; and the creation of the regional level of government. All of these factors, albeit often indirectly, had important consequences for the relationships between parties, institutions and civil society. There thus occurred a de-ideologization of political conflict; a decline in the importance of unions and other flanking organizations; a change in electoral attitudes; the creation of new regionally based political and economic power centres; and an increasing, mainly media-induced, personalization of politics.[23] At least on the surface, it seemed clear that the party elites were conscious of the need to adjust their organizations to these new circumstances, and one evident symptom of this could be seen in the generalized and protracted calls for the 'opening up' of parties to civil society. At the same time, however, the party statutes themselves and other formalized internal reforms had very little impact on the party organizations in practice. Most often, such reforms responded only superficially to social demands, and were in fact catering only to the needs of party elites at various levels, and the various party leaderships actually exerted very little control over the most important party organizational changes in this period. Rather, the changing conceptions of membership, the alternating membership trends, and the declining importance of basic territorial basic units all tended to reflect the actions of either the members themselves or the party sympathizers and, if anything, could be seen as resulting from the lack, or inadequacy, of formal reforms. At another level, however, as this analysis has tried to illustrate, the parties, albeit informally, did adapt very effectively to environmental changes. Indeed, in some cases, as was the case with the build-up of the public sector, they responded by modifying the environment themselves.

Following *mani pulite* and the referendum of April 1993, which became the first decisive step in the major change of the electoral law, the whole scenario changed both radically and rapidly. The investigations themselves did of course have a direct effect on the political parties and their organizations and, even in itself, the complete disruption of the illegal system of party financing effectively rendered the old party models and the old party system obsolete. In addition, there were also a number of more indirect effects, including the potential for electoral damage which was to be realized so extensively in the elections of March 1994. More than anything else, however, and in much the same way that the wider developments in the Communist world had acted upon the PCI, the investigations served as a catalyst for changes that were simply long overdue. For many years, the party elites had successfully attempted to conceal the organizational inadequacies of their parties; now, however, such tactics no longer proved viable, and the older outward images and the traditional organizational models appeared to be completely destroyed. This was also due to other important institutional changes which were made possible or at least facilitated by the same catalyst, such as the electoral and party financing reforms, which had been advocated in vain for many years by intellectuals and even by some of the politicians themselves.

In this perspective, the most salient question is how it was possible to maintain such an expensive, cumbersome and overdeveloped system of party organizations for such a long time. On the one hand, the main explanations might echo classical themes concerning the role of the vested interests developed by the institutions and the simple role of inertia; on the other hand, a more systemic explanation might highlight the survival of an internalized Cold War bipolarization (DC vs. PCI), as well as the development of a new sort of bipolarization between the two governmental parties (DC and PSI) during the 1980s. Above all, however, in the wake of the events of 1989 in the former Soviet bloc, and in a context of economic crisis and widespread popular dissatisfaction, there was clearly no sense in bearing the costs of the sort of institutions which had been revealed so completely by the *mani pulite* judges.

Notes

1 This chapter is an early version of a larger work in progress, which is concerned with the development of the party organizations and the party system in the period which finally ended with the major transformation in 1994. We are therefore dealing with the party organizations of what is now referred to as the 'First Republic', and we deliberately exclude any analysis of the 1994 election and its aftermath. The research on which it is based was supported by funds from the Italian Ministry for Scientific Research and the National Research Council (CNR).

2 Class, religion, and centre/periphery tensions have proved the main sources of the traditional cleavages in Italian politics since 1946, with the first of these being the most salient for decades (see also Bardi and Morlino, 1992; Sartori, 1982: esp. Ch. 1).

3 The same could now be said for the more recently established *Forza Italia*. It should be pointed out, however, that recent research on the Lega Nord suggests a contrasting view, attributing great importance to organizational efficiency in explaining the Lega's success. See Tarchi (forthcoming [b]).

4 In addition, one representative of the MPs was entitled to participate in the meetings of the national executive. For all the data concerning MSI see Ignazi (1989: 253–310), as well as the official documents of the party included in Vallauri (1981).

5 Total *Lega* membership in mid-1993 was estimated to be 140,000 (Tarchi, forthcoming [b]). Tangentially, it can be noted that the evidence of membership collapse in the traditional parties may also have been due to the parties' recent inability to inflate the figures to the same degree that was done in the past.

6 Although the importance of membership as a financial resource remains relevant, the official figures reflect just a fraction of the actual incomes of most parties, the bulk of which often goes unrecorded. Fake registration figures may even provide a means of laundering illegal revenue by disguising it as membership dues.

7 The party's capacity to encapsulate the working class actually increased during this period (Baccetti, forthcoming).

8 Total PDS membership was 989,708 in 1991 and 769,944 in 1992, as opposed to 1,319,905 for the PCI in 1990 (figures are based on official PCI/PDS figures; see also Baccetti, forthcoming).

9 The law provides for four different types of subvention (see also Table 10.1): (a) the subvention to the parliamentary group (basically this is *the* party subvention); (b) the national election campaign fund; (c) the sub-national election campaign fund; (d) the European election campaign fund. Only the first two were applicable between 1974 and 1979. The theoretical maximums refer to election years. From 1980 they refer to years in which the unlikely coincidence of three elections should occur.

10 Provincial feuds found their expression in the casting of preference votes in the 1992 Chamber of Deputies election, with local candidates often obtaining more preference votes and defeating national leaders (such as the former PDS *capogruppo*, Giulio Quercini).

11 Eventually, the *Assemblea* exceeded 1000 members, a number justified by the claimed party leadership intention to open up the party to civil society, a goal which in practice was defeated by that body's loss of importance (Di Virgilio, forthcoming). In reality, however, the

huge expansion of the *Assemblea* resulted from the leadership desire to reward and appease the *rampanti*.

12 The swelling of representative and executive bodies was a very widespread phenomenon during the 1980s, affecting even the MSI CC, which grew to 340 members (Tarchi, forthcoming [a]).

13 In Craxi's monocratic heyday, the takeover of provincial federations and regional committees reflected the need by the central authority to re-establish some control over the periphery; given the clear division of authority that existed between the two levels, however, it was not a widespread procedure, and between 1983 and 1989 there were only between two and five cases each year. During 1990 and 1991, the phenomenon became more relevant (eleven and eighteen cases respectively), prefiguring the post-Craxi 1992–93 explosion, which, in turn, resulted from more ethical motives, that is, from concerns about the unprecedented levels of corruption reached in some areas. The best illustration of this change was provided by the takeover of the Milan federation, which was once practically identified with the central party elite (see Di Virgilio, forthcoming: Table 1).

14 Benvenuto had harshly criticized the decision by the Chamber of Deputies (backed by the crucial votes of many PSI deputies) to deny the judiciary the authority to try Bettino Craxi; a few weeks later PSI deputies openly defied Benvenuto's leadership when they voted against the choice of a single-member constituency two-ballot electoral system.

15 Even the DC 1992 *Direzione*, which, following the wishes of Secretary Mino Martinazzoli, had been reduced to just fifteen members, was designated on the basis of factional representation criteria. On DC factions in general see Leonardi and Wertman (1989).

16 DC leaders were very prominently represented among the politicians indicted as a consequence of anti-corruption investigations, but the most dramatic indictment came from the accusations of a former *mafioso* that linked Giulio Andreotti to the murder of journalist Mino Pecorelli.

17 It could be argued that the referendums, for the first time in Italian history, forced electors to make decisions on the basis of desired policy outcomes rather than ideological prejudice. On these grounds one could perhaps explain why sizeable minorities of Catholic voters supported divorce and abortion in extremely divisive referendums.

18 Union leadership positions in the CGIL were made incompatible with parliamentary mandates in 1968. Incompatibility was then extended in 1970 to party leadership positions (Ferrante, 1982: 685). Similar rules were adopted by the CISL and UIL during the same period.

19 The President of Montedison, Cefis, backed by DC prime minister, Fanfani, opposed the nomination of Bruno Visentini, who was general manager of Olivetti and a member of the Republican Party (Martinelli, 1980: 83).

20 The agreement disproportionately privileged the least qualified workers' categories, leading, in years of very high inflation, to a compression of salary differentials, and the first 'autonomous' unions were created as a reaction of the dissatisfied higher-level workers (Mattina, 1989: 19).

21 The communist and socialist components of the CGIL have since been disbanded.

22 The most evident example of this was provided by the total lack of discipline of rural PCI supporters in connection with the 1990 referendum to abolish gun permits; the referendum, called by the environmentalist movement and half-heartedly supported by the PCI, was primarily intended to effect a ban on hunting, an objective that ran totally counter to the interests of the very powerful hunting section of the ARCI, which was very strong in rural areas.

23 More specifically, for example, the expansion of the public sector of industry, and the consequent growth in the importance of *Intersind*, had a strong impact on the relationship between the DC, the small secular centre parties, and *Confindustria*; moreover, the Constitutional Court ruling against the state monopoly of radio and television broadcasting, as well as favouring the personalization of politics, created the conditions that gave the DC, the PSI, and eventually the PCI/PDS privileged access to public, and in the case of the PSI,

private television. Later, in the run-up to the 1994 election, there were frequent complaints that Silvio Berlusconi's private television empire was privileging the position of Forza Italia.

References

Accattoli, L. (1988) 'Il Movimento popolare: forza e limiti di un messianismo politico', in P. Corbetta and R. Leonardi (eds), *Politica in Italia*. Bologna: Il Mulino, pp. 293–314.

Alberoni, Francesco (ed.) (1968) *L'attivista di partito*. Bologna: Il Mulino.

Baccetti, C. (forthcoming) 'Il PCI/PDS', in L. Morlino (ed.), *I partiti italiani: adattamento e trasformazione (1960–1994)*.

Baldassarre, A. (1981) 'I gruppi parlamentari comunisti', in M. Ilardi and A. Accornero (eds), *Il Partito Comunista Italiano: Struttura e storia dell'organizzazione 1921–1979*. Milano: Annali della Fondazione Fetrinelli, pp. 445–98.

Bardi, L. and Morlino, L. (1992) 'Italy', in R.S. Katz and P. Mair (eds), *Party Organizations: A Data Handbook on Party Organizations in Western Democracies, 1960–90*. London: Sage, pp. 458–618.

Barnes, S. (1967) *Party Democracy. Politics in an Italian Socialist Federation*. New Haven: Yale University Press.

Bartolini, S. (1982) 'The Politics of Institutional Reform in Italy', *West European Politics*, 5 (3): 203–21.

Bettin, G. (1983) 'PSI: la leadership degli anni ottanta', *Città e Regione*, 3: 80–106.

Cartocci, R. (1990) *Elettori in Italia: Riflessioni sulle vicende elettorali degli anni ottanta*. Bologna: Il Mulino.

Casciani, E. (1981) 'Dieci anni di reclutamento nel PCI', *Il Mulino*, 30 (274): 310–26.

Cazzola, F. (1970) *Il partito come organizzazione. Studio di un caso: il P.S.I.* Roma: Edizioni del Tritone.

Cazzola, F. (1982) 'Il PSI negli anni Settanta: un lungo viaggio alla ricerca dell'identità perduta', *Schema*, 5 (9–10): 19–47.

Cazzola, F. (1988) *Della corruzione: Fisiologia e patologia di un sistema politico*. Bologna: Il Mulino.

Cotta, M. (1979) *Classe politica e parlamento in Italia*. Bologna: Il Mulino.

D'Alimonte, R. and Chiaramonte, A. (1993) 'Il nuovo sistema elletorale italiano: quali opportunità?', *Rivista Italiana di Scienza Politica*, 23 (3): 513–47.

D'Amore, C. (forthcoming) 'La DC', in L. Morlino (ed.), *I partiti italiani: adattamento e trasformazione (1960–1994)*.

Di Virgilio, A. (forthcoming) 'Il PSI', in L. Morlino (ed.), *I partiti italiani: adattamento e trasformazione (1960–1994)*.

Farneti, P. (1983) *Il sistema dei partiti in Italia 1946–1979*. Bologna: Il Mulino.

Ferrante, G. (1982) 'Interscambio di dirigenti tra partito e sindacato', in M. Ilardi and A. Accornero (eds), *Il Partito Comunista Italiano: Struttura e storia dell'organizzazione 1921–1979*. Milano: Annali della Fondazione Feltrielli, pp. 673–92.

Galli, G. (1966) *Il bipartitismo imperfetto: Comunisti e Democristiani in Italia*. Bologna: Il Mulino.

Galli, G. (1976) *Storia del PCI*, 2nd edn. Milano: Bompiani.

Ghini, C. (1981) 'Gli iscritti al partito e alla FGCI, 1943/1979', in M. Ilardi and A. Accornero (eds), *Il Partito Comunista Italiano: Struttura e storia dell'organizzazione 1921–1979*. Milano: Annali della Fondazione Feltrielli, pp. 227–92.

Giglioli, P.P., and Mazzoleni, G. (1990) 'Processi di concentrazione editoriale e sistema dei media', in R. Catanzaro and F. Sabetti (eds), *Politica in Italia*. Bologna, Il Mulino. pp. 191–210.

Graziano, L. (1980) *Clientelismo e sistema politico: Il caso dell'Italia*. Milano: Angeli.

Hellmann, S. (1985) 'The Italian Communist Party between Berlinguer and the Seventeenth Congress', in R. Leonardi and R. Nanetti (eds), *Italian Politics: A Review*. London: Frances Pinter.

Ignazi, P. (1989) *Il polo escluso: Profilo del Movimento Sociale Italiano*. Bologna: Il Mulino.

Ignazi, P. (1992) *Dal PCI al PDS*. Bologna: Il Mulino.

Kirchheimer, O. (1966) 'The transformation of the Western European party systems', in J. LaPalombara and M. Weiner (eds), *Political Parties and Political Development*. Princeton: Princeton University Press, pp. 177–200.

Landolfi, A. (1968) *Il socialismo italiano: Strutture comportamenti valori*. Roma: Lerici.

LaPalombara, J. (1964) *Interest Groups in Italian Politics*. Princeton: Princeton University Press.

Leonardi, R. and Wertman, D. (1989) *Italian Christian Democracy: The Politics of Dominance*. New York: Macmillan.

Mannheimer, R. (1989) *Capire il voto: Contributi per l'analisi del comportamento elettorale in Italia*. Milano: Angeli.

Mannheimer, R. and Sani, G. (1987) *Il mercato elettorale: Identikit dell'elettore italiano*. Bologna: Il Mulino.

Maraffi, M. (1991) *Politica ed economia in Italia: La vicenda dell'impresa pubblica dagli anni trenta agli anni cinquanta*. Bologna: Il Mulino.

Marletti, C. (1987) 'Partiti e informazione televisiva: La nomina di Enrico Manca a presidente della Rai', in P. Corbetta and R. Leonardi (eds), *Politica in Italia*. Bologna: Il Mulino.

Martinelli, A. (1980) 'Organised Business and Italian Politics: Confindustria and the Christian Democrats in the Postwar Period', in S. Tarrow and P. Lange (eds), *Italy in Transition: Conflict and Consensus*. London: Frank Cass, pp. 69–87.

Massari, O. (1987) 'Le trasformazioni nella direzione del PSI: la direzione e i suoi membri (1976–1984)', *Rivista Italiana di Scienza Politica*, 17 (3): 399–432.

Mattana, S. (1981) 'La struttura e la base sociale del PSI', *Quaderni del Circolo Rosselli*, 1: 55–75.

Mattina, L. (1989) *I gruppi imprenditoriali, i sindacati e lo stato nella crisi e riaggiustamento del sistema industriale italiano (1969–1985)*. Firenze: DISPO (mimeo).

Merkel, W. (1987) *Prima e dopo Craxi: Le trasformazioni del PSI*. Padova: Liviana.

Morlino, L. (ed.) (1991) *Costruire la democrazia: Gruppi e partiti in Italia*. Bologna: Il Mulino.

Morlino, L. (forthcoming) 'Is there another side of the fascist legacy?' in S. Larsen (ed.), *Europe After Fascism*. Oslo: Universitetsforlaget.

Parisi, A. and Pasquino, G. (1980) 'Changes in Italian electoral behaviour: the relationships between parties and voters', in P. Lange and S. Tarrow (eds), *Italy in Transition: Conflict and Consensus*. London: Frank Cass, pp. 6–30.

Pasquino, G. (1980) 'Italian Christian Democracy: a party for all seasons?' in S. Tarrow and P. Lange (eds), *Italy in Transition: Conflict and Consensus*. London: Frank Cass. pp. 6–30.

Pasqunio, G. (1985) *La Complessità della politica*. Bari: Laterza.

Pasquino, G. (1987) 'Party government in Italy: achievements and prospects', in R.S. Katz (ed.), *Party Governments: European and American Experiences*. Berlin and New York: Walter de Gruyter, pp. 202–42.

Pasquino, G. (1991) *Programmatic Renewal and Much More: From the PCI to the PDS*. Bologna: The Johns Hopkins University Bologna Centre, Occasional Paper No. 66.

Pasquino, G. and Rossi, M. (1980) 'Quali compagni, quale partito, quale formula politica? Un'indagine sul PSI', *Il Mulino*, 29 (267): 74–101.

Poggi, G. (ed.) (1968) *L'organizzazione partitica del PCI e della DC*. Bologna: Il Mulino.

Regini, M. (1980) 'Labour unions, industrial action, and politics', in S. Tarrow and P. Lange (eds), *Italy in Transition: Conflict and Consensus*. London: Frank Cass, pp. 49–68.

Rossi, M. (1979) 'Un partito di "anime morte"? Il tesseramento democristiano tra mito e realtà', in A. Parisi (ed.), *Democristiani*. Bologna: Il Mulino.

Rossi, M. (1987) 'Sezioni di partito e partecipazione politica', *Polis*, 1 (1): 67–102.

Sartori, G. (1982) *Teoria dei partiti e caso italiano*. Milano: Sugarco.

Sebastiani, C. (1983) 'I funzionari', in A. Accornero, R. Mannheimer, and C. Sebastiani (eds), *L'identità comunista: I militanti, le strutture, la cultura del PCI*. Roma: Editori Riuniti, pp. 79–178.

Tarchi, M. (forthcoming [a]) 'Il MSI', in L. Morlino (ed.), *I partiti italiani: adattamento e trasformazione (1960–1994)*.

Tarchi, M. (forthcoming [b]) 'La Lega Nord', in L. Morlino (ed.), *I partiti italiani: adattamento e trasformazione (1960–1994)*.

Tarrow, S. (1967) *Peasant Communism in Southern Italy*. New Haven: Yale University Press.

Vallauri, C. (ed.) (1981) *L'arcipelago democratico: Organizzazione e struttura dei partiti italiani negli anni del centrismo (1949–1958)*. Roma: Bulzoni.

11

The Vulnerability of the Modern Cadre Party in the Netherlands

Ruud A. Koole

The Dutch political system achieved international renown within political science when it was first identified by Arend Lijphart (1968) as a system of 'consociational democracy'. Dutch society was seen to be deeply divided, not only on the political level, but also in most other domains, with the various political parties constituting the political expression of a network of societal organizations which, in turn, were bound together by a common religion or ideology. These networks were the so-called 'pillars' or *zuilen*, with the overall clustering of networks being known as 'pillarization' or *verzuiling*. The Catholics and the Protestants constituted the most pillar-ized of the major political families, the socialists somewhat less so, and the liberals only reluctantly. Nevertheless, despite these sharp socio-political divisions, the political system itself proved very stable, a paradox which Lijphart explained by emphasizing the independent effect of elite behav-iour. Thus, following Lijphart, it was the degree of cooperation between the elites from the different pillars, which was exercised within specific rules of the game, and which stemmed from a recognition of the dangers inherent in non-cooperation, which prevented the system from falling apart. Although other authors disagreed with this self-denying prophecy as an explanation for the coalescent elite behaviour by pointing, for example, at a consensual tradition that already existed long before the emergence of the different pillars at the beginning of the twentieth century (Daalder, 1974), the general image of a divided country with cooperating elites was itself never challenged.

Lijphart published his study of the Netherlands at the very moment when the system he described seemed to be coming to an end. Profound changes had taken place at the mass level during the 1960s. The pillarized system itself had begun to disintegrate and evidence of a growing individualization began to be apparent. The growth of the welfare state, changes within the churches, the impact of television and so on, had begun to open up a hitherto rather closed society. In this process, a formerly conservative society became quite permissive, and class and religion appeared to become much less effective predictors of partisan choice. Whereas 72 per cent of the popular vote had been determined by religion or class in 1956, this figure had fallen to 60 per cent in 1968, to 56 per cent in 1977, and to just 47 per cent in 1986 (Irwin and van Holsteyn, 1989: 39). Electoral competition became more open, and even at the elite level things began to change. Parties to the left of the political spectrum in particular sought to break with consensual politics and advocated a 'strategy of polarization' in order to offer the voters a more effective choice. But while the atmosphere clearly became more adversarial in the late 1960s and the 1970s, the traditional consensual elite behaviour returned once more in the 1980s. Indeed, given the apparent absence of difference between parties in this period, some observers even went so far as to suggest that the Netherlands had effectively become a 'one-party state'.

The central theme of this chapter concerns the way in which the organizations of Dutch political parties have reacted to the profound social changes which have occurred during the last three decades, for even though Dutch political parties were generally quicker to adopt new ideas than to change their structures, organizational adaptation did nevertheless take place, albeit at a rather limited pace. In brief, the three most important such changes were first, the reinforcement of the position of the parliamentary party, which was already quite strong by 1960; second, the dramatic decline in party membership, even though members remained important as far as the party organization was concerned; and third, due in part to 'de-pillarization' and to the introduction of state subventions, the growing cross-party harmonization of organizational structures which, prior to the 1960s, had varied according to differences in the parties' historical origins. These and other changes have resulted in the development of what I define to be *modern cadre parties*, characterized principally by a relatively small membership and a democratic internal organization. These are also parties which are under pressure regarding their intermediary role in the political system, and hence, despite an increasing opportunity to transform themselves into semi-state institutions, they are also vulnerable.

In this chapter, which draws heavily on an earlier study (Koole, 1992), I will deal primarily with the four major contemporary Dutch political parties and their predecessors: the Anti-Revolutionary Party (ARP), the Christian Historical Union (CHU), the Catholic People's Party (KVP), the Christian Democratic Appeal (CDA – a merger of the ARP, CHU and KVP), Democrats 66 (D66), the Labour Party (PvdA) and the Liberal Party (VVD). Other parties will sometimes be referred to, but will not be treated in detail. Most of the contemporary major parties can trace their organizational roots back to the last century and, even though all have changed names and political orientations since then, their general organizational structures nevertheless long continued to be determined by their own initial experiences or by those of their predecessors (Koole, 1992: 23–61). Indeed, it was only when societal developments in the 1960s had eroded the pillarized system in the Netherlands, that the formal structure of the mass party was eventually embraced by parties such as the

Protestant CHU and the conservative liberal VVD, which had originated in parliament and which, prior to the 1960s, had retained much of the character of nineteenth-century political 'clubs'. Thus, of the major parties, it was clearly the Protestant ARP and the social democratic PvdA, both of which had originated outside parliament, which had the strongest organizations at the beginning of the 1960s. The Catholic KVP is less easily categorized, however. The foundation of its predecessor party had certainly been initiated by Catholic parliamentarians, but any sense of its being a cadre party was belied by both the power of the local party organs and by the special position of Catholic social organizations within the party. Moreover, of all Dutch parties, the KVP had by far the largest membership.

Changes in and after the 1960s

Since the 1960s, however, and as noted above, differences between the formal structures of the party organizations tended to erode, with all of the parties formally adopting a mass party structure, building branches at the local level and relying on a national congress as the highest authority within the party.

Thus the Protestant CHU and ARP which, until around 1970, still officially described themselves as 'federations' of local election committees, now embraced the terms used by the other parties, while the KVP sought to do away with the special position of the 'congenial' social organizations within the party. In the latter case, however, its efforts were overshadowed by the attempts from 1967 onwards to form a new pan-Christian Democratic party together with the CHU and the ARP. The protracted negotiations between the three parties were often difficult, but they eventually led to a common list of candidates at the parliamentary elections in 1977 and to a complete merger of the three party organizations into the CDA in 1980 (ten Napel, 1992; Verkuil, 1992). The new party was established on the model of a mass party, with the strong organization of the former ARP furnishing a good basis for its new structure.

The PvdA was also hit by the profound changes in Dutch society, which lay at the basis of much of the party's political turmoil in late 1960s (van Praag, 1990). Within the PvdA a group of young members, calling themselves the New Left, managed to wield considerable influence, challenging the older generation with appeals for the recognition of North Vietnam and the German Democratic Republic, for the thorough democratization of society and of the party itself, and for a more antagonistic approach in politics. The party organization was reformed, which gave more power to the lower echelons of the party to the detriment of the national party elite, the impact of which was particularly visible in the recruitment of parliamentary candidates (see p. 294). The PvdA's radical phase drew to a close in the mid-1980s, however, with consensual politics once again replacing the antagonistic 'polarization strategy'. In 1989, the party returned once more to government, ending a period of exclusion in which it had served just six years in office in the three decades following 1958. Governmental participation did not appear to reap any electoral dividends, however, and even a number of profound organizational changes in 1992 (the nomination process was centralized once again, for example, and the national party council was abolished) failed to stem the large losses being indicated by polls, and which were also being experienced in elections at the local and national level.

The conservative-liberal VVD also changed considerably, albeit more in character than in its formal structure. Though still remaining a sort of political *club* in the 1960s, it grew rapidly during the 1970s, taking advantage of the losses of the major religious parties which were being hit by the process of secularization. During the 1980s, however, it lost some of these gains, suffering both internal disputes and a strong challenge from the new CDA. It regained strength during the 1990s.

One important new actor on the political stage emerged in the form of D66, which was founded in 1966 as a result of both the democratization wave and the 'end of ideology' movement. The new party aimed to do away with the 'old-fashioned ideologies of the nineteenth century' which were embodied in the other major parties and, like the New Left in the PvdA, it pushed for a profound democratization of Dutch society. It also was one of the first political movements to stress the need for environmental protection. In organizational terms, D66 has the structure of a mass party, but the atmosphere has always had something of a *club* character. That said, however, its appeal for democratization has also left its marks on the party's own internal life. Thus strong elements of direct democracy were introduced, with all members being allowed to speak and to vote at the national congress of the party, and being able to participate in a postal ballot on the rank order of the lists of candidates for representative bodies. Electorally, it has always proved unstable, but since the return in 1985 of its first leader, the charismatic Van Mierlo, the goddess of electoral fortune appears to be on the side of D66 once more.

The more minor parties in the Dutch system reflect a variety of ideological and religious groupings, including on the left the small Communist Party (CPN), the Pacifist Socialist Party (PSP), a left-wing grouping which emerged in 1957 as a protest against both the capitalist West and the Stalinist East, and the Radical Party (PPR), which was established in 1968 by a group of progressive Catholics who had become disenchanted by the alleged conservative direction of the KVP, and who were also joined by some equally progressive and equally disenchanted members of the ARP. The electoral fortunes of these three minor parties have been modest. Their 'finest hours' were in the 1970s, but they fell back considerably during the 1980s, particularly the PSP and the CPN. The latter parties' efforts at party renewal, both in ideological and organizational terms, failed to stem their ebbing electoral tide, and in 1990 the three parties agreed to cooperate in the creation of one new party, the Green Left (GL). The organizational structure of GL, as finalized in 1991, was based on the mass party model, and failed to include many of the elements of direct democracy which D66 had introduced into the Netherlands and which many Green parties in other countries had also incorporated.

The three other small parties which deserve a mention are the SGP (founded in 1918), the GPV (in 1948) and the RPF (in 1975). All are orthodox Calvinist parties, but with differing denominational backgrounds. They take a very conservative stance towards ethical and moral questions, and often also with regard to socio-economic issues (except perhaps for the RPF), and play a minor, albeit stable role in politics. The organizational structure of all three parties differs from the other Dutch parties in the sense that they remain federations, giving much power to the local or regional 'election associations'.[1]

Political parties in the Netherlands were originally organized around two cleavages: class and religion. As noted above, these cleavages accounted for roughly four different families of parties: Protestants, Catholics, socialists and liberals, none of which has ever won a majority on its own. In this sense, the Netherlands clearly was, and still is, a country of (political) minorities. In time, of course, the political families themselves changed. Thus, for example, the merger of the three major religious parties into the CDA was but one result of the de-pillarization of Dutch society. The advent of D66 was another. At the same time, however, we should be cautious in assuming that this has led to a major transformation of the party system. The new CDA, for example, played the same pivotal role which had earlier been the prerogative of the KVP, and was always in government (in coalition with other parties) until 1994. It remains to be seen whether the, in 1994, new so-called 'purple' coalition of PvdA, D66 and VVD has permanently ended the pivotal role of the CDA. Moreover, although the 'floating vote' has also become an important phenomenon in the Netherlands, most 'floating' voters tend to remain within the same bloc of parties (left or non-left) rather than shifting across the left–right divide (Mair, 1990). Thus while individual parties have therefore tended to become more vulnerable, the party system as a whole has remained quite stable.

The constitutional setting of the political parties

In the Netherlands elections are held for the Second Chamber (*Tweede Kamer*) of parliament at the national level, for the Provincial States at the regional level, for the municipal councils at the local level, and for the European Parliament. The First Chamber (*Eerste Kamer*) of parliament is elected indirectly by the Provincial States, and no elections are held for public functions such as those of mayor, prime minister or head of state (the Netherlands is a constitutional monarchy).

Since 1917 the Dutch electoral system has been characterized by extreme proportional representation. The threshold in this system is very low, and since the enlargement of the Second Chamber in 1956 from 100 to 150 seats, it has been set at only 0.67 of the national vote, that is, at the percentage which is necessary to obtain one seat in the Second Chamber. Some parliamentary fractions consist of only one member, to elect whom 39,997 votes, possibly scattered all over the country, were sufficient in 1963. As a result of demographic growth and the lowering of the voting age from 23 to 21 and then to 18, and notwithstanding the abolition of compulsory attendance at the ballot box in 1970, this figure has grown irregularly to 59,289 votes in 1989. The voter casts a single preferential vote for any candidate on one of the lists presented by the parties. The entire country is regarded as one constituency, but is also divided into nineteen administrative electoral sub-districts (*kieskringen*) in which the parties, if they so desire, can put forward different lists of candidates. The totals in these sub-districts are added up nationally and the number of seats awarded to each party is based on this national sum. If the party uses different lists, as most parties do, a very complex procedure is applied to assign the seats to specific individuals. Nonetheless, given that preference votes have virtually no impact on the list order as decided by the party,[2] it is almost always the candidates who are most favoured by the party who win seats. Dutch elections are therefore not candidate-oriented, and only the head-of-the-list receives substantial attention from the campaign leaders and the media. The voters decide only on the strength of the respective parties, with the actual competition for a parliamentary seat taking place within the party rather than on election day.

Political parties do not enjoy a special constitutional status in the Netherlands. Instead, they are treated in the law simply as ordinary voluntary associations, and are subject to the stipulations in the Civil Law concerning these associations. No specific stipulations are made with respect to the selection of candidates by the parties, their democratic character, or their finances. In this sense, and formally speaking, parties do not exist. In recent years, however, important changes have been made in both the Civil Law and the Electoral Law which affect the functioning of the parties. Since 1988, for example, the Civil Law states that any organization that 'disturbs the public order' in its goals or by its actions must be forbidden and dissolved. In addition, the new Electoral Law of 1989 contains stricter demands regarding the 'political groupings' that wish to present lists of candidates at elections. This 'hidden process of codification' is further fostered by the regulations concerning the public financing of political parties and their affiliated organizations. In 1971 a public subsidy for the research institutes of the parties was introduced, and similar subsidies for the parties' educational work and their youth movements were introduced in 1975 and 1981 respectively. In formal terms, scarcely any state subvention is given directly to the parties; rather, special foundations, closely linked to the parties, but formally independent of them, receive funds from the public purse for these specific purposes. In 1990 another subvention was introduced, albeit on a temporary basis, entitling the Dutch parties to funds which can be used to help their sister parties in Eastern Europe (see also p. 288).

The parties as membership organizations

All major parties in the Netherlands are characterized by the classic mass-party structure (Duverger, 1954): in all cases, political recruitment is party-controlled and party finance is a largely a matter of a fee-paying membership, and in all cases there is a striking similarity in structure. All major parties are also nationally organized.[3] Although the first party with a genuine national organization was already established in 1879 (ARP), it was only after the introduction of the system of proportional represen-tation in a single district in 1918, that all major parties moved to adopt a national structure in an effort to coordinate the presentation of lists of candidates. No fundamental changes in the main structure of party organizations have occurred since that time (see Koole and van de Velde, 1992: Table IX.D.1, for a basic organigram showing the main structural features of all the parties).

Each party organization consists of three levels, corresponding more or less to the three administrative layers of the state: the local, the regional and the national party bodies. The *afdeling* (branch) is not only the basic element for the national organization, sending its delegates to higher levels, it is also the supreme party body with regard to municipal politics. This dual task puts the *afdeling* under a constant pressure, in that it has to deal with all local affairs as well as discussing and deciding on supra-local issues. In practice, however, the tendency is to concentrate on local affairs, especially among the smaller branches.

The national congress (*congres* or *algemene vergadering*) is the highest authority within the party, convening between twice a year and once every two years, and consisting of the delegates of the branches and very often also of members of the *partijbestuur* and/or the *partijraad*. D66, however, has introduced an element of direct democracy in its structure by giving the right to speak and vote at the national congress to all party members. Some parties also allow simple party members to be present and sometimes to speak (VVD) at the congress, but reserve voting rights to the delegates and other members of the congress. Especially within the major denomin-ational parties there has been a shift of political power from the congress to the *partijraad*. The ARP simply abolished its congress in 1971, and congress was reduced to a more symbolic role in the CDA.

The *partijbestuur* or *hoofdbestuur* (national committee) is in charge of the political conduct of the party, and is generally elected by the national party congress and the regional party bodies. In the early 1960s, older integration parties such as the KVP and, to a lesser extent, the PvdA, reserved a special place on the *partijbestuur* for representatives from 'congenial' organizations (as, for instance, in the case of the chief editor of the daily *Het Vrije Volk* in the PvdA; or for those 'who enjoy the confidence of Catholic social organizations' in the KVP). During the 1960s, however, in line with the process of de-pillarization, these ties between parties and other organizations were severed. Although the size of the national committee varies considerably from one party to another, there has been a slight tendency towards the development of somewhat smaller bodies. The day-to-day business of the party is dealt with by a small *Dagelijks Bestuur* (national executive), which constitutes the core of the *partijbestuur*, and includes some five members: the chairman of the party (who is the most important person within the extra-parliamentary party organization in political terms), one or more secretaries, the treasurer and 'ordinary' members.

Another characteristic of the structure of the Dutch parties is the so-called *partijraad* (party council). In one sense this is a smaller version of the national congress, but its composition is completely different. Whereas the national congress mainly consists of delegates from the local branches, the party council is dominated by the delegates from the regional party bodies. Even D66, which had no proper party council during its early years, developed an 'Advisory Council' in 1978, consisting of regional delegates. Prior to that, D66 maintained a peculiar party organ (*steekproefvergadering*), in which a randomly selected sample of party members offered an opinion on organizational and political affairs. And although a fear of Michel's iron law of oligarchy lay behind the creation of this unique body, its malfunctioning pushed D66 towards a more conventional procedure. A party council devotes itself not only to intra-party domestic business, but can also play an important political role between the regular congresses. Indeed, in 1992, in an effort to break the power of the regional oligarchies in the party, the PvdA abolished its party council. This measure was part of a more generalized attempt to reorganize the party following a series of serious local electoral losses in the early 1990s.

While the *regional bodies*, consisting of delegates or members of the local branches, have grown in importance in all the parties during the last three decades, a counter-development began to be apparent in the beginning of the 1990s, especially within the PvdA and the VVD. In the late 1960s and 1970s, 'democratization' had been translated by the parties to mean 'decentralization'. That said, decentralization ceased when it hit the regional level, with the local branches and the ordinary members failing to profit from this development (Koole and Leijenaar, 1988 – D66 constituted one exception in this regard). Around 1990, however, there emerged a new tendency towards a re-centralization of internal decision-making procedures. The perceived negative effects of too much regional power in the party (especially with regard to its impact on the composition of the parliamentary fractions), combined with electoral losses, led both the PvdA and the VVD to opt for a more decisive role for the central party bodies. In this respect, at least, there appears to have been a successful intra-party coalition between the national committee and the local branches against an all too ambitious middle-level elite. A shift in D66 can also be read as an attempt at greater centralization, in that in order to guarantee a more 'balanced' composition of the parliamentary fraction, the party introduced a system of 'advice' by a special commission during the nomination process. In the CDA, on the other hand, the national committee already had enough power to be able to influence internal decision making.

Ancillary and affiliated organizations

All parties have ancillary and/or affiliated organizations. All maintain *youth organizations* (D66 only since 1984), for example, which always have an affiliated character (no direct membership link), except in the CDA. Most also maintain *women's organizations*, with those of the CHU, PvdA, CDA and VVD having (had) an ancillary status (complete membership overlap). D66, on the other hand, claiming to be opposed in principle to all categorial organizations within the party, has no women's organization. That said, the foundation of a D66 youth organization in 1984 would appear to have undermined the sacredness of this principle.

In addition, as indicated above, Dutch parties also maintain special *foundations* for specific purposes. Although having no membership of their own, these foundations often play an important role in intra-party politics. All parties maintain research foundations and educational foundations, and, since 1989, most also maintain special foundations to help the sister parties in Eastern Europe. Apart from the research foundations of the major parties, most of these bodies were created after the introduction of a public subsidy for research foundations in 1971, that for educational foundations in 1975, and that for 'Second World' foundations in 1989. Some of the parties also run other, smaller foundations, such as the special Third World foundations in the PvdA and the CDA. The intensity of the relationships between these foundations and the parties varies. The research institutes operate relatively autonomously, but, as is the case with all other foundations that receive a public subsidy, they must nevertheless be recognized by the parliamentary party in the Second Chamber in order to be able to claim their subvention.

Organizational presence and party membership

Although most parties have not kept a precise record of the development of their number of branches, the available data would appear to suggest that the number of branches organized by the parties has declined in parallel to the decline in the number of municipalities from 994 in 1960 to 714 in 1988.[4] Although some parties have more than one branch in cities such as Amsterdam and Rotterdam, it seems that the vast majority of the municipalities were organized by the PvdA and the major religious parties at the beginning of the 1960s (in 1960, the PvdA had 938 branches; the

CHU, 869; the ARP, some 850; the KVP, some 830), with the extent of the VVD network being much less (just 407 branches in 1960). Since then, however, the VVD, whose figures are exceptionally precise, appears to have caught up with its rivals, growing to more than 600 branches in the 1980s. This phenomenon must be explained by the processes of secularization and de-pillarization. In the religiously homogeneous regions, for example, the confessional parties had occupied a particularly dominant position, especially in the catholic south, which virtually belonged to the KVP, and where the only challenges came from the rather small branches of the PvdA and by so-called 'local lists' (lists of candidates presented by local 'parties', that did not participate in supra-local elections). After the 1960s, however, the VVD also proved capable of winning voters and members in this area, and was thus in a position to establish branches in this formerly catholic bastion, a trend which was also true, albeit to a lesser extent, for the PvdA and D66. The 'national coverage' of D66 in particular originally lagged behind, but its number of branches has increased rapidly in recent years. Thus today, although geographic strongholds continue to exist for each party, signs of organizational absence have declined considerably for all the major parties.

In the period between 1960 and 1990 the total number of party members has declined rapidly, albeit unevenly. In the 1960s, for example, and not least as a result of de-pillarization, the largest exodus affected the parties of 'social integration' – the major religious parties, especially the KVP, and the PvdA. In 1960, some 745,000 people were members of a political party; by 1970, by contrast, this figure had fallen to some 400,000. Even if one takes into account that the records for membership figures before 1970 were not always very accurate, and that the introduction of centralized and automatized administration of membership around 1970 resulted in a considerable 'cleaning-up' of these records, the dramatic decline in membership remains very evident (Koole and Voerman, 1986; complete figures are reported in Koole and van de Velde, 1992: Tables IX.B.1.a–j). During the 1970s, on the other hand, the total number of members remained more or less stable, with the atmosphere of 'politicization' and adversarial politics tending to compensate for the general trend towards individualization. The change in the political culture in the 1980s, however, when politics returned to a more consensual and business-like style, coincided with yet another period of decline, and only the small orthodox Calvinist parties and D66 have managed to grow in recent years. At the beginning of the 1990s, for example, fewer than 320,000 people were members of a party.

This decline is even more dramatic when set against the number of voters and the number of potential voters. Thus, in 1946, the total number of party members was equivalent to some 15 per cent of the total number of voters, falling to 14 per cent in 1956, to 8 per cent in 1967, to 5 per cent in 1977, and to not even 4 per cent in 1989. That said, this member/voter ratio does vary considerably across the parties, with smaller parties tending to have a higher ratio than bigger parties, and with right-wing parties tending to have a higher ratio than left-wing parties. The ratio of members to the overall electorate is even more diminished, of course. Indeed, the low membership/electorate ratio was already evident at the beginning of the 1960s, when the then biggest party, the KVP, was unable to convince even 5 per cent of the potential voters to join the party. Moreover, at the end of the 1980s, the CDA, which was by then the largest party, and which was also electorally more successful than the KVP had ever been, could muster a membership of just over 1 per cent of the electorate.

One reason for this low organizational presence is the fact that corporate membership has never existed in the Netherlands,[5] with parties counting only individual members. A more important reason, however, is the fact that during the period of the *verzuiling*, voters were already organized within the *zuilen* themselves, without necessarily becoming members of a party. Moreover, the strength of the *zuil*, even in electoral terms, was not exclusively dependent upon the organizational presence of the parties, in that voters could also be mobilized by other organizations within the *zuil*. Thereafter, once *verzuiling* had begun to erode, the parties found themselves unable to make good their organizational arrears.

A third factor which may be relevant here is the near-absence of a spoils system in the Netherlands. Apart from relatively few senior functions in politics and the bureaucracy, party membership is not a requirement for obtaining employment or preferment. Nor are party members privileged by other possible forms of *patronage*, such as housing, social insurance, access to recreational facilities and so on. Clientelism, in short, hardly exists.

Finally, and especially in light of the low member/voter ratios, it is also important to recognize the enormous increase in the size of the Dutch electorate during the past three decades. Partly as a result of the lowering of the voting age, and especially because of the enormous demographic growth, the number of people entitled to vote increased from some 6.7 million in 1963 to some 11.1 million in 1989, an expansion which, even by comparison to other west European democracies, is clearly exceptional. Moreover, notwithstanding the lower levels of turn-out, and the fact that compulsory attendance at the ballot box was abolished in 1970, the number of those actually voting also increased – from 6.4 million (95.1 per cent turn-out) in 1963 to 8.9 million (80.2 per cent turn-out) in 1989. The parties are apparently still capable of mobilizing voters, even if they are much less able to convince these voters to become party members.

The finances of Dutch parties

While the numbers of members may have fallen, and while particular state subventions may have been introduced in the 1970s, membership fees remain an important source of party income, modest as this is (Koole, 1989, 1990). As can be seen from Table 11.1, for example, which

Table 11.1 *Sources of income of national party organizations, including affiliated foundations, in 1989*

Party	Membership fees (%)	State subvention (%)	Other[a] (%)	Total (Dfl.)
CDA	64	17	19	7,276,343
PvdA	62	14	24	10,418,799
VVD	61	25	14	3,980,471
D66	48	31	21	1,666,103

[a] Refers to income from interest, fund-raising activities among the ordinary party members, 'party taxes' on the salaries of politicians (especially in the PvdA), etc.

Source: Koole, 1992: 211; Koole and van de Velde, 1992: Tables IX.E.1.b–k

summarizes the position in 1989, the three largest parties rely on membership dues for some 60 per cent of their total income, with state subventions contributing substantially less. As noted above, most of these subventions are specified for the special party foundations – the research institutes, educational institutes and youth organizations – with maximum levels varying according to the number of party seats in the Second Chamber. Moreover, the foundations are also required to be able to raise a certain amount of their own money in order to be eligible for state support (matching funds). Apart from these subventions, the parties also receive free time on radio and television as well as financial support for the costs of these broadcasts. Finally, the parties have also received public funds for projects promoting the position of women within their ranks and for projects which aim to increase the awareness (even within the party organization itself) of problems in developing countries.

Private donations from business now hardly exist at the national level (no data are available for the sub-national level), although prior to de-pillarization some political parties, and especially the KVP, were in receipt of this kind of support. One reason for this is perhaps the (neo-)corporatist structure of the Dutch political system, which gives business and trade unions direct access to the political process without requiring the inter-mediation of party. Moreover, democratization in the 1960s and 1970s has placed an almost ethical ban on these kinds of donations, even though they would be completely legal in the formal sense. They are also officially tax deductible, as are the fees and other contributions from individual members.

Although this large-scale dependence on membership fees may be laudable from a democratic point of view, it nevertheless places the parties in a difficult position when they are faced with a continuing exodus of party members. It is for this reason that they have recently requested further state aid. In response, however, a special commission advised the Minister of Home Affairs against any considerable increase in the total subsidy, and although it suggested that the system of state subvention be given a special legal status, the commission also argued that the 'intermediary role' of political parties in the society required a relatively low 'degree of dependence' on state finances (*Waarborg van Kwaliteit*, 1991).[6]

The party as a professional organization?

If the number of salaried staff is taken as a criterion, then the extra-parliamentary organizations of Dutch political parties have scarcely become more professionalized since the early 1960s. On the contrary, their main characteristic remains that of voluntary associations, relying heavily on the good will of their members to carry out tasks on an unpaid basis. There are in fact relatively few paid staff. At the sub-national level, for example, paid staff scarcely exist, although in this case information is difficult to obtain, and at the national level the numbers of staff in the party central offices (clerical as well as political) have hardly grown, except for the PvdA and D66. Indeed, in some parties, the numbers have even appeared to decline.[7]

The PvdA central office has always been that most oriented towards professional staff. At the end of the 1950s, more than 60 persons worked in its national secretariat, falling to little more than 30 at the beginning of the 1970s, and increasing again to about 50 in the middle of the 1980s. D66, on the other hand, is an almost perfect example of an amateur organization. Lack of sufficient members, and hence lack of income, limited the size of its paid staff to an average of some four persons (mostly part-time) in its first years, increasing to eight at the beginning of the 1980s, where it has since remained. At the national headquarters of the three denominational parties, the ARP, the CHU and the KVP, the number of salaried staff in the beginning of the 1960s was 15, 7 and 38 respectively. In the ARP this number increased to about 20 at the end of the decade, after which it remained more or less stable, while numbers were reduced in the CHU and the KVP. When the CDA was founded as the successor of the three major religious parties in 1980, the number of staff was not much higher than the sum of those employed by the constituent parties, and then declined from an average of 43 in the early 1980s to about 35 in the second half of the decade. The VVD, on the other hand, increased from having very few full-time staff to about 20 in the beginning of the 1970s, and then to 24 in the early 1980s, declining once again to 16 in subsequent years.

All in all, therefore, and not least as a result of declining membership, the party central offices tend to have fewer staff than before (except in the case of the PvdA which, however, has also recently begun to trim its numbers). To some extent, however, this loss is compensated for by the rapid growth of parliamentary party staff (see p. 291), as well as by the more modest growth in the numbers of staff in affiliated foundations, which has been facilitated by the introduction of the special state subventions. At the end of the 1960s, for example, the research foundations of the PvdA employed some 11 persons (full-time and part-time), with even smaller numbers in the other party foundations. Following the introduction of the public subsidies, however, these numbers grew, with the PvdA being again to the forefront. Thus, by the end of the 1980s, the number of the various PvdA foundation staff had grown to more than 33, and those in the CDA foundations had increased to more than 25. The number of staff in the VVD foundations also expanded significantly, from just 4 at the end of the 1960s to 12 at the end of the 1980s, and the D66 foundations grew from having virtually no staff in the years after its formation to an all-time, but nonetheless modest, high of 5 at the end of the 1980s.

Other than the help which can be obtained through these foundations, which may indeed be regarded as internal party resources, the Dutch parties do not tend to avail themselves of much outside expertise. Nor are there any real signs that such a practice is increasing. For even though the major parties do sometimes buy in expertise from PR agencies, especially in the context of election campaigns, this is not in itself a new phenomenon, being already the practice, for example, of the VVD and its predecessor in the 1940s, and of the PvdA at the end of the 1950s. But even if it is a reasonably long-established practice, the size and importance of this kind of expertise has remained rather minimal, with election campaigns always being managed by a small circle consisting of the political leadership and the party's own PR officer (see p. 296). That said, and from about the 1970s onwards, the major parties did begin to use expertise from market research agencies and sometimes from specialists at universities in order to base their electoral strategies on refined empirical data. Even then, however, all of this occurred on a very modest scale, not least because of scarce financial resources, on the one hand, and because of the availability of free expertise from (professionally qualified) party members, on the other hand.

The advent of a professional 'parliamentary party complex'

As noted above, one of the most important changes with respect to the organization of political parties in the Netherlands is the emergence of a 'parliamentary party complex' (*fractie complex*), consisting of both full-time MPs and large numbers of salaried personnel. This development was facilitated by a decision in 1968 to substantially augment the salaries of MPs as well as by the introduction of state subsidies for the assistance of individual MPs and parliamentary parties (Koole and van de Velde, 1992: Table IX.E.3). As a consequence, the balance of power between the extra-parliamentary party organization and its representatives in parliament shifted to the advantage of the latter. Prior to these decisions, of course, the individual MPs could always call on the services of the Clerk of the House (*Griffier*), whose office was, and remains, relatively small. But with the increasing workload of a parliament in a welfare state, extra assistance was felt to be necessary. In 1964 the parliamentary party as a collectivity could claim some money for its office; and from 1965 onwards money was also made available to the parliamentary party to hire staff, with the size of this support depending on the total number of party seats. In 1974 this system of collective assistance was supplemented by a programme of personal assistance for the individual MPs, such that by the end of the 1970s each MP was entitled to one full-time assistant. Although the systems of individual and collective help were established separately, they tend to be integrated financially into one personnel fund which, by late 1991, was providing a total of some 256 staff (121 full-time and 135 part-time) for the four major parliamentary parties.[8]

Parties, society and de-pillarization

Relationships with the media

There is no question but that the societal changes in the 1960s have had an impact on the links between the parties and the print media. In 1967, for example, the formal tie between the daily *Het Vrije Volk* and the PvdA was severed, after which this daily paper was reduced to the status of a local Rotterdam newspaper. The PvdA-oriented newspaper *Het Parool* has also developed in practice into a local Amsterdam newspaper, with *De Volkskrant* informally taking over the position of the most important national left-wing newspaper, albeit without having a formal link with any party (prior to the mid-1960s *De Volkskrant* had been the Catholic daily, linked to the KVP through a series of personnel connections). The protestant daily, *Trouw*, which had had a close but informal link to the ARP, also cut loose and became a more open, but still Christian, newspaper. The readership of *Trouw* is now mainly supportive of the CDA, and the paper's political orientation lies somewhere between the PvdA and the CDA. The VVD, on the other hand, has never had any formal ties with any newspaper, but many of the so-called 'neutral' dailies have a liberal outlook. The *Telegraaf*, the biggest-selling paper, has always been conservative, while the *NRC/Handelsblad*, a leading 'quality' paper, has no special sympathy for any party. Indeed, the only party-owned newspaper which continued to exist through the 1970s and 1980s was the small CPN-backed *De Waarheid* which, faced with an ever-shrinking readership, eventually closed down in 1989.

The relationships between the parties and the electronic media have also been subject to profound changes, although unlike the print media, the Dutch broadcasting system has long retained its pillarized character. This unique system is based on the rule that broadcasting associations win time on the airwaves in proportion to their numbers of members (and not their proportion of listeners or viewers), which have always been considerably higher than the number of party members. From the very beginnings of the radio in the 1920s, ideologically oriented broadcasting associations developed which belonged to the various *zuilen*, including the Protestant NCRV, the Catholic KRO, the socialist VARA and the 'neutral', but liberal, AVRO. And although the formal ties between these associations and the political parties had been severed by the early 1960s, the different political sympathies persisted, as they still do today.

During the 1960s, however, there emerged new broadcasting associations (TROS and the former pirate Veronica) which had no link whatsoever with the disintegrating *zuilen*, nor with parties. A further, but more profound, change occurred in the early 1990s, when the commercial television channel RTL4, founded in 1989, was able to attract about a third of the television audience, a success which put the traditional public broadcasting system under severe pressure.

Nevertheless, despite these changes, the continued existence of the traditional system has certainly eased the access of the political parties to the media. Thus, as the importance of television in particular increased, the political parties found themselves in a position where they could adapt to the new situation without too many difficulties or too much cost. The new broadcasting organizations also adopted a very cooperative stance in this regard. Moreover, as has been noted above, the parties also receive free broadcasting time on radio and television. During election campaigns, for example, those parties which present lists in all of the electoral subdistricts are entitled to equal time on the airwaves, while in inter-election periods all parties that occupy one or more seats in parliament also have free access to radio and TV, again irrespective of size. But although television may have replaced the press as the major channel of communication between the parties and the voters, and although the parties do enjoy privileged access, the recent diversification of television channels (which has increased even more so since the very successful introduction of cable TV), has nevertheless made it more difficult for the parties to formulate an efficient media strategy, and especially to formulate a strategy which can reach the increasingly common 'zapping' voter.

Parties and other societal organizations

More generally, de-pillarization has also led to a weakening of the ties between parties and other societal organizations, in that what is true for the media is equally true as far as relations with the trade unions, employers' organizations, churches, etc., are concerned. In short, the powerful binding force of a common religion or ideology has clearly evaporated in a society characterized by a pronounced process of individualization and secularization. Thus formal links between parties and societal organizations effectively no longer exist, and interlocking directorates, which existed at the beginning of the 1960s (Lijphart, 1968), have diminished considerably.

Another important reason for this trend is the very fact of professionalization in both the parties and these other organizations. Leadership positions have become full-time functions, and fulfilling two or more of these functions at the same time has become almost impossible. In addition, and as a part consequence of the 'democratization wave' of the 1960s, many of the personnel links between parties and societal organizations had become taboo, with all of the parties increasingly emphasizing the unacceptability of multiple office-holding in their standing orders. In this sense, the accumulation of power was conceived to be detrimental to democracy. In the case of D66, for example, the party demanded of all its parliamentary candidates a written declaration that they would give up all other functions in society (and in the party) at the moment of their election as an MP. Reciprocal sympathies, on the other hand, do continue to exist, and, particularly in the case of the CDA, informal contacts with the former affiliated organizations are believed to continue to play an important role (Duffhues, 1991). The parties themselves also change. In the early 1990s, for example, the PvdA, which had wanted to become an 'action party' in the 1970s by concentrating itself very much on progressive 'action groups', now openly questioned the fact that MPs scarcely involved themselves in (other) functions in society. Other parties have also discussed how to improve their relations with societal organizations as a means of escaping their otherwise growing isolation from society.

The party as a political organization

Candidate selection and leadership selection

Political parties in the Netherlands wholly control the selection of candidates for representative bodies. But although this is as true today as it was in 1960, there are nevertheless two important developments which have taken place in this regard. First, as noted above, the parties have become more independent – or, perhaps, more isolated – from societal organizations, and hence the influence of the latter on the process of candidate selection has declined considerably since the 1960s. Second, within various parties, the process of candidate selection has become decentralized, with the influence of the regional party bodies in particular becoming more important, not least as a result of the wave of democratization in the late 1960s and early 1970s which had stressed the need to bring politics closer to the grassroots. This process of regionalization was formally introduced in the PvdA in 1969 and later became manifest in the other major parties. In the VVD, for example, a special 'party council' consisting of delegates from the regional party bodies was given the greatest voice in the selection process. And although the three religious parties hesitated, the newly formed CDA placed the local party branch in a decisive position. D66 has gone further than any other party in this respect, with all party members being given the right to participate via a postal ballot in decisions regarding the ordering of the lists of candidates (except for the head-of-the-list).

Since 1990, however, this move towards decentralization has tended to be reversed, with the VVD and the PvdA formally changing their rules in order to give the central party organs more influence on the selection processes. In the PvdA the party congress will henceforth decide on the final list order, based on a proposal by the national committee. In the VVD a comparable procedure was introduced. It is also remarkable to observe that these changes were effected using the same arguments about the need to bring politics closer to the grassroots. Attempts at centralization are also evident in the case of D66. While the postal ballot has been retained, the members now receive not only the alphabetical list with the names of the candidates, but also (since 1986) an advisory list with a certain order proposed by a special commission appointed by the national committee. The steering power of this advisory list is clear, in that the results of the postal ballot are virtually identical to it (Hillebrand, 1992).

In contrast to the decentralization of candidate selection, leadership selection has always remained a matter for the party elite. Although the process itself has scarcely been analysed (but see Toonen, 1992), it is nevertheless clear that certain common practices do prevail. As noted above, for example, there is an unwritten rule that the political leader (party leader) of a Dutch party is either (vice) prime minister in a cabinet or chairman of the parliamentary party. The chairman of the extra-parliamentary party organization is in this sense subordinate, a practice which once again underlines the dominant position of the parliamentary fraction. Only in the PvdA does the role of the party chairman sometimes come close in importance to that of the political leader, although never really matching it.

Once selected as such, the political leader will almost automatically become the head-of-the-list at the next elections, if he or she expresses the wish to be a candidate at those elections. Thus it is only when the incumbent party leader is no longer available that the party organization may perhaps exert more influence. Even then, however, the selection of a new head-of-the-list, who will become the new political leader after the elections, is mainly organized by a small circle within the party elite, thus confronting the party organization with a *fait accompli*; since no other candidate is presented, the organization cannot but approve. This was the case, for example, with the succession of Lubbers by Brinkman (in 1994) as the incoming political leader of the CDA. It is only under very exceptional circumstances, therefore, that there is real and open competition to become head-of-the-list and, consequently, political leader of a party (as was the case in the new Green Left prior to the parliamentary elections of 1994). That said, it is also important to note that most of the parties had different heads-of-list in the various electoral sub-districts until around 1970, and that the political leader of the party was drawn from among this group. But this has changed since the age of television has made it absolutely necessary to emphasize the electoral appeal of one and the same political leader.

The composition of the Second Chamber has also changed considerably during the past three decades. Thus professionalization and de-pillarization have turned MPs into full-time politicians who very often have had a previous career in the public bureaucracy, transforming the parliament in the 1970s from being 'a representation of the organized society into a working place for professional politicians' (van den Berg, 1983). Prior to de-pillarization, the parties selected many of their candidates from among the ranks of the various 'congenial' societal organizations; thereafter, however, the candidates tended to come from a less 'pillarized' background, and were increasingly drawn from within the party organizations themselves. Moreover, because the number of party members has declined so rapidly in the last decades, the available pool for recruitment has also diminished, with the result that complaints began to surface in the 1980s concerning the 'one-sidedness' of the parliamentary intake. This was, however, not only the result of shrinkage in the recruitment pool, but was also because new groups began to claim representation on a proportional basis.

Women, who were and still are particularly under-represented, were especially critical in this regard (Leijenaar, 1989). In this case, however, the demands proved quite successful, although equal representation is still far from being a reality: in 1963 only 14 (9.3 per cent) out of 150 members of the Second Chamber were women, a figure which increased steadily to 35 (23.3 per cent) in 1989 (Koole and van de Velde, 1992: Table IX.D.10). All of the major parties have expressed the wish to increase the number of women in parliament, but it is only the PvdA which has formally set an obligatory ratio (a minimum of 25 per cent in 1986 and 33 per cent in 1992).

The drafting of election manifestos and the organization of campaigns

Unlike the selection of candidates, policy formation has scarcely been subject to a process of decentralization. According to the formal rules it has always been the national congress, consisting of delegates from the local party branches, which determines the party platforms. In practice, however, there are variations. Whereas until the late 1960s the national executive (and, in the VVD, the party leader) drafted the proposal for the platform, the preparatory work has since been taken over by special committees which are installed by the party executive but approved by congress. Nevertheless this development is more an example of a process of deconcentration than it is of decentralization, and the drafting of the manifesto remains a matter for the top levels of the party (Koole, 1992; Zielonka-Goei, 1989). Indeed, notwithstanding a higher degree of participation, the manipulative power of the original draft appears to be such that the impact of sub-national levels on the final programme remains very limited, although it is greater than was the case in the early 1960s.

More evident changes can be seen in the organization of election campaigns, albeit mainly as a result of the advent of television and the growing importance of the floating vote. As was the case around 1960, the campaign teams of today remain quite small, but they are now obliged to respond more quickly to events which occur during the campaign itself. Free publicity on television programmes has become an important goal for the campaign teams, and more attention is also given to the head-of-the-list. The result is that campaigns have now become more personalized.

Table 11.2 *Campaign expenditures of national party bureaus in national elections (Dfl. '000, 1980 prices)*

	ARP	CHU	KVP	PvdA	VVD	D66
1963				1462.4	387.6	–
1967	763.6*	94.6*	709.2*	1226.1	687.9*	70.9*
1971	1134.6*	472.8*	945.5*	1169.0	113.5*	160.7*
1972				394.4		159.1
		CDA				
1977		1386.0*		1519.5	808.5*	254.5
1981		1504.2		2544.2	1088.5	604.0
1982		1904.7		1258.8	866.1	452.7
1986		1100.1		1357.9	1126.7	325.1
1989		1138.8		1074.7	828.7	455.3

Source: Koole, 1992: 370; Koole and van de Velde, 1992: Table IX.E.6. The figures marked with * are derived from Brants et al. (1982: 56)

New techniques (such as public opinion polling) have also been introduced, albeit on a rather modest scale. Campaign expenditures have also always been relatively limited, although, if anything, and perhaps partly as a result of a scarcity of resources, more recent campaigns have tended to become even cheaper than before (see Table 11.2).

The advent, and the future, of the modern cadre party

It is clearly difficult to interpret the development of Dutch party organizations over the past thirty years wholly within the confines of what have now become the conventional frameworks for understanding. In other words, it is difficult to characterize the parties in terms of the familiar distinction between mass-integration parties and catch-all parties (Kirchheimer, 1966) or, on the other hand, in terms of the more recent distinction between mass-bureaucratic parties and electoral-professional parties (Panebianco, 1988).

The position of the top leaderships inside the parties, for example, was already strong in the Netherlands in 1960. And though this position did indeed strengthen in some areas (campaigns, leadership selection), as Kirchheimer hypothesized, it nevertheless weakened in others (notably in the selection of candidates and, albeit very slightly, in policy formation), until the central party organs once again regained control around 1990. Thus, the leadership position is a strong one, but is not really stronger than was the case in 1960. Moreover, the central role of the (hardly professionalized) bureaucracy also remains intact, and has not been lost to specialized professionals in the extra-parliamentary organization, as Panebianco suggests would be the case. The pre-eminence of the public representatives also remains very evident. Although a general feature of the Dutch political system has been that the position of the parliamentary parties always predominates in policy-formation, nevertheless the advent of a professional parliamentary party complex of full-time MPs and salaried assistants has further strengthened the position of the parliamentary party vis-à-vis the extra-parliamentary party organization, in a way which is only partly compensated for by the influence which the latter can exert through the internal nomination processes. Personalized leadership has also become more important, especially since the advent of television, even though it should be added that there is no sense in which personalized campaigns may be regarded as a wholly new phenomenon. Indeed, the parties of popular prime ministers such as Colijn in the 1930s or Drees in the 1950s also conducted very personalized campaigns. That said, the 'need for a face' has now become a structural feature, and the campaigns of all parties now tend to depend increasingly on the electoral appeal of their heads-of-list.

Membership figures, on the other hand, have certainly evidenced a drastic decline, and the influence of ordinary members has clearly not increased. In financial terms, however, party members remain very important, and the parties' income still depends heavily on membership dues. The introduction of limited public subsidies may have lessened this dependence to some extent, but it nevertheless has not replaced the membership as the principal source of income. Financing through interest groups, which very probably had taken place in the era of the *verzuiling*, has not re-emerged as an additional source of party revenue. The parties are also clearly less concentrated on the traditional 'electorate of belonging', and voters have become more volatile. In addition, it is clear that the mass media are tending to drive parties towards personalized campaigns and that the parties also address themselves towards a more heterogeneous public ('opinion electorate'). Indeed, television has also become a more important link between parties and voters, albeit a very precarious one. As against this, however, it must be emphasized that this volatility is highly constrained with certain blocks of parties (i.e. within the left or within the right), and in this sense the recruitment of voters from among the population *at large*, as foreseen by Kirchheimer, has therefore not become a dominant feature (except perhaps in the case of the CDA). Thus although the individual parties are increasingly vulnerable, this nevertheless has not (yet?) forced them toward the electoral-professional model through imitative and reciprocal adjustment processes, as Panebianco predicts will be the case. Finally, there has also been little evidence of the need for access to interest groups as a means of securing electoral support, which both Kirchheimer and Panebianco stress as a vital element for party survival. On the contrary, the process of de-pillarization has pushed the parties in the opposite direction, with recent efforts on the part of interest groups to influence the behaviour of the voters having virtually no impact.[9]

If they are neither catch-all parties, nor electoral-professional parties, how then are we to classify the Dutch parties at the beginning of the 1990s? In my view, the developments which have been reviewed in this chapter suggest that they are in fact more like *modern cadre parties* (Koole, 1992). This emphasis on *modern* is important, since it is necessary to distinguish the contemporary Dutch parties from the nineteenth-century cadre party, as depicted by Duverger (1954). But although modern, they are nevertheless *cadre* parties, mainly as a result of the fact that the low numbers of members render the notion of a 'mass party' quite inappropriate, and since this also allows us to conceive of their being vehicles for the active members only (the 'cadre'), rather than devices for mass encapsulation. The organizational characteristics of these modern cadre parties can be listed as follows:

1 predominance of the professional leadership groups (especially the parliamentary party), but with a high degree of accountability to the lower strata in the party;
2 a low member/voter ratio, although members remain important as a source of finance, as a means of recruiting candidates for political office and as the bodies who are required simply to maintain the party apparatus in working order;
3 a strong and broad-ranging orientation towards voters, but with a strategy which is neither catch-all, on the one hand, nor focusing on a *classe gardée*, on the other;
4 the maintenance of the structure of a mass party (with vertical organizational ties), not only to maintain a specific image, but also in order to guarantee a certain degree of internal democracy;
5 the reliance for financial resources on a combination of both public subsidies and the fees and donations of members.

One of the most important differences between the modern cadre party, on the one hand, and the old cadre party, the catch-all parties and the electoral-professional parties, on the other, is clearly the strong emphasis within the former on (formal) internal democracy. And even though the evident tension between internal party democracy and electoral and political effectiveness does add to the vulnerability of the modern cadre party, it nevertheless also makes the party that much less likely to develop into a catch-all party, as Kirchheimer both described and feared.

   Although each of the major Dutch parties can currently be regarded as a modern cadre party, there are of course some differences between them. The predominance of leadership groups is true for all, in that public money has stimulated the professionalization of all parliamentary parties in a proportional way; but the position of the national executive is stronger in the PvdA, the CDA and the VVD than is the case in D66, where the parliamentary party is even less subject to the challenge of a powerful executive than in the other parties. Internal 'party democracy' is also strong in all parties, and each now maintains the structure of a mass party, through which the party elite can be held responsible and eventually even sanctioned by the lower strata in the party. But in D66, and to a lesser extent in the PvdA, elements of direct democracy are also present, and these do not exist in the other parties. That said, more direct democracy is not necessarily the same as more democracy per se. The member/voter ratio is the lowest in D66, but is increasingly modest in the other parties also. And although the electoral tactics of all the major parties have been adapted to the more open electoral situation, none has seriously embraced an approach intended to catch votes from right across the left–right spectrum (the CDA, which always refuses to accept the relevance of the left–right distinction, comes closest to such an appeal). Differences in the types of financial resources are negligible, and in this sense de-pillarization has had a standardizing effect, as have had state subventions. No party now receives substantial funds from business circles or from trade unions.

A future situation in which the established parties constitute a cartel against newcomers and rely increasingly heavily on the state for their survival (Katz and Mair, 1992) must of course be regarded as one possible, but not necessarily inevitable, development. To be sure, Dutch parties are moving closer to the state in the sense that they have developed what I have referred to as the parliamentary party complex, but their financial situation in particular prevents them removing themselves entirely from a membership base. It is here that the modest scale and format of state subventions in the Netherlands play such an important role. Dutch modern cadre parties therefore still act as intermediaries between the state and the citizens, although it is certainly true that this position has been put under pressure.

The parties are also still capable of mobilizing voters, at least at the national level: since the abolition of compulsory voting in 1970, voting turn-out has fluctuated between 80 and 88 per cent, notwithstanding the massive increase in the size of the electorate. No clear development is discernible to suggest a structural growth in the support of what in Germany is referred to as the 'party of non-voters'. It is only at sub-national and supranational (European) elections that a recent drop in turnout has become visible, and it is simply too early to conclude that the rate of abstention at the national level will follow the trend at these other levels. Indeed, it is equally possible that voters make a rational distinction in relation to the importance of the various elections.

Dutch parties have also been very successful in integrating new political demands into their electoral platforms, even though their organizational structures have only gradually changed. When the pillarized system disintegrated in the 1960s, and when the political system seemed to be in turmoil, the major political parties adapted themselves very quickly to demands that have since been labelled as those of the 'New Politics' with the result that no new major party emerged to promote these ideas (Thomassen and van Deth, 1989). Indeed, it was the very threat that existing smaller parties or new parties might capitalize on these new issues, which is always present in an extreme proportional electoral system, that led the existing major parties to opt for change. This sort of flexibility, which is induced by the electoral system, may also continue to work in the future.

Nevertheless, as we have seen, the parties are also vulnerable. And, as in other countries, they have become subject to severe criticism. Anti-party sentiment, which does seem to have become more pervasive in the wider society, and which, of course, is difficult to measure with any precision, tends to concentrate on the alleged gap between the voters and the government. Parties, in other words, are seen to be failing to fulfil their intermediary role. Whether such a perception is accurate is difficult to say; indeed, parties have always been subject to criticism in this regard. Moreover, when the crisis of a particular party appears to work to the advantage of other parties, this would not seem to indicate that parties in general are malfunctioning. In this sense, the recent growth of support for D66 cannot easily be read as a sign of protest against the parties *tout court*, although it could well reflect an uneasiness with the traditional established parties in particular, as would a growth in the support for the xenophobic Centre Democrats.

Anti-party sentiment, such as it is, can also be largely explained as the result of factors which lie outside the parties themselves. One factor might be the economic crisis, for example, and the high rates of unemployment. Another might be the demystification of politics through the direct televising of political debates and statements. A third might be the process of individualization, and the loosening of ties between the individual citizen and collective organizations, including political parties. A fourth, and related factor might be the increasing fragmentation of society, weakening the ability of government to act in various domains, and leading to disappointment with politics in general. All of these factors contribute to a certain public hostility to politics and parties, although the parties can often hardly be held responsible for them. That said, it must be emphasized that the parties themselves have also provoked criticism. A common complaint is that they are too inward-looking, and that they pay too much attention to their own functioning and to that of the governmental machine, and too little to what is happening in society. This sometimes leads them to reactions which are too little and/or too late. In the end, however, and for all their vulnerability, the Dutch parties remain dependent on their members, and remain committed to internal democracy. And it is both of these core characteristics in their make-up which may well dissuade them from developing into semi-state institutions, and may well prevent them from becoming completely isolated from the wider society.

Notes

1 Other minor parties have also been represented in parliament over time. In the 1960s, a poujadist Farmers' Party made some short-term inroads and, at the beginning of the 1970s, right-wing members of the PvdA left the party to form the Democratic Socialists 1970 (DS '70), which participated briefly in a government coalition, but which soon lost its electoral appeal. Finally, an extreme right-wing occupied one seat in parliament from 1982 to 1986 and again since 1989. The party first called itself the Centre Party and later the Centre Democrats (CD). This xenophobic party was able to increase its electoral support in 1994 from one to three MPs.

2 Some 90 per cent of voters cast their vote for the first person on the list.

3 No regional party has ever won a seat in the national parliament. Indeed, regional parties generally do not even participate in national elections.

4 The number of municipalities was reduced as a result of administrative reforms. As far as the decline in the number of party branches is concerned, one exception would appear to be the case of the CHU, although this may well be due to the unreliability of these sparse data. Indeed, it otherwise seems surprising to see a growing number of branches, even outnumbering the total number of municipalities, especially in such a loosely organized party as the CHU.

5 Between 1975 and 1980 members of the KVP, CHU and ARP were automatically deemed to be members of the new CDA; this was a transitional phenomenon, however, and is not considered as a form of corporate membership.

6 The report of the commission was not in fact followed by a special ministerial decision, and hence the already existing rules on state subvention continue (including no special law on party finances, no direct subvention of political parties, and only 'indirect' subsidies for specific purposes to special foundations).

7 Exact calculations are difficult given that the data are not always complete, and sometimes fail to distinguish full-time and part-time personnel.

8 Including 101 for the CDA, 91 for the PvdA, 42 for the VVD and 22 for D66. See Koole (1992: 214).

9 Thus the efforts of the Interconfessional Peace Council (IKV) in 1982, of the biggest labour union (FNV) in 1986, and of the main organization of entrepreneurs (VNO) in 1989, have been generally regarded as unsuccessful, even by these organizations themselves.

References

Brants, K., Kok, W. and van Praag, Ph. (1982) *De strijd an de Kiezersgunst: verkiezings- campagnes in Nederland*. Amsterdam: Kobra.

Daalder, H. (1974) 'The Consociational Democracy Theme', *World Politics*, 26: 604–21.

Duffhues, T. (1991) 'Confessionele politieke partijen en maatschappelijke organizaties: aspecten van een duurzame relatie', in P. Luykx and H. Righart (eds), *Van de pastorie naar het Torentje: een eeuw confessionele politiek*. Den Haag: SDU, pp. 124–46.

Duverger, M. (1954) *Political Parties*. London: Methuen.

Hillebrand, R. (1992) *De antichambre van het parlement: kandidaatstelling in Nederlandse politieke partijen*. Leiden: DSWO Press.

Irwin, G.A. and van Holsteyn, J.J.M. (1989) 'Decline of the Structured Model of Electoral Competition', in H. Daalder and G.A. Irwin (eds), *Politics in the Netherlands: How Much Change?* London: pp. 21–41.

Katz, R.S. and Mair, P. (1992) 'Changing Models of Party Organization: The Emergence of the Cartel Party', paper prepared for the ECPR Joint Sessions in Limerick.

Kirchheimer, O. (1966) 'The Transformation of the Western European Party Systems', in J. LaPalombara and M. Weiner (eds), *Political Parties and Political Development*. Princeton: Princeton University Press, pp. 177–200.

Koole, R.A. (1989) 'The "Modesty" of Dutch Party Finance', in H.E. Alexander (ed.), *Comparative Political Finance in the 1980s*. Cambridge: Cambridge University Press, pp. 200–19.

Koole, R.A. (1990) 'Political Parties Going Dutch: Party Finance in the Netherlands', *Acta Politica*, 25: 37–65.

Koole, R.A. (1992) *De opkomst van de moderne kaderpartij: veranderende partijorganizatie in Nederland 1960–1990*. Utrecht: Het Spectrum.

Koole, R.A. and Leijenaar, M. (1988) 'The Netherlands: The Predominance of Region- alism', in M. Gallagher and M. Marsh (eds), *Candidate Selection in Comparative Perspective: The Secret Garden of Politics*. London: Sage, pp. 190–209.

Koole, R.A. and van de Velde, H. (1992) 'The Netherlands', in R.S. Katz and P. Mair (eds),

The Modern Cadre Party in the Netherlands 303

Party Organizations: A Data Handbook on Party Organizations in Western Democracies, 1960–90. London: Sage, pp. 619–731.

Koole, R.A. and Voerman, G. (1986) 'Het lidmaatschap van politieke partijen na 1945', in R.A. Koole (ed.), Jaarboek 1985 Documentatiecentrum Nederlandse Politieke Partijen. Groningen: pp. 115–76.

Leijenaar, M. (1989) De geschade heerlijkheid: politiek gedrag van vrouwen en mannen in Nederland, 1918–1988. 's-Gravenhage: SDU.

Lijphart, A. (1968) The Politics of Accommodation: Pluralism and Democracy in the Netherlands. Berkeley: University of California Press.

Mair, P. (1990) 'Organisatorische veranderingen en electorale stabiliteit', Beleid & Maatschappij, 1: 27–34.

Panebianco, A. (1988) Political Parties: Organization and Power. Cambridge: Cambridge University Press, (orig. in Italian, 1982).

ten Napel, H.-M. (1992) 'Een eigen weg': de totstandkoming van het CDA (1952–1980). Kampen: Kok Press.

Thomassen, J. and van Deth, J. (1989) 'How New is Dutch Politics?', in H. Daalder and G.A. Irwin (eds), Politics in the Netherlands: How Much Change?, London: Cass, pp. 61–78.

Toonen, J.A.M. (1992) Op zoek naar charisma: Nederlandse politieke partijen en hun lijsttrekkers 1963–1986. Amsterdam: VU Uitgeverij.

van den Berg, J.Th.J. (1983) De toegang tot het Binnenhof; de maatschappelijke herkomst van Tweede Kamerleden tussen 1849–1970. Weesp: van Holkema en Warendorf.

van Praag jr., Ph. (1990) Strategie en illusie: elf jaar intern debat in de PvdA (1966–1977). Amsterdam: Het Spinhuis.

Verkuil, D. (1992) Een positieve grondhouding: de geschiedenis van het CDA. 's-Gravenhage: SDU.

Waarborg van Kwaliteit: Rapport van de Commissie Subsidiëring Politieke Partijen (1991) 's-Gravenhage: Ministry of Home Affairs.

Zielonka-Goei, M.L. (1989) Uitzicht op de toekomst. Delft: DSWO Press.

12

Change and Adaptation in Norwegian Party Organizations

Lars Svåsand

Since 1960 the Norwegian party system has been characterized by, first, the loss of the Labour Party's dominant position; second, the erosion of the political centre through the virtual elimination of the Liberals and the slow decline of the Centre Party; third, a right-wing shift since the mid-1970s which has benefited the Conservative Party; and fourth, the emergence of new parties, the Socialist Left and the Progress Party, on the wings of the old party system. These changes have been accompanied by increased voter mobility and by an increasing share of those voters who decide their preferences very late in the campaign. Moreover, it has become rare for a government to survive the whole four-year period. While all of this might suggest that Norway has joined the club of countries facing a 'crisis of party' (Daalder, 1992), such 'instability in the electoral arena' should not be taken to indicate a 'decline of parties' as such.

Two processes have strengthened the role of the parties: the organizations of those parties that traditionally had weak structures have been strengthened, and 'new' organizational models have successfully been incorporated; and the linkages between party and the state have developed in such a way that it has become relevant to speak of the 'stateness of the parties' as well as the 'partyness of the state'.

The parties as organizations

Party as hierarchy

The party organization proper has three levels, corresponding to the administrative structure of the state, in which the basic unit is the municipal branch, serving the *local and regional party organization*. Recruitment to the parties usually takes place through the municipal branch, although ward organizations also serve this purpose in the larger cities. By proposing amendments to the party programme and voicing its opinion on current policy matters, the branch is also important in shaping party policy. The branches are also expected to communicate the views of the grassroots to the party leadership, nominate candidates for municipal council seats, run local campaigns and run the national election campaigns.

In 1965 a major reform of local government structures forced smaller communities to merge, reducing the number of municipalities from 732 to 465. Since then, the number has fallen further to 439 (in 1993). This strengthened the parties' grip on local politics in that many smaller communities with non-partisan local elections were combined with larger party-politicized units. Although there are still some lists of non-party candidates for local elections, the importance of such lists has declined rapidly, and in 1991 non-partisan lists polled only 3 per cent of the votes.[1] At the same time, it is only the Conservative Party which claims to have branches in all municipalities, and the smaller parties tend not to have branches in much of the country. The socialist parties, on the other hand, have two kinds of basic units, both territorial and workplace. The Labour Party and the main trade unions in Norway, the LO (*Landsorganisasjonen*), developed as sections of the 'labour movement', and until 1992, Labour allowed corporate membership via the unions, with the result that it had more than 2000 basic units (the non-socialist parties, which maintain territorial organizations only, have correspondingly fewer basic units). At workplace level, LO-unions may decide to affiliate with a local Labour Party branch. Union members may also opt out, in which case the union cannot use their fees to pay the party membership subscription. Unions do not have a block vote in party meetings. It is, however, an informal rule to include union representatives in provincial delegations to the national congress. The party and the unions are also connected at the top of the hierarchy in two important joint committees, the Committee of Cooperation between the Labour party and the LO, and the Labour Movement's Committee for International Cooperation. In addition, the unions are represented in the party's governing bodies and hold cabinet posts in Labour governments.

Norway's nineteen provinces (*fylket*) also serve as the constituencies for parliamentary elections, and the provincial branch of each party therefore serves several functions. First, it is the basis for representation in the national conventions and national committees within the party. Second, the provincial branch nominates candidates for *Storting* elections and the provincial council (*fylkesting*) elections. Third, the 1975 reform that introduced direct elections to the *fylkesting* simultaneously gave the provinces responsibility for several policy areas, thus obliging provincial parties to develop political priorities for sectors that were previously managed by national or local government.

Although there are no formal direct links between the local and the national levels, recent technological changes have altered the picture. All parties now maintain centralized and computerized membership archives. Previously, the central level knew *how many* members there were, but not *who* they were; now, the central office can use direct mail to by-pass local and regional party units and is much better equipped to challenge local branch claims for membership-based central support. Television has also reduced the ability of local and regional leaders to control communication between national leaders and the grassroots. The focus on the central party leadership during election campaigns – also during local and provincial council elections – adds to the weight of the top and the centre of the party. However, local and regional activists in all parties have learned to use television's appetite for internal party conflicts to promote their own aims. It is therefore doubtful that television alone has increased party centralization.

The national extra-parliamentary organization

The national conventions of Labour and the Socialist Left have a fixed or maximum number of delegates (300) while the number of delegates in the non-socialist party congresses varies in accordance with membership strength and/or electoral support. Labour formerly assigned delegates to the provincial parties based on membership strength alone before shifting in 1973 to a system in which 200 of the 300 delegates were allocated on the basis of membership and the remainder according to electoral strength, thus clearly increasing the party's 'electoral orientation'. In the non-socialist organizations, the conventions also include representatives from ancillary organizations (women, youth, students, etc.), as well as members of parliament and cabinet members on an ex officio basis. In the Labour party, however, all voting delegates (including those from the women's organization) must be elected as part of a provincial party delegation or as part of the parliamentary group representation of one delegate for every ten members. This may be intended to enhance the importance of the party organization proper and prevent its role from being diluted by representatives whose main loyalty lies elsewhere in the broader party movement. In the Socialist Left Party it is only elected representatives from the local branches (and the current national council) who may take part and vote, while the parliamentary representatives may attend and speak. The youth movement has up to eight representatives but, following the bad experience of the party's forerunner, the Socialist People's Party (see p. 311), these can vote only on matters relating to the party's programme of principles. Finally, while the Socialist Left Party does not afford any representation to party employees, Labour allows central party functionaries to attend, without voting rights, and the non-socialist parties have given party secretaries ample representation at several levels. Officially, the national convention is the 'highest organ' of each party (see Heidar, 1988). It elects the party leadership and has the sole right to change the party statutes. Further, the convention adopts the party platform for each parliamentary term.

Since 1960, the structures of the party organizations have become more similar across parties in what might be seen as a process of adaptation to Labour's organizational model. In the Conservative, Liberal and Christian

People's parties there used to be only one national committee, with an internal subcommittee. All of these parties changed in the early 1970s to the established Labour Party practice of having two committees: a larger national committee with representation from the provincial (and ancillary) organizations, and a smaller executive committee, often with a still smaller subcommittee. There are probably several explanations for this development, including the arrival in the late 1960s of a new generation of leaders concerned with the functioning of the extra-parliamentary organization that took over the Conservative Party (Sejersted, 1984). Labour, in particular, served as a model for these leaders. Second, the 1960s witnessed an uproar against elitist rule and authority, and the reorganization of the top level of the parties extended the opportunities for participation and influence. Third, the introduction of state subsidies for party organizations in 1970 made it that much easier for parties to maintain more complex organizations.

Compared to the other 'old' parties, the Conservatives have undergone numerous and extensive organizational changes, many of which can be associated with the conflicts between the party's traditional 'parliamentary orientation' and a new 'organizational orientation'. These changes also reflect the strains caused by a rapid growth in membership and geographic coverage. The standardization of the party structures towards the 'Labour Party model' is also evident in the cases of the two new parties, the Socialist Left Party (SV) and the Progress Party (FRP). The SV organization originally (1975) had two special characteristics: individuals could not serve in the same office for more than four years, and the parliamentary group had only a limited number of seats on the national executive committee. By 1984 both of these had been dropped. The term limitation rule underestimated the importance of 'organizational memory' and also the difficulties of finding people willing and able to take on organizational roles, while the restriction on parliamentary representation in the national executive committee conflicted with the need for coordination inside and outside parliament. One novelty which was introduced by the SV was a gender quota, which required the national convention and committees on all levels to have at least 40 per cent of each gender and the list of candidates for public offices to alternate between men and women. This requirement has since spread to other parties (Liberals, 1981, Labour, 1983, Centre Party, 1989) and in reality is also observed in the Christian People's Party and the Conservatives, even without a formal rule.

The FRP originally (1973) represented another type of organization. As a protest against the dominant political consensus in Norway, the party – or rather movement – revolted against the 'old-fashioned' type of bureaucratic parties and organizations. The party's founder, Anders Lange, believed in 'spontaneous action' (Harmel and Svåsand, 1989) and rejected the idea of formal party organization. After his death in 1974, however, the party rapidly lost electoral support, and a new leadership took over with the idea of building an organization which would make the party credible in the eyes of the voters as well as among other parties. Although still struggling with internal conflicts over organization and policy, the party has now developed a set of rules and organizational units which are like those of the other parties.

Parties as parallel structures

Each of the parties represented in the *Storting* has a parliamentary party organization (*stortingsgruppe*), which is separate from, but of course linked to, the regular party organization, and which is headed by the party's parliamentary leader (*parlamentarisk fører*). Even just one representative is sufficient to constitute a parliamentary group, and even when there are just two members, one acts as parliamentary leader. The parliamentary leader is the main spokesperson for the party and plays therefore a vital role in inter-party negotiations; that person can also take part in the parliament's 'extended committee on foreign affairs and constitutional matters'.

Government members are recruited partly from parliament and partly from outside parliament, and members of parliament who are appointed to cabinet posts have to resign (temporarily) their seats. If the person is parliamentary leader, the group elects a replacement, and when the person leaves government office and returns to parliament, he or she has to be re-elected group leader. Thus, the positions of party chair and chair of the parliamentary group may be combined, as may those of party chair and cabinet member, but the combination of cabinet member and MP is impossible. In the Labour Party, it is normal for the party leader to be also parliamentary leader, and hence the party's candidate for prime minister; thus while the Labour parliamentary leader is officially elected by the parliamentary group, in many cases the choice is effectively made by the national council of the party. In the past thirty years, it has only been in the tumultuous years following the EC debacle (1975–81) that the two posts have not been held by the same person.

The Conservatives used to follow the opposite pattern, with the parliamentary wing clearly dominant; in the late 1980s, however, a new pattern developed with the same person holding both offices. The party leaders of the other non-socialist parties tend to be re-elected for several terms: Johan J. Jacobsen was leader of the Centre Party for twelve years; in 1993, Carl I. Hagen had been leader of the Progress Party for thirteen years, and Kjell Magne Bondevik was in his ninth year as chair of the Christian People's Party. The Conservative Party, however, is known for its 'leadership cannibalism', with eight chairmen between 1962 and 1993. The rapid changes in party rules, the battle between the parliamentary wing, the party organization and the ancillary organizations, together with rapid membership growth in the 1970s and early 1980s, have clearly made it difficult to find persons who are able to reconcile the different elements in the party. This problem has probably been exacerbated by the party's need to compromise in government while at the same time meeting the Progress Party's challenge from the right.

While most parties try to manage party–parliament relations through cross-membership and the representation of organizational leaders at meetings of the parliamentary group, the potential for conflict was illustrated by the experience of the Liberal Party in 1972. This party was particularly badly divided on the question of EC membership, with the national council being dominated by the anti-EC group and the parliamentary fraktion by the pro-EC group. When the minority Labour government resigned after the defeat of the referendum on EC membership, the national council of the Liberals ordered the parliamentary group to take part in the formation of an interim anti-EC government. This was rejected by the pro-EC fraktion in parliament, for reasons of both politics and principles. The minority fraktion nevertheless joined the other non-socialists in forming a government, and eventually this proved to be the final straw breaking the party apart (Garvik, 1982). It is inconceivable that the parliamentary wing could claim such autonomy in the socialist camp.

From the right as well as from the left, the position of the parliamentary group has been changing from either dominance in the party organization or total exclusion from it, to some kind of middle position. Conservative parliamentarians have lost their majority position within their party's executive and national committees as representatives from various sub-groups within the party have been added. The Socialist Left has moved in the opposite direction, no longer excluding the parliamentary group per se from the party's senior bodies. In 1985 a clause limiting MPs or party employees to less than 50 per cent of the representation on the executive and national council members was removed. Simultaneously, the statutes made it mandatory for the parliamentary leader and his/her deputy to meet in the national council, while also allowing access to other MPs. These changes, as well as the party chairman's desperate search for nomination in a 'safe' district in 1989, underline the importance of the parliamentary group to the party as a whole. In Labour, the national executive committee organizes the parliamentary group and is represented at its board and meetings. Several of the non-socialist parties, although always affording ample representation to MPs, altered their rules to ensure that the leader of the parliamentary group was represented on the national committees even if not otherwise elected.

The Progress Party represents a clear exception here. Since 1990, the national executive has been represented in the parliamentary group by five members and has the final say on the political strategy and budget; it also even functions as a source of appeal for the minority in the parliamentary group. Moreover, from 1994, the rules regulating the structure and functions of the parliamentary group will become part of the party organizational statutes, which means that the parliamentary group cannot change the rules regulating its own activity. The reason for this probably lies in the sudden increase in the size of the parliamentary group in 1989, growing from two to twenty-two seats. By subordinating the group to the party organization, it is more likely that the party leader, Carl I. Hagen, can maintain control of the fraktion. While it is unlikely that a majority in the executive committee would oppose him, a vastly expanded parliamentary group in which few people owe their nomination to him or to the central leadership in general certainly provides a potential for the sort of revolt which has already happened in the Danish Progress Party (see Harmel and Svåsand, 1991)

Party discipline is tight in all parties and party voting therefore very high (see Shaffer, 1991). The statutes of the two socialist parties require that the party's MPs vote according to the party programme, and the Socialist Left Party has made it clear from the start that the party's national committee can instruct the parliamentary group how to vote on other matters as well. While such a requirement is not explicit in the rules of the non-socialist parties, it is nevertheless expected. That said, there are occasions when voting along party lines breaks down. These involve, first, issues which pit region against region, such as the location of large public projects such as airports, and in which the party line is often relaxed. Second, on issues which concern moral and ethical questions, such as abortion, the individual members are often free to vote according to their consciences – particularly if they made their views known when nominated. Formal rules notwithstanding, the parliamentary groups control important assets that may give them the upper hand. The most important of these are professionalism, experience and the fact that the MPs are a small group meeting frequently, whereas their potential 'opponents' represent different organizational elements and/or are geographically dispersed.

The party as complex organization

The party organization proper is supplemented by a complex web of ancillary organizations, three of which – the women's movement, the youth movement and the educational organization – are found in most parties. Also linked to the parties are 'associations of newspapers' and, in the case of Labour, the trade unions.

All parties have a youth organization; with the exceptions of Progress and the Socialist Left, they also have a women's organization, the exceptions here being explained by their being new parties, whereas special organizations for women in the other parties reflect a traditional view of women as voters but not as active participants in the parties themselves. With the increasing political mobilization of women these organizations have become more active at the same time as they come to be seen as obsolete. In the SV a special women's organization was seen as incompatible with the party's conception of women's political and social roles, and for different reasons the Progress Party arrived at the same conclusion, insisting that women should compete with men for office and nomination. In fact, as a result of its recruitment practices and its opposition to the welfare state, the Progress Party scores lower on women's representation than any other party.[2] In a recent effort to change its image, however, the party has established a women's committee at the central level and has sought female candidates for one of the two deputy leader positions. Here too, then, there has been a convergence of party organizations, in that changes in the representation rules for women and the widespread acceptance of women's political interests (Skjeie, forthcoming) have placed the traditional women's branches under strain. Membership has been declining faster than in the regular party branches. Membership in the women's branches accounted for 25 per cent of total Conservative Party membership in 1970, for example, but only 6 per cent in 1980, and the party's women's organization decided to disband in 1994. Similar proposals in the Centre Party have been rejected, however, mainly due to opposition from the women's organizations themselves, which have found them an excellent focus for mobilization and as a means of ensuring organizational and political representation.

Although most of the current top leadership in the parties emerged from the various youth branches, the relationship between the two organizations is often conflictual, with the youth organization being frequently more radical than the main party. In the Liberal, Centre and Christian People's parties, scepticism towards cooperation with the Conservatives has always been more pronounced within the youth organization than in the main party. In the Labour and Liberal parties the youth organizations have been opposed to NATO membership and strategy, and both strongly opposed EC membership, whereas the Labour Party officially favoured Norwegian membership. In the Socialist People's Party, the forerunner of the Socialist Left Party, the youth organization broke with the party and formed the nucleus of the Marxist-Leninist Party, an experience which was not lost on the Socialist Left. Thus, the Socialist Left Party is now the only party where the representatives of the youth branch do not have voting rights in the party's executive committee.

In 1965 the *Storting* established a set of subsidies for adult courses run by voluntary associations and, as a result, all parties established their own *educational associations*. In theory, these offer courses for the general public, but in practice most serve as mechanisms to educate the parties' own memberships. These educational organizations are not based on individual membership but are made up of other organizations, such as the party proper, and the youth and the women's branches. While their size, measured in terms of the number of courses and participants, generally follows the general membership fluctuations in the parties, the Socialist Left Party nevertheless illustrates how an 'activist' party can use this opportunity to improve its otherwise weak organizational apparatus. In 1981/82, for example, and with just one-sixth of the membership of the Christian People's Party, the SV had twice as many courses and participants. The SV (and the SF) mobilized strongly among young voters, and particularly among university students and graduates. The 'law on adult education' was therefore perfect for its members, compared, say, to the Christian People's Party, with its strong presence among older women in rural areas.

New ancillary organizations have also emerged. In the Conservative Party in 1978, against the will of the central leadership, the elderly succeeded in gaining recognition as an ancillary organization, which guaranteed them representation at the national convention. They have not, however, been allocated representation at higher levels in the party hierarchy. The parties also maintain branches for students which, in the socialist parties, affiliate with a municipal party, while in the non-socialist parties they have direct representation at the national level. Finally, unions of party employees have also gained internal representation. These organizations have developed as a result of professionalization and because of legal rules that regulate relationships between employers and employees; and although they probably do not indicate attempts by the bureaucrats to establish a niche for themselves in the party hierarchy, they may very well have this consequence. In the Labour and Socialist Left parties, such representation is limited to sending non-voting delegates to the national congresses, while in the non-socialist parties, employees have also obtained representation on the governing boards.

In general, however, the parties are sceptical about fragmentation into separate units, and the initiatives to abolish the women's organizations and replace them with some kind of 'committee', as is already the case in the Socialist Left and the Progress parties, is likely to be repeated. Labour is unique in being formally linked to an external organization, the LO. Through interlocking committees at the top, and corporate membership at the local level, the party and the unions have been (until now) inextricably linked. Although other parties lack such formal organizational connections, there is nevertheless extensive personnel overlap and, most importantly, ideological overlap, with 'their' organizations. Indeed, it is only the Socialist Left, the Progress Party and the old Liberals that have lacked a distinct foothold in a major part of the corporate society.

The press and the parties: from partners to independent actors

The press in Norway has always been closely identified with the parties, albeit not necessarily under their ownership. Only the Labour Party, the Socialist Left and the traditional Communist Party run newspapers from the central party office, although several local papers are also run as companies in which the local party organization is one among several owners.[3] On the non-socialist side the parties rarely own newspapers, but local branches may be part shareholders. More frequently, while ownership is non-partisan, newspapers subscribing to a particular 'ideology' nevertheless become members of party-affiliated organizations.

Party-affiliated newspapers accounted for 32 per cent of total newspaper circulation in 1990 (NOU, 1992: 38), as against 82 per cent in 1950 (Høyer, 1982: 161). Moreover, press representation within the parties is also clearly in decline. The Conservatives admitted nine (in 1960) and later thirteen (in 1979) delegates representing the Conservative press association to their national congress, but abolished press representation completely in 1983. In the Liberal Party, the press continues to be represented, but the formal rules conceal the fact that there are now few officially liberal newspapers. Even the Labour Party newspaper is less tied to the party than used to be the case. Faced with increasing competition, declining class identification and tumbling circulation, the Labour newspaper has explicitly begun to criticize the party leadership and has even published information confidential to the party. One symptom of the weakening linkage between party and press came in 1983 when Labour changed its statutes in order to drop the newspaper editor from the party's executive committee. In the Socialist Left, a revision of the party statutes in 1987 removed the editor of the party newspaper as a voting member of the executive committee.

The membership party

Norwegian political parties have a long tradition as membership-based parties. The 'model' here has been the Labour Party, which features massive membership figures, a powerful central bureaucracy, a strong organizational culture and a sense of 'belonging' that links party leaders closely to the grassroots. This mass membership model has also been adopted by bourgeois parties. Some 16 per cent of the Norwegian electorate claim membership in a political party, a figure which was relatively stable over the thirty-year period from the end of the 1950s to the end of the 1980s (see Figure 12.1). Only in the early 1970s, amidst the turbulence of the EC membership struggle, did membership drop significantly. The overall figure nevertheless hides significant variations between the parties, with some experiencing substantial growth, and others decline. That said, the most recent figures again point towards decline for the larger parties.

While the Labour, Centre and Liberal parties have all lost members more or less consistently, it has been for different reasons. Labour suffered a severe shock when it lost a third of its members after the 1972 EC debacle. Even before then, however, the party had been in continuous decline since the immediate post-war period. Since the early 1970s there has been some recovery, both electorally and organizationally, and in 1985 the membership levels, at about 174,000, were more or less the same as they had been in the early 1950s. Thereafter, membership has again declined to less than 130,000, the lowest level in the post-war period. Both individual and corporate membership has fallen, but the latter is particularly striking, falling by 50 per cent between 1971 and 1988. In 1971

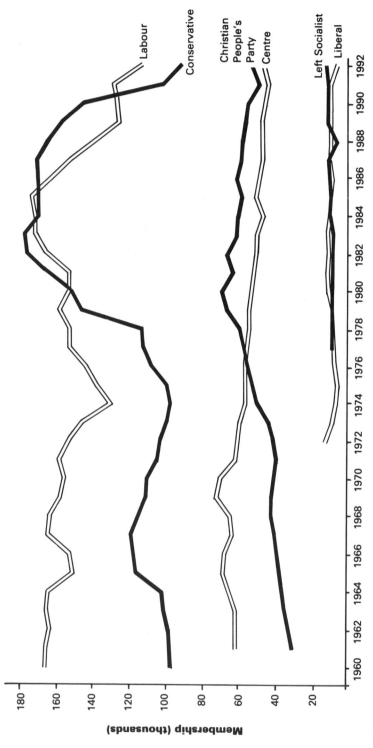

Figure 12.1 *Trends in party membership. (Progress Party not included due to lack of time-series data. Membership in 1989 was 16,874.)* (Norwegian Social Science Data Services)

corporate members accounted for half the total membership in the party; in 1989 this had fallen to just 24 per cent.

One factor lying behind this gradual separation of party and unions is surely the declining linkage between social class and voting (Listhaug, forthcoming) which, in turn, is reflected in the membership figures. In addition, there have also been changes in the union movement itself. First, the number of local union branches has declined considerably as local branches have merged to form larger units, and as smaller unions have merged they have tended not to affiliate with the party. Second, trade unionism is no longer identical with the LO, and the Labour affiliated unions have been losing members to new, politically neutral, unions. In 1976 the LO had 80 per cent of the membership of the three largest peak organizations, but in 1993 this figure had fallen to 58 per cent. Moreover, faced with competition from the new unions, the LO has had to loosen its ties to Labour, and the close links which once existed between the two, and which were once a source of strength for both parts of the labour movement, have now become a mutual liability. In 1992 the unions and the party agreed to phase out collective membership over a four-year period, as had already happened in Sweden.

The Centre Party has also experienced a modest, but consistent decline in membership, a decline which is rooted in the party's 'sectarian' character. Unlike similar parties in Finland and Sweden, the Norwegian party has not managed to attract urban voters (Christensen, 1992), and remains deeply entrenched within the agricultural community: a third of its voters in 1985 were farmers or fishermen, occupational groups which accounted for between 40 and 66 per cent of the party's provincial branch members. As this population has declined, so has the 'natural' constituency of the party. Presently, however, the party claims a strong increase in membership, although this does not necessarily imply that the trend has been reversed. The break-up of the government in late 1990 had been provoked by the EC issue, and the party now benefits from its consistent opposition to 'the drift towards EC membership', with which it had to live so long as it took part in the government. Increasing membership may therefore reflect the salience of the EC issue in Norwegian politics, rather than a long term affiliation to the Centre Party.

The third party in organizational decline, the Liberals, is again a different case. As a party that has always appealed to a broad range of social groups, the Liberals have not been similarly affected by changes in social structure. Organizationally the party was weak, and at the electoral level it has suffered from voter disloyalty – even in the politically tranquil 1950s and 1960s (Valen, 1981). Nor was it able to cope with the EC issue in the early 1970s, when internal conflicts reinforced already existing political and personal rivalries (Garvik, 1982), and resulted in an actual split. Neither the splinter party nor the remaining Liberal Party has since proved able to recover (Leipart and Svåsand, 1988), and in 1988 they again merged, albeit to little avail.

Until recently, the overall losses of these three parties have been compensated for by an increased membership in the Conservative and Christian People's parties, and by the formation of new parties. In 1990 the Labour and the Centre parties together had about 43,000 fewer members than they had in 1965, and during the same time-span Conservative and Christian People's party membership grew by 49,000. In the Conservative Party a downward trend in membership was reversed in the early 1970s, when the party rapidly expanded its organization and proved successful in mobilizing voters as well as members. But while membership figures almost doubled from 1960 to 1983, they have since declined to the 1979 level. The same pattern was true in the Christian People's Party, where membership more than doubled from 1961 to 1980, but then slowly declined. While there are several factors that may account for this development, it appears that in the case of the Conservative Party, new leaders introduced a different conception of the party organization (see Sejersted, 1984). The Conservative Party had always had an ambivalent view of its organization, which was not regarded as being an activist movement like Labour. Yet, some Conservative leaders acknowledged that what the party needed was precisely that: a large group of followers that could be mobilized at election time. In addition, the style and culture of the party organization had to adapt to the rapid changes in social structure brought about by educational expansion and geographic and social mobility. Thus, to some extent, the growth in membership reflects a change in party philosophy whereby the mass organization received much more attention from the central party leadership. But what is also interesting to note is that the electoral effect of membership expansion has differed across the two parties. Electoral support for the Christian People's Party has remained remarkably stable. In the Conservative Party, however, the organizational build-up occurred more or less simultaneously with a dramatic increase in voting support, from 17 per cent in 1973 to 32 per cent in 1981.

The total national membership figure has also been maintained to some extent by the rise of new parties: the Socialist People's Party (1961), its successor, the Socialist Left Party (1975), and the Progress Party (1973). Although these parties together polled more than 23 per cent of the votes in 1989, they have proved considerably weaker as mass membership organizations, having each some 13,000 members. Moreover, despite occupying the opposite ends of the left–right continuum, both the SV and the FRP share a certain number of organizational features, albeit for different reasons. The SV has sought to build an organizational alternative to the top-heavy bureaucratic machine they perceive in Labour, and hence the emphasis has been on activity rather than on formal organization. Similarly, the FRP began as a protest movement opposed to the very idea of formal organization (Harmel and Svåsand, 1989), and particularly in the early phase of its history, attracted people with a rather low interest in politics.

These aggregate membership figures should not mislead us into believing that all is well in the Norwegian parties, however, in that the gross figures disguise two important aspects of the party organization: stability and activity. As one investigation has shown, for example, membership turnover can be very high, and in 1981 only 46 per cent of respondents claiming party membership had also been members four years earlier (Selle and Svåsand, 1991). Moreover, while synchronic surveys have shown that 16 per cent of the electorate are party members, Rose and Waldahl (1982) found that between 1965 and 1973 31 per cent of their respondents claimed to have been party members at one stage or another. In this sense, party membership is surprisingly volatile.[4]

There are also several indicators of passivity in the party organizations. Membership attendance at meetings is low and it is difficult to get members to accept nominations to party as well as public (particularly municipal) office (Hellevik and Skard, 1985: Ch. 6), and a 1983 survey comparing activity levels in various types of organizations found that fewer than 10 per cent of party members could be defined as 'active'. Indeed, only in trade unions and housing cooperatives was the level of activity as low as that in the parties. In a similar vein, a report to the 1983 national Labour Party convention stated that 'almost independent of the total number of members there are only 15 to 30 activists, and membership attendance at meetings is seldom higher than 25 per cent' (DNA, 1983). These problems are not specific to Labour, of course, but run across the entire party spectrum. In the Socialist Left, for example, the number of non-paying members has averaged 20 per cent for the last three years, which is quite high for a party emphasizing active participation. In addition, a recent Conservative Party report claims that 'most (60–70 per cent) of members of the Conservative party are first of all interested in supporting the party through paying the fees. They do not really wish to be active . . .'.[5] Finally, in a recently completed survey of party members, Heidar (1994) found that 53 per cent of all party members never attended any party meeting or party function in 1990.[6] Given the absence of adequate time-series data on this question, however, it is difficult to ascertain whether it is a growing problem.

Centralization of party organizations

Although the party statutes specify what tasks the national conventions must perform, each convention is in theory free to establish its own rules of operation regarding both the *control of the congress itself and the election of leadership*. In reality, however, the central party leadership controls much of the agenda. Similarly, while the leader of the party organization is elected at the national convention, the process begins with the report of an official search committee to the national council which, in turn, includes its recommendation on the agenda of the national convention. Nevertheless, leadership control is far from complete. The search committee receives proposals for candidates from various units in the party organization, as well as from individual members, and both the election of office-holders and the revision of the party programme also are open to initiatives from the floor.

As far as the *nomination of candidates* is concerned, the provincial branches nominate candidates for parliamentary and provincial council elections, while municipal nomination is a matter for the municipal branch and, following the electoral law of 1920, the government is committed to pay travel and accommodation expenses for delegates to these nomination meetings provided that these are constituted according to certain rules of proportionality. But while this law does not prevent the influence of the central party leadership on the nomination process, nevertheless most province associations are fairly independent in this respect in practice (Valen, 1988). This can be explained in part by the pre-1952 requirement that candidates reside in the constituency where they are nominated. Even after this clause was removed, however, the provincial associations have remained quite autonomous, and attempts to centralize the nomination processes have proved unsuccessful. In 1973 the Labour Party introduced a rule requiring provincial associations to submit a list of candidates to be cleared by a national coordinating committee before the final nomination. This proved both unpopular and impractical, however, and the rule was repealed in 1983. Even when a provincial party has violated internal party rules, as happened in 1985 in the Labour Party, the central party office is unable to force a new nomination meeting. Similarly, the Socialist Left has limited central level involvement in a committee that may propose new nominations if a province violates the gender quota rules.

Given the almost 'extreme' attention paid in Norway to geographic representation, attempts on the part of the central party leadership to influence the selection, or to parachute candidates, are rare. In 1989 the leader of the Socialist People's Party lost the bid for nomination in his own district and, desperately wanting to be elected to parliament in order to exert more control over the parliamentary wing of the party, he succeeded in being nominated in another constituency. This was quite exceptional, however.

Even if not formally, *election campaigns* are becoming more centralized due to changes in campaign techniques and in the structure of the media. Strategy is settled at the national council and executed by the party on the ground. The campaign may of course be adapted to local contexts, but the main message and partly also the main actors are dominated by the central party leadership. Moreover, the expansion in physical communication in Norway in the last decades has made it possible for the national party leadership to tour the whole country, which would have been unthinkable in the 1950s. Second, the introduction of television in 1960 gave national leaders a primary role in election programmes, which not only added to the strength of the national party apparatus but also, it is claimed, increased the importance of personalities in party politics. Traditional campaign meetings are certainly in decline, except when a senior national politician appears, and even campaigns for local and province council elections are being 'nationalized' in this way. That said, further changes may yet be wrought through the proliferation of local television and radio stations. Third, the newspaper market is becoming more 'nationalized' as a result of both changes in the publishing industry and improved communications. The three largest Oslo dailies – which for all practical purposes have become national papers – alone control some 40 per cent of the total newspaper circulation in Norway.

As far as *policy formulation* is concerned, the national convention in all parties is the supreme party body, and among its tasks is the adoption of the party programme. There are two types of programmes: the programme of principles, and the election programme. In the first, the parties outline their views on how society ought to be organized, their main party values, and so on. Such programmes are revised very infrequently. Election programmes, on the other hand, tend to be quite voluminous booklets and are mixtures of specific policies or policy targets and more general viewpoints. A draft is prepared about a year in advance and is usually sent to the grassroots organizations in the party, which may then submit proposals for changes, or new items to be included. The programme committee then submits a revised draft to the national committee, before a final draft is presented to the convention. The debate at the convention may result in further changes. This long process is possible because there is never any doubt about the timing of elections. However, there is also usually little conflict over the main policy lines developed in the programme, and as Heidar (1988) reports, an astounding 87 per cent of congress delegates report that there was no discussion of, or disagreement with, the central party's proposal in their own local party branches.

Party rules may be changed only at the national convention. In the non-socialist parties proposals for changes must be submitted to the national executive committee some months in advance of the convention. This rule is not included in the statutes of the socialist parties, which therefore allow the leadership to propose last minute changes in the party statutes. This happened in the Labour Party in 1989, when a conflict over the election of a new deputy leader was 'solved' by changing the rules in order to allow two deputy leaders rather than one, after which both contestants for the post were elected. Rule changes in the non-socialist parties require a two-thirds majority, whereas a simple majority is sufficient in the socialist parties.

More generally, any assessment of *the power balance between national and lower levels* must recognize the capacity of party units at the lower levels to assert themselves more strongly against the central level, a capacity which has been enhanced by the financial independence accruing from the provision of state funds earmarked for local and regional party organizations. Moreover, in several parties, all income from fee-paying members is retained by the local units (the reverse of this, of course, is that the national office may also be more independent of the grassroots). From another perspective, it is often argued that modern communication techniques have contributed to the centralization of the parties, and this is certainly true in the sense that the mass media allow national leaders to speak directly to voters and members, by-passing the party apparatus. Here too, however, the lower levels have also benefited, and successful campaigns to effect a change of party leaders and party policies have begun at grassroots, funnelled by sensation-hungry journalists. Moreover, with the loosening of the ties between the newspapers and the parties, it is increasingly impossible for party leaders to prevent the publication of critical articles.

Political alliances have been also formed at the local and regional levels between parties that are opposed to one another at the national level. In one city, for example, the Conservatives allied themselves with the Progress Party, while the national leadership was under pressure to distance themselves from the same party. Later, in Oslo, the Conservatives succeeded in building an alliance with Progress and the Christian People's Party, even though the national leadership of the latter unsuccessfully attempted to prevent the party's participation. More generally, rather than arguing that the balance between national and lower level units has been tilted in a certain direction, it is probably more correct to say that parties have become increasingly fragmented internally, and that the distribution of power has become correspondingly more stratarchic.

The state and the parties

Although political parties are not explicitly protected by the constitution, it may be argued that their existence is assumed by a proportional electoral system, and they are assumed to be covered by constitutional guarantees of the right to associate and freedom of expression. Parties are acknowledged in ordinary laws, of course, but Norway lacks a specific law that applies explicitly to parties as organizations. There are no rules regulating what parties can do, for example, or about how to conduct election campaigns, and so on. On the other hand, the rules governing the nomination of candidates for public office allow parties to have part of the expenses for nomination meetings covered if they follow certain rules,[7] and the introduction of public finance for parties can also be read as an explicit recognition of their role in the political system. From a legal point of view, however, Norwegian parties have only a marginal relationship to the state.

That said, the real picture is something different, for ever since the introduction of public party finance, Norwegian parties have become almost totally dependent on the state for their existence. The 'stateness' of the parties is therefore one of the most significant changes in the Norwegian political system, which could potentially have many conse-

Table 12.1   *State subsidy per vote and total sums appropriated for national party organizations*

Year	Nkr. per vote	Total subsidy (Nkr. million)
1970	3.7	8.0
1971	3.7	8.0
1972	4.6	10.0
1973	5.1	11.0
1974	6.1	13.0
1975	6.5	14.0
1976	8.4	18.2
1977	8.6	19.6
1978	8.6	19.6
1979	9.1	21.0
1980	9.1	21.0
1981	12.0	27.5
1982	12.5	31.3
1983	13.6	34.0
1984	14.4	36.0
1985	15.6	39.0
1986	16.5	43.0
1987	18.8	49.0
1988	21.1	55.0
1989	21.4	56.7
1990	22.1	58.7
1991	22.1	58.7

Source: *Storting* reports 1970–91

quences for the way parties function. Nevertheless, it is difficult to talk of causal effects in this case, in that the time span between the 'cause' (public subsidies) and the 'effect' (say, declining membership activity) is such that a number of different factors may have come into play. One effect that is easily visible, however, is increased bureaucratization in the form of an expanded corps of salaried personnel; but how this might have affected party activity is more difficult to judge.

Party finances: from voluntary associations to 'state institutions'?

Despite the provision of public subsidies, the parties are still not required to publish their accounts, and therefore information about their income and expenditures is difficult both to compare and to assess. The most important change in party finance occurred in 1970 when state subsidies for national party organizations were introduced (see Table 12.1), although parliament began to support staff for the parliamentary groups about a decade earlier. In addition, there are various other types of direct and indirect support that contribute to the whole picture of state subventions.

When the members of the *Storting* introduced public subsidies to party organizations, they must have realized that the decision would affect the internal life of the parties, particularly insofar as the decision undermined one of the rationales for a mass party. Public finance was necessary, the parties argued, because political parties played such an important role in a democratic society. Moreover, public subsidies would reduce the dependency of parties on large donors. The Conservatives were hesitant about the proposal, and there were, and still are, disagreements about the criteria for allocating the funds. However, only the Progress Party now opposes the idea of state subventions (Svåsand, 1991). All registered parties nominating candidates in at least one constituency in at least two consecutive elections are eligible on a per vote basis for general support with no strings attached. The sums for this purpose are included in the government's annual budget proposal, and both these amounts and the rules for their allocation have been subject to several modifications over the years.

In 1975 financial support was limited to parties that polled at least 2.5 per cent of the vote,[8] and from 1975 onwards subsidies have also been given to municipal and provincial branches, based on election results at those levels. In 1978 support was further extended to include the parties' youth organizations. The amounts involved have also changed, and annual subsidies to party organizations have climbed from Nkr. 8 million in 1970 to more than Nkr. 121 million in the early 1990s. Moreover, with time, the share of all state subvention has been tilted towards the upper level. In 1976 the national party organizations received about 39 per cent of the total subventions, as against 47 per cent in 1988. Indeed, each vote at national level is now worth three times that at local level (in 1970 the parties received Nkr. 3.70 per vote; today they receive Nkr. 21.10). It is also revealing to note that a majority in parliament almost always adds money to the ministry proposal, regardless of which party controls the government. Only in the beginning, and then again in 1978 and 1979, was parliament actually satisfied with the proposed budget, and in all other years the final appropriations exceeded the government proposal. In 1987, for example, the Labour government proposal of a 4.5 per cent increase was supported only by the Conservative and Progress parties; not even the Labour group supported the suggested level.

State subventions for the parties themselves tell only half the story, however, for there are also additional subsidies that are not targeted to parties per se, but which nevertheless are important for their activities, such as the support for parliamentary groups, the support for the press and the support for educational associations. Opponents of the general subvention of parties used the existence of these measures as an argument against further subventions, claiming that they were sufficient to support the parties' main functions. Supporters of general subvention used them to support expanding the government's responsibility for party finance. They argued that these indirect measures proved that the state had recognized the contribution of parties to the democratic system, and hence it was natural for the state to make sure the parties were well equipped to carry out their tasks. The political parties certainly benefit from the state subsidies to the *press* which were introduced in 1969 (the subsidy totalled

Nkr. 277 million in 1989) and which are aimed at maintaining a 'differentiated press' by subsidizing both the production and distribution of newspapers. All parties have an internal newspaper and have organized press bureaus. In addition, Labour and the Socialist Left Party run their own newspaper and many other newspapers continue to lean towards a party or certainly a block of parties. The principle of government support for the press is therefore of vital importance to the parties for, in addition to any indirect support the parties receive through subsidies for 'friendly' newspapers, there is also support for their own internal newspapers. In 1989, for example, some Nkr. 21 million was allocated to a set of publications, almost all of which were party newspapers. Similarly, parties represented in parliament received more than Nkr. 4 million for their press offices.

Public support for *voluntary education* has a long tradition in Norway, and in this sense the political parties are just another type of voluntary organization that runs educational programmes (which, with the exception of Progress, is true for all of the parties). Nevertheless, prior to the 1960s, there was a tendency to differentiate between the parties' general political activity and their educational purposes. Without such differentiation, it was argued, party organizations in general would be supported while other types of organizations would be denied support. With time, however, it became impossible to maintain such a differentiation, and in 1967 Nkr. 7.2 million was appropriated for adult education, and in 1989 almost Nkr. 155 million, of which the party-affiliated organizations received close to 50 per cent. But while it is certainly true that the parties would have been unable to carry on their extensive educational arrangements without subsidy, it is also the case that there have been allegations of fraud, in which party-affiliated educational associations are said to have been paid excessively for courses which were never held.

Support for the *parliamentary groups* was first introduced in the 1960s when parliament allocated secretarial assistance to the parties, and while these secretaries were originally assumed to be at the disposal of the parliament as such when it was not in session, the party groups nevertheless quickly took complete control of the positions. In spite of this support, the parliamentary parties also have come to depend on extra support from the party organization itself. The Norwegian parliament has relatively few resources to cope with the increasing amount and complexity of cases submitted by the government, as well as with issues raised by the public, and dependence on the party organization is especially pronounced in the smaller parties. Another important subsidy is free travel for parliamentarians. In clause 65 in the Constitution, members of parliament are given the right to free domestic travel, without regard for its purpose. As there is considerable overlap between the parliamentary groups and the top of the organizational apparatus in the parties, this prerogative is in reality a considerable subsidy which makes it possible for the party leadership to communicate with various levels and parts of the party organization.

Parties are still autonomous in the sense that the state does not direct their internal business, but they are no longer autonomous in the sense that their activities could be carried out without state support. Directly and indirectly, the parties have become tied to the state via the government budget, and the important question concerns the extent to which this has affected their internal operations.

National party income and expenditure

Although variations in the accounting practices of the parties make it difficult to effect comparisons between them and over time, it is still possible to point to some important trends. Until 1970, for example, the parties relied for their main income on membership dues, donations and lotteries. The Conservative Party was somewhat exceptional here, in that the central party did not, and does not, receive any share of the membership dues, which were divided between the municipal and provincial levels, and until 1970, 'contributions' made up almost 100 per cent of party income. After 1970, with the exception of election years, when it again increased substantially, the absolute level of 'contributions' fell by almost 50 per cent, with the difference being made up by state subventions. Indeed, state subventions became increasingly important as the Conservative vote increased in the 1980s: accounting for one-third of total income in 1970, they were usually 50 per cent in the 1980s and reached 60 per cent in 1989. Along with the increasing importance of state subventions, the Conservative central office sought to diversify its income by taking a portion of advertising income in party publications and by 'selling' rather than just 'performing' office functions for affiliated organizations. However, all such income is very marginal when compared to contributions and state subventions.

From the available data it appears that state subventions have become the major source of income for all the national party offices, even though their significance varies from party to party. The Progress and Labour parties seem to be most dependent on state subsidies. In the Progress Party (in the period 1985–88) state subventions were four times higher than all other income categories combined, one major reason for this being the very low member/voter ratio and the absence of links to interest organizations. In the Labour Party, state subsidies in 1977–80 were twice other income sources, and compared to earlier years, this share has been increasing. In the other parties state subsidies are less dominant, but are always more important than membership dues.

One evident effect of public subsidies is that the political parties are now richer than before. In the Christian People's Party, for example, total income increased by 60 per cent from 1969 to 1970. Moreover, while there may have been a decline in voluntary contributions immediately after the introduction of public subsidies, these have since picked up again. Central party offices have also become less dependent on lower organizational levels. Again in the Christian People's Party, for instance, membership dues accounted for more than half the total income of the central organization in 1967, as against just 8 per cent in 1982. On the other hand, with funding also earmarked for provincial and local level units, these have increased their autonomy vis-à-vis the central offices. Judging from the share of total income now coming from the public purse, there can be no doubt that it would be disaster if the Progress Party proposal for phasing out all state funding were to be accepted.

It is of course difficult to say whether the state subventions have contributed, or even caused, the 'malaise' that most party organizations seem to be presently experiencing. On the positive side, these subsidies may well have strengthened the influence of party organizations in relation to the extensive network of contacts between large interest organizations and the state bureaucracy. Certainly, when compared to the trade unions and industrial organizations, the political parties are both poor and small. In the unions alone, there are more than 1000 full-time employees (NOU, 1982: 88), three times as many as in all the parties taken together. One reason for this relative disparity is that unions are able to charge their members much higher membership fees both because they provide tangible benefits for their members (such as influencing wages and working conditions, and providing services such as insurance benefits) and because the tax deductibility of union fees passes the cost of their bureaucracy on to the taxpayers. Neither of these options is open to the parties, and in this sense public party finance may be seen as a counterweight to the professionalization of other types of organizations.

Professionals and amateurs in party organizations

As parties have become richer, so they have been able to employ more staff, and there has been an expansion of the party bureaucracy particularly after 1975, when public subventions were allocated to the province and municipal levels. In 1969 the Christian People's Party maintained ten full- or part-time staff at provincial level; in 1975, by contrast, they maintained provincial secretaries in all nineteen electoral districts, with some provinces also being able to employ additional personnel out of their own funds. With the exception of the Labour Party, the local and province party secretaries are appointed by the local and regional levels, respectively. Their salaries, however, often come, at least in part, from the central level, and in this respect the central office functions as a redistributor of resources. Provincial organizations which cannot support a full-time secretary themselves transfer some funds for this purpose to the central office, which then adds money of its own, thus enabling all provinces to employ personnel on roughly the same terms, regardless of the resources of the individual provincial branch.

The professionalization process is apparent in all parties, but can perhaps be best illustrated by the Socialist Left, which began in 1975 by espousing an anti-bureaucratic and anti-hierarchical image, much as the Greens were later to do in Germany. The first party statutes specified an equal pay principle, in which all employees were to be paid the same, regardless of the type of job, qualification or position in the party hierarchy. Reality has been different, however. Already in 1975 political secretaries earned 28 per cent more than clerical secretaries, and a claim in the party's annual report in 1979 that equal pay had been introduced at the central office, with the wage level set to 'the average industrial wage' in Oslo, did not survive for long. At the same time as the party dropped its emphasis on the rotation of office holders (1985), the equal pay statute was modified to become one in which the people determining wage levels at the party central office were asked to 'pay attention' to the equal pay principle. Moreover, throughout the years there has been a difference in wage levels between clerical staff and those performing political functions, with the reference being no longer to the 'average industrial wage in Oslo' but to the Union of Clerical Personnel. (It should be noted, however, that clerical personnel in the party are paid well above those in similar positions in the government administration, while top party leaders are paid less.) Until 1981 the party did not pay employees for working overtime, and overtime compensation was again dropped for political office-holders in 1987, even though the salary differentiation between various staff positions continued. As the party became gradually institutionalized, it is evident that it also abandoned some of its anti-hierarchical characteristics.

Similar traits can be found in other parties. The Centre Party recently stressed the need for a 'clearer division of work and communication lines'. The General Secretary of the party was relieved of 'routine organizational tasks' and assigned a more pronounced political role, with his administrative functions being transferred to a new head of administrative services. Simultaneously, the central office was reorganized in three departments: information and marketing, administration and economy, and training and development. The party acknowledged that it needed to deal more professionally with on-the-job training, wage policy, and organizational simplification, and as part of the latter, the educational association was incorporated into the training department. An attempt to reduce the women's organization to the status of a standing committee was strongly resisted, however.

Administratively, the parties have also become more centralized. All parties have developed, or are developing, a central register of individual members. Computerization of membership files enables the central offices to by-pass the regional and local levels in communicating with individual members and thus strengthens the national leaders. Opposition within the parties to such central registration has focused mainly on the potential for misuse rather than on their organizational consequences. Moreover, all parties claim to make use of commercial advertising companies to develop election propaganda; most subscribe to regular opinion polls; and all make use of special polls around election time. There also seems to be occasional use of consultancy firms on various issues, particularly on organizational development.

Organizational change and adaptation

Over time, as the parties have become more similar to one another, they have also each become more like the Labour Party, the 'model' party organization. Yet there is also movement in other directions. In the Socialist Left, there is now less emphasis than in the beginning on office rotation and on the organizational limits to the influence of the parliamentary party. In the Labour Party, collective membership has been relegated to history. The Progress Party, beginning as a party opposed, politically as well as organizationally, to the prevailing orientation in the party system, has adapted to the 'normal' organizational model. In addition, recent trends indicate that the parties are declining as membership organizations, even though what is perhaps the most disturbing sign is the low level of party membership activity. This is also reflected in the recruitment of candidates for local offices, particularly in the larger towns, where previous worries about 'ruling elite groups' have been replaced by worries about finding people who are willing to be elected to political offices.

The principal philosophy underlying the formal structure of the party organization is representation and control from below, but the extent to which reality matches these ideas is open to dispute. There is no doubt that the top party leaderships exert formidable influence on organizational developments as well as on day-to-day politics. Their position in the party is first of all enhanced by the fact that they are full-time participants, commanding both information and communication skills that the regular party member lacks. Although the party convention is formally the highest authority, representatives in parliament and government are able to dominate the party apparatus, and this goes in particular for people who hold dual positions. Conflicts between the group of representatives and the party organization are reduced by extensive overlap of positions: generally, about one-third of the parties' representatives in parliament have also been members of a national party body, and among cabinet members the figure is one half (Eliassen, 1985). There seem to be only marginal differences between the parties in this respect.

Yet, leadership also means responsibility. Fairly or unfairly, the party leaders must take the blame when things go wrong. Thus the falling opinion poll ratings of the Conservatives in late 1989 and early 1990 precipitated, or fuelled, a wave of demands for a change of leadership. Regardless of how much support the national leader was able to mobilize in the central party bodies, regional power brokers and aspiring candidates, aided by the media, made it clear that re-election was unlikely. Similarly, Labour had to accede to the national convention when finding a new deputy leader: only by arm-twisting could it induce the convention to accept its candidate, and then only as part of a wider change in the party. When Odvar Nordli announced his resignation as prime minister in 1981, the party leadership first looked to Rolf Hansen rather than Gro Harlem Brundtland as his successor, but a coalition of party secretaries and regional party leaders wanted it otherwise. In the case of the Conservatives, Jo Benkow announced his candidacy for re-election as party chairman in 1985, yet a movement among regional party secretaries and chairmen succeeded in having their candidate elected. The national conventions are certainly more active bodies than the iron law of oligarchy would lead us to believe, and there are numerous examples of the need for the leadership to fight 'brush-fires' (for example, to prevent the adoption of undesirable policies in the party platform – see Heidar, 1988). Central–local relations also indicate that the party hierarchy allows considerable freedom from central direction.

Finally, while there is little scope here to give a full account of the 'partyness' (Katz, 1986) of Norwegian governments, there are a number of factors which can be identified as pulling the system one way or the other. As far as the limitations to party government are concerned, there are three major relevant considerations. First, the geographical dimension, which is present in all political issues in Norway. Whenever parliament has to decide on location of institutions or policies that implicitly favour or disfavour one or other region, there is a breakdown of voting along party lines. Second, Norway is among the most 'corporatist' political systems (Williamson, 1989), with hundreds of standing committees, and as many non-standing committees, which function as arenas for political representation, bargaining and policy implementation. Although the parties in parliament may make the final decision, in many cases the details are worked out in the committee meetings. At the same time, in their survey of this field, Lægreid and Roness (forthcoming) point out that the corporate channel performs as a supplement as much as a competitor to the parties, and even when it is seen a competitor, this may not necessarily be true across all policy sectors. Third, the Norwegian civil service is strongly professionalized (Lægreid and Roness, forthcoming). And while it would be wrong to state that the civil service acts as a barrier to policy implementation in general, it has been very successful in obstructing policy implementation whenever vital interests of the civil service itself are at stake, as in the case of a relocation of governmental institutions (Sætren, 1980). Moreover, there has been a tendency to increase the number of full-time elected positions at the local level, on the grounds that this is necessary in order to keep the bureaucracy from controlling policy formulation too much.

There are also indicators pointing towards an increased partyness of government. First, the reduction in the number of municipalities from the early 1960s has reduced support for non-party lists of candidates. The Labour Party was the first to politicize municipal elections, beginning in the 1930s (Hjellum, 1967), and in the 1950s and 1960s local candidate lists of 'non-socialist coalitions' were increasingly replaced by regular party lists. Indeed, with the increasing predominance of party lists, local elections have also become quasi-referenda on the government of the day, being dominated by national media and hence by national party leaders, and according national political issues greater attention than specific local concerns. In the 1991 local elections, for example, the question of Norway's relationship with the EC again surfaced as a hot issue, and the Centre and Socialist Left parties, both strongly resisting future EC membership, significantly improved their electoral support. Second, a 1975 reform created a new administrative unit, transforming the provincial councils into directly elected bodies, and assigning them policy responsibility in a number of fields, such as education, health care, transportation and cultural affairs. The provinces therefore became important arenas for policy-making and thereby increased the role of the parties. Kvavik and Mydske (forthcoming) have shown that most provincial councillors see themselves acting on behalf of their parties, rather than as representatives of their municipalities, organizations or professions.

The decline of parties has therefore occurred simultaneously with their strengthening. As movements which are able to incorporate their supporters into a tightly connected web of organizations with an overarching ideology, parties have to a large extent failed; as organizations competing with other types of organizations for control of the political system, on the other hand, they have proved very successful.

Notes

1 Because of the local government reforms there are fewer units in some parties today than in 1960. However, this does not mean that the party organization has become weaker, only that it has adapted to the official administrative structure.

2 Only 12 per cent of their local council representatives, elected in 1991, were women, compared to 28 per cent for all parties, and only a fifth of the seats on the national executive committee were held by women compared to at least a third in other parties.

3 In 1946 half of the local Labour party newspapers were owned directly by the local party branches, but by 1960 only one-fifth were owned this way (Høyer, 1982: 182).

4 The Socialist Left Party in 1991 reported that it lost as many members as it recruited in the two-year period 1989–91: c. 1500 or 15 per cent of the total membership. While this figure could be higher for that party than for other parties, because of strong recruitment among young voters, it is also worth noticing that the high turnover occurred in a period with strong increase in support for the party in elections.

5 *Fornyelse av partiarbeide. Innstilling fra Høyres strukturkomite* (1991: 11).

6 The extremes were represented by the Socialist Left Party, 36 per cent, and the Conservatives, 69 per cent.

7 Subsidies for party nomination meetings are provided if the meeting is constituted on the basis of the proportional representation of the party's municipal branches. It was feared (in 1920) that the nomination meeting otherwise would be dominated by the larger municipalities, and that the smaller branches would be unable to pay for their representatives' expenses. Most parties follow these rules, even if they are not obliged to do so. However, the basis for representation is the party's share of the votes in each municipality – not its membership size.

8 This had also been one of the original proposals from the Commission on party finance.

Its adoption in 1975 is quite clearly a response to the proliferation of new party initiatives following the EC struggle.

References

Christensen, Dag Arne (1992) 'Bondeparti, Distriktsparti eller Folkeparti; Ei komparativ analyse av fornyinga av bondepartia i Noreg og Sverige', unpublished thesis, Department of Comparative Politics, University of Bergen.

Daalder, Hans (1992) 'A Crisis of Party?' *Scandinavian Political Studies*, 15 (4): 269–88.

DNA (1983) Organisasjonskomiteens Innstilling (Document for the National Convention).

Eliassen, Kjell A. (1985) 'Rekrutteringen til Stortinget og regjeringen 1945–1985', in T. Nordby (ed.) *Storting og regjering 1945–1985. Institusjoner – rekruttering*. Oslo: Kunnskapsforlaget, pp. 109–30.

Garvik, Olav (1982) *Da Venstre sprakk*. Oslo: Aschehoug.

Harmel, Robert and Svåsand, Lars (1989) 'From Protest to Party: Progress on the Right in Denmark and Norway', Paper prepared for the Annual Conference of American Political Science Association, Atlanta.

Harmel, Robert and Svåsand, Lars (1991) 'Party Leadership and Party Institutionalization: from "Preacher" to "Stabilizer"', paper prepared for the Annual Conference of the American Political Science, Washington, DC.

Heidar, Knut (1988) *Partidemokrati på prøve*. Oslo: Universitetsforlaget.

Heidar, Knut (1994) 'The Polymorphic Nature of Party Membership', *European Journal of Political Research*, 25 (1): 61–86.

Hellevik, Ottar and Skard, Torild (1985) *Norske kommunestyrer – plass for kvinner?* Oslo: Universitetsforlaget.

Hjellum, Torstein (1967) *Partiene i lokalpolitikken*. Oslo: Gyldendal.

Høyer, Svennik (1982) 'Pressen – Økonomisk utvikling og politisk kontroll', in NOU No. 30. *Maktutredningen. Rapporten om massemedier*. Oslo: Universitetsforlaget, pp. 133–247.

Katz, Richard S. (1986) 'Party Government: A Rationalistic Conception', in F.G. Castles and R. Wildenmann (eds), *Visions and Realities of Party Government*. Berlin: de Gruyter, pp. 31–71.

Kvavik, Robert and Mydske, Per K. (forthcoming) 'Political Parties and Norwegian Provincial Government', in Kaara Strøm and Lars Svåsand (eds), *Challenges to Political Parties: The Norwegian Case*. Ann Arbor: University of Michigan Press.

Lægreid, Per and Roness, Paul (forthcoming) 'Political Parties, Bureaucracies and Corporatism', in Kaara Strøm and Lars Svåsand (eds), *Challenges to Political Parties: The Norwegian Case*. Ann Arbor: University of Michigan Press.

Leipart, Jørn Y. and Svåsand, Lars (1988) 'The Norwegian Liberal Party: From Political Pioneer to Political Footnote' , in Emil J. Kirchner (ed.), *Liberal Parties in Western Europe*. Cambridge: Cambridge University Press, pp. 304–25.

Listhaug, Ola (forthcoming) 'The Decline of Class Voting', in Kaara Strøm and Lars Svåsand (eds), *Challenges to Political Parties: The Norwegian Case*. Ann Arbor: University of Michigan Press.

NOU (1982) No. 3. *Maktutredningen. Sluttrapport*. Oslo: Universitetsforlaget.

NOU (1992) No. 14. *Mål og midler i presspolitikken*. Oslo: Statens Forvaltningstjeneste.

Rose, Lawrence E. and Waldahl, Ragnar (1982) 'The Distribution of Political Participation in Norway', *Scandinavian Political Studies*, 5 (4): 285–315.

Sejersted, Francis (1984) *Opposisjon og posisjon (1945–1981). Høyres historie*, 3. Oslo: Cappelen.

Selle, Per and Svåsand, Lars (1991) 'Membership in Party Organizations and the Problem of Decline of Parties', *Comparative Political Studies*, 23 (4): 459–78.

Shaffer, William R. (1991) 'Interparty Spatial Relationships in Norwegian Storting Roll Call Votes', *Scandinavian Political Studies*, 14 (1): 59–84.

Skjeie, Hege (forthcoming) 'Women in Political Parties' , in Kaara Strøm and Lars Svåsand (eds), *Challenges to Political Parties: The Norwegian Case*. Ann Arbor: University of Michigan Press.

Svåsand, Lars (1991) 'State Subventions for Political Parties in Norway', in Matti Wiberg (ed.), *The Public Purse and the Political Parties: Public Financing of Political Parties in the Nordic Countries*. Helsinki: The Finnish Political Science Association, pp. 119–46.

Sætren, Harald (1980) *Utflytting av statsinstitutsjoner*. Bergen: Universitetsforlaget.

Valen, Henry (1981) *Valg og politikk – Et samfunn i endring*. Oslo: NKS-Forlaget.

Valen, Henry (1988) 'Norway', in M. Gallagher and M. Marsh (eds), *Candidate Selection in Comparative Perspective*. London: Sage Publications.

Williamson, Peter J. (1989) *Corporatism in Perspective*. London: Sage Publications.

13

Party Organizations in Sweden: Colossuses with Feet of Clay or Flexible Pillars of Government?

Jon Pierre and Anders Widfeldt

Our concern in this chapter is focused on the question of party and party system change in a political system which, to a significant extent, is shaped by the presence of the political parties. This close, almost symbiotic relationship between the political parties and the state emerged primarily because both elements had a strong interest in the creation and mainten-ance of a stable and institutionalized system of party government. Thus, in order to understand the changes that have occurred within the party system and the party organizations we must look not only at the parties and the party system, as such, but also at those changes which concern the role(s) played by parties at the level of the state and, more generally, at changes in the parties' dependency vis-à-vis the state (Katz and Mair, 1992).

We advance three basic arguments. First, the Swedish case highlights the relevance of public subventions to the party organizations for the position of the parties themselves in the system of political representation. The effects of these subventions are as many as they are influential, affecting the role of the party membership, organizational strength and staffing, and the introduction of professional party campaigning; they also help to create and/or sustain a continuous organizational life in an era when voluntaristic involvement in such organizations has lost much of its former appeal for the citizenry.

Second, the financial and legal institutionalization of the Swedish party system – produced mainly by state and local subventions to the party organizations and by the imposition of thresholds for new parties in the electoral system – has helped to create a false sense of stability and control among the party elites, an image of stability which probably obstructed organizational development and change for a long period of time. For example, despite the introduction of new campaign techniques and the need for more coordinated action, the parties nevertheless maintained their original stratarchic organizational model. That said, it should be emphasized that it did not become obvious that the 'old' parties no longer had a political oligopoly in Swedish politics until the late 1980s.

The third and final argument relates to the interdependence between the level of the party system and the level of the state. Given the Swedish system of parties as semi-institutionalized actors in the political system, changes in the structure and stability of the party system in a political system must in some way affect the *modus operandi* of the political system *tout court*, and vice versa. This implies that the analysis of the Swedish party organizations must employ factors related to the state at large – for example, the policy-making process, changes in state finances, and the party composition of parliament and cabinet – as independent elements in our analysis. The basic argument here is that the organizational development and adaptation of party organizations is more closely geared to the need to adapt the organizations to the state rather than to civil society. We also suggest that the emergence of new parties challenging the existing order has resulted to a large extent from this insensitivity to demands and opinions among the electorate and the party memberships. While the parties have gradually moved closer to the state they have also been very careful to maintain their original mass party image, not least because this was the model which originally legitimated the parties as linkage agencies between civil society and the state. The challenge of the new parties is now aimed at this very inconsistency between the model and the performance.

Overview

The Swedish party system and the system of government is one of the stronger cases of party government covered in this book (cf. Sjöblom, 1987). There are two main indicators on this, one related to the system of representation and the other to the linkages between party standpoints and public policy. First, although some differences exist among the parties, all subscribe to the basic idea of party democracy, which implies at least some organizational leverage over the parliamentary party and party policies as executed in parliament and/or in government. Here, differences among the parties do not primarily refer to whether the organization should be democratic in nature; rather, the variations concern the extent to which members of parliament should be committed to work in the party organization (Pierre, 1986b), the de facto centralization on matters of party policy, and the question of the basis of political representation (that is, the extent to which party activists and members of parliament feel that representation should be individual or collective, or indeed determined by the constituency or region).

A second important factor concerns the relationship between party policies and public policy, or more specifically, the party determinants of public policy. Here, too, we assume that Sweden emerges as a case of strong party government, or as one with a high 'partyness of government' (Katz, 1986). The corporatist style of policy-making in Sweden has to a large extent evolved as corporatism *through the political parties* (cf. Rothstein, 1986). Strong bonds exist between several organized interests and various political parties, such as those between the blue-collar unions and the Social Democratic Party, as well as between agricultural producer organizations and the Centre Party, linkages which underline the phenomenon of party organizations evolving within an already highly organized society (see below). As a result, the political parties and their organizations dominate both the process of political representation and the process of policy-making.[1] As Holmberg (1989: 27), has emphasized, 'the Swedish system is far from any model of popular representation from below. A more elitist model, with a clear emphasis on policy leadership on the part of political parties, fits . . . much better.'

Over time, of course, and mainly at the local level, other channels of political participation, such as single-issue movements or local action groups, have significantly challenged this position of the parties (Westerståhl and Johansson, 1981; Petersson et al., 1989: 336f). At the national level, however, and despite the recent changes which suggest that the stability of the party system is eroding, the fact that some new social movements are adopting the formal status, objectives and organizational structure of parties is proof enough of the latter's significance.

The political and social origins of the party system

As a Scandinavian country and, as such, as one of the cases that provided Stein Rokkan with the empirical foundation for his 'freezing' hypothesis, Sweden displays three significant political and social characteristics that have played a key role in shaping the political parties and their organizations. The first of these factors is related to what Olsen (1983) has referred to as 'organized democracy', which is here used as a metaphor for a society characterized by strong interest organizations and a corporatist style of policy-making. Collective action, be it related to religion, temperance, trade unionism or partisan activity, is a key feature of Swedish social and political behaviour, and many of the types of organizations involved in these activities preceded the formation of the party organizations. When they did emerge, therefore, the party organizations capitalized on the existence of an overall civic inclination towards collective behaviour. The best example of this relationship between a party organization and organized interests is the close linkage between the Social Democratic Party (SAP) and the LO (Confederation of Blue-Collar Unions). Drawing on a long experience of concerted activities within a wide range of areas, the SAP and the LO exchange resources, political ideas and support. The long period of corporate affiliation of LO union members to the Social Democrats also underlines the close relationship between the two organizations, and except for a small number of public disagreements the two organizations devote much effort to heralding their joint interests and objectives. There is also a close connection between the Centre Party and farmers' interest organizations. Although there are no formal links between the party and these organizations, the informal contacts are undisputed and have a history dating back to the formation of the Centre Party, thus helping to sustain the party's links with the rural population (cf. Back and Berglund, 1978: 89f; Elvander, 1969: 279ff; Holmberg and Esaiasson, 1988: 65–8; Winqvist et al., 1972: 185f).

The institutionalization of aggregated social interests and demands into interest organizations developed through a process of organization and counter-organization. Thus, in the labour market, the emergence of trade unions at the local and later also the national level was counteracted by the creation of various organizations for employers and capital. Similarly in the political arena, the strong extra-parliamentary organization of the Social Democratic Party catalysed a process of nation-wide organizations among the Conservative and Liberal parties. Over time, then, there developed a system of organized interests balancing each other's powers in various sectors of society, a process which has been cited as an explanation for the consensual style of political decision-making which many see as the trademark of Swedish politics (Elder et al., 1982; Rustow, 1955). In addition, the model of mutually balancing organized interests has also been seen as conducive to the introduction of proportional representation in Sweden, seen here as a method of accommodating conflicting interests in a situation in which no single interest or organization controls a majority of the population.

The presence of strong organizations both in politics and other areas of social action has provided a marked degree of political stability in Sweden. Thus, the party system remained essentially stable from around 1920 till the mid-1980s. Few new parties entered the political scene, and those which did were unable to establish themselves as viable and consistent actors. A high level of electoral stability, sustained by strong class identification among the electorate and high thresholds of parliamentary representation, effectively forestalled any attempts by new political parties to gain a foothold in Swedish politics. That said, this scenario of a remarkable political stability eventually gave way to a more transient, dynamic and unpredictable state of affairs, as we will later show.

The second important feature of Swedish politics is the predominant position of the Social Democrats during the twentieth century and, most importantly, during the post-war period, a dominance which has led to Sweden being referred to as a 'one-party dominant regime' (Krauss and Pierre, 1990; cf. Sartori, 1976). This refers to more than just the mere fact that one of the parties controls a stable majority and/or is incumbent for an extended period of time. Rather, what is conspicuous about such regimes is the way in which the dominant party seems to become perpetually associated with government and the public bureaucracy. Incumbency and dominance seem to reinforce one another, with the border between the dominant party and the governmental apparatus becoming increasingly blurred as a result of the party's control over the political agenda, its strong position in the bureaucracy with bona fide officials in key positions, and its transformation of key elements of party ideology into values above and beyond partisan conflict (Pempel, 1990). Swedish politics displayed many of these features for a long period after 1945, and it was not until the mid-1970s that the Social Democratic government was replaced by a coalition consisting of the three non-socialist parties.

The third factor, finally, and as noted above, is the predominant position of the political parties in the Swedish system of government and, in particular, in the system of representation and the public policy-process. That said, it should be emphasized that Swedish public administration is far less politicized than is, for instance, the case in the UK or France (Pierre, 1994). In this sense, the focus here is on the parties as formative agents in the process of interest aggregation and also in the policy-process up until the implementation phase.

Taking these three factors together – a long tradition of strong organizations in all areas of society, the dominant position of the Social Democrats for most of the post-war period, and the strength of party government – sets the scene for the development of the party organizations, on the one hand, and for the new challenges that these organizations encountered during the 1970s and 1980s, on the other. Clearly, the strong social inclination towards collective behaviour and the stability of the party system were both very conducive to a rapid development of the party organizations. Thus, by capitalizing on pre-existing organizations and learning from them the method of creating stable and powerful organizations, the political parties in Sweden (and probably in Scandinavia at large) developed their organization in a more favourable political and social setting than in most other countries. Furthermore, once created these organizations also helped sustain this very stability.

The party organizations

Not least as a result of their historical origins, the five traditional parties can be divided into two basic organizational groups, with the Centre, Social Democratic and Communist parties emanating from popular movements outside parliament, and with the Conservatives and Liberals originating from inside the Riksdag and consequently having less of a movement tradition. The two different party organizational cultures do not therefore parallel the basic ideological cleavage in the party system.

Origins and developments

The organizational development of the Swedish parties can be divided into three phases. The first phase (1880–1920) witnessed emerging party organizations strongly characterized by the original dichotomy between mass parties and cadre parties. Over time, parties originating outside parliament gained parliamentary representation. Conversely, parties of parliamentary origin began developing extra-parliamentary organizations.

During the second phase (1920–65), there was an emerging organizational convergence, while in the third phase (1965 onwards), this process of convergence was accentuated. This third phase gradually transformed into a fourth phase in the mid- to late-1980s, when the established parties were challenged from the outside by new parties with significantly different organizational models: the Green Party and later also the right-wing populist New Democracy.

Formed in 1889, the *Social Democrats* constituted one of the most electorally successful socialist parties in Europe, mobilizing the emerging working class into a party advocating democratic socialism through parliamentary reformism. From the start, there was a close link with the blue-collar trade unions. At the formal level, the links between the two branches of the labour movement include corporate membership, in which local union members were affiliated with the Social Democratic party by default (this type of membership was abolished in 1990). More informally, the LO made significant financial and other contributions to the party, especially during election campaigns. The *Centre Party* – until the late 1950s the 'Farmers' League' – was formed following a merger of two separate parties in 1922. Compared to the SAP, the Centre Party leaned more towards elite organizational models, and in its early years only persons with direct connections to the peasant community were admitted as party members (Thermaenius, 1933: 45). Once this restriction was abolished in the 1930s, the party enjoyed a rapid growth in membership, and over a period of twenty years, from 1930 to 1950, the membership figures quadrupled. Despite twice having formed coalition governments with the Social Democrats – in the 1930s and again in the 1950s – the party has been careful not to become associated with the socialist ideology; indeed, for many years they even denied having any ideological allegiance whatsoever. Today, the Centre Party is a typical catch-all, middle-of-the-road party, albeit with a clear non-socialist political orientation and identity. But even in a comparative perspective, the party's transformation from a party of vertical to one of horizontal mobilization is remarkable. The *Communist Party*, formed after a defection from the Social Democrats in 1917, experienced several splits during the 1920s and 1930s. The party which was to survive in the long run, the Communist Party of Sweden (SKP), was affiliated to the Communist International in 1919, and this was clearly reflected in the party organization, modelled after the pure vanguard party. Up until the 1960s, the SKP was built upon the principles of democratic centralism. The party rules dictated a degree of loyalty and activity on the part of its members which was unparalleled by any other significant political party in Sweden.

The Liberal and Conservative parties originated within the parliament during the later half of the nineteenth century, with national extra-parliamentary organizations being formed in 1902 and 1904 respectively. The *Liberal Party* has a dual background, based on Free Church and temperance supporters, on the one hand, and radical Liberals, primarily

from the bigger cities, on the other. This dualism eventually provoked a
party split in the inter-war period and although reunited in 1934, it remains
a salient feature of the party to this day. When the party was formed it
adopted a structure close to that of the cadre party model. The selection of
candidates was not confined to party members and party finances were to a
significant extent based on donations from private industry. The *Conservative Party* was primarily formed as a counterweight against the emerging
working-class mass parties and only reluctantly adopted the traits of an
organized political party. The extension of the suffrage clearly suggested
that if conservatism were to remain a significant political force, the party
had little choice but to engage in organizational development. However,
the cadre tradition was slow to die, and for over half a century, the party
was heavily financially dependent on private industry.

   This organizational dichotomy in the Swedish party system should
not of course be confused with the basic ideological divide, and the (non-
socialist) Centre Party's close association with social movements and
organized interests clearly rejects any hypothesis of a 'contagion from the
left'. That said, the Conservative and Liberal party organizations did
gradually become more membership-based as their organizational development progressed, and following an initial period of clear differences,
the party system entered the second phase of slow organizational convergence in the inter-war period.[2] The convergence was towards a stratarchical organizational model, giving the party leadership extensive autonomy
on policy matters, regional party organizations control over candidate
nomination processes, and leaving tasks related to voter mobilization,
meetings and other continuous organizational functions to the local
organizations.

Convergence and challenge

In 1965, the Riksdag introduced a new system of national state subventions
for the political parties (Gidlund, 1983). The proposal was supported
mainly by the Social Democrats and the Centre Party, arguing that strong
and extensive party organizations were a precondition of a democratic
system. The plan involved two kinds of subventions, one to the national
party organizations and one to the parliamentary fraktions, and was soon
followed by additional elements. Thus, in 1969, subventions to parties
represented in local and regional assemblies were introduced, and in 1973
and 1975 substantial extensions of the subventions to the parliamentary
parties were implemented. In the present context it should also be noted
that 1972 saw the introduction of public support for the daily press, which,
indirectly, also offered an additional subvention to the parties, who had
spent substantial amounts on their affiliated newspapers.

   It is our contention that this new system of public subventions (in which
the amounts paid via each subvention continually increased) acted to fuel
the process of organizational convergence. The Liberals, for example, first

introduced compulsory party membership for all public office candidates in 1971, while the Conservatives first began charging membership dues to the central party in 1965, and subsequently increased the significance of these payments. Both parties abandoned their systems of donations from private companies in 1971 and 1977 respectively. In 1967, the Communists abandoned the principles of democratic centralism by means of a profound revision of the party rules, which transformed the party into the group of new left parties based on participatory ideals, as was illustrated by the change of the party name to the Left Party Communists (VPK). By the mid-1970s, therefore, the Swedish party system consisted of five remarkably similar parties, all with the formal weight on membership democracy and with their main financial dependence on subventions from the state.

Although some of these organizational changes may well have been caused by factors other than the public subventions, we nevertheless maintain that the influx of state funds into the party organizations acted to trigger off a process of organizational development which was very similar in each of the different parties. Even today, despite several differences in detail, the five traditional Swedish parties are remarkably similar in terms of their organizational structure and style. In brief, they are based on a structure which is *simplistic, stratarchic* and *stable*: simplistic in the sense that the organizational levels are relatively few and easily distinguishable; stratarchical in the sense that each organizational level operates relatively independently of other levels; and stable in the sense that the parties do not alter their statutes very often, preferring instead to effect profound revisions at quite extended intervals.

The period from the 1920s until the mid- to late 1980s was characterized by this tendency towards organizational convergence, which, at the same time, was also a period of marked party system stability. Efforts to establish new parties were short-lived, and eventually failed. There were, to be sure, a number of disconcerting factors. Survey research, for example, indicated a slow but continuous decline in party identification and in the level of trust in politicians (Holmberg, 1989). Nevertheless, this was a fairly slow trend and was not generally seen as alarming. Moreover, electoral turn-out was continuously high: having topped 90 per cent throughout the 1970s and in 1982, it fell to 86 per cent – still a very high figure by international standards – in 1988.

At the same time, however, the party system was beginning to show serious signs of weakness. The 1988 election campaign was dominated by environmental issues, and the Green Party, formed in 1981, exceeded the 4 per cent threshold and gained representation in the Riksdag. With the exception of a short-lived splinter party from the Liberal, Centre and Conservative parties in the 1960s, this was the first break in the five-party hegemony since the 1930s. Moreover, the 1988–91 election period proved to be even more testing for the old parties. Surveys indicated dramatic decline in levels of trust, in party identification and so on. Regardless of the measure, these were unmistakable signs of a crisis for the parties, with the

340 How Parties Organize

governing Social Democrats facing an enormous loss of support (Holmberg, 1989).

New challengers also entered the scene and, in consequence, the party system can be said to have entered a fourth phase, in which the five old parties remain comparatively similar but are now challenged from the outside by three new parties. One challenger was the Christian Democratic Party, formed in 1964 but lacking electoral significance until now. In 1988 they polled 2.9 per cent, their best ever result, and in 1991 they increased to 7.1 per cent, comfortably above the threshold. In late 1990, plans were announced to launch a populist party, similar to the Progress parties in Denmark and Norway. The party, *New Democracy*, was formed in February 1991, gained strong support in the opinion polls, and eventually won 6.7 per cent of the vote in 1991. Even though the Greens lost their Riksdag status by falling little more than half of one per cent below the threshold, the traditional five-party system, which had only very recently looked very stable, had been clearly demolished.

In organizational terms, the three new entrants offered some very contrasting pictures. The Christian Democrats (KDS), which began as a confessional party with close links to the Free Churches, made a conscious effort to modernize its image in the mid-1980s, and are now ambitious to form part of the European family of Christian Democratic parties. On the whole, their organization is similar to that of the traditional Swedish parties and, even before the national electoral breakthrough, the party had enjoyed a reputation of being remarkably well organized. The KDS has been represented in a variety of local and regional assemblies since the 1960s, and for many years its membership strength has exceeded that of the Greens or the Left Party.

The other two new entrants reflect challenges which are more in line with two mainstream criticisms levelled against the old established parties. The Green Party has a very flat organization with participatory ideals. Rather than one executive committee[3] and one leader, there are four executive committees with a division of labour but equal status, and two national spokespersons, one from each gender. Interestingly, New Democracy represents precisely the opposite pattern. Lacking a formalized structure, its explicit ambition is to run the party as a business operation with quick decisions and few organizational layers. The regional party level, for example, has been almost totally omitted, and the organizational culture is emphatically top-down, with the party leader enjoying a dominance unequalled in any other Swedish party (Taggart and Widfeldt, 1993).

The parties, civil society and the state

As noted above, the Swedish political system and policy-process are strongly characterized by the presence of the political parties. The parties emerged as organizations within civil society and constituted the key political link between civil society and the state. Over time, however, as we also noted, the parties and their organizations moved closer to the state, creating an effective symbiosis between the two. In this symbiosis, the parties fulfil key functions related to the state, representing aggregated social and political interests and helping to sustain the legitimacy of the political system. In return, the state provides the financial and legal resources to sustain the party system. Above all, it is through the inclusion of the parties into the political, financial and legal sphere of the state that the state itself helps to sustain the status quo in the party system.

Most of the developments in the party organizations are to a greater or lesser extent adaptations to the needs of the state rather than to those of civil society and the traditional representative role of the parties. To take this argument one step further, we contend that this organizational development and the stratarchical organization model of the parties have precluded vertical integration of the party organizations, and that this has indirectly facilitated the emergence of new parties which, in turn, capitalize on popular discontent with the old system.

The main features of organizational development and change which can be observed during the period from 1960 to 1990 include the decreasing significance of party membership; the increasing centralization of party organization; the centralization of the process of policy formulation; the strengthening of the parties' financial situation; and the increasing autonomy of the parliamentary parties. And while these changes have directly or indirectly contributed to making the parties more efficient components in the state, they have also perhaps made them less able to fulfil their traditional representative role.

The declining significance of party membership

In 1960, the parties claimed a total of approximately 1.5 million members; in 1989, the number was almost exactly the same. Relative to the Swedish demographic development, however, this reflects a decline from 21 to 18 per cent of the population. Hence, although the size of the party membership has fluctuated between 1960 and 1989 – in aggregate terms as well as for most of the individual parties – the current situation is very much one of decline, with a particularly sharp drop at the end of the 1980s. Moreover, the Social Democrats have experienced severe difficulties in replacing the members lost following the recent abandonment of corporate membership and, should this trend continue, party membership will become very drastically reduced as we advance through the 1990s. Not surprisingly, the situation of recent years has often been referred to as a 'crisis for the parties', and these are also the terms in which the parties themselves view the situation.

In all parties, internal documents clearly testify to an organizational effort to recruit and maintain membership. A positive membership development indicates that the party is enjoying tail-winds and is popular among the voters. However, given the decreasing significance of membership dues in the parties' finances, increasing membership figures are remarkably similar to increases in a public company's share prices on the stock market: that is, while indicating that the market trusts the project, this does not in itself enhance profitability. Therefore, the important point to emphasize here is that no party appears to be terribly anxious to maintain its mass party character simply because membership dues provide its principal financial input; rather, and more importantly, the parties seem to want to maintain the *image* of a mass party, with a positive membership development being taken as proof that the party is perceived as a viable channel for political representation.

Albeit to varying degrees, it is also the case that the parties in Sweden have all been highly membership oriented. This was less true some thirty years ago in the case of the Conservatives and Liberals, but during the 1960s and 1970s they developed in a direction which conformed to the more traditionally membership-based Centre and Social Democratic parties. In 1965 the Conservatives introduced the payment of membership dues to the central party organization, a controversial step at the time. Similarly, at its Congresses in 1969 and 1971, the Liberals decided that party membership should be compulsory for those wishing to be nominated by the party for any public position.[4]

The membership orientation is also reflected in the importance which is attached to the need for an educated membership cadre, with the parties offering a wide range of courses to their members. With the exception of the Greens, all the major parties have at least one conference centre which is used for these and many other activities by both the rank and file members and the leadership. In order to maintain contact with the membership, the leading personalities of the parties are also expected to attend as many meetings as possible, and not only within their own constituencies. It is thus not uncommon for a cabinet minister to attend a basic unit meeting in his/her own party with less than twenty people present. That said, in all the major parties there is a dissatisfaction with the extent to which MPs engage in the constituency party organization's activities (Pierre, 1986a).

But while all parties are very membership-oriented in a formal sense, the practice of membership involvement does tend to be somewhat different, with the channels available to the member to influence party policies being significantly more limited than is suggested by the party statutes. And while the qualitative aspects of membership influence warrant an extensive study of their own, it nevertheless remains clear that the party leaderships still hold a firm grip on their parties. Although the debates in the Social Democratic congress, for example, are often long and hard, almost 100 per cent of the policy proposals of the national executive are carried by congress (Pierre, 1986a; see also p. 345). Moreover, should the leadership sense the danger of defeat on an important issue, they are very skilful at getting the congress to arrive at a less precise decision, which then leaves sufficient room for manoeuvre for forthcoming encounters with other parties and with the electorate.

The centralization of party organizations

It is far from easy to assess the degree of centralization in party organizations of the Swedish type. A quick glance at any party's organizational structure clearly indicates that the party congress, which is composed of representatives elected by the party membership, is the supreme decision-making body in the organization. Furthermore, the party leadership is elected by and accountable to the congress. At the same time, however, it would not seem very controversial to assert that the parties are highly and increasingly centralized organizations.

The key question, it seems, is the extent to which the nominal mass culture of the parties is compatible with the workings of modern Swedish democracy. Because of the increasing political dependence on the performance of the economy – an artefact of the growth in the public sector – as well as increasing internationalization, political decision-making has become less predictable than before. In addition, the growth in electoral volatility, the electorate's increased political awareness and, not least, the close attention paid by the media to the handling of political issues, are all factors which make the traditional model of party congresses convening at long intervals and laying down party policies both awkward and obsolete. Instead, what we see emerging is a centralization of the short-term policy-making process in the hands of the top party leadership, and these are also the person(s) who come to epitomize the party in the eyes of the media.

In some respects, of course, the party organizations have always been highly centralized, and while the party congresses have developed into important forums for ideological debate, their influence over the day-to-day politics of the party should not be overstated (Albinsson, 1986; Gustafsson, 1973; Pierre, 1986; Uddman, 1987). Instead, the party leaderships ensure they have substantial discretion, and hence party policies have to a very large extent evolved from within the national executive, the parliamentary party and the party leadership, and have then been approved of, post facto, by the party congresses. Whenever the congress has revolted and adopted resolutions which clearly deviate from the preferences of the party leadership, the three key organs mentioned above always have the de facto option of deciding which resolutions to act on. We will return to these questions below; for now, suffice it to say that there are strong mechanisms both within and without the party organization which seem to place effective power in the hands of the top leadership.

There are also a number of important changes which suggest that this process of centralization has been further increased in recent years. First, the role and impact of the media has grown considerably (Asp, 1986).

From the point of view of the political parties, the most significant changes in this respect seem to have taken place during the 1960s, when the parties' election campaigns were organized to an increasing extent in order to cater for the interests of the media (Esaiasson, 1990: 341). Indeed, the extent of media coverage of election campaigns roughly doubled between 1960 and 1988 (Esaiasson, 1990: 372f), a process which was accompanied by an increasingly autonomous and assertive journalistic style. This process has also proved very conducive to an indirect centralization in the parties. The approach of the media is predominantly on persons rather than on organizations, and this has inevitably enhanced the profile of the party leader and his or her closest associates. It remains a more open question as to whether this pattern also applies to day-to-day party–media relations, however. Nevertheless, although election campaigns may be said to constitute a special type of political event, it seems plausible to suggest that the general pattern noted here also applies to the normal, routine media coverage of politics and the political parties.

A second factor suggesting an increased centralization of the party organization concerns the control over the party's financial resources. This control rests completely in the hands of the national executive committee and the parliamentary party, with the party congresses auditing the accounts and approving the national executive's financial reports. Thus, the congresses make no decisions regarding the deployment of the party's financial resources. Given the dramatic increase in these resources following the introduction of state subventions, this centralized power of the purse adds to the overall internal predominance of the party leadership.

The centralization of influence over party policy

The extensive activities and the supposedly powerful political influence exercised by the Swedish party organizations make them important potential loci of political power. Moreover, serving as key reservoirs of elite recruitment, intra-party positions are also often strategic springboards for careers in politics and government. In this perspective, analysing the distribution of power in the organizations should generate insights into the relationship between the party and the governmental apparatus, on the one hand, and the organizations' changing relationship to the state and to civil society, on the other.

Having played a fairly insignificant role in the party's external image for a long period of time – indeed, they were not open to non-members, let alone the media, until the 1950s or 1960s – the party congresses have since developed into huge meetings, maximizing media coverage and other types of external contact. At the same time, the congresses are supposed to formulate policy in a wide range of areas, as well as to elect the party leader, the national committee, the national executive and a variety of other party officials. There is thus an increasingly apparent conflict between party congresses as intra-party policy-making meetings, on the one hand, and as significant occasions for political marketing, on the other. The latter function currently seems to prevail.

Despite these changes in the political functions of the party congresses, the systems of rules applying to the congress and to the intra-party decision-making process have remained remarkably stable over time. Party statutes regulate in great detail both the relationship between the party organization and the various 'side organizations', as well as the process of leadership selection. All parties ascribe major decision-making mandates to the party congress, the powers of which rest with the national executive between congresses. The congresses also elect the national executive, which is the most important locus of power in the organization. Beyond these similarities, the parties employ slightly different models of interest representation.

These formal powers of the party congresses are certainly impressive. That said, however, studies of intra-party decision-making clearly suggest that the effective powers of the party leadership and the national committee are overwhelming; close to 100 per cent of the decisions favour the national executive (Pierre, 1986b; cf. also Albinsson, 1986; Gustafsson, 1973; Uddman, 1987). And even though some of these decision outcomes may of course reflect anticipated concessions made by the national committee to ensure congress's approval, these studies nonetheless bring the notion of a vivid party democracy into serious question.

In all party organizations, decision-making processes are very formalized, particularly with regard to matters related to the party congresses. Thus, the party statutes describe in great detail who has the right to submit motions to the party congresses and which bodies in the organization should consider these motions. As noted above, the regulatory framework for these processes has remained by and large unchanged for a very long period of time and, with some variations, the processes themselves distinctively bottom-up in character. Thus, members submit their motions to the respective local branch, which comments on them and forwards them further up in the organization. In theory, at least, this decision-making model therefore highlights the values and norms associated with the traditional mass party.

As can be seen from Table 13.1, the number of motions submitted to the congresses of all the parties has also increased dramatically between 1960 and 1990, a trend which underlines the increasing attention paid by the membership and the local organizations to the congresses as forums for intra-party debate and policy-making. Whereas the party congresses up to the 1970s were fairly peaceful occasions dominated by leadership speeches, the congresses since then have been much more vigorous. The most probable cause of this rapid change is the increasing organizational activity at the local level, with local organizations developing in number and activity during the period studied. The flow of demands has also confronted the party leadership with a more assertive activist cadre (for

Table 13.1   *Number of motions to party congresses, selected years*

Year	Comm.	SAP	Centre	Lib	Cons	Greens
1960	*	131	n/a	3	7	
1964	63	175	28	29	52	
1967	160	113[a]	52	52	71	
1969	107	404	57	136	12(+63[a])	
1972	182	474	88	497	127	
1975	325	1186	222	275	140	
1978	361	728	250	357	283	
1981	310	727	327	*	308	762
1985	232	*	317	*	*	110
1987	336	896	300	316	242	129
1990	268	912	272	440	259	157

[a] Indicates an extraordinary congress. Years indicated by * are those in which no congress was held.

further analyses, see Albinsson, 1986: 112; Gustafsson, 1973; Pierre, 1986a: Ch. 3; Uddman, 1987: 300).

Such a formalized bottom-up process does not in itself ensure the local party branches a corresponding influence over party policies, however. In terms of the 1960–90 period, for example, the most significant change with regard to the party congresses has been the transformation from intra-party, policy-making conventions to what Gustafsson (1973) calls 'congresses of manifestation', the main function of which is to spread the party's image and ideology to the outside world. It is also interesting to note that this change, which has occurred slowly but consistently, has been accomplished within a stable regulatory framework. Indeed, it could be argued that the fairly rigid regulation of the intra-party decision-making process has in fact proved to be an effective instrument for ensuring party leadership control over the debates and decisions of congress, which, along with increasing media interest, has become one of the most important factors in this change. Thus, the party statutes may be said to have played the ideal role in the eyes of the party leadership: while allowing for desirable changes they have also helped to obstruct other and less desirable ones.[5]

The increasing financial strength of the parties

From a comparative perspective one of the most conspicuous changes in the Swedish party organizations is the advent of state subventions, which over time have developed into huge transfers of financial resources from the state to the parties and their organizations.

With the exception of the Conservative and Liberal parties, that is, of those parties closest to a cadre-type origin, membership income used to play a fairly important role for all Swedish parties. For the Communists and Social Democrats, for example, this accounted for some 20 and 30 per cent respectively of the total central party income. In the case of the Centre Party, membership income accounted for almost 50 per cent of total party income in the early 1960s. At the other extreme lay the Conservatives, who did not begin to charge membership fees to the central organization until 1965. In the case of the Liberals, membership fees fluctuated between 3 and 7 per cent of total party income.

The introduction of state subventions drastically changed the picture for the three parties which relied to a substantial extent on membership income. The most obvious example is the Centre Party, which has not even nominally increased the membership fee charged by the central organization since 1962, and which has gone from top to bottom in the membership reliance league, with membership contributions now accounting for less than 2 per cent of total income. Similarly, the Social Democrats and Communists also display a roughly decreasing trend in terms of their reliance on membership fees (from 31 to 10 per cent and from 19 to 4 per cent respectively), stabilizing in the 1970s. Since its introduction, the proportion of membership income for the Conservatives has steadily increased from just under 6 per cent in the mid- to late 1960s to about 10 per cent in the late 1980s. This increasing trend is unique among the Swedish parties, and the 10 per cent proportion of total income is, as also with the Social Democrats, the highest proportion for all parties at the end of the 1980s.

Donations also constitute an important source of party income. Traditionally, the Liberals and Conservatives have received financial support from private companies, while the Social Democrats and, to some extent, Left Party Communists have been supported by blue-collar unions. The Conservative and Liberal dependence on private donations used to be virtually total, accounting for close to 100 per cent of the Conservative Party income up to 1965. Following the introduction of state subventions, this proportion dropped immediately to 46 per cent, and gradually declined further to just 30 per cent in 1976. In absolute terms, however, private donations remained quite stable until they were finally abandoned altogether (Albinsson, 1986: 53–8). Available data suggest that donations were almost as important for the Liberals, and, judging by the somewhat unspecific economic reports from the early 1960s, accounted for 97 per cent of total party income in those years (the remainder coming from membership). In 1968, following the introduction of state subventions, party records indicate that donations had sunk to 30 per cent (see also Olivecrona, 1968: 180).

In the election year of 1968, some 30 per cent of SAP income is reported to have come from trade union donations (Olivecrona, 1968: 175ff), and in 1988 and 1989, the Social Democrats claimed to have received donations amounting to a total of SEK 20 and 19 millions respectively, amounting to some 18 per cent of the total central party income. The Communists have also received donations from trade unions, but it has not been possible to establish exactly how much and the development over time. It may well have been fairly substantial in the late 1940s and early 1950s, when the Communists were quite strong in some unions, but even then it was likely to have been significantly lower than in the case of the Social Democrats. The Communists soon lost their position in the unions, and the donations have most certainly dwindled over time (cf. Winqvist et al., 1972: 291). Certainly in 1968, only about 8 per cent of the total income of the VPK central party plus the regional organizations came from trade unions (Olivecrona, 1968: 174f).

State financial support for the party organizations therefore completely changed the preconditions for their activities. Over time, the subvention system has diversified and has become quite complex. Today there are two basic kinds of subventions, each of which can be further sub-divided into another two categories. First, there are state subventions which are included in the national budget. Paid directly to the central office of the parties, they divide into a general (*Partistöd*) subsidy and a parliamentary party (*Kanslistöd*) subsidy.[6] The state subventions have 'cushion' rules, which means that gains as well as losses in seats have a gradual and lagged effect on the subventions received, and will have full effect only after three years. In the introductory year of 1966, a total of SEK 24.4 million was paid to the parties, which increased to over 50 million in 1973 and to nearly 80 million in 1983. In the fiscal year 1989/90 the total amount paid exceeded SEK 130 million. The second major source of state subventions is paid by the administration of the Riksdag to the parliamentary parties, although in practice these subventions are also paid via the national budget, since this is also the source of the Riksdag finances. These party subventions are specified in the national budget of the Riksdag.

The parliamentary party fraktion subvention (*Partigruppsstöd*) was introduced in 1975. It is very similar to the parliamentary party subvention, but smaller in size, and consists of a Basic and a Seat-based subvention. Until 1988 the seat-based element was differentiated between governing and non-governing parties, but today there is an identical sum per seat for all parties which, in 1990, involved a total sum of SEK 19.2 million. In the fiscal year 1989/90 a total of SEK 39.6 million was therefore paid to the parties via the parliamentary budget, and a total of SEK 170 million taking all of these subventions together. At the time, this was roughly equivalent to $34 million or £17 million.

In addition to these state subventions, however, there are also local and regional subventions, which were introduced in 1969. In 1986, a total of SEK 161 million were paid out by the municipalities and SEK 86 million by the regional councils (*SOU*, 1988: 47). This total of SEK 247 million paid by the sub-national governments can be compared with the SEK 107.6 million paid out by the state and Riksdag in 1985/86. It is hardly surprising, then, that these subventions have become the dominant income source for all the major parties, and have allowed them to build up a reasonably solid financial base.

The construction of the subventions, which are based largely on the number of party seats in parliament, means that election results play a fundamental role not only in terms of the political significance of the party, but also in terms of its overall financial situation.[7] In this sense, the economic incentive is clearly to win votes rather than to gain or keep members, with the corresponding likelihood that party effort will be directed less towards the mass membership organization and more towards election campaigns. Once again, therefore, there would seem to be an increasing emphasis on the external world of the party.

The increasing autonomy of the parliamentary parties

In all mass parties, formal and effective control of the parliamentary party constitutes a complicated problem in several respects. First, the parliamentary party is a basically anomalous element in the hierarchial structure of the party organization, with no self-evident position on the organizational ladder. Second, the parliamentary party owes its legitimacy not only to the party organization but also to the electors and the electoral process. Third, being the linkage between the party organization and the loci of political power, the parliamentary party operates within two organizational frameworks, the party organization, on the one hand, and the parliament, on the other. In addition, there is also a distinct possibility that members of the parliamentary party will increasingly identify with parliamentarians from other parties rather than with the rank-and-file members of the party from which they are supposed to get their cues. In sum, the parliamentary party faces the dilemma of double organizational identification. From the point of view of the party organization, control over the parliamentary party is a crucial element in ensuring that party policies are transformed into public policy, a control which, at the same time, may alienate the parliamentarians from the party.

Given the elaborated rules concerning the relationships between parties and their ancillary and affiliated organizations, the sheer absence of rules regarding the relationship with the respective parliamentary parties is intriguing. To be sure, the Swedish parties do differ significantly with respect to the question of organizational control over the parliamentary party. In none of the parties, however, does the party congress enjoy a mandate to control the activities of the parliamentary party. In the case of the Conservatives and Liberals, the autonomy enjoyed by the parliamentary parties may partially be due to their being primarily 'internally created' parties (Duverger, 1954: xxii–xxxvii), that is, parties which began inside parliament and which, as such, are dominated by their parliamentary wings.[8] In the case of the Social Democrats, on the other hand, which is a typical 'externally created' party in Duverger's terminology, other factors are involved, for in this case the party organization has long attempted to increase its control over the parliamentary fraktion. Indeed, according to the party statutes, the parliamentary party is responsible to the congress. In practice, however, the congress has had very limited opportunity to exercise control over the parliamentary fraktion, and it was not until 1972 that the latter opened its minutes to congress committee

Table 13.2	*Financial status and autonomy of parliamentary parties*

Party	Formal employer	Party taxes	Own budget	Financial autonomy
Conservatives	No	Insig.	(No)	Medium
Centre Party	No	SEK 200	No	Weak
Liberals	No	Insig.	No	Weak
Social Democrats	Yes	SEK 600	Yes	Strong
VPK (Comm)	Yes	SEK 800	Yes	Strong
Green Party	Yes	SEK 1000	Yes	Medium

Sources: Information is based on personal communications with senior administrative officials of the parliamentary parties, 7–8 August 1991. 'Insig.' indicates that the party tax is used only for social functions.

auditing (Pierre, 1986a: 70f). Prior to that, the parliamentary party simply submitted a report to congress. Thus, the autonomy of the Social Democratic parliamentary party with respect to the party organization is to a large extent the result of the successful defence of its autonomy, rather than deriving from any organizational consensus favouring its discretion in the field of parliamentary politics.

Although a high degree of overlap in the leadership of the party organization and that of the parliamentary party ensures policy coordination, the issue of parliamentary accountability has not yet been settled for once and for all. The decision of the parliamentary party in 1972 to allow congress committees access to its minutes was certainly a response to consistent demands from the party organization; but it is not clear why this decision was made then, and not earlier.[9] One possible explanation is that the media coverage of the parliamentary party had by then become so intense that most of its major debates and conflicts were being widely reported, and hence in any case it was no longer possible to hold debates and decisions in camera.

The financial autonomy of the parliamentary party also constitutes an important dimension of its relationship to the party organization and to the party leadership, and here we find an intriguing variation among the parties. Three different aspects of this autonomy are shown in Table 13.2, together with a summary indication of overall financial autonomy. While this assessment offers only a very broad overview of the question, it is nevertheless intriguing to note the contrasts between the parties. Thus the Social Democrats and the Communist Party, both of which subscribe to the general idea of strong congress control over the parliamentary party, and in both of which the issue of external control has been most salient, both have financially autonomous parliamentary fraktions. As has been noted elsewhere in this chapter, this also suggests that the original distinction between 'exterior' and 'interior' is rapidly losing all practical significance in the case of the Swedish party organizations.

Within the broader context, of course, the financial autonomy of the parliamentary party is only one aspect of its relative independence, and what is perhaps more important is its increasingly important role as a reference group or sounding board for the party leadership. In day-to-day politics the parliamentary party is often the key body where the leadership ensures approval of its actions, much more so than is the case of the national committee, for example. We can thus assume that the most important changes relating to the parliamentary parties are, first, their autonomy with respect to the party organization – which is clearly increasing; and, second, their relationship to the party leadership, where we would suggest that they are gradually becoming more influential. Part of the explanation for this is the increasing pace and stress which characterizes parliamentary politics: the parliamentary party is quickly and easily accessible to the leadership; it includes expertise on all major areas of public policy; it represents experience and skill in inter-party negotiations; and, perhaps most importantly, it is not antithetical but complementary to the party leadership, which itself normally comprises the leadership of the parliamentary party. From this perspective, the parliamentary party is likely to share the basic values and objectives of the party leadership.

Conclusions

The five general trends in the Swedish party organizations which have been discussed here – the decreasing significance of party membership, the overall centralization of the party organization, the centralization of the intra-party policy-process, the increased financial resources, and the growing autonomy of the parliamentary parties – share a number of very interesting features. First, whether directly or indirectly, they all illustrate a movement by the parties towards the state and away from their traditional role as linkage agencies between civil society and the state. Second, these changes have evolved gradually and in a very subtle form over an extensive period and, with only minor exceptions, have occurred within the existing system of party statutes and rules. Third, these changes have meant the parties have to some extent abandoned most of their mass-party characteristics.

To be sure, the parties still report impressive membership figures, and the intra-party decision-making process remains nominally membership-based. As we have seen, however, both of these mass-party features have lost much of their significance within the party organization, and what is carefully maintained instead, most tellingly so, is the *image* of the mass party. This image is essential to the parties in that it relates directly to the traditional role of the parties in a party government model, and to the role upon which their legitimacy is ultimately based: a role played by parties with large numbers of members, continuous organizational activities, a formalized bottom-up model of intra-party decision-making, extra-parliamentary control of the parliamentary party and so on.

Thus, while the changes we observe all tend to modify this traditional role of the political parties and their organizations, the fact that they have occurred over such a long period of time while remaining within the existing formal organizational framework has meant that the parties' legitimacy has not been jeopardized. Indeed, it has not been until very recently that new parties have emerged to challenge the older parties on issues which relate to these changes – their loss of contact with grassroots and rank-and-file members, their insensitivity to changes in civil society, their reluctance to change their organizations or to broaden their base, and so on – and that many of the negative effects of these changes have surfaced.

The 'stratarchic' model of party organization (Eldersveld, 1964) assumes that, to a large extent, different organizational levels operate independently of one another, that they fulfil distinctively different functions in the organization and that they enjoy a substantial mutual autonomy in their inter-relationships. As we have seen, this is in fact a very accurate depiction of the Swedish party organizations. Thus, the local branches are the chief instruments for membership recruitment and meetings; the regional level is primarily involved in coordinating the activities at the constituency level and candidate nomination; and the central level's most important functions include party leadership and policy-making.

There are two important implications of this arrangement. First, it means that different organizational levels face different environments and also different types of challenges from their respective environment. Thus, organizational change has different objectives and takes different forms, depending on the level of the organization. It is only when a certain type of problem assumes a substantial magnitude that it is also reflected in the activities of other organizational layers. Second, and derived from this, the conception of party organizations as stratarchies indicates substantial organizational inertia. Thus, by relating different functions to different organizational levels, organizational change becomes more difficult to effect and hence, despite changes in civil society and in the political landscape, the structure of the party organizations has remained almost completely unchanged throughout the last three decades, and, indeed, also further back in time.

Moreover, while some processes of organizational change may be identified as adaptation to external changes, there remain a number of contending explanations, such as, for example, unsuccessful or partial adaptation, or organizational change which has been wholly triggered by intra-organizational factors. Indeed, in a study on organizational change in the Conservative Party between 1960 and 1985, Albinsson (1986: 167) concludes that changes were triggered more by internal than by external factors.

In referring to the party organizations as 'colossuses' in the title of this chapter it was our intention to highlight the overall strength of these organizations. The Swedish party organizations enjoy a great deal of state, regional and municipal financial support. In addition to these resources, most party organizations can also rely on support – the extent of which is almost impossible to measure – from other organizations or actors in their respective political and social constituencies. Over time, of course, the precise mixture of these inputs has varied – indeed, state subventions to political parties were in part introduced in order to make the parties less dependent on these other types of resources – but the end result remains that the parties have always ensured large and seemingly stable financial support for their organizations. That said, and from the point of view of the parties themselves, a close relationship with the state may easily become a two-edged sword, especially in a period of retrenchment in the public sector. Indeed, in this sense the 'fiscal crisis of the state' (O'Connor, 1973) also becomes the fiscal crisis of the parties, and in the austerity pro-grammes implemented in 1992 and 1993, the parties for the first time in their history experienced a reduction in state subventions.

For a long period of time finance was one of the key factors stabilizing and sustaining the party system. Together with the relatively high thresh-old which stood in the way of new parties seeking to obtain parliamentary representation, state subventions for existing parties created a moat around the political establishment of the existing parties which new parties found difficult to cross. As such, the parties gained control over their organizational environment to such an extent that 'adaptation' effectively became the synonym for organizational responses to changes which were triggered in fact by themselves.

As the parties gradually moved closer to the state, however, organiz-ational adaptation changed from adaptation to civil society into adaptation to the state. More specifically, the parties changed in ways which would make them more able to play the role of parties closely associated with the state. The state's interest with regard to the political parties typically includes some level of stability at the level of the party system (Bartolini and Mair, 1990). Furthermore, from the point of view of the state there is also an interest in having efficient parties as gate-keepers in the political system: parties as capable sets of decision-makers; parties, or party leaderships, operating in a manner which is free of any major policy constraints from their party organizations, and hence making unbiased decisions; parties socializing voters and rank-and-file members, and so on. And, as we have seen, the major trends and developments in the Swedish party organizations during the past thirty years do seem to point in this direction.

This argument now also helps to explain the new and increasing instability in the system. Given the stabilizing impact of state subventions, and given the barrier placed by the electoral threshold, it may appear counter-intuitive to see a number of new parties making their entrance on the political stage, as has been the case during the late 1980s and early 1990s. In practice, then, it may simply be that these recent changes have occurred not *because of* but *despite* the state subventions. However, a more intriguing and provocative explanation may be that when the established parties moved closer to the state, they left behind a 'gap' between themselves and civil society. This 'gap' can then be understood as reflecting an increasing frustration with the established parties on the part of the citizenry, a decreasing concern with the opinions and the demands of 'ordinary people' on the part of the parties, and a resulting organizational inability, or unwillingness, to adapt to changes in civil society. And this frustration, in turn, proved a catalyst for the emergence of the new challengers.

Finally, by looking at party organizational change as – at least in part – a process of adaptation to the state, we may also understand changes in the parties' performance at the grassroots level. During the 1970s and 1980s, for example, the party organizations experienced increasing problems recruiting new members and maintaining high levels of attendance at local party meetings. The main competitors to the parties have been different local action groups, often single-issue-oriented groups (Westerståhl and Johansson, 1981; Petersson et al., 1989: 336f). Partly as a result of this development, some of the parties have developed new forms of participation and activity inside the party organization. Thus, the Liberals have recently opened up the opportunities for single-issue activities within the framework of their own party organization and, in a similar vein, the Conservatives have relaxed central control of the constituency organizations' electoral campaigning.

In both instances the aim has been to encourage internal participation in non-traditional ways. Hence engaging in party activities should be defined by the individual's interests in various issues, and the package of party standpoints should not be imposed on single-issue participants but rather should help to 'coopt the single-issue movements'.[10] It is of course premature to assess the long-term consequences of this project and, currently, such organizational responses to declining party participation should be seen merely as experiments. Indeed, the party organizations themselves employ that very label for these changes.

Nevertheless, these same experiments may well be the first steps towards new patterns of interaction between the public and the parties, particularly since increasing electoral discontent with the parties (Holmberg and Gilljam, 1987: 235ff) and decreasing or stabilizing participation in party organizational activities (Petersson et al., 1989: 336) suggest that the parties are not seen as viable channels of political representation. These are both long-term trends towards which the parties have not so far responded efficiently, and to the extent that measures have been taken to reverse these trends, they have clearly proved inadequate. To be sure, it is difficult to detect the existence of any such measures. Much of the decentralization in the parties has primarily been structural rather than procedural, and hence has not been geared to inspire participation and political involvement. On the contrary, many of the organizational changes which we noted have been geared towards increasing the efficiency of the parties in their relations with the state, and not with civil society.

Notes

1 Policy implementation, on the other hand, is less guided by partisan factors: instead, in a comparative perspective the Swedish public administration emerges as a fairly autonomous and elitist type of bureaucracy (Pierre, 1994).

2 Important differences between the parties remained, however, as, for example, can be seen in the balance between income from membership and from donations, which is discussed later in the chapter.

3 Although, in 1993, such a national executive committee is in the process of being established.

4 The practical side of the problem of wanting to be represented by members rather than by independents became evident after the electoral success in 1985, when the Liberal Party experienced major difficulties in recruiting people to the resulting number of public positions. Interestingly, no other party has such a ruling, simply because it is taken for granted that no-one would ever even think of nominating non-members to party-contested positions.

5 Interestingly, this may be a key explanation for the dramatically increasing number of amendments as, for example, at the SAP party congresses (Pierre, 1986a: Ch. 3). If a member who is also a conference delegate is unable to have her motion accepted by her local and/or constituency organization, she still has the option of presenting her proposals directly at the congress debate.

6 In the beginning these subsidies were both seat-based, that is, a sum was paid out for every seat in parliament, the requirement being parliamentary representation and 2 per cent of the national vote in the latest parliamentary election. Since 1970 (when the threshold for parliamentary representaiton was raised to 4 per cent), the general subsidy has remained seat-based, but a party outside parliament still qualifies for some money if it has gained at least 2.5 per cent of the national vote in the most recent election.

7 The local and regional party subsidies, which are exclusively seat-based, act in the same direction (see Gidlund, 1985; SOU, 1988: 48).

8 This result is corroborated by studies on expectations of constituency party organizations regarding the MP's involvement in various organizational activities. Generally speaking, Liberal and Conservative constituency organizations do not see MP participation in these activities as important. Conversely, Social Democratic constituency organizations to a large extent adopt the opposite perspective, advocating extensive MP involvement in all organizational activities (cf. Pierre, 1986a: 101ff).

9 The SAP employs a strict twenty-year limit for outside access to the minutes of all party bodies including the parliamentary party, except the party congress.

10 Interview with Liberal party official. Encouraging single-issue based involvement in the party is clearly inconsistent with traditional (cross-issue and programme-oriented) party work. However, the problem of accommodating various types of participation in the same organization has not so far been seen as a serious dilemma.

References

Albinsson, Per (1986) *Skiftningar i Blått: Förändringar inom Moderata Samlingspartiets Riksorganisation 1960–1985*. Lund: Kommunfakta Förlag.

Asp, Kent (1986) *Mäktiga Massmedier*. Stockholm: Akademilitteratur.

Back, Pär-Erik and Berglund, Sten (1978) *Det Svenska Partiväsendet*. 4th edn. Stockholm: Almqvist & Wiksell.

Bartolini, Stefano and Mair, Peter (1990) *Identity, Competition and Electoral Availability*. Cambridge: Cambridge University Press.

Duverger, Maurice (1954) *Political Parties: Their Organization and Activity in the Modern State*. London: Methuen.

Elder, Neil, Thomas, Alastair and Arter, David (1982) *The Consensual Democracies?* Oxford: Martin Robertson.

Eldersveld, Samuel J. (1964) *Political Parties: A Behavioral Analysis*. Chicago: Rand McNally.

Elvander, Nils (1969) *Intresseorganisationerna i Dagens Sverige*. Lund: CWK Gleerup.

Esaiasson, Peter (1990) *Svenska valkampanjer 1866–1988*. Stockholm: Allmänna Förlaget Publica.

Gidlund, Gullan (1983) *Partistöd*. Lund: Gleerups.

Gidlund, Gullan (1985) 'Det Kommunala Partistödet', *Ds C*, 8.

Gustafsson, Agne (1973) 'Partikongresser och Medlemsinflytande', in Pär-Erik Back (ed.), *Modern demokrati*. Lund: Gleerups, pp. 119–69.

Holmberg, Sören (1989) 'Political Representation in Sweden', *Scandinavian Political Studies*, 12, 1–36.

Holmberg, Sören and Esaiasson, Peter (1988) *De Folkvalda*. Stockholm: Bonniers.

Holmberg, Sören and Gilljam, Mikael (1987) *Väljare och Val i Sverige*. Stockholm: Bonniers.

Katz, Richard S. (1986) 'Party Government: A Rationalistic Conception', in Francis G. Castles and Rudolf Wildenmann (eds), *Visions and Realities of Party Government*. Berlin: de Gruyter, pp. 31–71.

Katz, Richard S. and Mair, Peter (1992) 'Changing Models of Party Organization: The Emergence of the Cartel Party', paper presented at the 1992 ECPR Joint Sessions of Workshops, Limerick, Ireland, 30 March–4 April.

Krauss, Ellis S. and Pierre, Jon (1990) 'The Decline of Dominant Parties: Parliamentary Politics in Sweden and Japan During the 1970s', in T.J. Pempel (ed.), *Uncommon Democracies: The One-Party Dominant Regimes*. Ithaca and London: Cornell University Press, pp. 226–59.

O'Connor, James (1973) *The Fiscal Crisis of the State*. New York, NY: St Martin's Press.

Olivecrona, Gustaf (1968) *Hur Väljarna Vanns*. Stockholm: Wahlström & Widstrand.

Olsen, Johan P. (1983) *Organized Democracy*. Oslo and Bergen: Universitetsforlaget.

Pempel, T.J. (1990) 'Introduction', in T.J. Pempel (ed.), *Uncommon Democracies: The One-Party Dominant Regimes*. Ithaca and London: Cornell University Press, pp. 1–32.

Petersson, Olof, Westholm, Anders and Blomberg, Göran (1989) *Medborgarnas Makt*. Stockholm: Carlssons.

Pierre, Jon (1986a) *Partikongresser och Regeringspolitik*. Lund: Kommunfakta Förlag.

Pierre, Jon (1986b) 'Riksdagsledamöterna och de Regionala Partiorganisationerna', *SOU*, 27: 89–128.

Pierre, Jon (1994) 'Governing the Welfare State: Public Administration, the State and Society in Sweden', in Jon Pierre (ed.), *Bureaucracy in the Modern State*. Cheltenham: Edward Elgar Publishing Ltd, pp. 140–60.

Rothstein, Bo (1986) *Den Socialdemokratiska Staten*. Lund: Arkiv Förlag.

Rustow, Dankwart (1955) *The Politics of Compromise*. Princeton: Princeton University Press.

SOU (1988) 'Kommunalt Stöd till de Politiska Partierna', *SOU*, 47.

Sartori, Giovanni (1976) *Parties and Party Systems*. Cambridge: Cambridge University Press.

Sjöblom, Gunnar (1987) 'The Role of Political Parties in Denmark and Sweden, 1970–1984', in Richard S. Katz (ed.), *Party Governments: European and American Experiences*. Berlin: de Gruyter, pp. 155–201.

Taggart, Paul and Widfeldt, Anders (1993) '1990s Flash Party Organization: The Case of New Democracy in Sweden', paper presented at the PSA conference, University of Leicester, England, 20–22 April.

Thermaenius, Edvard (1933) *Sveriges Politiska Partier*. Stockholm: Hugo Gebers Förlag.

Uddman, Paula (1987) 'Arbetsbörda och Regeringsansvar: Centerpartiets Riksstämmor under 1970-talet', in Lars-Göran Stenelo (ed.), *Statsvetenskapens Mångfald. Festskrift till Nils Stjernquist*. Lund: Lund University Press, pp. 293–300.

Westerståhl, Jörgen and Johansson, Folke (1981) 'Medborgarna och Kommunen', *Ds Kn*, 12.

Winqvist, Kay-Vilhelm, Wickléus, Jan-Åse, Uddman, Paula, Bengtsson, Lars and Lund-ström, Berndt-Ola (1972) *Svenska Partiapparater*. Stockholm: Bonniers Aldus.

14

Transnational Party Federations, European Parliamentary Party Groups, and the Building of Europarties[1]

Luciano Bardi

Both the history and development of the European model of democracy have been closely associated with the history and development of political parties. Thus expressions such as 'party government' or 'party democracy' now appear routinely in the literature on European governance, with few if any aspects of political life being seen as removed from the important role played by political parties.[2] It is therefore hardly surprising that hopes for the democratic growth and development of the European Community (EC)/European Union (EU) often rest on the expectation that there will develop genuinely European political parties, that is supranational or at least transnational political parties. Indeed, the years immediately surrounding the first direct election of the European Parliament (EP), when trends towards the transnationalization of European political parties were predicted by many experts, witnessed a widespread feeling that direct elections might provide the equivalent stimulus at the European level that during the late nineteenth and early twentieth centuries had fostered the birth of political parties at the national level. In the early 1970s, and perhaps as a consequence of such convictions, all three major European party families, the Socialists, the Liberals and the Christian Democrats, created EC-specific transnational federations: the Confederation of the Socialist Parties of the European Community (CSPEC), the European Federation of Liberal, Democratic and Reform Parties of the European Communities (ELDR), and the European People's Party (EPP – the Federation of Christian Democratic Parties in the European Community). The result was that academic expectations grew even higher, as is testified by the considerable volume of books and articles that touched more or less directly on the topic.[3] Since 1979, however, no formal steps of any importance towards the transnationalization of European parties have been taken,[4] and the progress of the EC has been, at least in certain crucial institutional aspects, slower than many expected or hoped. At the same time, the recent challenges posed by the completion of the single European market and the ratification of the Maastricht agreements clearly imply the need to reconcile sovereignty and compliance, and serve once more to remind us of the problem of the democratic deficit.

Building democracy in the late twentieth century, especially within a quasi-federal system such as the EC, whose components are already endowed with all the institutional elements of democracy, cannot be based on a model deriving from the development of national democracies in late nineteenth and early twentieth-century Europe. This certainly applies to political parties, and it is clear that EC-based political parties cannot be expected to develop in ways reminiscent of the development of their national counterparts. National political party organizations were created either to provide pre-existing parliamentary parties with support, or to channel demands of emerging social groups and/or non-political organizations (Duverger, 1954: xxiv, passim). Moreover, the building of strong national party organizations was made desirable and even necessary by the growing importance of parliaments. Thus a strong party organization proved a prerequisite to winning a parliamentary majority and, ultimately, to winning government and political power.

The EC situation is quite different, however. To be sure, it is clear that the EP will have to play a crucial role if the democratic deficit is eventually to be overcome; indeed parliamentary groups, which are not quite the same thing as Duverger's parliamentary parties, had already been formed as early as 1952 in the predecessor to the EP, the Assembly of the European Coal and Steel Community (ECSC), and this was almost twenty years prior to the creation of the transnational federations. It is also quite reasonable to assume that any intensification of supranational political processes will find its primary focus in the EP and its party groups, and will probably at the same time foster the strengthening of the extra-parliamentary transnational party organizations. Moreover, as EC-level decisions become more and more far-reaching, the need for European-level accountability becomes increasingly evident. Euro-summit decisions are now, perhaps for the first time, directly in the public eye, and decisions that deeply affect the lives of citizens in all twelve member-states, and of which those very citizens are now keenly aware, can no longer be perceived as being imposed by the prime ministers of particular countries. In this case, then, we witness the *prospective* need for a new EC-level democratic system, involving an enhancement of the role and powers of the EP, and creating one of the conditions for more assertive and powerful European parties. The societal and institutional character of the EC nevertheless remains quite incomparable to that of the developing national democracies in late nineteenth-century Europe. And even if, for analytical purposes, we consider the EC as a fully autonomous political system, then the most important institutional condition for political party development, the centrality of parliament, does not pertain. For while national parliaments may be said to be losing real powers in many contemporary political systems, the importance of the EP itself is even further depressed by its lack of formal powers, a defect which is only marginally relieved by the institutional provisions of the Single European Act or by the broad guidelines of the Maastricht Treaty. Finally, whereas the European parties of the nineteenth century were unique organizations in their respective political systems, the new Europarties would form only a second coexisting and, to an extent, competing party system. In this sense, a clear analogy can be seen in the genesis of the Canadian federal party system, where 'national organizations were gradually superimposed upon sectional factions', but where provincial organizations remain the 'continuing and effective units' within the political parties (Hougham, 1972: 13–14).

Parties in the EC system

Both the homogeneity and cohesiveness of European party families are usually considered to be decisive in discussions about the adequacy and efficacy of any future European parties. But while some of these family federations (the ELDR and the EPP in particular) already appear to be very cohesive, this does not necessarily mean that they will become fully integrated Europarties. It is normally assumed, for example, that parties belonging to the same families are produced in each national context by the same cleavages. Even in this case, however, the cleavages that produced parties at the national level may not be relevant at the European level, with the principle of subsidiarity, according to which national governments and the EC will continue to have different and clearly separate domains, making certain policy areas and even some national cleavages politically irrelevant at the European level. Indeed, were the EC to develop its own autonomous political system, the present embryonic party system, which reflects those characteristics that are common to most national systems, would probably evolve into one with very different features and components (Marquand, 1979: 121). The degree of cohesiveness of the present transnational federations may therefore prove irrelevant to the future development of the EC system.

In addition to party-system differences, the emerging European parties would also differ substantially from their national counterparts in the relative importance of the various elements of their organization. Parties now operate at the EC level through three main types of structures: first, the national party organizations and their components (sub-national organizations, which are sometimes relevant even at the EC level, are included in this category); second, EP party groups; and third, either transnational organizations (in the case of the larger and longer established party families), or less formal structures of international coordination (in the case of the smaller, newer, party families, such as the Greens and the Right). Although these formally correspond to three different components in national party organizations (respectively: membership, parliamentary party and extra-parliamentary party), their mutual relationships depart rather sharply from the national model.

This is especially the case when it comes to the role of national parties in the EC system. Beyond their formal role as federation members, national parties are autonomously very active in the EC context, and this makes them much more than simple Europarty components. In fact, they may well be the most powerful obstacle to the development of genuine Europarties. Moreover, there are also differences even with respect to the other two, more genuinely European, components. The EC institutional structure tends to enhance the organizational importance of the EP party groups, and EC legislation, as well as ignoring national parties, makes practically no mention of extra-parliamentary party organizations.[5] Parties are therefore not obliged to develop large extra-parliamentary structures in order to respond to legal requirements; in other words, unlike their national counterparts, extra-parliamentary parties in the EC context do not have to 'adapt to the state'. Conversely, EP party groups are created and operate in a highly regulated context, with EP regulations imposing some restrictions (for example, the minimum number of members), but mainly providing incentives for party group formation and operation, and with national party delegations gaining both important material (resources and funding) and political (better committee and EP leadership positions) advantages from EP group membership (see, for example, Attinà, 1990; Jacobs and Corbett, 1990). EP groups are thus financially independent, even to the extent that they are in a position to transfer funds to their national affiliates and to contribute substantially to the financing of transnational federations.

These factors make EP party groups the organizational foci of EC level parties and offer a ready explanation of some of the marriages of convenience among otherwise rather heterogeneous national party delegations (for example, Fianna Fáil and the Gaullist RPR or, between 1979 and 1989, the PCI and the PCF). To be sure, these extreme cases are unlikely to produce anything more than EP party groups, and then for reasons of pure administrative convenience. But other and potentially more important processes, such as those which will probably fully incorporate the Italian PDS and the British Conservatives into the recently renamed Party of European Socialists (PES) and the EPP respectively, were actually initiated within the EP groups themselves. In this case, political action in the EP provides ample opportunities to produce and/or verify convergence between the new potential members and the party groups.

On the other hand, similar opportunities for the federations seem to have manifested themselves in recent years in the course of the Intergovernmental Conferences (IGCs) which were held during the negotiations of the Maastricht Treaties (Hix, forthcoming). Intergovernmental processes are a grey area in which transnational federations and, perhaps more effectively, national parties, may play a role. It is thus very plausible to suggest that membership in the EPP (but also in the PES and the ELDR) may have facilitated the achievement of common positions by several European heads of government, and sometimes even by opposition leaders. At the same time, however, IGC-related decisions were always prepared in federation leaders' summits, and do not seem to have had any impact on the institutionalization of the federations themselves as autonomous organizations, and the decisions were eventually underwritten by the federation leaders as heads of government, sometimes with the help of coalition partners from different parties holding relevant cabinet posts. If anything, therefore, they tended to act as members of their national parties whose positions happened to be close to those of most other European parties, with similar situations occurring for many years within another EC intergovernmental forum, the Council of Ministers. Finally, as the early history of the EC demonstrates, membership in the same party family has always facilitated the actions taken by European heads of government in pursuit of European integration, without at the same time having had any lasting positive effect on the Europarties as such. In fact, by enhancing the role of national party leaders, the continuing importance of intergovernmental decision-making is probably more of a hindrance than an incentive for the development of Europarties.

Transnational party federations

While data on transnational federations are rather scarce and difficult to obtain, their comparability to data regarding national parties nevertheless allows us to test the extent to which the three federations are in fact like real parties. As a preliminary attempt which simply aims to 'find out more' about transnational party federations, however, this discussion will be limited to a description and assessment of some of the more structural features of these federations, namely membership, staffing, finance and internal organization.

The EC notion of party membership clearly differs from that of parties at the national level. To be sure, much as was the case with most national parties in their earlier phases of development, the statutes of all three federations indicate a heavy reliance on membership fees and contributions for their financial needs (Bardi, 1992). Indeed, within the EPP and the PES, the only real obligations of membership are financial. Nevertheless, unlike national parties, individual membership is virtually non-existent at the EC-party level. Rather, membership is strictly collective and consists of national parties from EC member-states belonging to the three party families. Only the EPP's statutes also provide for individual membership, but it is very doubtful that anyone ever took advantage of this opportunity as no individual membership records are kept, and two of the federations, the EPP and the ELDR, report only national party membership figures.[6] Were the federations to add up these national figures, which is not done in their official records, they would correspond to millions of individual members, but there is no reason to believe that the national card-carrying adherents are aware of this dual membership, and hence there is no reason to expect them to be committed to activities for, or on behalf of, 'their' transnational federation. The situation is even more straightforward in the case of the PES, which lists only the member parties, and which does not keep, or simply does not make available, records of their memberships. Obviously, this means that transnational party federations cannot avail themselves of the resource represented by individual members: they have no grassroots organization, no local branches and virtually no direct contact with European society. The only partial exception is again the EPP, owing to its impressive (by comparison) array of ancillary organizations. Besides the customary youth and women's organizations, the most interesting of these appear to be the UEAL (European Union of Local Administrators) and the AECM (European Independent Business Confederation), which have at least the potential to by-pass the bottleneck represented by national parties and interest groups in the linkage between European society, on the one hand, and the EC level of representation and government, on the other.

The weakness of transnational federations as organizations is also confirmed in terms of staffing levels. A growing salaried staff is normally taken to be an indicator of increasing party professionalization. This could, of course, have positive or negative implications, but in either case it is usually taken to indicate the existence of a consolidated organization. Obviously our attention here must be limited to the federations' central offices, since at all other levels of their organization they rely on national parties.[7] During the period covered by the study, all three organizations have expanded (considerably so in the cases of the EPP and the PES) the numbers of their paid staff. Nevertheless, these numbers remain almost embarrassingly low, with the most recent figures indicating thirteen paid staff in the PES, ten in the EPP and just six in the ELDR, figures which even include the federations' General Secretaries and, in the EPP case, an Assistant General Secretary. These figures clearly suggest the marginal character of the transnational federations in comparison to the organizations of some of their national counterparts and, perhaps ironically, their components. Indeed, the only national party which appears to be less endowed than its federation is the Irish Labour party, with nine paid staff, while, still in Ireland, even the relatively small Fine Gael boasts twenty-five employees. Staffing levels in all other national parties easily surpass those of the federations (see Katz and Mair, 1992). The limited institutionalization of the federation is also underlined when it is realized that only the PES directly pays all of its own staff, with both the EPP and the ELDR passing the tab on to their member parties and to the EP party groups. Indeed, some of the staff are actually employees of the member parties who are 'lent' to the transnational federation, as certainly appears to be the case with one EPP advisor who actually spent most of his time working at the DC headquarters in Italy.

An analysis of federations' finances is even more difficult than that of the national political parties, which are notoriously secretive in this regard.

But while national laws, especially in recent years, have forced parties to publish at least some of their financial records, there are no such obligations which apply to the European federations, and the only official data which proved obtainable concerned ELDR expenditures.[8] In 1991, for example, the ELDR spent 11.6 million Belgian francs, more than three times the level in 1982, and of this, only some 4.5 million was spent on political activities. In 1989, a year for which comparable national party figures are available, ELDR expenses amounted to 9.8 million Belgian francs, and this figure, when adjusted according to the relative size of the federations, would suggest an estimate for EPP and PES expenditures to be higher and even double. Even so, this is just a pittance when compared to the expenditures of the national parties. In 1989 in Germany, for example, expenditures of the SPD amounted to 275.5 million marks, that of the CDU to 235 million marks, that of the CSU to 54 million marks, and that of the FDP to 43.5 million marks.

Over and above the dues paid by the member parties, the income of the transnational federations derives from the corresponding EP party groups. Federation statutes indicate that either the Bureau of the federation (in the case of the EPP and the PES), or the Executive Committee (in the case of the ELDR), determines the membership fees of each member party, although the criteria (presumably size must be important) and the amounts are not specified. Few national parties report transfers to supranational party organizations in their budgets, although some figures are available from Italy in 1989 (the DC, 856 million Lire; the PLI, 31 million Lire), and from the Netherlands in 1988 (the PvdA, 81,000 guilders; the CDA, 82,000 guilders; the VVD, 69,000 guilders). These are not large amounts, however, and probably also include contributions to other organizations, such as the various Internationals. The statutes of the PES and the ELDR also explicitly indicate EP party groups as sources of income, and it is estimated that some 50 per cent of the income of all three federations derives from EP party groups.

An overall estimate of the income of the EP party groups themselves can be obtained by looking at specific subventions provided by the EC. Although the official EC budget reports only the total amount of annual subventions, reasonably accurate estimates of the amount given to each group can be based on the fact that the main criterion for distribution is party group size. In 1991, for example, the EC transferred about 27 million Ecus to EP party groups, of which 12 million was allocated to the European Information Campaign. Such funds, which are much more relevant in years preceding European elections, are usually transferred to national parties to finance campaign activities. This leaves about 15 million Ecus as the actual share for the EP party groups. On the basis of the distribution of seats in the EP, the three party groups related to transnational federations probably together obtained about two-thirds of that amount, or some 10 million Ecus (7 million in 1989). This was a respectable amount, but was also relatively small when compared to the contributions to national party groups, which, again in the German case in 1989, totalled to 67 million marks for the three corresponding party groups.

At least on the surface, the organizational structures of the transnational federations bear some resemblance to those of the national parties. All organize 'party' congresses, with the function of representing the membership, one or two executive bodies and a president. Moreover, all of these bodies have tasks that formally correspond to those of their national counterparts. However, a closer look at the statutes of the federations reveals significant departures from the national party organizational model, with the most evident differences concerning the relationships among the various components of the federations, that is, the relationships among the national parties (equivalent to the membership at national level), the EP party groups (equivalent to the parliamentary parties), and the federations' other bodies (equivalent to the extra-parliamentary parties).

Formally speaking, a high degree of reciprocal independence characterizes the relationship between the two properly European components of the transnational parties: although EP party group heads are normally ex-officio members of the executive bodies of the federations, there are practically no other formal rules determining the relationships between the parliamentary and the extra-parliamentary component. In particular, unlike some of the national extra-parliamentary parties, the federations have no say in the internal rules of the EP groups. EP group independence is, however, constrained by the national parties, for while the percentage of members of the European Parliament (MEPs) who are also national party officials is decreasing, it nevertheless remains relatively high. Thus, for example, recent research on the EP delegations of the most important parties in Italy and Germany (Verzichelli, 1991: 488–92) has found that about 17 per cent of the German MEPs hold national party offices (as against about 23 per cent of German national MPs), as do some 42 per cent of Italian MEPs (as against some 41 per cent of Italian national MPs). Moreover, and most importantly, national parties also have the capacity to control their EP delegations by means of selecting EP election candidates, and it is only in the statutes of the ELDR that there exists a provision for the involvement of that organization's Executive Committee in the selection procedure. Even then, however, this statute only requires national parties to communicate the lists of candidates to the ELDR Executive Committee, which has no power of ratification.

Party groups in the European Parliament

Even if national parties still appear to be the predominant actors, EP groups nevertheless show more potential to provide the core of Euro-parties than do the federations. As noted above, party groups had already been formed in the first ECSC Assembly, but they acquired a new importance with the first direct elections to the EP in 1979. Since that first election, however, the EP based 'party system' has been characterized by substantial instability, as, for example, was demonstrated by the disappearance of two of the original groups, the European Democrats (ED) and the Group for the Technical Coordination and Defence of Independent Groups and Members (CDI), and by the emergence of three new groups (Rainbow, Greens and the European Right [ER]). A sixth group, the Communists, survived for two terms and then split into two different groups respectively built around the French (Left Unity – LU) and Italian (United European Left – EL) communist delegations. In addition, all of the other groups, the Socialist group (referred to hereafter with its federation's new acronym: PES), the European Democratic Alliance (EDA), the group of the European People's Party (EPP), and the Liberal, Democratic and Reformist group (LDR) also underwent important changes of composition either as a result of either EC enlargements or inter-group realignments. In fact, inter-group realignments accounted for 91 seat changes between 1984 and 1989 (17 per cent of the total), as opposed to 40 (7.7 per cent of the total) which were the consequence of elections. This trend continued during the third elected term of the EP with the demise of the ED and EL groups and with their incorporation respectively into the EPP and the PES. Should these most recent mergers prove successful, however, the EP group system might well have achieved a satisfactory level of stability. In fact most groups have now reached a rather high level of ideological or political homogeneity, and there are currently only three noteworthy cases of intra- and inter-group incongruence, which at the same time are unlikely to provide the basis for further change in the short term. Thus Fianna Fáil's membership in the EDA still remains the lesser evil for the party, given Fine Gael's veto of its original intention to join the EPP. Similarly, the rather heterogeneous Danish anti-EC cartel is the largest (four-member strong) delegation in the Rainbow group, and can be readily accepted by the numerous smaller regionalist and nationalist parties making up the rest of the group. Finally the ER's founding party, the Italian Social Movement (MSI), left the group and joined the non-attached members because of deep conflicts with the German *Republikaner* over the question of Alto-Adige (in German, Südtirol), the predominantly German-speaking Italian region where the MSI functions as the staunchest defender of the Italian-speaking minority. The differences between the two parties are not likely to be easily settled.

The importance of EP groups in the evolution of the 'Europarty system' is perhaps confirmed by the widespread academic attention which they have received. In general, the creation of cohesive party groups is considered a prerequisite for, or at least an indicator of, the building of transnational parties, with the result that much of the research in this area has concentrated on the study of EP party groups. Some of these studies have attempted to infer party group cohesiveness and potential for transnationalization through the analysis of EP roll-call data (Attinà, 1986,

1990, 1992; Wolters, 1986; Quanjel and Wolters, 1993), while others have pursued similar goals by attempting to probe MEP attitudes (Kirchner, 1985; Bardi, 1989; Bowler and Farrell, 1993b).

The two approaches are not incompatible, and both sets of data can perhaps be profitably integrated in an effort to assess the real potential of this new Europarty system. The first set of data which is relevant here is that gathered by Attinà on the first and second directly elected parliaments. Attinà considered six major party groups, based on ideological affinity, which were present in the first directly elected EP: the PES, the LDR and the EPP groups, which included representatives from most EC countries; the Communists, who were present in Italy, France, Greece and Denmark; the EDA group, which was built around the French Gaullists (fifteen out of a total of twenty-two members in the first EP) and had members from Ireland, Denmark and Northern Ireland; and the ED, which included the British Conservative Party, the Ulster Unionist party (with one representative) and the Danish Conservatives. In the second elected EP two new groups were formed and included in the research: the European Right (ER), with representatives from France (ten out of the total of eighteen members), Italy, Greece, Portugal and the UK; and the Rainbow Group which, in the second EP, was a twenty-strong and rather heterogeneous coalition of ecologist and regionalist parties from six countries.

Cohesiveness is likely to be influenced by the number of national components in each party group. Generally, as a result of successful concertations and compromises in the relevant committees, votes on most proposals are taken unanimously in the EP and records are usually limited to the overall (positive or negative) outcomes. Given the symbolic importance of the majority of such resolutions, a very high level of agreement on such a high number of votes can hardly be considered a reliable indicator of intra-group, or even inter-group, cohesiveness. On the other hand, on a number of more important or controversial issues, votes are taken by roll-call, and in these cases official records report the vote of each individual MEP. Attinà examined 936 resolutions which were voted upon during the first directly elected term. Of these, only 142, or about 15 per cent, were taken by roll-call (110 during the second term).[9] In most cases, while overt conflicts occur among different party groups, a certain degree of intra-group disagreement can often be detected.

Attinà calculated Agreement Indices for all party groups on five categories of resolutions (the indices were not calculated if at least one-third of the group's membership did not take part in a sufficient number of votes), and the figures in Table 14.1 report the averages of the five indices for all relevant groups in the first and second elected terms, as well as an overall EP index for the second term.[10] In general, first term figures are very high, being extremely high in the case of the EPP, only slightly lower for four other groups, and only comparatively small in the case of the Socialists. The EPP figures are all the more remarkable considering that

Table 14.1 *Overall indices of agreement in the first and second directly elected European Parliaments*

	EP I	EP II
SOC (now PES)	65.8	62.2
EPP	83.2	84.1
ED	77.3	82.9
COMM	71.9	71.2
EDA	75.7	70.8
Rainbow	na	67.8
ER	na	96.1
Overall		25.9

Source: Attinà, 1990: 574. The overall EP II index was not included in the original source, and has been calculated on the basis of data kindly supplied by Fulvio Attinà.

the group then consisted of twelve different national parties from nine member states (the United Kingdom was the exception). Similar considerations apply to the LDR, which included eleven parties from eight member states. In the cases of the ED and the EDA, on the other hand, a high level of agreement on EP votes may be explained by the dominance within each group of one national party (the British Conservatives and the French Gaullists respectively). In the case of the Communist group, the sharp disagreements between the French and Italian delegations on institutional matters (the French being still predominantly anti-EC and the Italians being solidly in favour of the initiative by Altiero Spinelli, then an independent member of their group) are minimized by the near unanimous positions on international matters. Finally, the PES display of the lowest, even if still very high, level of agreement probably reflects its extremely fragmented composition. The PES then consisted of fifteen different parties, and was the only group with representatives from all member states.

The second term data do not reflect many significant changes for the 'old' groups, although average indices evidence a slight decline for four of the six groups. Again, the relative stability of the indices is remarkable, especially given the magnitude of some of the newly incorporated delegations from the Portuguese and Spanish member parties: the 36-strong Spanish delegation in the PES was the largest single delegation, and accounted for 20 per cent of the total group membership; the nine-member Portuguese delegation in the LDR was the second largest, and accounted for 18.4 per cent of the total. Of the new groups, the ER proved to be the most cohesive, while the slightly below average showing by the Rainbow Group is still very high considering its evident heterogeneity. All of these index figures are substantially higher than the overall EP figure.

In sum, the analysis of EP roll-call data suggests a very high degree of intra-group cohesiveness. Nevertheless, a more careful evaluation of the way votes are taken in the EP, and of how these particular data were collected, suggests that such conclusions should be treated very cautiously. Intra-group quasi-unanimity is usually guaranteed by long preparatory committee and party-group sessions which have the stated purpose of smoothing out most disagreements. What is even more important, however, is that most MEPs consider quasi-unanimity necessary for the projection of a strong image vis-à-vis other EC or national institutions, and it is quite possible that MEP voting behaviour is distorted by the paramount importance which is attributed to this goal. In such circumstances, intra-group cohesiveness as such may lose most of its meaning, at least as an indicator of Europarty institutionalization, particularly because inter-group differences would themselves be blurred.[11] Moreover, it should be noted that the overall EP index figure still indicates that an average of considerably more than half of all MEPs voted according to one single modality. Finally, as was noted above, the votes of certain party groups on many resolutions could not be included in the data-set because of an insufficient number of cases. While absenteeism is a problem in the EP as in many other parliaments, in some cases it may nevertheless reflect dissent on the part of parliamentary minorities. If roll-call data only portray situations where intra-group or at least intra-party discipline has been maintained, any conclusions they might suggest clearly need to be supported by further evidence.

This is confirmed by some of the other approaches to the study of EP party groups which, though not useful as measures of the practice of group discipline, deal with attitudinal data which reveal potential intra-group conflicts and disagreements within all of the party groups in the first directly elected parliament.[12] In particular, while the relative positions of the various groups are the same in terms of cohesiveness, the absolute agreement indices for all groups appear to be much lower. Such a divergence from the impression suggested by roll-call data may be due to a number of factors. For one thing, the roll-call analysis is based on a large sample of resolutions, only a handful of which are likely to be highly controversial, and any effects of less than conformist voting behaviour on such issues would naturally be offset by the very high number of quasi-unanimous decisions on the less divisive questions. The attitudinal data probes, on the other hand, were selected from a battery of questions specifically designed to bring out differences of opinion among MEPs. But even allowing for this important caveat, some other useful considerations are possible. Thus the attitudinal data confirm that groups like the EPP and the LDR have a much higher potential for cohesiveness than the PES, although on questions having implications for national sovereignty or public morality, country-based differences may have an impact even for these groups. Moreover, if the transnationalization of the European party system does indeed take place, it is likely that it will be in response to a growth in the importance of the supranational dimension of European politics. In that case, the number of controversial issues voted upon in the EP is very likely to increase. For example, the high levels of PES-group agreement on votes concerning international resolutions (Attinà, 1990: 573) were certainly favoured by the inconsequential nature of most such resolutions. The cohesiveness of the group on more problematic international issues, on the other hand, such as European defence, which would no doubt present themselves in a new institutional context, would be less than certain in a more powerful EP.

Conclusion

Given the particular nature of the EC political system, it would be inappropriate to formulate hypotheses on the genesis of Europarties based on traditional national party models. At least one Europarty 'component', the national one, appears to be quite independent of the overall Europarty organization; indeed, national parties can even be seen as competitors for the emerging transnational organizations. It would also be difficult and perhaps futile to speculate on when and how this situation might change. Europarties are therefore more likely to develop from the institutionalization of at least one of the other two components, the transnational federations and/or EP party groups, with 'exogenous' party-formation processes being very unlikely to occur. At the same time, the transnational federations themselves, in terms of political relevance and organizational structure, appear to be little more than expressions of a generic sense of commonality shared by national parties with comparable histories and similar sets of values. The rather minor role played by the federations even during EP election campaigns, when common manifestos are practically ignored by nationally selected EP candidates, offers an appropriate illustration. At least on the surface, therefore, it is the EP party groups which appear to show more potential for lasting transnationalization, even though the persistent powerlessness of the EP contrives to render intragroup cooperation ineffective. Moreover, even if, at the very symbolic and formal level typical of the EP, a strong degree of cooperation does occur, MEP attitudes still reveal potential contrasts that would probably make cooperation more difficult in 'real life' situations. Given the present institutional arrangements in the EC, the formation of genuine 'Europarties' is thus rather unlikely.

As against this, however, and possibly as a result of demands imposed on the supranational level by the completion of the internal market, it is often argued that the new institutional arrangements might endow the EP with greater powers, and were this to be the case then it is likely that the present party groups would find more incentives for increased cooperation. Not all EP groups would be able to face this new situation with equal efficacy, however, and further steps towards a transnational European party system would probably be conditioned by the present 'two-speed' character of the EP system of party groups. The EPP group and, to a slightly lesser extent, the LDR group, already evidence very well developed attitudes towards the creation of cohesive European parties. In the case of the EPP, however, the process might well be slowed down by a possible desire to fully absorb the British Conservatives, in much the same way that the least cohesive of the major groups, the PES, might be slowed down through its absorption of the former Italian communists (PDS). Even disregarding problems of this kind, and those posed by the further enlargement of the EC, individual party identities would still have to be maintained (it is difficult to imagine why the CSU, for example, having jealously and successfully defended its identity for over four decades at the national level, would now prove willing to lose its independence at the European level). This problem is compounded by the presence in several European countries, including the United Kingdom and France, of important national parties which have only weak links outside their own national boundaries: the wholesale integration of the British Conservatives into the EPP, for example, which is already problematic under the present predominantly intergovernmental EC, would certainly become even more difficult in a genuinely supranational institutional context. National peculiarities would probably be even more disruptive for the more recent, less homogeneous party groups. Finally, as has been suggested, even a display of high intra-group cohesiveness in the present system may not be maintained when and if the institutional context changes. It is in this sense that the obstacles to the transnationalization of the European party system appear to be stronger than the incentives.

Notes

1 This chapter is based on work supported in part by funds from the Italian Ministry for University and Scientific Research. An earlier version was presented to the Workshop on 'Inter-party Relationships in National and European Parliamentary Arenas', ECPR Joint Sessions, University of Leiden, 1993, and I am grateful to the participants in that workshop for their useful comments and insights. I also wish to thank Fulvio Attinà for allowing me access to his original research data.

2 In more recent years, to be sure, contrasting views have emerged in the political and academic debates: the views of some authors (e.g. Lawson and Merkl, 1988) have implied, and the recent experiences of some countries (Italy and, to an extent, France) have suggested the possible demise of the party government model, while other observers and commentators are of the view that these more recent developments are actually better understood as manifesting party change and/or adaptation.

3 Among these, and excluding single-country and single-party studies, are: Bonvicini and Solari (1979); Burban (1979); Fitzmaurice (1975, 1978); Guidi (1983); Henig (1979); Marquand (1979); Pridham (1975); Pridham and Pridham (1981); Vredeling (1971). See also and more recently Attinà (1990, 1992); Jacobs and Corbett (1990); Nugent (1991).

4 The only noteworthy exception, the Green Coordination (or European Greens) is not an EC-specific but rather a pan-European organization, the heterogeneity of whose membership hardly markes it comparable to the three transnational federations (see Bowler and Farrell, 1993a).

5 While politically noteworthy, the vague references to parties in Art. 138a in the Maastricht Treaty should not make a substantial difference for the evolution of EC party organizations.

6 It is interesting to note that these data as provided by the federations seldom coincide precisely with those officially provided by several of their member parties (see the figures in Katz and Mair, 1992).

7 In practice, this is often limited to the existence of an international liaison office attached to the national party headquarters. These offices are usually very sparsely staffed and are also obliged to maintain contacts with the other international organizations to which the national party belongs.

8 All three federations initially demonstrated a great willingness to provide financial information, especially when confronted with evidence of national parties' cooperation, but inevitably various 'technical' problems led them to withhold the data.

9 See Attinà (1990). These findings are also analysed more extensively in Attinà (1986, 1992).

10 The index varies between −33 and +100. Positive values indicate that at least half of the group members have voted according to the same modality, the three modalities being in favour, against and abstention (Attinà, 1990: 564).

11 Similar problems are created by the development and growth of the so-called 'intergroups', which organize MEPs on the basis of their interests in specific issues rather than on the basis of EP group membership. Intergroups have facilitated the creation of cross-group coalitions (which could actually be detrimental to intra-group cohesiveness), and have at the same time become a 'rival centre of attention to official parliamentary activities' (Jacobs and Corbett, 1990: 148).

12 The data were collected as part of the European University Institute Study of the European Parliament, directed by the late Rudolf Wildenmann, and conducted by an international team of scholars including Luciano Bardi (Italy), Patrice Manigand (France), Philomena Murray (Ireland), Karlheinz Reif and Hermann Schmitt (Germany), Carsten Sorensen (Denmark), and Martin Westlake (United Kingdom). Benelux interviews were conducted by Edi Clijsters (Belgium) and Mario Hirsch (Luxembourg). In all, 331 out of 410 MEPs were interviewed in the spring of 1983, with a further 11 out of 24 Greek MEPs being interviewed by Eurodim in 1984. Among other things, MEPs were asked to express their positions on a number of policy questions comparable to those in at least four of Attinà's five issue categories.

References

Attinà, F. (1986) *Il parlamento europeo e gli interessi comunitari*. Milano: Angeli.

Attinà, F. (1990) 'The Voting Behaviour of European Parliament Members and the Problem of the Europarties', *European Journal of Political Research*, 17: 557–79.

Attinà, F. (1992) *Il sistema politico della Comunità Europea*. Milano: Giuffrè.

Bardi, L. (1989) *Il Parlamento della Comunità Europea*. Bologna: Il Mulino.

Bardi, L. (1992) 'Transnational Party Federations in the European Community', in R.S. Katz and P. Mair (eds), *Party Organizations. A Data Handbook on Party Organizations in Western Democracies, 1960–1990*. London: Sage.

Bonvicini, G. and Solari, S. (eds) (1979) *I partiti e le elezioni del Parlamento Europeo*. Bologna: Il Mulino.

Bowler, S., and Farrell, D.M. (1993a) 'The Greens at the European Level', *Environmental Politics*, 1 (1): 132–7.

Bowler, S., and Farrell, D.M. (1993b) 'Legislator Shirking and Voter Monitoring: Impacts of European Parliament Electoral Systems Upon Legislator–Voter Relationships', *Journal of Common Market Studies*, 31 (1): 45–69.

Burban, C. (1979) *Le Parlement européen et son élection*. Brussels: Bruylant.

Duverger, M. (1954) *Political Parties*. New York: Wiley & Sons.

Fitzmaurice, J. (1975) *The Party Groups in the European Parliament*. Farnborough: Saxon House.

Fitzmaurice, J. (1978) *The European Parliament*. Farnborough: Saxon House.

Guidi, G. (1983) *I gruppi parlamentari del Parlamento Europeo*, Rimini: Maggioli.

Henig, S. (ed.) (1979) *Political Parties in the European Community*. London: Policy Studies Institute.

Hix, S. (forthcoming) 'The European Party Federations: From Transnational Party Cooperation to Nascent European Parties', in J. Gaffney (ed.), *Political Parties and the European
Community*.

Hougham, G.M. (1972) 'The Background and Development of National Parties', in H.G.
Thorburn (ed.), *Party Politics in Canada*. Scarborough: Prentice-Hall.

Jacobs, F. and Corbett, R. (1990) *The European Parliament*. Harlow: Longman.

Katz, R.S. and Mair, P. (eds) (1992) *Party Organizations. A Data Handbook on Party
Organizations in Western Democracies, 1960-90*. London: Sage.

Kirchner, E. (1985) *The European Parliament. Performance and Prospects*. Aldershot:
Gower.

Lawson, K., and Merkl, P. (eds) (1988), *When Parties Fail: Emerging Alternative Organizations*. Princeton: Princeton University Press.

Marquand, D. (1979) *Parliament for Europe*. London: Cape.

Nugent, N. (1991) *The Government and Politics of the European Community*, 2nd edn.
Houndmills: Macmillan.

Pridham, G. (1975) 'Transnational Party Groups in the European Parliament', *Journal of
Common Market Studies*, 13: 266–79.

Pridham, G. and Pridham, P. (1981) *Transnational Party Cooperation and European
Integration*. London: Allen & Unwin.

Quanjel, M. and Wolters, M. (1993) 'Growing Cohesion in the European Parliament', paper
presented at the ECPR Joint Sessions of Workshops, Leiden.

Verzichelli, L. (1991) 'Autonomia e peso politico della classe parlamentare europea: i casi di
Italia e Germania', *Studi Senesi*, 103 (3): 456–503.

Vredeling, H. (1971) 'The Common Market of Political Parties', *Government and Opposition*, 6 (4): 448–61.

Wolters, M. (1986) 'The Role of European and National Interests in the European
Parliament's Decision-making', paper presented at the ECPR Joint Sessions of Workshops,
Gothenburg.

Index